Project Economics Analysis Tool (PEAT)

User Manual & Visual Guide
(Version 2016 & Later)

Johnathan Mun, Ph.D., MBA, MS, BS, CQRM, FRM, CFC, MIFC

Real Options Valuation, Inc.

REAL OPTIONS VALUATION, INC.

Table of Contents

GETTING STARTED VISUAL GUIDES

1. PROJECT ECONOMICS ANALYSIS TOOL (PEAT)

1.1 Welcome to PEAT

T his Project Economics Analysis Tool (PEAT) software was developed by Real Options Valuation, Inc., to perform a comprehensive Integrated Risk Management analysis applying Project Economics Analysis, Monte Carlo Risk Simulation, Risk Analytics, Strategic Real Options Analysis, Stochastic Forecasting, Business Intelligence, and Portfolio Optimization.

To help you get started quickly, we recommend watching the PEAT Getting Started Video available on our website at *www.realoptionsvaluation.com* or accessible by simply starting the PEAT software and clicking on **Knowledge Center | Getting Started Videos | Quick Getting Started Video.**

1.2 Installation Requirements and Procedures

To install the software, follow the on-screen instructions. The minimum requirements for this software are:

- Pentium IV processor or later (dual core recommended)
- Windows 7, Windows 8, Windows 10, or later
- 500 MB free space
- 2 GB RAM minimum (4 GB recommended)
- Administrative rights to install software

There is a default 3-day trial license file that comes with the software. To obtain a full corporate license, please contact Real Options Valuation, Inc., at *admin@realoptionsvaluation.com* or call +1 (925) 271-4438.

1.3 Licensing

If you have installed the software and have purchased a full license to use it, you will need to e-mail us your Hardware Fingerprint so that we can generate a license file for you. Follow these instructions:

- After installing the software, start the PEAT tool and click on **Help | License.**

- You will be greeted with the Enter Key dialog (Figure 1.1). Write down the HWF or Hardware Fingerprint (8-alphanumeric characters) and e-mail it to admin@realoptionsvaluation.com. We will send a Name and Key to enter corresponding to the HWF you provided.

- Once you receive the Name and Key combination, repeat the first step above, enter the information exactly as provided, and click OK. Your software will be licensed immediately.

- In the event you need a temporary license key, use the following 3-day trial for PEAT:

    o Name = PEAT 3 Day Trial

    o Key = 7257-3CB2-A1D8-3C6A

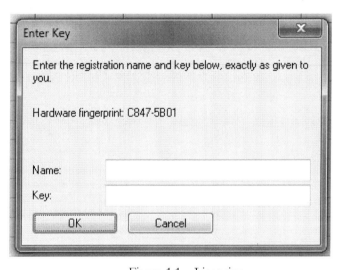

Figure 1.1 – Licensing

2. GETTING STARTED

T his chapter provides details on how to get started quickly using the PEAT tool. Instead of starting from a new file, we use an existing default example model to explain the concepts and steps to replicate and create your own model.

2.1 Overview of the PEAT Menu and Navigation Tabs

Create or Open a New File, or Load an Example

Follow the steps below to get started:

1. Start the PEAT software by double clicking on the desktop PEAT icon, or click the Windows button + C | Search and type in PEAT. Click on ROV PEAT to start.

2. **Select a Module** you wish to run (e.g., Discounted Cash Flow Model or Oil and Gas Project Economics on the main splash screen (Figure 2.1); additional Modules will be added in future releases).

3. Select **New** (to start a new model from scratch), **Open** (open an existing model), or **Load Example** to load an already completed example model (this latter choice is useful when trying to learn the functionalities of the software). To follow along with the examples, select **Corporate Investments Stochastic DCF** and **Load Example**.

Figure 2.1 – PEAT Splash Screen

TIPS on Reading This User Manual

This User Manual is divided into chapters and technical appendices. The first chapter covers the installation and licensing procedures of PEAT, and this current second chapter covers the navigation, functionality, description, and application of PEAT. To simplify the use of this manual, the subsections in this chapter parallel the tabular view of PEAT. Also, locations of certain elements appear in **purple**, and step-by-step procedures appear in **blue**.

In addition, this User Manual covers as much material as is deemed necessary to get the new user comfortable with the PEAT software, but it is not meant to be a comprehensive resource for all the analytics available in PEAT. For more technical details, refer to Dr. Johnathan Mun's books: *Modeling Risk*, Third Edition (Wiley 2015) and *Real Options Analysis*, Second Edition (Wiley 2006).

TIPS on Input Data

The PEAT software's menu items are fairly straightforward (e.g., **File | New** or **File | Save**). The software is also arranged in a tabular format. There are three tab levels in the software and it is recommended that you proceed from top to bottom and left to right when performing your analysis. Complete the lowest level from left to right first before moving up a level. Referring to Figure 2.2, for instance, start with the **Project Economics** (Level 1) tab, select **Global Settings** in (Level 2), and begin entering your inputs in the **Global Assumptions** (Level 3) tab. Then proceed to the **WACC** (Level 3) and **Beta** (Level 3) subtabs. When you have completed the lowest level subtabs, proceed up one level and continue with **Custom Calculations** (Level 2), **Option 1** (Level 2), **Option 2** (Level 2), and **Portfolio Analysis** (Level 2). When these tabs at Level 2 are completed, continue up a level to the **Applied Analysis** (Level 1) tab, and proceed in the same fashion.

Note that all Level 1 tabs are identical regardless of the Module (e.g., Discounted Cash Flow [DCF] Model or Oil and Gas [O&G] Model) chosen, except for the first tab (Project Economics).

Navigating Inside the PEAT Software

The PEAT software has the following modules or tabs:

- **Main Module: Discounted Cash Flow** or **Project Economics**. Depending on the module selected when the software first starts, the contents of this Level 1's tab and its subtabs will change.

  - **Custom Calculations**. Allows you to enter your own custom model and calculations, and link certain cells to the other subtabs.

  - **Options/Projects**. This tab is at the heart of the software's input assumptions. You can insert, delete, edit, or reorder these Options tabs by first clicking on any Option tab and then selecting **Options/Projects | Add, Delete, Duplicate, Rearrange,** or **Rename Option** from the menu. An Option tab is indicative of a project, an implementation path, or an alternative strategic decision. Within each Option tab, the following subtabs are available depending on the module selected:

    - **DCF: Discounted Cash Flow Model.** Revenues, expenses, capital investments, starting and ending years for the cash flow model, discount rate, and tax rates can be entered here.

    - **DCF: Cash Flow Ratios.** Additional balance sheet data can be entered (e.g., current asset, shares outstanding, common equity, total debt, etc.) and the relevant financial ratios will be computed (EBIT, Net Income, Net Cash Flow, Operating Cash Flow, Economic Value Added, Return on Invested Capital, Net Profit Margin, etc.).

- **DCF: Economic Results.** This tab returns the computed economic and financial indicators such as Net Present Value (NPV), Internal Rate of Return (IRR), Modified Internal Rate of Return (MIRR), Profitability Index (PI), Return on Investment (ROI), Payback Period (PP), and Discounted Payback (DPP). It also features a dynamic chart where you can view the NPV Profile (calculated NPV values depending on different discount rates), time-series of cash flows for the Option, and other calculated financial metrics.

- **DCF: Information and Details.** Here you can enter information and notes for the Option or project.

- **O&G: Input Assumptions.** Revenues, expenses, capital investments, starting and ending years for the cash flow model, discount rate, and tax rates can be entered here.

- **O&G: Escalation and Depreciation.** The capital investments, revenues, and expenses are automatically escalated and depreciated accordingly over time. You can copy these computed results to paste into another software (e.g., Microsoft Excel).

- **O&G: Cash Flow Model.** The intermediate calculations (i.e., cash flow model and tax consequences) are automatically computed and shown in this tab.

- **O&G: Economic Results.** This tab returns the computed economic and financial indicators such as NPV, IRR, MIRR, PI, ROI, PP, and DPP. It also features a dynamic chart where you can view the NPV Profile (calculated NPV values depending on different discount rates), time-series of cash flows for the Option, and other calculated financial metrics.

- **O&G: Information and Details.** Here you can enter information and notes for the Option or project.

o **Portfolio Analysis.** This tab returns the computed economic and financial indicators such as NPV, IRR, MIRR, PI, ROI, PP, and DPP for all the Options combined into a portfolio view. The Economic Results (Level 3) subtabs show the individual Option's economic and financial indicators whereas this Level 2 Portfolio Analysis view shows the results of all Options' indicators and compares them side by side. There are also two charts available for comparing these individual Options' results.

o **Applied Analytics.** This section allows you to run Tornado Analysis and Scenario Analysis on any one of the Options previously modeled—this analytics tab is on Level 1, which means it covers all of the various Options on Level 2. You can therefore run Tornado or Scenario on any one of the Options.

- **Static Tornado.** Tornado Analysis is a static sensitivity analysis of the selected model's output to each input assumption, performed one at a time, and ranked from most impactful to the least. This analysis tests all precedent variables in the model independently.

- **Scenario Analysis.** Scenario Analysis is also a static sensitivity model that can be easily performed through a two-step process: set up the model and run the model. This analysis tests one or two variables through a range of scenarios to determine the outcome of the selected output.

- **Scenario Input Settings.** This is where you would set up the variables to test and their ranges or scenarios.

- **Scenario Output Tables.** This is where you would run the saved scenarios and obtain color-coded scenario tables ("sweetspots" and "hotspots").

o **Risk Simulation.** Set up and run Monte Carlo risk simulations on any of your Options. Specifically, you can set up probability distribution assumptions on any combinations of inputs, run a risk simulation tens of thousands of trials, and retrieve the simulated forecast outputs as charts, statistics, probabilities, and confidence intervals in order to develop comprehensive risk profiles of the Options.

- **Set Input Assumptions.** Start the simulation analysis by first setting simulation distributional inputs here.

- **Simulation Results.** Shows the simulated forecast charts (PDF/CDF), simulation risk statistics, percentiles, probabilities, and confidence intervals of your simulation.

- **Overlay Results.** Multiple simulation output variables can be compared at once using the Overlay Results tab.

- **Analysis of Alternatives.** This subtab shows the results of the simulation statistics in a table format as well as a chart of the statistics such that one Option can be compared against another.

- **Dynamic Sensitivity.** After a simulation is run, this is where a dynamic sensitivity analysis is performed.

o **Options Strategies.** This is where you can draw your own custom strategic map or strategic real options paths. This section only allows you to draw and visualize these strategic pathways and does not perform any computations. The next section, Options Valuation, actually performs the computations.

o **Options Valuation.** This tab performs the calculations of Real Options Valuation models.

- **Options Valuation.** Here is where you start by choosing and setting up the real options model to compute.

- **Strategy View.** Provides a visual exemplar of the selected real option.

- **Sensitivity.** Runs a static sensitivity table of the real options model.

- **Tornado.** Develops the Tornado chart of the real options model.

- **Scenario.** Runs a scenario table of the real options model.

o **Forecast Prediction.** This is a sophisticated Business Analytics and Business Statistics module with over 150 functionalities.

- **Dataset.** Enter and edit your data here.

- **Visualize.** You can chart any data variable you have entered.

- **Command.** Provides an alternative and quicker way of executing models in the Forecast Prediction module.

- **Analysis.** Set up the analytical models (choose the model, provide it with the relevant data variables, and set the model parameters).

- **Results.** Shows the results of the analytical model, if applicable.

- **Charts.** Charts the results of the analytical model, if applicable.

- **Statistics.** Returns the statistics of the analytical model, if applicable.

○ **Portfolio Optimization.** In the Portfolio Optimization section, the individual Options can be modeled as a portfolio and optimized to determine the best combination of projects for the portfolio.

- **Optimization Settings.** Start the analysis by setting up the portfolio's objective, decision variables, and constraints here.

- **Optimization Results.** This tab returns the results from the portfolio optimization process.

- **Advanced Custom Optimization.** In this tab, you can create and solve your own customized optimization models.

○ **Knowledge Center.** To assist you in quickly getting up to speed in using the software, here you will find quick getting started guides and sample procedures that are straight to the point.

- **Step by Step Procedures.** Here you will find some quick self-paced lessons on how to use PEAT.

- **Basic Project Economics Lessons.** This section provides an overview tour of some common concepts involved with cash flow analysis and project economic analysis such as the computations of NPV, IRR, MIRR, PI, ROI, PP, and DPP, as well as the basics of interpreting PDF/CDF simulation forecast charts.

- **Getting Started Videos.** Here you can watch a short description and hands-on examples of how to run one of the sections within this PEAT software.

2.2 Project Economics

The **Project Economics** section is at the heart of your input assumptions. Here you would enter your input assumptions, set up the project economics model, identify and create the various Options, and compute the economic and financial results such as Net Present Value (NPV), Internal Rate of Return (IRR), Modified Internal Rate of Return (MIRR), Profitability Index (PI), Return on Investment (ROI), Payback Period (PP), and Discounted Payback (DPP). This section will also auto generate various charts, cash flow models, intermediate calculations, and comparisons of your Options within a portfolio view.

TIPS on NPV, IRR, MIRR, PI, ROI, PP, and DPP

Refer to the Technical Appendix for more technical specifications and examples of project economics analysis as well as the most common results, including NPV, IRR, MIRR, PI, ROI, PP, and DPP.

2.2.1 Global Settings

The **Global Settings** section is only available in the Oil and Gas module, and comprises the following subtabs:

- **Global Assumptions.** This subtab requires you to enter the global inputs (Figure 2.2) that apply across all Options to be analyzed later, such as the various discount rates, depreciation rates, decimal settings, simulation settings, etc.

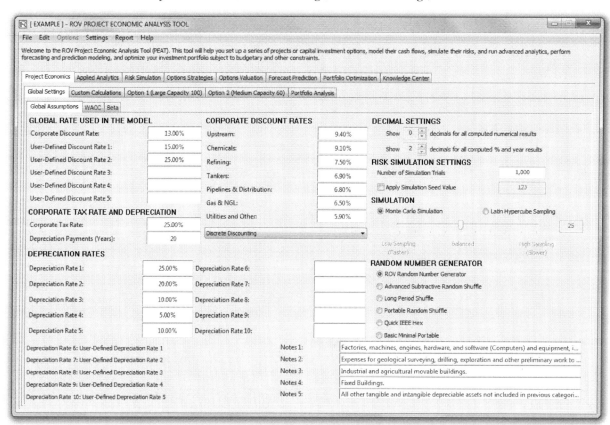

Figure 2.2 – Oil and Gas Model: Global Assumptions

- **Weighted Average Cost of Capital (WACC).** This is an optional set of analytics whereby you can compute the firm's WACC to use as a discount rate (Figure 2.3). Start by selecting either the **Simple WACC** or **Detailed WACC Cost Elements**. Then, you can either enter the required inputs or click on the **Load Example** button to load a sample set of inputs that you can then use as a guide to entering your own set of assumptions.

- **Beta.** This is another optional subtab used for computing the Beta risk coefficient by pasting in historical stock prices or stock returns to compute the Beta (Figure 2.4). The resulting Beta is used in the Capital Asset Pricing Model (CAPM), one of the main inputs into the WACC model. Start by selecting whether you have historical **Stock Prices** or **Stock Returns**, then enter the number of **Rows** (periods) of historical data you have, and **Paste** the data into the relevant columns and click **Compute**. The Beta result will update and you can use this Beta as an input into the WACC model.

TIPS on WACC and BETA

In the Discounted Cash Flow module, the **WACC** and **BETA** calculations are available under the **Discount Rate** subtab of the main **DCF** tab.

When deciding on the periodicity and length of historical stock price data to use, we recommend using daily stock prices with a historical period either commensurate with the Options analysis period or a representative period in the past (similar risks and market conditions in the past that are expected to repeat themselves in the near future).

Figure 2.3 – Oil and Gas Model: WACC Discount Rate

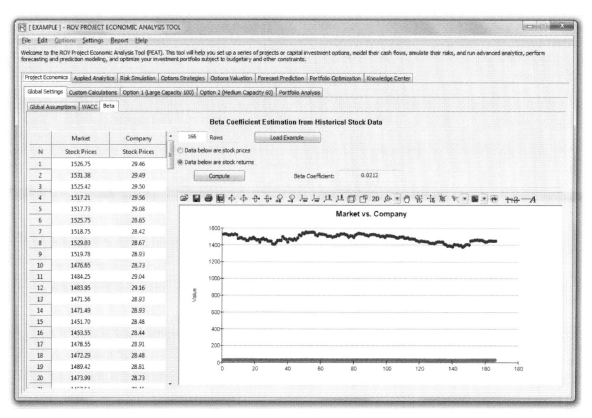

Figure 2.4 – Oil and Gas Model: Beta

2.2.2 Custom Calculations

A **Customs Calculation** tab (Figure 2.5) is also available for making your own custom calculations just as you would in an Excel spreadsheet. Clicking on the **Function F(x)** button will provide you with a list of the supported functions you can use in this tab. Other basic mathematical functions are also supported, such as =, +, -, /, *, ^. If you use this optional Custom Calculations tab and wish to link some cells to the input tabs (e.g., Option 1), you can select the cells in the Custom Calculations tab, right-click, and select **Link To**. Then proceed to the location in the Option tabs and highlight the location of the input cells you wish to link to, right-click, and select **Link From**. Any subsequent changes you make in the Custom Calculations tab will be updated in the linked input assumption cells.

Example 1: In the Custom Calculations tab, enter the following: **1, 2, 3** into cells **A1, B1, C1**, respectively. Then in cell **D1**, enter **=A1+B1+C1** and click on any other cell and it will update the cell and return the value 6. Similarly, you type in **=SUM(A1:C1)** to obtain the same results. The preset functions can be seen by clicking on the **f(x)** the button.

Example 2: In the Custom Calculations tab, enter the following: **1, 2, 3** into cells **A1, B1, C1**, respectively. Then, **select these three cells**, **right-click**, and select **Link To**. Proceed to any one of the **Option** tabs, and in the **Discounted Cash Flow** or **Input Assumptions** subtabs, **select three cells across** (e.g., on the Revenue line item), **right-click** and select **Link From**. The values of cells A1, B1, C1 in the Custom Calculations tab will be linked to this location. You can go back to the Custom Calculations tab and change the values in the original three cells and you will see the linked cells in the Discounted Cash Flow or Input Assumptions subtabs change and update to reflect the new values.

Figure 2.5 – Custom Calculations

TIPS on the Custom Tab

- The Custom tab is where you can replicate your Excel models with multiple worksheets or multiple Excel workbooks in this Custom tab, so that all the preliminary calculations linked to your project will be stored in one convenient place, ready for auditing and archiving the models.

- In PEAT, click on **Help | Extras | PEAT Visual Guide 08 – Custom Tab and Excel Links** for a visual guide of these Custom tab's tips.

- Click on the Custom tab and then right-mouse-click to **Add** additional tabs, **Delete** existing tabs, **Duplicate**, **Rename**, and **Rearrange** Custom tabs.

- You can manually move and resize the column widths or click the **Grid...** button to select **Auto Fit** or set a specific width size.

- You can click on the **FX** icon to bring up a list of currently supported functions (e.g., ABS, AVERAGE, CONCATENATE, LEFT, LEN, LN, LOG, LOG10, MAX, MIN, POWER, RIGHT, ROUND, SUM, SUMIF, SUMPRODUCT, IF, AND, OR, +, -, /, *, ^).

- You can **Name Cells** (select one or more cells, type in the name you want in the cell **Name** box on the top left of the data grid and hit **Enter**). These named cells will appear later in Tornado, Scenario, and Risk Simulation tabs for easier recognition. If more than one cell is selected, then the cells will have the same name followed by an index (e.g., MyName1, MyName2, MyName3, etc.).

- Note that you can have multiple Custom tabs and rename them as you wish, each tab also has an internal name such as **xls1**, **xls2**, and so forth. These internal names are used in the software's internal algorithms as well as when you cross link cells (linking across different Custom tabs, see below).

- You can copy existing calculations and worksheets from Excel and paste them into the Custom tabs. Simply select the cells or area in the Excel model worksheet you wish to copy, then **CTRL+C** or **right-mouse-click Copy** or click on the **Copy** icon in Excel… Then, select a cell in the Custom worksheet and hit **CTRL+V** or **right-mouse-click Paste** to paste into the Custom worksheet… Note that this approach will only paste the Texts and Values… Colors, equations, functions, live calculations, and formatting will not be included.

- Alternatively, you can paste a **Live Excel Model** with computations into the Custom worksheet:

  o In your Excel model, click **CTRL~** (hold down the **Control** key while hitting the **Tilda ~** key, which is usually located to the top left of the number 1 and letter Q keys) to change the Excel view from values and results to Equation View where you can see all the equations and functions. Once you are in the Equation View, you can Copy from Excel and Paste into PEAT's Custom worksheet as usual, and the equations will carry forward into the Custom tab… Equations will be pasted into the Custom worksheet and be updated/calculated as live links.

  o Please note that PEAT Custom worksheet now supports the main basic functions which are sufficient for most users.

  o Uncheck the **Auto Calculate** box to temporarily turn off auto update before pasting a large model but remember to turn it back on afterwards. The Custom tab will paste the model more quickly.

  o Be careful with the specific cell locations where you copy and paste. For example, if you copy cells A1:C10 in Excel, make sure to paste it into the same cell locations in the Custom tab so that the equations, links, and their computations will be preserved.

  o You can **Cross Link** cells among tabs (i.e., one custom tab has cells linked to another custom tab inside PEAT). In order to cross-link among tabs, you have to use the internal Custom tab naming convention. For example, you can use equations like: =xls2!a3 or =100*xls3!c35 and so forth. This is similar to Excel's cross worksheet linking convention.

  o If you are copy and pasting a live model with multiple worksheet cross linking via the CTRL~ approach above, make sure to **first rename your Excel worksheets to xls1, xls2, and so forth**. This will auto-rename the links inside Excel, and hence, when you paste the live equations, the cross Custom tab links will be maintained.

  o Another approach is to **Link to an External Excel Model**. This means the Excel model is kept separate and external from PEAT, and will be maintained external to PEAT. These external Excel files can then be linked to PEAT and when the Excel source models are updated, the Custom tab's values will also be updated. In the Custom worksheet, click the **Excel** button to **Add an Excel Link** (or to Edit/Delete existing links). Then **Browse the Excel File** you need, select the **Excel Worksheet** and **Excel Cell Range** to link from, and enter the **Starting Cell** in the Custom worksheet to link to. Enter a **Name** and **Notes** for easy reference in the event you have multiple links (you can link multiple Excel workbook files and Excel worksheets) into one or more Custom worksheets… Be careful with the specific cell locations where you copy and paste. For example, if you copy cells A1:C10 in Excel, make sure to paste it into the same cell locations in the Custom tab so that the equations, links, and their computations will be preserved.

- Custom tab's results and values can also be used to Link From/To another Option tab within the PEAT software. For instance, the Custom tab is used as a scratch location where your own custom computations are done. And some of these resulting computations need to be used in the Project Options tabs. You can always copy and paste static values to these Project Options tabs or create a dynamic updatable link. Multiple links can be performed, where each link can take on multiple cells at once.

    o The first step is a Link To. In the Custom worksheet, select the data area (one or more contiguous cells) and right-mouse-click Link To… to generate a link from this Custom worksheet… Notice the blinking marquee border around a live Linked To data area…

    o The second step is a Link From. In the Project Option tab, select the cells/location you wish to link the data into and right-mouse-click then select Link From… You can also Remove Link later if required. Notice the Yellow highlights indicating a live link. Changing the values in the Custom worksheet will change the values here…

- Miscellaneous Tips

    o You right-mouse-click to Copy Formula and then right-mouse-click Paste the Formula with Relative versus Absolute cell addressing. This is the same as $ cell addressing in Excel. You can also paste data with Signs Reversed (e.g., expenses with -100 values will be pasted as 100 with signs reversed) or paste its Absolute Values regardless of signs.

    o You can also select cells with basic input values and via the right-mouse-click, and Set as Simulation Assumptions. These cells will turn green and show up later in the Risk Simulation | Set Input Assumptions tab. In the event these set assumption cells in the Custom tabs do not show up, save the file and reopen to reestablish their internal links.

    o Change cell colors or font colors by using the color droplist icons.

    o Use the Up/Down/Left/Right arrows on the keyboard to navigate the data grid.

    o Use F2 or double click on a cell to access the contents of the cell for editing.

    o Click on the top left corner of the data grid to select all cells at once.

    o You can increase/decrease the column width as required (simply drag the columns to change its width or use the Grid… button to Auto-fit columns).

    o You can click on and select multiple rows or columns at once.

    o Do not change the source Excel file name or folder location if you are performing a live link from Excel.

    o By default the Live Links from source Excel files are updated every time the *.rovprojecon file opens (this checkbox is default selected when you click on the Excel button in the Custom worksheet).

    o Live Excel links when updating, will locate the same file name in the absolute folder path (e.g., c:\your folder\subfolder name\filename.xlsx) first and if the file does not exist, it will locate the same file name in the relative folder path where your *.rovprojecon file is stored. The latter comes in handy when you have to e-mail the model file as well as the Excel source file to another individual, and s/he may save the files in a different subdirectory/location/path but as long as both files reside in the same subfolder, the links will still update and work.

o The best way to update any externally linked Excel files is to SAVE and restart the *rovprojecon file.

o Manually inputted cells (black font) can be overridden easily by simply typing over the cell's values (type over the cell, double click, or F2 to access and edit the cell). Linked cells (blue font) are intentionally created to prevent accidental overrides (you cannot simply type over existing cell values) and you can only intentionally override Excel linked cells by selecting the cell and editing its contents in the Formula bar.

2.2.3 Options

When in any of the Options tabs, the Options menu will become available, ready for you to add, delete, duplicate, or rename an option or rearrange the order of the Option tabs by first clicking on any Option tab and then selecting **Options | Add, Delete, Duplicate, Rearrange,** or **Rename Option** from the menu. All the required functionalities such as input assumptions, adding or reducing the number of rows, selecting discount rate type, or copying the grid are available within each Option tab.

The input assumptions you enter in these Option tabs are localized and used only within each tab, whereas input assumptions entered in the Global Settings tab (Figure 2.2) apply to all Option tabs simultaneously. When setting up your model in the Options tab (Level 2), proceed from left to right of the Level 3 subtabs. Required input assumptions are shown as input boxes (e.g., seen as white input boxes in Figure 2.6) and computed results are shown as data grids. Finally, if your model is large, you can click on the **View Full Grid** for a pop-up view of the entire model.

DCF: Discounted Cash Flow Model

Revenues, expenses, capital investments, starting and ending years for the cash flow model, discount rate, and tax rates can be entered here (Figure 2.6).

TIPS on the DCF Model

- Enter all the required inputs, and if certain cells are irrelevant, enter zeros. You can also select some data from Excel and right-click on any cell and paste the data for the entire row or multiple rows and columns. You can also right-click and select Paste Absolute Values or Paste with Signed Reversed if required (e.g., these are valuable if your Excel data uses negative values to represent expenses whereas PEAT requires positive values as expenses).

- You can increase or decrease the number of rows for each category as required.

- The DCF Starting Year input is the discounting base year, where all cash flows will be present valued to this year.

- The main categories are in boldface, and the input boxes under the categories are for you to enter in the line item name/label.

- Remember to scroll down the user interface to continue entering additional required critical inputs (e.g., **Capital Expenditures**).

- You can either apply a constant tax % rate to compute taxes or use your own custom inputs.

- See the Technical Appendix for some example cash flow models and cash flow calculations.

- As usual, you can click on **Copy Grid** to copy the results into the Windows clipboard in order to paste into another software application such as Microsoft Excel or Word.

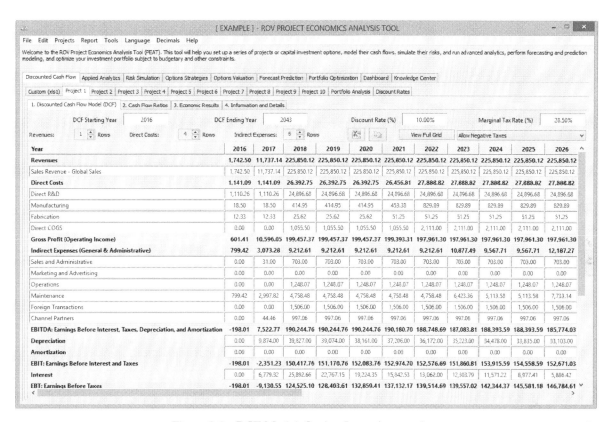

Figure 2.6 – DCF Model: Option Input Assumptions

O&G: Input Assumptions

Revenues, expenses, capital investments, starting and ending years for the cash flow model, discount rate, and tax rates can be entered here (Figure 2.7).

TIPS on O&G Input Assumptions

- Enter the required inputs, not forgetting the special **Depreciation** % and **Escalation** % columns.

- Remember to scroll to the right to continue entering input assumptions in the out-years.

- The **Discount Rate drop-down list** defaults to the **Corporate Rate** entered in the **Global Settings** tab, but you can change the rate to use here for this Option. Each Option can have a different discount rate (e.g., if the Options have different risk structures, their respective discount rates should be allowed to differ, with the exception that when all Options are considered at par in terms of risk or a global corporate weighted average, cost of capital is used).

- You can select the **Auto-Fill** checkboxes if required. The auto-fill function allows you to enter a single value on a line item and all subsequent years on the same line item will be automatically filled with the same value.

- Note that the green input cells are for the ERA period whereas the purple cells are for the ERC period. This separation of colors makes it easier to identify the periods when entering or pasting data.

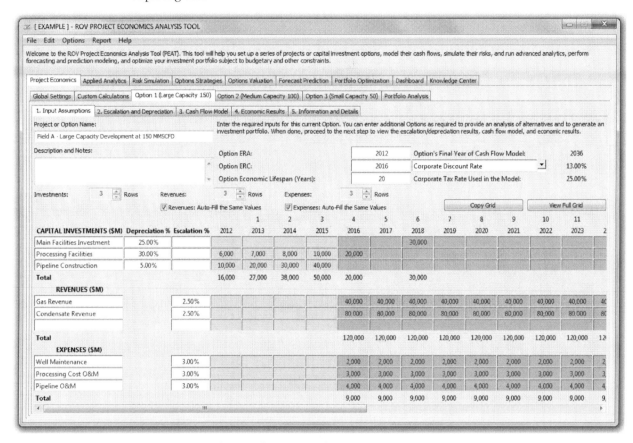

Figure 2.7 – Oil and Gas Model: Option Input Assumptions

TIPS on Viewing the Full Grid

You can also click on the **View Full Grid** to see the entire model as a pop-up screen (Figure 2.8). This facilitates viewing of a large model and reduces the need for scrolling horizontally and vertically. It also helps when you are attempting to take a screenshot of the entire model.

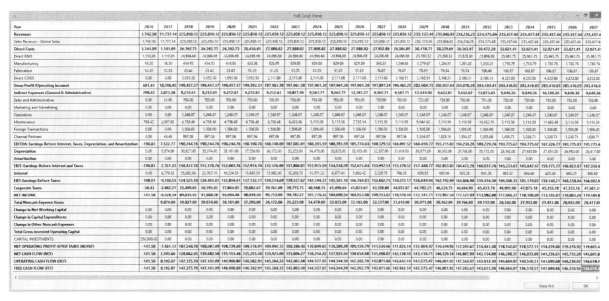

Figure 2.8 – View Full Grid

DCF: Cash Flow Ratios

Additional balance sheet data can be entered here (e.g., current asset, shares outstanding, common equity, total debt, etc.), as seen in Figure 2.9, and the relevant financial ratios will be computed (EBIT, Net Income, Net Cash Flow, Operating Cash Flow, Economic Value Added, Return on Invested Capital, Net Profit Margin, etc.). Computed results or intermediate calculations are shown as data grids. Data grid rows are color coded by alternate rows for easy viewing. As usual, you can click on **Copy Grid** to copy the computations to the Windows clipboard from which you can then paste into another software such as Microsoft Excel.

TIPS on Modeling Cash Flow Ratios

- Enter the input assumptions as best you can; you can guess at some of these figures to get started. The inputs entered in this **Cash Flow Ratios** subtab will be used only in this subtab's balance sheet ratios.

- There are two sets of results available. The first and larger results grid shows the time-series of cash flow analysis for the Option for multiple years. These are the cash flows used to compute the NPV, IRR, MIRR, and so forth.

- The smaller grid at the bottom of the screen returns the balance sheet ratios, which apply the input parameters at the top of the tab. These are single-point estimates and represent a snapshot in time for either the firm or the project's balance sheet.

- The first project requires you to enter the eleven balance sheet input assumptions, whereas all other projects' balance sheet inputs either can be linked to the first project or uniquely entered (if these are projects under a different balance sheet scenario such as international projects or a different year).

- You can show the results as cash flow values and ratios or as percentage of sales revenue (use the Show Earnings droplist to make your selection).

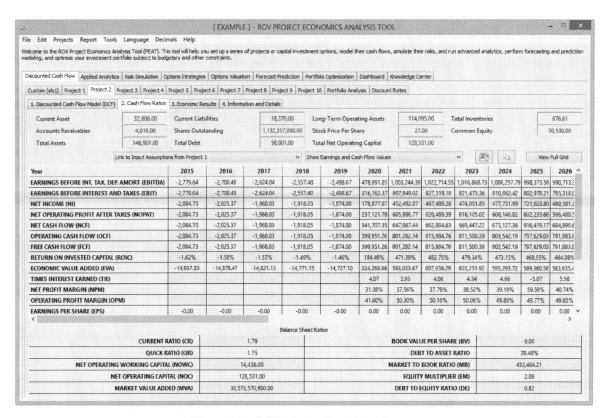

Figure 2.9 – DCF Model: Cash Flow Ratios

O&G: Escalation and Depreciation

The capital investments, revenues, and expenses are automatically escalated and depreciated accordingly over time (Figure 2.10). You can copy these computed results to paste into another software application (e.g., Microsoft Excel).

O&G: Cash Flow Model

Additional intermediate calculations (i.e., cash flow model and tax consequences) are automatically computed and shown in this tab (Figure 2.11).

TIPS on Escalation, Depreciation, and Cash Flow Model

- The Escalation and Depreciation subtab returns the input assumptions' escalation and depreciation schedule of the cash flow series over time.

- The results in the grid are automatically computed and you cannot modify its contents.

- Alternate rows are color coded for easier visual identification and the colors do not represent anything specific.

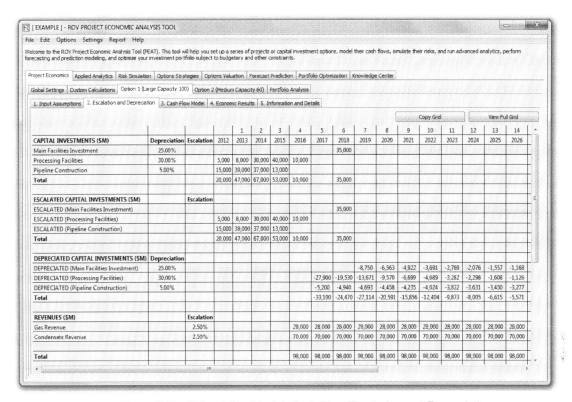

Figure 2.10 – Oil and Gas Model: Cash Flow Escalation and Depreciation

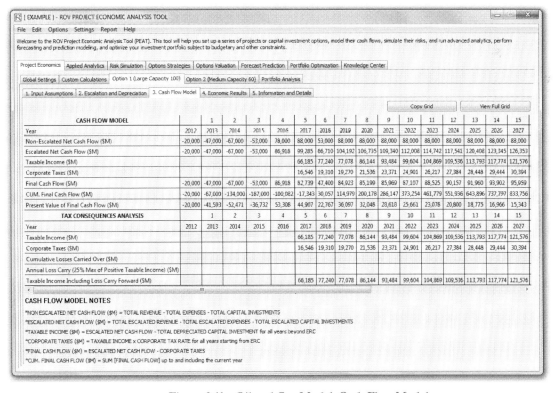

Figure 2.11 – Oil and Gas Model: Cash Flow Model

DCF and O&G:
Economic Results

This Economic Results (Level 3) subtab shows the results from the chosen Option and returns the Net Present Value (NPV), Internal Rate of Return (IRR), Modified Internal Rate of Return (MIRR), Profitability Index (PI), Return on Investment (ROI), Payback Period (PP), and Discounted Payback Period (DPP), as seen in Figures 2.12 and 2.13. Refer to the Technical Appendix for details on each of the calculation methods.

An NPV Profile table and chart are also provided, where different discount rates and their respective NPV results are shown and charted. You can change the range of the discount rates to show/compute, copy the results, and copy the NPV Profile chart, as well as use any of the chart icons to manipulate the chart's look and feel (e.g., change the chart's line/background color, chart type, chart view, or add/remove gridlines, labels, and legend).

You can also change the variable to display in the chart. For instance, you can change the chart from displaying the NPV Profile to the time-series charts of net cash flows, escalated net cash flows, taxable income, final cash flows, cumulative final cash flows, or present value of the final cash flows. You can then click on the Copy Chart button to take a screenshot of the modified chart that you can then paste into another software application such as Microsoft Excel or Microsoft PowerPoint. *As a note of caution, when you click this copy chart button, please do give it an extra second before moving the mouse and pasting into another software because on slower computers, the native Windows imager services will need to run in the background and may take the added second or two to complete.*

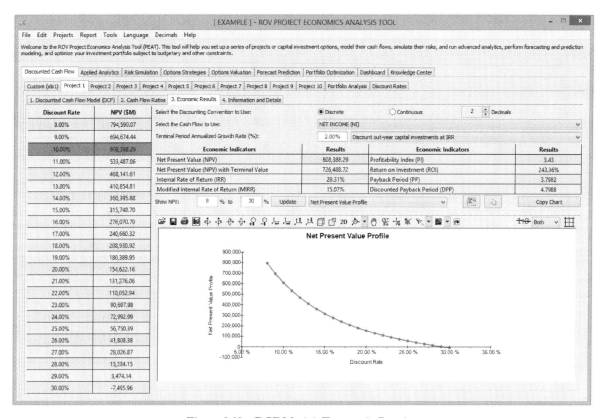

Figure 2.12 – DCF Model: Economic Results

TIPS on Reviewing Economic Results

- The Economic Results are for each individual Option, whereas the Portfolio Analysis tab compares the economic results of all Options at once.

- The Terminal Value Annualized Growth Rate is applied to the last year's cash flow to account for a perpetual constant growth rate cash flow model, and these future cash flows are discounted back to the base year and added to the NPV to arrive at the NPV with Terminal Value result.

- You can change the Show NPV percentages and click Update to change the NPV Profile results grid and chart (assuming you selected the NPV Profile chart, as shown in Figure 2.13).

- As usual, there are chart icons for you to modify the chart (bar chart color, chart type, chart view, background color, rotation, show/hide labels and legends, show/hide gridlines and data labels, etc.). Also available are the Copy Results and Copy Chart functionalities. Again, on slower or older computers, remember to give it an additional second after you click the copy chart before moving the mouse and pasting into another application.

- In the Oil and Gas module, we have multiple discount rates, and these rates and their respective NPV results are highlighted in the data grid (Figure 2.13), as well as the discount rate equivalent to the IRR (i.e., the discount rate where NPV = 0).

- There is a discount out-year capital investments drop-down list using the IRR Method or Discount Rate Method. The IRR result that is computed will depend on the method chosen. The traditional method is to use IRR as the reinvestment rate (default selection in the drop-down list) defined as the discount rate where the $NPV = 0$ (this can be verified in the NPV and Discount Rate grid on the left of the screen). This approach works in most traditional models but will return a null result if the IRR requirement is violated. IRR has a requirement that the initial Cash Flow (CF) at time 0 compared to Capital Investments (INV) at time 0 be such that $INV_0 > CF_0$, otherwise the concept of IRR and its math do not work. This method works well in most business situations (capital investments come early and positive cash flows come later in time), but one can also have a situation where $INV_0 < CF_0$ making the *Total Net Cash Flow* or $CF_0 - INV_0 > 0$. Therefore, the traditional IRR, defined as the Discount Rate where $NPV = 0$, will not return a valid result (this situation of the initial cash flow being greater than the investment can, in fact, occur in real-life, albeit seldom). There are two ways to solve this problem. The first is that you manually push the positive CF_0 one period into the future using some discount rate or reinvestment rate, or discount all future INV_T amounts at the discount rate back to time zero, thereby making the *Total Net Cash Flow* or $CF_0 - INV_0 < 0$ as the present value of the $\Sigma INV_T > CF_0$. This is essentially the approach undertaken in the second item on the drop-down list (please be aware that in this situation, the computed IRR is really a quasi-IRR and therefore will not be the discount rate making the $NPV = 0$; it will, nonetheless, at least provide you a computed metric). Of course, in a highly profitable project where the present value of the $\Sigma INV_T < CF_0$, neither the traditional IRR nor the quasi-IRR works.

  - IRR calculations require that *Total Initial Cash Flow* $(CF_0 - INV_0) < 0$. This value has to be NEGATIVE. The IRR Method stops if $(CF_0 > INV_0)$ or $NET CF_0 > 0$. This value cannot be POSITIVE.

  - The IRR Method is better in most cases except when the following occurs, then the IRR Method cannot return a value, and only the Discount Rate Method will return a result (although this is a quasi-IRR and not the traditional IRR): $(CF_0 > INV_0)$ or $NET CF_0 > 0$, and if *Present Value of the* $\Sigma INV_T > CF_0$. If *Present Value of the* $\Sigma INV_T < CF_0$, neither method works.

To summarize, we see the following effects on IRR calculations:

No Cash Flow at Time 0 *(CF₀ = 0):*

Large Investments in Year 0	IRR Method = DR Method, both work, same results
Large Investments in Year 0, 2, 5	IRR Method runs and is correct; DR Method runs quasi-IRR
Large Investments in Year 2, 5	IRR Method runs and is correct; DR Method runs quasi-IRR
Small Investments in Year 0	IRR Method = DR Method, both work, same results
Small Investments in Year 0, 2, 5	IRR Method runs and is correct; DR Method runs quasi-IRR
Small Investments in Year 2, 5	IRR Method stops; DR Method stops

Some Cash Flow at Time 0 *(CF₀ > 0):*

Large Investments in Year 0	IRR Method = DR Method, both work, same results
Large Investments in Year 0, 2, 5	IRR Method runs and is correct; DR Method runs quasi-IRR
Large Investments in Year 2, 5	IRR Method stops; DR Method runs quasi-IRR
Small Investments in Year 0	IRR Method stops; DR Method stops
Small Investments in Year 0, 2, 5	IRR Method stops; DR Method runs quasi-IRR
Small Investments in Year 2, 5	IRR Method stops; DR Method stops

The subscripts above represent $CF_0 = 0$ and $CF_0 > 0$.

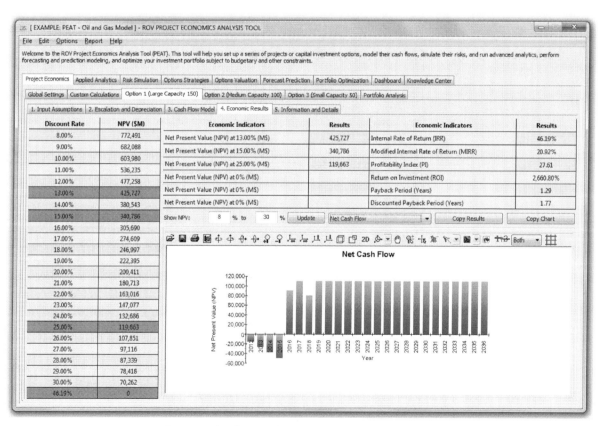

Figure 2.13 – Oil and Gas Model: Economic Results

DCF and O&G: Information and Details

In this tab, you can enter information and notes of the Option or project. The default settings have category labels such as Project or Option Title, Corporate Objective, and so forth. However, you can click on the Categories button to edit and modify these category titles as required (Figure 2.14).

TIPS on Using Information and Details

- Use this tab for entering justifications for the input assumptions used as well as any notes on each of the Options. For numerical calculations and notes, use the Custom Calculations tab instead.

- You can also change the labels and categories of the Information and Details tab by clicking on Categories and editing the default labels.

- The formatting of entered text can be performed in the Description box by clicking on the various text formatting icons.

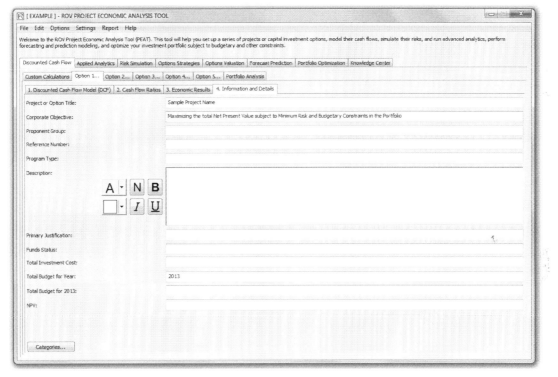

Figure 2.14 – Information and Details

2.2.4 Portfolio Analysis

This Portfolio Analysis tab (Figure 2.15) returns the computed economic and financial indicators such as NPV, IRR, MIRR, PI, ROI, PP, and DPP for all the Options combined into a portfolio view. The Economic Results (Level 3) subtabs show the individual Option's economic and financial indicators whereas this Level 2 Portfolio Analysis view shows the results of all Options' indicators and compares them side by side. There are also two charts available for comparing these individual Options' results.

TIPS on Using Portfolio Analysis

- The Portfolio Analysis tab is used to obtain a side-by-side comparison of all the main economic and financial indicators of all the Options at once. For instance, you can compare all the NPVs from each Option in a single results grid.

- What appears to be a chart graphic in the upper right (Figure 2.15 shows the DCF module's default example's Portfolio Analysis results) is actually a placeholder such that when there are multiple Options, the data results grid will expand in width to cover said graphic.

- The **bubble chart** on the left provides a visual representation of three main variables at once (e.g., the y-axis shows the IRR, the x-axis represents the NPV, and the size of the bubble may represent the capital investment; in such a situation, one would prefer a smaller ball that is in the top right quadrant of the chart).

- As usual, **chart icons, Copy Grid,** and **Copy Chart** and available for use in this tab.

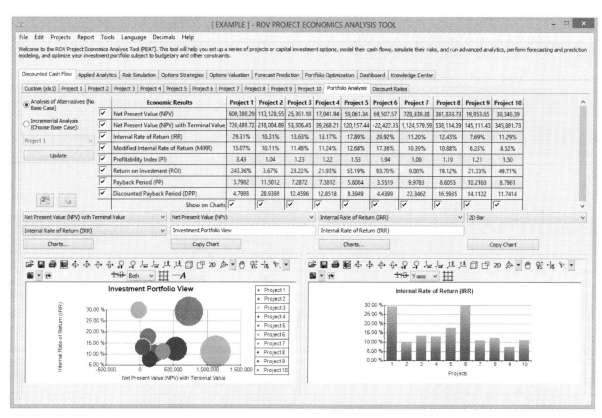

Figure 2.15 – Portfolio Analysis

2.3 Applied Analytics

The **Applied Analytics** section allows you to run Tornado Analysis and Scenario Analysis on any one of the Options previously modeled—this analytics tab is on Level 1, which means it covers all of the various Options on Level 2. You can, therefore, run Tornado or Scenario on any one of the Options.

2.3.1 Static Tornado

Tornado Analysis (Figure 2.16 shows the DCF module's default example's Tornado Analysis result) is a static sensitivity analysis of the selected model's output to each input assumption, performed one at a time, and ranked from most impactful to the least. Start the analysis by first choosing the output variable to test from the drop-down list.

You can change the default sensitivity settings of each input assumption to test and decide how many input assumption variables to chart (large models with many inputs may generate unsightly and less useful charts, whereas showing just the top variables reveals more information through a more elegant chart). You can also choose to run the input assumptions as unique inputs, group them as a line item (all individual inputs on a single line item are assumed to be one variable), or run as variable groups (e.g., all line items under Revenue will be assumed to be a single variable). Remember to click **Compute** to update the analysis if you make any changes to any of the settings. The sensitivity results are also shown as a table grid at the bottom of the screen (e.g., the initial base value of the chosen output variable, the input assumption changes, and the resulting output variable's sensitivity results). As usual, you can **Copy Chart** or **Copy Grid** results into the Windows clipboard for pasting into another software application.

TIPS on Interpreting Tornado Analysis Results

- Each horizontal bar indicates a unique input assumption that constitutes a precedent to the selected output variable.

- The x-axis represents the values of the selected output variable. The wider the bar chart, the greater the impact/swing the input assumption has on the output.

- A green bar on the right indicates that the input assumption has a positive effect on the selected output (conversely, a red bar indicates a negative effect).

- As another example, in Figure 2.16, we see the following:
  - The output tested is Option 1's NPV with Terminal Value.
  - Each of the precedent or input assumptions that directly affects the NPV with Terminal Value is tested ±10%; the top 10 variables are shown on the chart, with a 2 decimal precision setting; and each unique input is tested individually.
  - The results indicate that the Discount Rate has the highest impact, naturally, with the highest swing (widest horizontal bar), with a red bar on the right, indicating that the lower the discount rate (**Input Downside** in the grid and on the red right chart: 13.50%), the higher the NPV (**Output Downside** in the grid and on the red right bar chart's x-axis: 186.41). Conversely, the higher the discount rate (**Input Upside** in the grid and on the green left bar chart: 16.50%), the lower the NPV (**Output Upside** in the grid and on the red right bar chart's x-axis: 140.84).

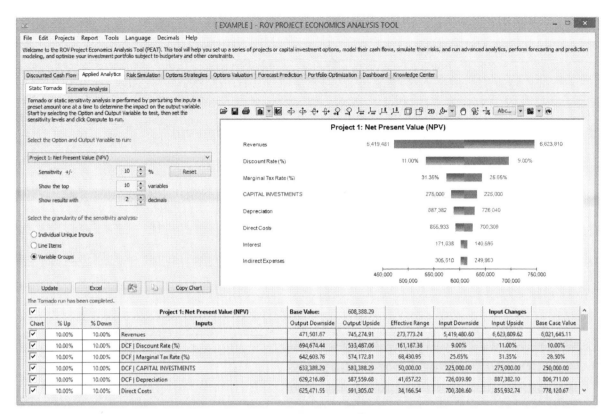

Figure 2.16 – Static Tornado Analysis

2.3.2 Scenario Analysis

Scenario Analysis can be easily performed through a two-step process: set up the model and run the model. In the **Scenario Input Settings** subtab (Figure 2.17 shows the DCF module's default example's Scenario Input Settings), start by selecting the output variable you wish to test from the drop-down list. Then, based on your selection, the precedents of the output will be listed under two categories (**Line Item**, which will change all input assumptions in the entire line item in the model simultaneously, and **Single Item**, which will change individual input assumption items). **Select one or two checkboxes** at a time and the inputs you wish to run scenarios on, and enter the plus/minus percentage to test and the number of steps between these two values to test. You can also **add color coding** of sweetspots or hotspots in the scenario analysis (values falling within different ranges have unique colors). You can create multiple scenarios and **Save As** each one (enter a **Name** for each saved scenario).

Proceed to the **Scenario Output Tables** (Figure 2.18) to run the saved analysis. Click on the **drop-down list** to select the previously saved scenarios to run. The selected scenario table complete with sweetspot/hotspot color coding will be generated. **Decimals** can be increased or decreased as required, and you can **Copy Grid** or **View Full Grid** as needed. To facilitate review of the scenario tables, pay attention to the NOTE, which provides the information of which input variable is set as the rows versus columns.

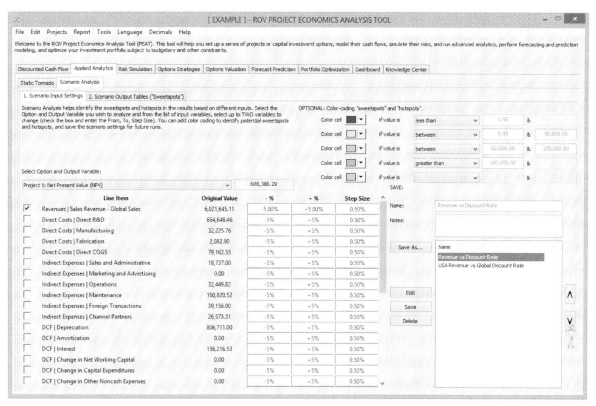

Figure 2.17 – Scenario Analysis: Scenario Input Settings

TIPS on Running a Scenario Analysis

- You can create and run **Scenario Analysis** on either one or two input variables at once.

- The scenario settings can be saved for retrieval in the future, which means you can modify any input assumptions in the Options models and come back to rerun the saved scenarios.

- You can also increase/decrease decimals in the scenario results tables, as well as change colors in the tables for easier visual interpretation (especially when trying to identify scenario combinations, or so-called sweetspots and hotspots).

- Remember to scroll down the form for additional input variables.

- **Line Items** can be changed using $\pm X\%$ where all inputs in the line are changed multiple times within this specific range all at once., **Individual Items** can be changed $\pm Y$ *units* where each input is changed multiple times within this specific range.

- You can either double click on a saved model to retrieve it settings or click on the **Edit** button to edit the settings. Do not forget to click **Save** to save any changes you made or use **Save As** to duplicate the model and create a new model with the modified settings.

- Sweetspots and hotspots refer to specific combinations of two input variables that will drive the output up or down. For instance, suppose investments are below a certain threshold and revenues are above a certain barrier, then the NPV will be in excess of the expected budget (the sweetspots, perhaps highlighted in green), or if investments are above a certain value, NPV will turn negative if revenues fall below a certain threshold (the hotspots, perhaps highlighted in red).

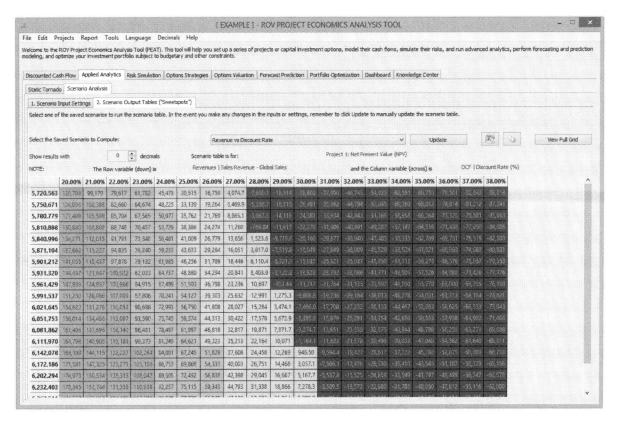

Figure 2.18 – Scenario Analysis: Scenario Output Tables

2.4 Risk Simulation

In the **Risk Simulation** section, you can set up and run Monte Carlo risk simulations on any of your Options' inputs. Specifically, you can set up probability distribution assumptions on any combinations of inputs, run a risk simulation tens of thousands of trials, and retrieve the simulated forecast outputs as charts, statistics, probabilities, and confidence intervals in order to develop comprehensive risk profiles of the Options.

2.4.1 Set Input Assumptions

In the **Set Input Assumptions** subtab, you start the simulation analysis by first setting simulation distributional inputs here (Figure 2.19 shows the DCF module's default example's Set Input Assumptions settings). Click on and **choose one Option at a time** to list the available input assumptions. Click on the **probability distribution icon** under the Settings header (see Figure 2.19 for the highlighted cell) for the relevant input assumption row, **select the probability distribution to use, and enter the relevant input parameters.** Continue setting as many simulation inputs as required (you can check/uncheck the inputs to simulate). Enter the **simulation trials** to run (start with 1,000 as initial test runs and use 10,000 for the final run as a rule of thumb for most models). You can also **Save As** the model (remember to provide it a **Name**). Then click on **Run Simulation**. Finally, in this tab, you can set simulation assumptions across multiple Options and **Simulate All Options at Once**, apply a **Seed Value** to replicate the exact simulation results each time it is run, apply pairwise **Correlations** between simulation inputs, and **Edit** a previously saved simulation model.

TIPS on Selecting Probability Distributions

- Refer to Dr. Johnathan Mun's *Modeling Risk: Applying Monte Carlo Risk Simulation, Strategic Real Options, Stochastic Forecasting, and Portfolio Optimization,* Third Edition (Wiley, 2015) for more technical details on selecting and understanding probability distributions.

- Although the software supports up to 50 probability distributions, in general, the most commonly used and applied distributions include **Triangular, Normal,** and **Uniform.**

- If you have historical data available, use the **Forecast Prediction** tab to perform a **Distributional Fitting** to determine the best-fitting distribution to use as well as to estimate the selected distribution's input parameters.

- You can also **Extract Simulation Data** when the risk simulation run is complete, and the extracted data can be used for additional analysis as required.

- You can **Save** multiple simulation settings such that they can be retrieved, edited, and modified as required in the future.

- Remember to select either **Simulate All Options at Once** or **Simulate Selected Option Only,** depending on whether you wish to run a risk simulation on all the Options that have predefined simulation assumptions or to run a simulation only on the current Option that is selected.

- The simulated results (e.g., distributional statistics, percentiles, confidence intervals, and probabilities) provide and create a risk profile of your Options. For more technical information on interpreting these results, refer to the Technical Appendix on simulation.

- Double clicking on a saved simulation model will run the simulation (or simply select the saved model and click **Run Simulation**), or selecting a saved model and clicking the **Edit** button allows you to make changes to the saved model.

- You can also click on the **Defaults…** button to set assumptions on all inputs at once with some generic parameter inputs (e.g., set all as Triangular distributions with +/- 10% or the most likely values).

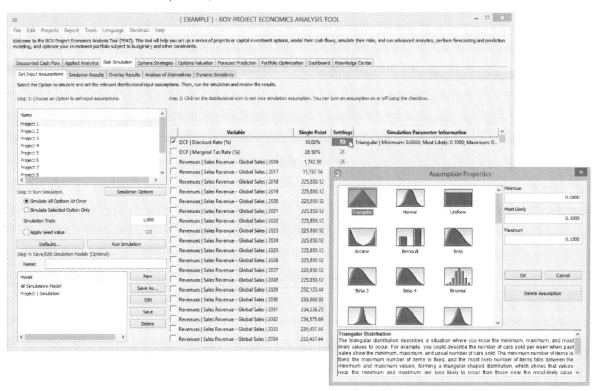

Figure 2.19 – Risk Simulation: Set Input Assumptions

2.4.2 Simulation Results

After the simulation completes its run, go to the **Simulation Results** tab (Figure 2.20 shows the DCF module's default example's risk simulation results after running the All Simulations Model). First **select the output variable** you wish to display using the drop-down list. The percentiles and simulation statistics are presented on the right, and the simulation forecast chart is shown on the left. You can change the chart type (e.g., PDF, CDF), enter **Percentiles** (in %) or **Certainty Values** (in output units) on the bottom left of the screen (remember to click **Update** when done) to show their vertical lines on the chart, or compute/show the **Percentiles/Confidence** levels on the bottom right of the screen (select the type, **Two Tail, Left Tail, Right Tail,** then either enter the percentile values to auto compute the confidence interval, or enter the confidence desired to obtain the relevant percentiles). Note that the bottom right section for percentiles and confidence levels are used to both show the vertical lines on the chart as well as to compute the statistical results (i.e., entering the percentile value automatically computes the corresponding confidence value whereas entering the confidence level automatically imputes the corresponding percentile value) as compared to the section on the bottom left where it is used only to draw the vertical lines on the chart.

You can also **Save** the simulated results and **Open** them at a later session, **Copy Chart** or **Copy Results** to the clipboard for pasting into another software application, **Extract Simulation Data** to paste into Excel for additional analysis, modify the chart using the chart icons, and so forth.

The simulation forecast chart is highly flexible in the sense that you can modify its look and feel (e.g., color, chart type, background, gridlines, rotation, chart view, data labels, etc.) using the chart icons. To illustrate, if you entered either a **Percentile** or **Certainty Value** at the bottom left of the screen and clicked **Update**, you can then click on **Custom Text Properties** (Figure 2.21), select the **Vertical Line**, type in some custom text, click on the **Properties** button to change the font size/color/type, or use the **A** icons to move the custom text's location. Please note that the custom text properties box will be empty unless you have at least one vertical line (bottom left section).

Finally, note that the **Simulation Results** forecast chart shows one output variable at a time whereas the **Overlay Results** compares multiple simulated output forecasts at once.

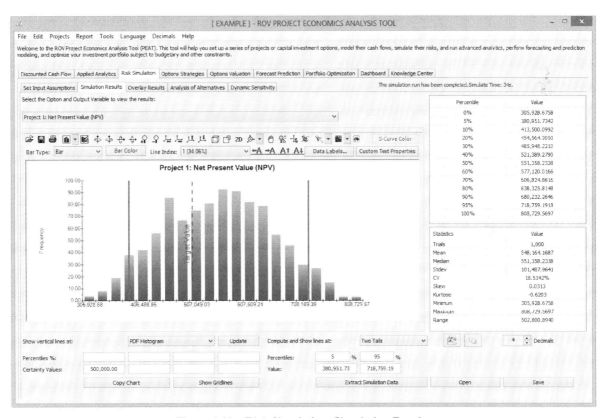

Figure 2.20 – Risk Simulation: Simulation Results

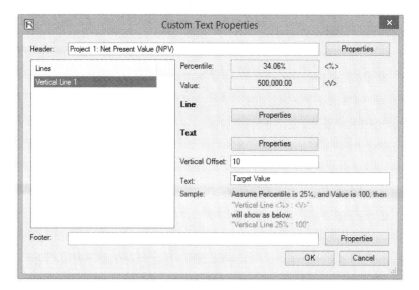

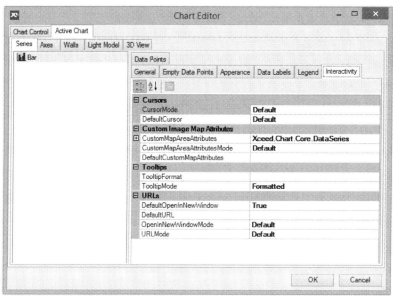

Figure 2.21 – Risk Simulation: Customizing Simulation Forecast Charts

2.4.3 Overlay Results

Multiple simulation output variables can be compared at once using the **Overlay Results** tab (Figure 2.22 shows the DCF module's default example's results after running the All Simulations Model, and then going to the Overlay Results, choosing the first two Option's NPV and selecting PDF Curve Overlay). Simply check/uncheck the simulated outputs you wish to compare and select the chart type to show (e.g., S-Curves, CDF, PDF). You can also add **Percentile** or **Certainty** lines by first selecting the output chart, entering the relevant values, and clicking the **Update** button. As usual, the generated charts are highly flexible in that you can modify the charts using the included chart icons.

TIPS on Interpreting Overlay Charts

- Typically, S-curves (CDF) curves are used in overlay analysis, when comparing the risk profile of multiple simulated forecast results. You can also change the chart into a PDF curve (see Figure 2.22) to see how one project stacks up against another (central tendencies showing the expected returns, the width showing the potential uncertainties and risks, the directional skewness of each project, the excess fatness in the tails or peakedness in the distribution, etc.).

- Refer to the Technical Appendix on Risk Simulation for more details on interpreting forecast distribution charts, statistical moments in the forecast charts, S-curves, PDFs, CDFs, and other associated charts.

- You can also view the **Basics of Project Economics Analysis** in the **Knowledge Center** for quick details on interpreting S-curves.

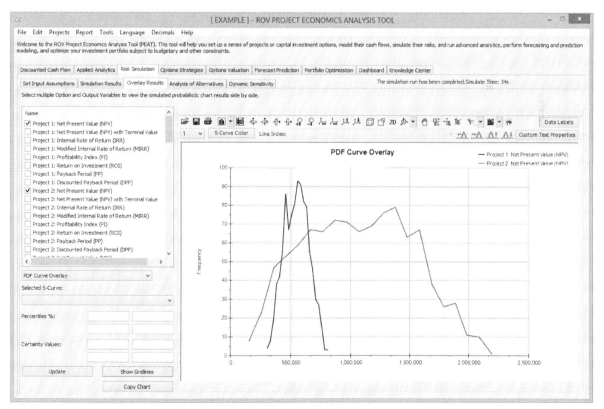

Figure 2.22 – Risk Simulation: Overlay Results

2.4.4 Analysis of Alternatives

While the **Overlay Results** show the simulated results as charts (PDF/CDF), the **Analysis of Alternatives** tab (Figure 2.23 shows the DCF module's default example's risk simulation Analysis of Alternatives results after running the All Simulations Model) shows the results of the simulation statistics in a table format as well as a chart of the statistics such that one Option can be compared against another. The default is to run an **Analysis of Alternatives** to compare one Option versus another, but you can also choose the **Incremental Analysis** option (remember to choose the **Base Case** to compare the results to). For instance, Figure 2.23 shows the relative coefficient of variation (a proxy for project volatility and relative risks) for all projects compared side by side.

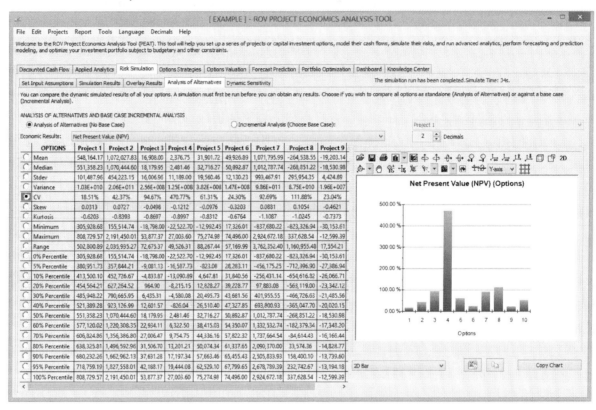

Figure 2.23 – Risk Simulation: Analysis of Alternatives

2.4.5 Dynamic Sensitivity

Tornado analysis and Scenario analysis are both static calculations. **Dynamic Sensitivity** (Figure 2.24 shows the DCF module's default example's Dynamic Sensitivity results after running the All Simulations Model), in contrast, is a dynamic analysis, which can only be performed after a simulation is run. Red bars on the **Rank Correlation** chart indicate negative correlations and green bars indicate positive correlations for the left chart. The correlations' absolute values are used to rank the variables with the highest relationship to the lowest, for all simulation input assumptions. **Contribution to Variance** indicates the percentage fluctuation in the output variable that can be statistically explained by the fluctuations in each of the input variables.

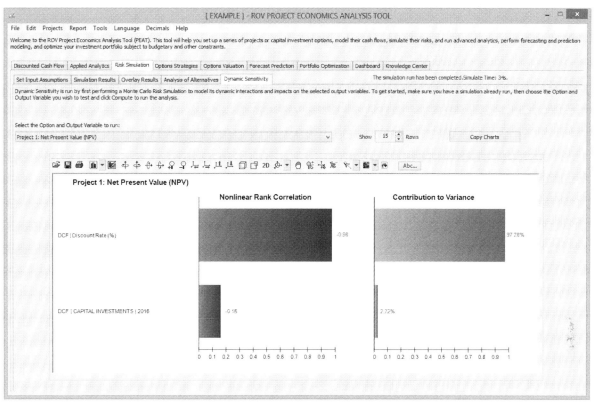

Figure 2.24 – Risk Simulation: Dynamic Sensitivity

2.5 Options Strategies

Options Strategies is where you can draw your own custom strategic map or strategic real options paths (Figure 2.25). This section only allows you to draw and visualize these strategic pathways and does not perform any computations. (The next section, **Options Valuation**, actually does the computations.) Feel free to explore this section's capabilities but we recommend viewing the **Video on Options Strategies** to quickly get started on using this very powerful tool. You can also explore some preset options strategies by clicking on the **First Icon** and selecting any one of the **Examples**.

The default methodology shown is that of a Strategy Tree (i.e., visual representations of strategic implementation pathways of investments and no computations are performed using this methodology. All quantitative computations and valuations are performed in the next tab, **Options Valuation**). Decision trees are also available by clicking on the **ROV Decision Trees** button or the **Last Icon** (decision trees can be used to perform basic decision models as well as other more advanced methods like risk simulation on decision nodes, Bayes' theorem applications and Bayes' updating, expected value of information, utility functions analysis, and so forth).

TIPS on Options Strategies

- *Insert Option* nodes or *Insert Terminal* nodes by first selecting any existing node and then clicking on the option node icon (square) or terminal node icon (triangle).
- Modify individual *Option Node* or *Terminal Node* properties by double-clicking on a node. Sometimes when you click on a node, all subsequent child nodes are also selected (this allows you to move the entire tree starting from that selected node). If you wish to select only that node, you may have to click on the empty background and click back on that node to select it individually. Also, you can move individual nodes or the entire tree started from the selected node depending on the current setting (right-click, or in the *Edit* menu, and select *Move Nodes Individually* or *Move Nodes Together*).
- The following are some quick descriptions of the things that can be customized and configured in the node properties user interface. It is simplest to try different settings for each of the following to see its effects in the Strategy Tree:
  - *Name*. Name shown above the node.
  - *Value*. Value shown below the node.
  - *Excel Link*. Links the value from an Excel spreadsheet's cell.
  - *Notes*. Notes can be inserted above or below a node.
  - *Show in Model*. Show any combinations of Name, Value, and Notes.
  - *Local Color* versus *Global Color*. Node colors can be changed locally to a node or globally.
  - *Label Inside Shape*. Text can be placed inside the node (you may need to make the node wider to accommodate longer text).
  - *Branch Event Name*. Text can be placed on the branch leading to the node to indicate the event leading to this node.
  - *Select Real Options*. A specific real option type can be assigned to the current node. Assigning real options to nodes allows the tool to generate a list of required input variables.
- *Global Elements* are all customizable, including elements of the Strategy Tree's *Background*, *Connection Lines*, *Option Nodes*, *Terminal Nodes*, and *Text Boxes*. For instance, the following settings can be changed for each of the elements:
  - *Font* settings on Name, Value, Notes, Label, Event names.
  - *Node Size* (minimum and maximum height and width).

- o *Borders* (line styles, width, and color).
- o *Shadow* (colors and whether to apply a shadow or not).
- o *Global Color.*
- o *Global Shape.*

- *Example Files* are available in the *first icon* menu to help you get started on building Strategy Trees.
- *Protect File* from the *first icon* menu allows the Strategy Tree to be encrypted with up to a 256-bit password encryption. Be careful when a file is being encrypted because if the password is lost, the file can no longer be opened.
- *Capturing the Screen* or printing the existing model can be done through the *first icon* menu. The captured screen can then be pasted into other software applications.
- *Add, Duplicate, Rename,* and *Delete a Strategy Tree* can be performed through right-clicking the Strategy Tree tab or the *Edit* menu.
- You can also *Insert File Link* and *Insert Comment* on any option or terminal node, or *Insert Text* or *Insert Picture* anywhere in the background or canvas area.
- You can *Change Existing Styles* or *Manage and Create Custom Styles* of your Strategy Tree (this includes size, shape, color schemes, and font size/color specifications of the entire Strategy Tree).

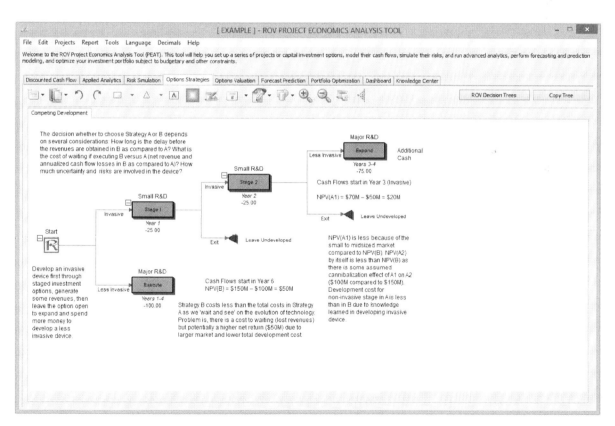

Figure 2.25 – Options Strategies

2.6 Options Valuation

This **Options Valuation** section performs the calculations of Real Options Valuation models (see Figures 2.26-2.29 show the results of using the default load example inputs). Make sure you understand the basic concepts of real options before proceeding. Briefly, start by choosing the **option execution type** (e.g., American, Bermudan, or European), select an option to model (e.g., single phased and single asset or multiple phased sequential options), and, based on the option types selected, enter the required inputs and click **Compute**. Some basic information and a sample strategic path are shown on the right under **Strategy View**. Also, a **Tornado** analysis and **Scenario** analysis can be performed on the option model and you can **Save As** the options models for future retrieval.

You can click on **Load Example** to load an example set of inputs you can use as a guide to implementing your own option model, or click on the **Manual Input** droplists to automatically compute the inputs based on the projects you selected (i.e., some of the real options inputs will be linked to and computed from the outputs of the DCF model and simulation results).

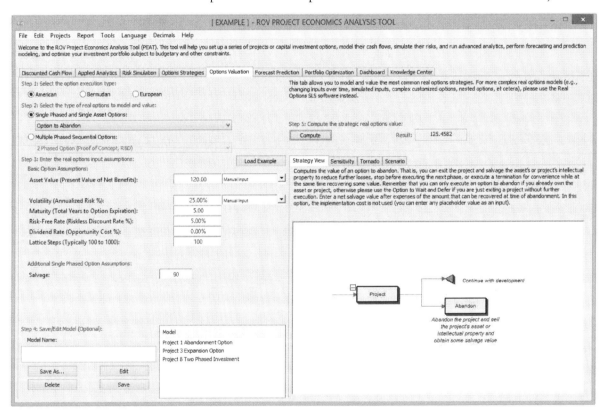

Figure 2.26 – Options Valuation: Input Assumptions and Strategy View

Options Execution Types

- **American Options** can be executed at any time up to and including the maturity date.

- **European Options** can be executed only at one point in time, the maturity date.

- **Bermudan Options** can be executed at certain times, and can be considered a hybrid of American and European Options. There is typically a blackout or vesting period when the option cannot be executed, but starting from the end of the blackout vesting date to the option's maturity, the option can be executed.

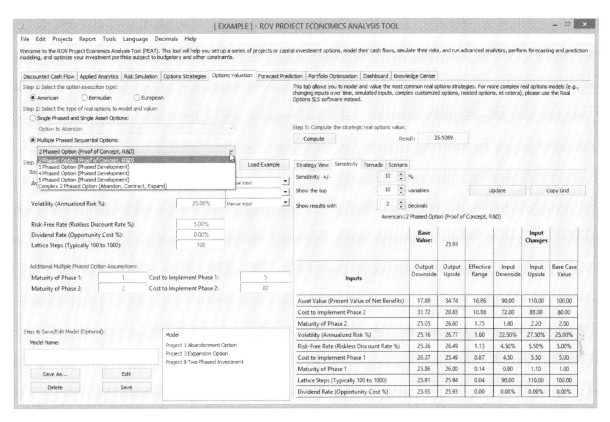

Figure 2.27 – Options Valuation: Sensitivity Analysis on Options

Option to Wait and Execute

Buy additional time to wait for new information by pre-negotiating pricing and other contractual terms to obtain the option but not the obligation to purchase or execute something in the future should conditions warrant it (wait and see before executing).

- Run a Proof of Concept first to better determine the costs and schedule risks of a project versus jumping in right now and taking the risk.

- Build, Buy, or Lease. Developing internally or using commercially available technology or products.

- Multiple Contracts in place that may or not be executed.

- Market Research to obtain valuable information before deciding.

- Venture Capital small seed investment with right of first refusal before executing large-scale financing.

- Relative values of Strategic Analysis of Alternatives or Courses of Action while considering risk and the Value of Information.

- Contract Negotiations with vendors, acquisition strategy with industrial-based ramifications (competitive sustainment and strategic capability and availability).

- Project Evaluation and Capability ROI modeling.

- Capitalizing on other opportunities while reducing large-scale implementation risks, and determining the value of Research & Development (parallel implementation of alternatives while waiting on technical success of the main project, and no need to delay the project because of one bad component in the project).

- Low Rate Initial Production, Prototyping, Advanced Concept Technology Demonstration before full-scale implementation.

- Right of First Refusal contracts.

- Value of Information by forecasting cost inputs, capability, schedule, and other metrics.

- Hedging and Call- and Put-like options to execute something in the future with agreed upon terms now, OTC Derivatives (Price, Demand, Forex, Interest Rate forwards, futures, options, swaptions for hedging).

Option to Abandonment

Hedge downside risks and losses by being able to salvage some value of a failed project or asset that is out-of-the-money (sell intellectual property and assets, abandon and walk away from a project, buyback/sellback provisions).

- Exit and Salvage assets and intellectual property to reduce losses.

- Divestiture and Spin-off.

- Buyback Provisions in a contract.

- Stop and Abandon before executing the next phase.

- Termination for Convenience.

- Early Exit and Stop Loss Provisions in a contract.

Option to Expand

Take advantage of upside opportunities by having existing platform, structure, or technology that can be readily expanded (utility peaking plants, larger oil platforms, early/leapfrog technology development, larger capacity or technology-in-place for future expansion).

- Platform Technologies.

- Mergers and Acquisitions.

- Built-in Expansion Capabilities.

- Geographical, Technological, and Market Expansion.

- Foreign Military Sales.

- Reusability and Scalability.

Option to Contract

Reduce downside risk but still participate in reduced benefits (counterparty takes over or joins in some activities to share profits; at the same time reduce your firm's risk of failure or severe losses in a risky but potentially profitable venture).

- Outsourcing, Alliances, Contractors, Leasing.

- Joint Venture.

- Foreign Partnerships.

- Co-Development and Co-Marketing.

Portfolio Options   Combinations of options and strategic flexibility within a portfolio of nested options (path dependencies, mutually exclusive/inclusive, nested options).

- Determining the portfolio of projects' capabilities to develop and field within Budget and Time Constraints, and what new Product Configurations to develop or acquire to field certain capabilities.

- Allows for different Flexible Pathways: Mutually Exclusive (P1 or P2 but not both), Platform/Prerequisite Technology (P3 requires P2, but P2 can be stand-alone; expensive and worth less if considered by itself without accounting for flexibility downstream options it provides for in the next phase), expansion options, abandonment options, parallel development or simultaneous compound options.

- Determining the Optimal Portfolios given budget scenarios that provide the maximum capability, flexibility, and cost effectiveness with minimal risks.

- Determining testing required in Modular Systems, mean-time-to-failure estimates, Replacement and Redundancy requirements.

- Relative value of strategic Flexibility Options (options to Abandon, Choose, Contract, Expand, Switch, and Sequential Compound Options, Barrier Options, and many other types of Exotic Options).

- Maintaining Capability and Readiness Levels.

- Product Mix, Inventory Mix, Production Mix.

- Capability Selection and Sourcing.

Sequential Options   Significant value exists if you can phase out investments over time, thereby reducing the risk of a one-time up-front investment (pharmaceutical and high technology development and manufacturing usually comes in phases or stages).

- Stage-gate implementation of high-risk project development, prototyping, low-rate-initial-production, technical feasibility tests, technology demonstration competitions.

- Government contracts with multiple stages with the option to abandon at any time and valuing Termination for Convenience, and built-in flexibility to execute different courses of action at specific stages of development.

- P3I, Milestones, R&D, and Phased Options.

- Platform technology.

Options to Switch   Ability to choose among several options, thereby improving strategic flexibility to maneuver within the realm of uncertainty (maintain a foot in one door while exploring another to decide if it makes sense to switch or stay put).

- Ability to Switch among various raw input materials to use when prices of each raw material fluctuates significantly.

- Readiness and capability risk mitigation by switching vendors in an Open Architecture through Multiple Vendors and Modular Design.

Other Types of Real Options   Barrier Options, Custom Options, Simultaneous Compound Option, Employee Stock Options, Exotic Options, Options Embedded Contracts, Options with Blackout/Vesting Provisions, Options with Market and Change of Control Provisions, and many others!

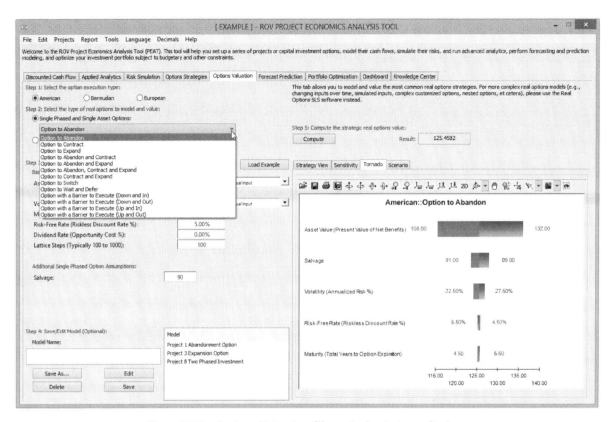

Figure 2.28 – Options Valuation: Tornado Analysis on Options

Options Input Assumptions

- **Asset Value.** This is the underlying asset value before implementation costs. You can compute it by taking the NPV and adding back the sum of the present values of capital investments.

- **Implementation Cost.** This is the cost to execute the option (typically this is the cost to execute an option to wait or an option to expand).

- **Volatility.** This is the annualized volatility (a measure of risk and uncertainty, denoted as a value in percent) of the underlying asset.

- **Maturity.** This is the maturity of the option, denoted in years (e.g., a two and a half year option life can be entered as 2.5).

- **Risk-free Rate.** This is the interest rate yield on a risk-free government bond with maturity commensurate to that of the option.

- **Dividend Rate.** The annualized opportunity cost of not executing the option, as a percentage of the underlying asset.

- **Lattice Steps.** The number of binomial or multinomial lattice steps to run in the model. The typical number we recommend is between 100 and 1000, and you can check for convergence of the results. The larger the number of lattice steps, the higher the level of convergence and granularity (i.e., the number of decimal precision).

- **Blackout Year.** The vesting period entered in years, during which the option cannot be executed (European), but the option converts to an American on the date of this vesting period through to its maturity.

- **Maturity of Phases.** These are the number of years to the end of each phase in a sequential compound option model.

- **Cost to Implement Phases.** These are the costs to execute each of the subsequent phases in a sequential compound option, and they can be set to zero or a positive value.

- **Expansion Factor.** The relative ratio increase in the underlying asset when the option to expand is executed (typically this is greater than 1).

- **Contraction Factor.** The relative ratio reduction in the underlying asset when the option to contract is executed (typically this is less than 1).

- **Savings.** The net savings received by contracting operations.

- **Salvage.** The net sales amount after expenses of abandoning an asset.

- **Barrier.** The upper or lower barrier of an option whereupon if the underlying asset breaches this barrier, the option becomes either live or worthless, depending on the option type modeled.

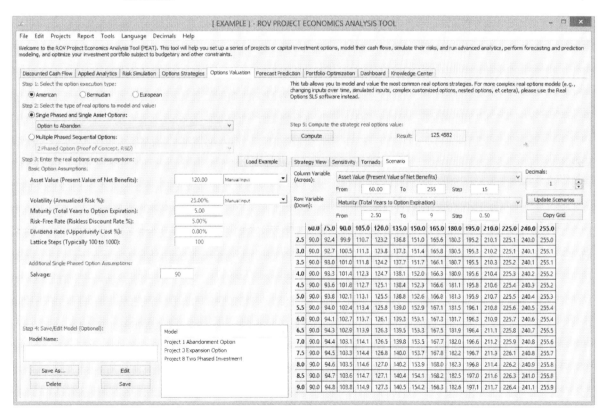

Figure 2.29 – Options Valuation: Scenario Analysis on Options

Real Options SLS Software Tool

PEAT's Options Valuation tab is a simplified version of options analysis in the sense that the most common strategic real options have been incorporated into the software, and all you need to do is select the option you want valued, enter the required assumptions, and compute. The analysis is also backed by **Tornado Analysis, Sensitivity Analysis,** and **Scenario Analysis.** However, for more advanced or customized options, please use our other software tool, Real Options Super Lattice Solver (SLS) as seen in Figure 2.30, where more advanced analytical models can be created (Figure 2.31).

Figure 2.30 – Real Options Super Lattice Solver (SLS) Software

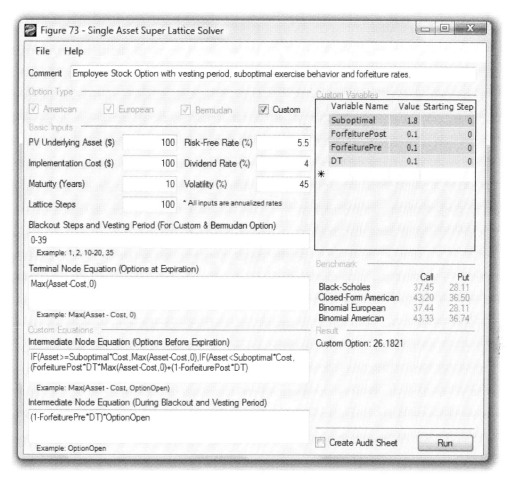

Figure 2.31 – Real Options Super Lattice Solver (SLS) Software: Sample Customized Option

2.7 Forecast Prediction

This section on **Forecast Prediction** (see Figures 2.32-2.34) is a sophisticated Business Analytics and Business Statistics module with over 150 functionalities. Start by entering the data in **Step 1** (copy and paste from Excel or other ODBC-compliant data source, manually type in data, or click on the **Options | Load Example** button to load a sample dataset complete with previously saved models). Then, choose the analysis to perform in **Step 2** and, using the variables list provided, enter the desired variables to model given the chosen analysis (if you previously clicked **Options | Load Example**, you can double-click to use and run the saved models in Step 4 to see how variables are entered in Step 2, and use that as an example for your analysis). Click **RUN** in **Step 3** when ready to obtain the **Results, Charts,** and **Statistics** of the analysis. You can also **Save** your model in **Step 4** by giving it a name for future retrieval.

The following provides a few quick getting started steps on running the Forecast Prediction module and details on each of the elements in the software, while there is a Technical Appendix dedicated to explaining and exploring some of the most critical statistical methodologies available in this module. Feel free to explore the power of this Forecast Prediction module by loading the preset **Options | Load Example**, or watch the Video to quickly get started using the module, and review the user manual for more details on the 150 analytical methods.

Forecast Prediction: Quick Procedures

- Proceed to the Forecast Prediction tab and click on **Options | Load Example** to load a sample data and model profile or type in your data or copy/paste from another software such as Excel or Word/text file into the data grid in **Step 1** (Figure 2.32). You can add your own notes or variable names in the first **Notes** row.
- Select the relevant model to run in **Step 2** and using the example data input settings, enter in the relevant variables. Separate variables for the same parameter using semicolons and use a new line (hit **Enter** to create a new line) for different parameters.
- Click **Run** to compute the results. You can view any relevant analytical results, charts, or statistics from the various tabs in **Step 3**.
- If required, you can provide a model name to save into the profile in **Step 4**. Multiple models can be saved in the same profile. Existing models can be edited or deleted and rearranged in order of appearance, and all the changes can be saved.
- If you use your own data and create your own models, you can save these models in **Step 4**.
- If you are playing with the example data/models and need to recover your saved data and models, click on **Options | Recover My Models**.
- Saving your data and multiple models in **Step 4** will be saved as part of the **rovprojecons* profile. In addition, if you click on **Options | Save/Open Profile** you can save the data and models as a standalone **.bizstats* file that can be opened in a separate software **ROV BizStats**.

TIPS on Using Forecast Prediction

- The data grid size can be set in the **Grid Configure** button, where the grid can accommodate up to 1,000 variable columns with 1 million rows of data per variable. The pop-up menu also allows you to change the language and decimal settings for your data.
- To get started, it is always a good idea to load the example file that comes complete with some data and precreated models. You can double-click on any of these models to run them and the results are shown in the report area, which sometimes can be a chart or model statistics. Using this example file, you can now see how the input parameters are entered based on the model description, and you can proceed to create your own custom models.
- Click on the variable headers to select one or multiple variables at once, and then right-click to add, delete, copy, paste, or visualize the variables selected.

- Models can also be entered using a **Command** console (Figure 2.34). To see how this works, double-click to run a model and go to the **Command** console. You can replicate the model or create your own and click **Run Command** when ready. Each line in the console represents a model and its relevant parameters.

- Click on the data grid's column header(s) to select the entire column(s) or variable(s), and once selected, you can right-click on the header to **Auto Fit** the column, or to **Cut, Copy, Delete,** or **Paste** data. You can also click on and select multiple column headers to select multiple variables and right-click and select **Visualize** to chart the data.

- If a cell has a large value that is not completely displayed, click on and hover your mouse over that cell and you will see a pop-up comment showing the entire value, or simply resize the variable column (drag the column to make it wider, double-click on the column's edge to auto fit the column, or right-click on the column header and select **Auto Fit**).

- Use the up, down, left, and right keys to move around the grid, or use the **Home** and **End** keys on the keyboard to move to the far left and far right of a row. You can also use combination keys such as **Ctrl+Home** to jump to the top left cell, **Ctrl+End** to the bottom right cell, **Shift+Up/Down** to select a specific area, and so forth.

- You can enter short notes for each variable on the **Notes** row.

- Try out the various chart icons on the **Visualize** tab to change the look and feel of the charts (e.g., rotate, shift, zoom, change colors, add legend, etc.).

- The **Copy** button is used to copy the **Results, Charts,** and **Statistics** tabs in **Step 3** after a model is run. If no models are run, then the **Copy** function will only copy a blank page.

- The **Report** button will only run if there are saved models in **Step 4** or if there are data in the grid, otherwise the report generated will be empty. You will also need Microsoft Excel to be installed to run the data extraction and results reports, and Microsoft PowerPoint available to run the chart reports.

- When in doubt about how to run a specific model or statistical method, start the **Options | Load Example** profile and review how the data is set up in **Step 1** or how the input parameters are entered in **Step 2**. You can use these as getting started guides and templates for your own data and models.

- Click the **Options | Load Example** button to load a sample set of previously saved data and models. Then double click on one of the **Saved Models** in **Step 4**. You can see the saved model that is selected and the input variables used in **Step 2**. The results will be computed and shown in the **Step 3** results area, and you can view the **Results, Charts,** or **Statistics** depending on what is available based on the model you chose and ran.

- The **Grid Configure** button allows you to change the number of rows or columns of the data grid in **Step 1**.

- Click **Report** only if you truly mean it! That is, this function will run all of the saved models in **Step 4** and extract the results to Microsoft Excel, Word, and PowerPoint. We say do it only if you mean it because if you have too many saved models, it will run all models and the entire process might take a few minutes to complete.

- You can save a model if required after setting up the model (entering the data, selecting the model, and configuring the input parameters in **Step 2**) after you give it a **Name** in **Step 4** and click **Save**. You can **Edit** or **Delete** saved models later.

- You can copy data from another software, such as Microsoft Excel, and paste it into the data grid in **Step 1**. Simply copy the data, click on the location you wish the data to be pasted, right-click, and select **Paste**.

- If your data contains large values (e.g., 10,000,000.00), right-click anywhere in the data grid and select **Auto Fit All Columns**.

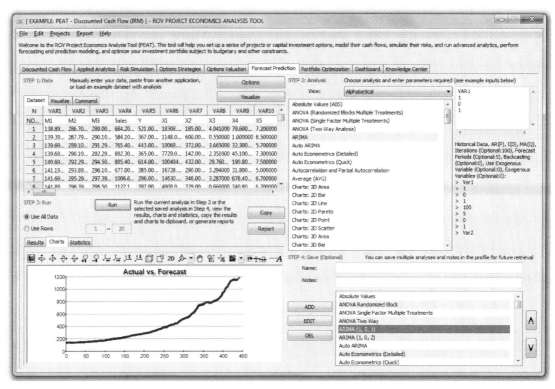

Figure 2.32 – Forecast Prediction: Module Overview

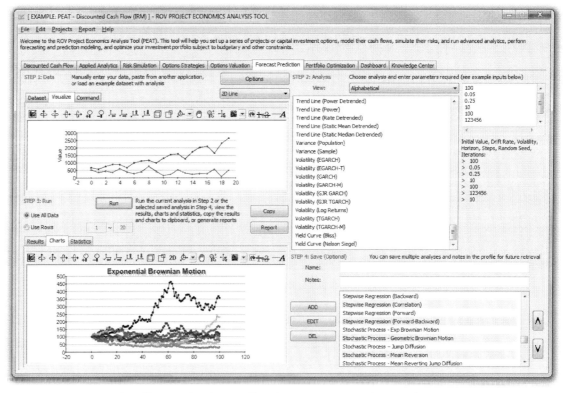

Figure 2.33 – Forecast Prediction: Data Visualization and Results Charts

- You can select a variable in the data grid by clicking on the header(s). For instance, you can click on **VAR1** and it will select the entire variable.

- When a variable is selected, click on the **Visualize** button or **right-click** and select **Visualize**, and the data will be collapsed into a time-series chart.

- Depending on the model run, sometimes the results will return a chart (e.g., in Figure 2.33, a stochastic process forecast was created and the results are presented both in the **Results** subtab and the **Charts** subtab).

- The charts subtab has multiple chart icons you can use to change the appearance of the chart (e.g., modify the chart type, chart line colors, chart view, etc.).

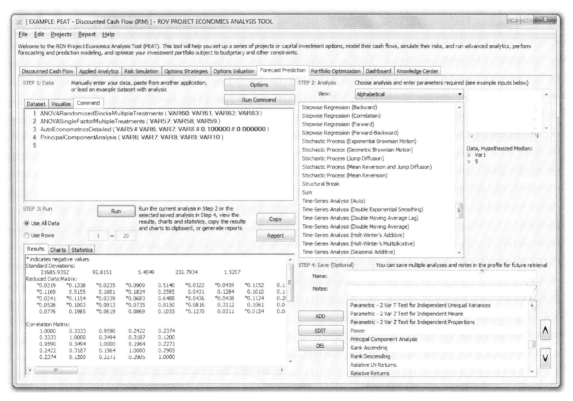

Figure 2.34 – Forecast Prediction: Command Console

- Sometimes you can also quickly run multiple models using direct commands (Figure 2.34) using the **Command Console**.

- For new users, we recommend setting up the models using the user interface, starting from **Step 1** through to **Step 4**.

- To start using the console, create the models you need, then click on the **Command** subtab, copy/edit/replicate the command syntax (e.g., you can replicate a model multiple times and change some of its input parameters very quickly using the command approach), and when ready, click on the **Run Command** button.

2.8 Management Dashboards

This section on **Management Dashboards** (see Figures 2.35-2.36) shows how the results from the PEAT software can be summarized into management dashboards. To follow along, we assume that you are continuing to use the default DCF example and have already run risk simulation and optimization models. Then, click on the in the **Dashboard** tab (Figure 2.35) and wait for a second or two while the software identifies and looks up the results in memory.

Then for each of the four available quadrants, select from the droplists what you would like to show (charts, data grids, text results, or your custom text). Remember to Save the dashboards when you are done setting them up. Then click on View Dashboards to view them (Figure 2.36). When viewing the dashboards, remember to click on the droplist to select which saved dashboard you wish to view. You can also click on the Capture Screen to copy the quadrants and subsequently paste them into another software like Microsoft PowerPoint and Excel.

As information, in future versions of PEAT, the dashboards will have additional available configurations and settings, as well as allows for saving and archiving of dashboard results.

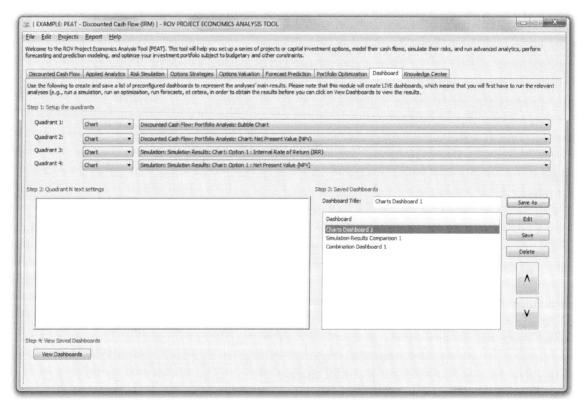

Figure 2.35 – Dashboard Settings

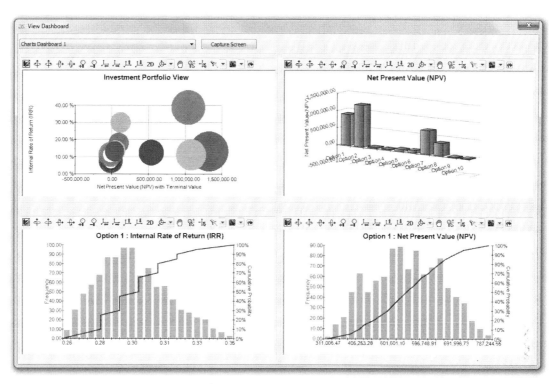

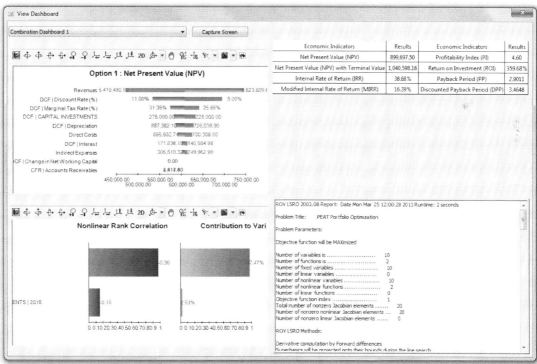

Figure 2.36 – Management Dashboards

2.9 Portfolio Optimization

In the **Portfolio Optimization** section, the individual Options can be modeled as a portfolio and optimized to determine the best combination of projects for the portfolio. In today's competitive global economy, companies are faced with many difficult decisions. These decisions include allocating financial resources, building or expanding facilities, managing inventories, and determining product-mix strategies. Such decisions might involve thousands or millions of potential alternatives. Considering and evaluating each of them would be impractical or even impossible. A model can provide valuable assistance in incorporating relevant variables when analyzing decisions and in finding the best solutions for making decisions. Models capture the most important features of a problem and present them in a form that is easy to interpret. Models often provide insights that intuition alone cannot. An optimization model has three major elements: decision variables, constraints, and an objective. In short, the optimization methodology finds the best combination or permutation of decision variables (e.g., which products to sell and which projects to execute) in every conceivable way such that the objective is maximized (e.g., revenues and net income) or minimized (e.g., risk and costs) while still satisfying the constraints (e.g., budget and resources).

Important Note: The Optimization Settings cannot be set and optimizations cannot be run if you do not first run a Risk Simulation. Make sure you have first run a risk simulation model before attempting to set up an optimization model.

2.9.1 Optimization Settings

The Options can be modeled as a portfolio and optimized to determine the best combination of projects for the portfolio in the **Optimization Settings** tab (Figure 2.37 shows the Optimization Settings of the DCF default example model after the All Simulations Model was run). Select the decision variable type of **Discrete Binary** (chooses which Options to execute with a Go/No-Go binary 1/0 decision) or **Continuous Budget Allocation** (returns % of budget to allocate to each Option as long as the total portfolio is 100%); select the **Objective** (e.g., Max NPV, Min Risk, etc.); set up any **Constraints** (e.g., budget restrictions, number of projects restrictions, or create your own customized restrictions); select the Options to optimize/allocate/choose (default selection is all Options); and when completed, click **Run Optimization**. The software will then take you to the **Optimization Results** (Figure 2.38).

Decision Variables   Decision variables are quantities over which you have control; for example, the amount of a product to make, the number of dollars to allocate among different investments, or which projects to select from among a limited set. As an example, portfolio optimization analysis includes a go or no-go decision on particular projects. In addition, the dollar or percentage budget allocation across multiple projects also can be structured as decision variables.

Constraints   Constraints describe relationships among decision variables that restrict the values of the decision variables. For example, a constraint might ensure that the total amount of money allocated among various investments cannot exceed a specified amount or at most one project from a certain group can be selected; budget constraints; timing restrictions; minimum returns; or risk tolerance levels.

Objective   Objectives give a mathematical representation of the model's desired outcome, such as maximizing profit or minimizing cost, in terms of the decision variables. In financial analysis for example, the objective may be to maximize returns while minimizing risks (maximizing the Sharpe's ratio or returns-to-risk ratio).

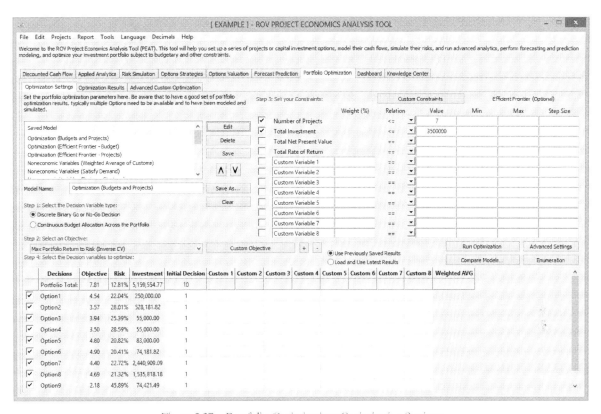

Figure 2.37 – Portfolio Optimization: Optimization Settings

2.9.2 Optimization Results

The **Optimization Results** tab (Figure 2.38 shows the results after running the saved *Optimization Efficient Frontier – Budget* model) returns the results from the portfolio optimization analysis. The main results are provided in the data grid (lower left corner), showing the final Objective function result, final Constraints, and the allocation, selection, or optimization across all individual Options within this optimized portfolio. The top left portion of the screen shows the textual details of the optimization algorithms applied, and the chart illustrates the final objective function (the chart will only show a single point for regular optimizations, whereas it will return an investment efficient frontier curve if the optional **Efficient Frontier** settings are set [min, max, step size] in the **Optimization Settings** tab).

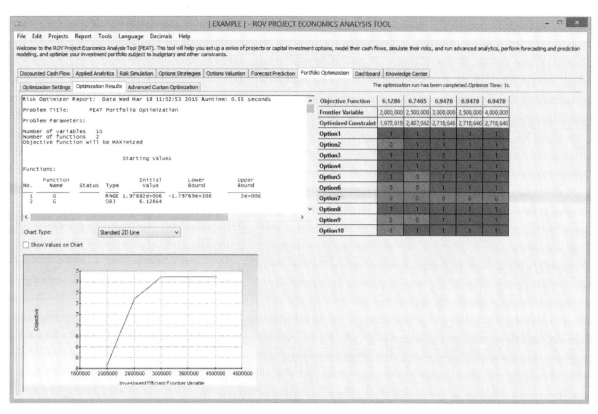

Figure 2.38 – Portfolio Optimization: Optimization Results

2.9.3 Advanced Custom Optimization

In the **Advanced Custom Optimization** tab (see Figures 2.39-2.43), you can create and solve your own optimization models. Knowledge of optimization modeling is required to set up your own models but you can click on **Load Example** and select a sample model to run. You can use these sample models to learn how the Optimization routines can be set up. Click **Run** when done to execute the optimization routines and algorithms. The calculated results and charts will be presented on completion.

When setting up your own optimization model, we recommend going from one tab to another, starting with the Method (static, dynamic, or stochastic optimization); setting up the Decision Variables, Constraints, and Statistics (applicable only if simulation inputs have first been set up, and if dynamic or stochastic optimization is run); and setting the Objective function.

Method: Static Optimization

As far as the optimization process is concerned, PEAT's Advanced Custom Optimization can be used to run a Static Optimization, that is, an optimization that is run on a static model, where no simulations are run. In other words, all the inputs in the model are static and unchanging. This optimization type is applicable when the model is assumed to be known and no uncertainties exist. Also, a discrete optimization can be first run to determine the optimal portfolio and its corresponding optimal allocation of decision variables before more advanced optimization procedures are applied. For instance, before running a stochastic optimization problem, a discrete optimization is first run to determine if there exist solutions to the optimization problem before a more protracted analysis is performed.

Method: Dynamic Optimization

Next, Dynamic Optimization is applied when Monte Carlo simulation is used together with optimization. Another name for such a procedure is Simulation-Optimization. That is, a simulation is first run, then the results of the simulation are applied back into the model, and then an optimization is applied to the simulated values. In other words, a simulation is run for N trials, and then an optimization process is run for M iterations until the optimal results are obtained or an infeasible set is found. That is, using PEAT's optimization module, you can choose which forecast and assumption statistics to use and replace in the model after the simulation is run. Then, these forecast statistics can be applied in the optimization process. This approach is useful when you have a large model with many interacting assumptions and forecasts, and when some of the forecast statistics are required in the optimization. For example, if the standard deviation of an assumption or forecast is required in the optimization model (e.g., computing the Sharpe ratio in asset allocation and optimization problems where we have mean divided by standard deviation of the portfolio), then this approach should be used.

Method: Stochastic Optimization

The Stochastic Optimization process, in contrast, is similar to the dynamic optimization procedure with the exception that the entire dynamic optimization process is repeated T times. That is, a simulation with N trials is run, and then an optimization is run with M iterations to obtain the optimal results. Then the process is replicated T times. The results will be a forecast chart of each decision variable with T values. In other words, a simulation is run and the forecast or assumption statistics are used in the optimization model to find the optimal allocation of decision variables. Then, another simulation is run, generating different forecast statistics, and these new updated values are then optimized, and so forth. Hence, the final decision variables will each have their own forecast chart, indicating the range of the optimal decision variables. For instance, instead of obtaining single-point estimates in the dynamic optimization procedure, you can now obtain a distribution of the decision variables and, hence, a range of optimal values for each decision variable, also known as a stochastic optimization.

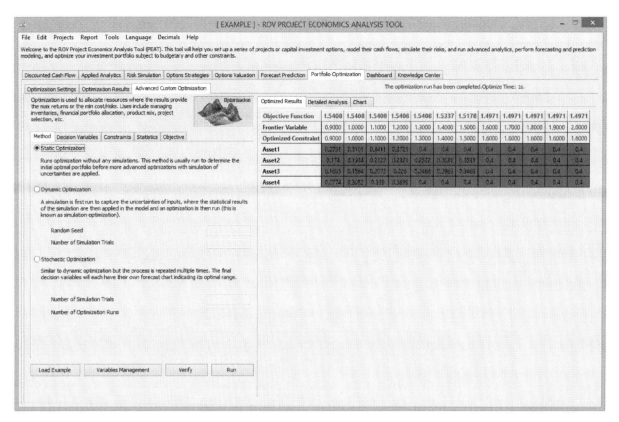

Figure 2.39 – Portfolio Optimization: Method

TIPS on Optimization Method

- You should always run a Static Optimization prior to running any of the more advanced methods to test if the setup of your model is correct.

- The Dynamic Optimization and Stochastic Optimization must first have simulation assumptions set. That is, both approaches require Monte Carlo Risk Simulation to be run prior to starting the optimization routines.

Decision Variables

Decision variables are quantities over which you have control; for example, the amount of a product to make, the number of dollars to allocate among different investments, or which projects to select from among a limited set. As an example, portfolio optimization analysis includes a go or no-go decision on particular projects. In addition, the dollar or percentage budget allocation across multiple projects also can be structured as decision variables.

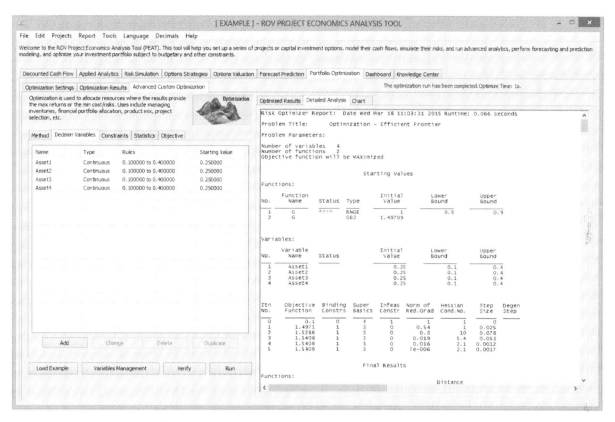

Figure 2.40 – Portfolio Optimization: Decision Variables

TIPS on Optimization Decision Variables

- Click **Add** to add a new **Decision Variable**. You can also **Change**, **Delete**, or **Duplicate** an existing decision variable.

- **Decision Variables** can be set as **Continuous** (with lower and upper bounds), **Integers** (with lower and upper bounds), **Binary** (0 or 1), or a **Discrete Range**.

- The list of available variables is shown in the data grid, complete with their assumptions.

Constraints

Constraints describe relationships among decision variables that restrict the values of the decision variables. For example, a constraint might ensure that the total amount of money allocated among various investments cannot exceed a specified amount or, at most, one project from a certain group can be selected; budget constraints; timing restrictions; minimum returns; or risk tolerance levels.

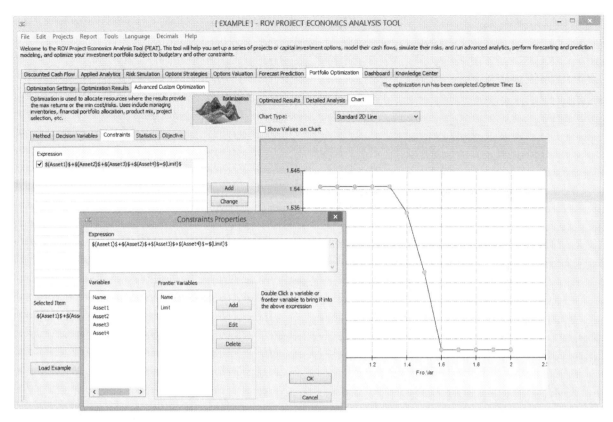

Figure 2.41 – Portfolio Optimization: Constraints

TIPS on Optimization Constraints

- Click **Add** to add a new **Constraint**. You can also **Change** or **Delete** an existing constraint.

- When you add a new constraint, the list of available **Variables** will be shown. Simply double-click on a desired variable and its variable syntax will be added to the **Expression** window. For example, double-clicking on a variable named "Return1" will create a syntax variable "$(Return1)$" in the window.

- Enter your own constraint equation. For example, the following is a constraint: $(Asset1)$+$(Asset2)$+$(Asset3)$+$(Asset4)$=1, where the sum of all four decision variables must add up to 1.

- Keep adding as many constraints as you need but be aware that the higher the number of constraints, the longer the optimization will take, and the higher the probability of your making an error or creating nonbinding constraints, or having constraints that violate another existing constraint (thereby introducing an error in your model).

Statistics   The Statistics subtab will be populated only if there are simulation assumptions set up.

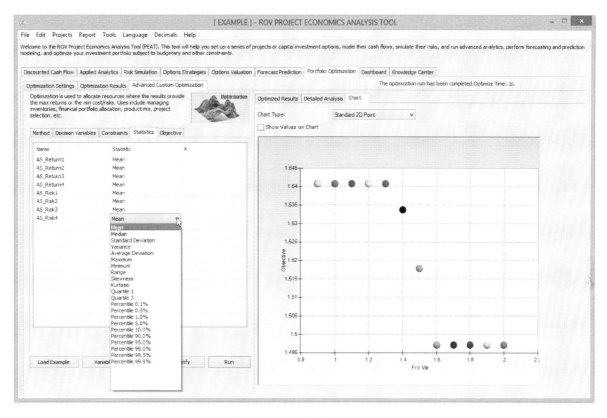

Figure 2.42 – Portfolio Optimization: Statistics

TIPS on Optimization Statistics

- The Statistics window will only be populated if you have previously defined simulation assumptions available.

- If there are simulation assumptions set up, you can run **Dynamic Optimization** or **Stochastic Optimization**; otherwise you are restricted to running only **Static Optimizations**.

- In the window, you can click on the statistics individually to obtain a drop-down list. Here you can select the statistic to apply in the optimization process. The default is to return the **Mean** from the Monte Carlo Risk Simulation and replace the variable with the chosen statistic (in this case the average value), and Optimization will then be executed based on this statistic.

Objective

Objectives give a mathematical representation of the model's desired outcome, such as maximizing profit or minimizing cost, in terms of the decision variables. In financial analysis, for example, the objective may be to maximize returns while minimizing risks (maximizing the Sharpe's ratio or returns-to-risk ratio).

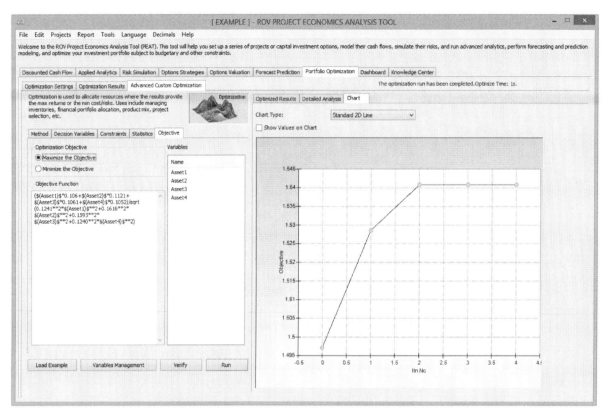

Figure 2.43 – Portfolio Optimization: Objective

TIPS on Optimization Objective

- You can enter your own customized **Objective** in the function window. The list of available variables is shown in the **Variables** window on the right. This list includes predefined decision variables and simulation assumptions.

- An example of an objective function equation looks something like: ($(Asset1)$*$(AS_Return1)$+$(Asset2)$*$(AS_Return2)$+$(Asset3)$*$(AS_Return3)$+$(Asset4)$ *$(AS_Return4)$)/sqrt((AS_Risk1)**2*$(Asset1)$**2+(AS_Risk2)**2*$(Asset2)$**2+$(AS_Ri sk3)$**2*$(Asset3)$**2+(AS_Risk4)**2*$(Asset4)$**2)

- You can use some of the most common math operators such as +, -, *, /, **, where the latter is the function for "raised to the power of."

2.10 Knowledge Center

In the **Knowledge Center** (see Figures 2.44-2.46), you will find quick getting started guides and sample procedures that are straight to the point to assist you in quickly getting up to speed in using the software. Click on the **Previous** and **Next** buttons to navigate from slide to slide or to view the **Getting Started Videos**. These sessions are meant to provide a quick overview to help you get started with using PEAT and do not substitute for years of experience or the technical knowledge required in the Certified Quantitative Risk Management (CQRM) programs.

2.10.1 Step by Step Procedures

The **Step-by-Step Procedures** (Figure 2.44) highlights some quick getting started steps in a self-paced learning environment that is incorporated within the PEAT software. Navigate to this subtab within the **Knowledge Center** and click on the **Previous** and **Next** buttons to navigate from slide to slide. There are short descriptions above each slide and key elements of the slide are highlighted in yellow for quick identification.

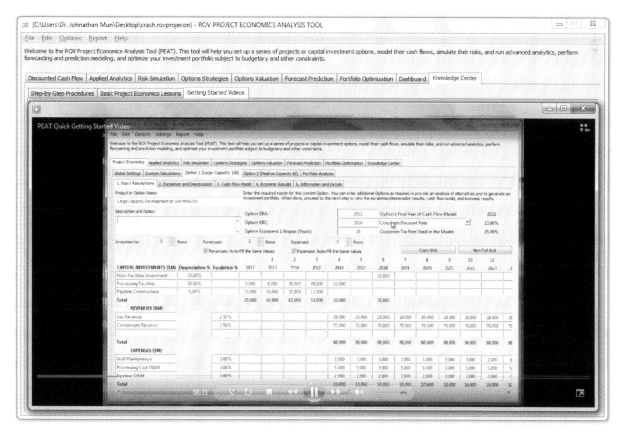

Figure 2.44 – Knowledge Center: Step by Step Procedures

2.10.2 Basic Project Economics Lessons

The **Basic Project Economics Lessons** (Figure 2.45) provide an overview tour of some common concepts involved with cash flow analysis and project economic analysis such as the computations of NPV, IRR, MIRR, PI, ROI, PP, DPP, and so forth.

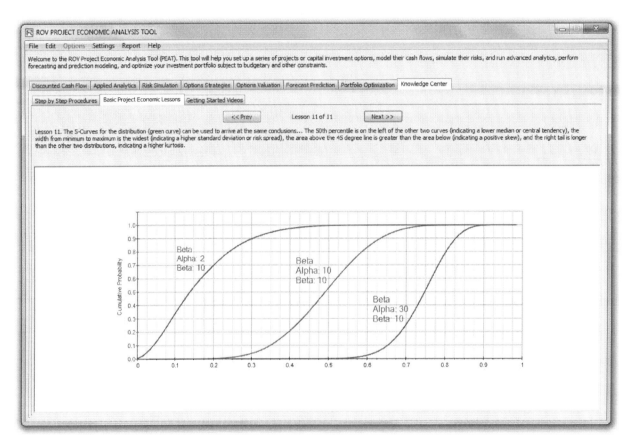

Figure 2.45 – Knowledge Center: Basic Project Economics Lessons

2.10.3 Getting Started Videos

Click on any one of the **Getting Started Videos** (Figure 2.45) to watch a short description and hands-on examples of how to run one of the sections within this PEAT software. The first quick getting started video is preinstalled with the software while the rest of the videos will have to be downloaded at first viewing. Make sure you have a good Internet connection to view these online videos.

Figure 2.46 – Knowledge Center: Getting Started Videos

TIPS on Knowledge Center

- The **Knowledge Center** files (videos, slides, and figures) are available in the installation path's three subfolders: **Lessons**, **Videos**, and **Procedures**. You can access the raw files directly or modify/update these files and the updated files will show in the software tool's **Knowledge Center** the next time you start the software.

- Use the existing files (e.g., file type such as *.BMP or *.WMV as well as pixel size of figures) as a guide to the relevant file specifications you can use when replacing any of these original **Knowledge Center** files.

- If you wish to edit the text shown in the **Knowledge Center**, you can edit the ***.XML** files in the three subfolders, and the next time the software tool is started, the updated text will be shown.

- If you wish to have any files updated/edited and be set as the default when a user installs the software tool, please feel free to send the updated files to *admin@realoptionsvaluation.com* so that we can create an updated build for you.

- The ***.WMV** (Windows Media Video) file format is preferred as all Windows-based computers can run the video without any additional need for Video Codec installations. This file format is small in size and, hence, more portable when implementing it in the PEAT software tool installation build, such that you can still e-mail the installation build without the need for uploading to an FTP site. There are no minimum or maximum size limitations to this file format.

3. TECHNICAL APPENDIX: RISK SIMULATION

3.1 Understanding the Forecast Statistics

Most distributions can be defined up to four moments. The first moment describes a distribution's location or central tendency (expected returns); the second moment describes its width or spread (risks); the third moment, its directional skew (most probable events); and the fourth moment, its peakedness or thickness in the tails (catastrophic losses or gains). All four moments should be calculated in practice and interpreted to provide a more comprehensive view of the project under analysis. PEAT provides the results of all four moments in its **Simulation Results** grid in the Risk Simulation tab.

Measuring the Center of the Distribution—the First Moment

The first moment of a distribution measures the expected rate of return on a particular project. It measures the location of the project's scenarios and possible outcomes on average. The common statistics for the first moment include the mean (average), median (center of a distribution), and mode (most commonly occurring value). Figure 3.1 illustrates the first moment—where, in this case, the first moment of this distribution is measured by the mean (μ), or average, value.

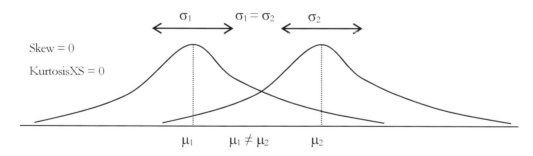

Figure 3.1 – First Moment

Measuring the Spread of the Distribution—the Second Moment

The second moment measures the spread of a distribution, which is a measure of risk. The spread, or width, of a distribution measures the variability of a variable, that is, the potential that the variable can fall into different regions of the distribution—in other words, the potential scenarios of outcomes. Figure 3.2 illustrates two distributions with identical first moments (identical means) but very different second moments or risks. The visualization becomes clearer in Figure 3.3. As an example, suppose there are two stocks and the first stock's movements (illustrated by the darker line) with the smaller fluctuation is compared against the second stock's movements (illustrated by the dotted line) with a much higher price fluctuation. Clearly an investor would view the stock with the wilder fluctuation as riskier because the outcomes of the more risky stock are relatively more unknown than those of the less risky stock. The vertical axis in Figure 3.3 measures the stock prices, thus, the more risky stock has a wider range of potential outcomes. This range is translated into a distribution's width (the horizontal axis) in Figure 3.2, where the wider distribution represents the riskier asset. Hence, width, or spread, of a distribution measures a variable's risks.

Notice that in Figure 3.2, both distributions have identical first moments, or central tendencies, but the distributions are clearly very different. This difference in the distributional width is measurable. Mathematically and statistically, the width, or risk, of a variable can be measured through several different statistics, including the range, standard deviation (σ), variance, coefficient of variation, and percentiles.

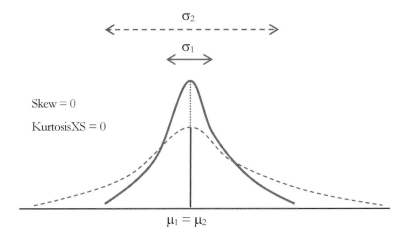

Figure 3.2 – Second Moment

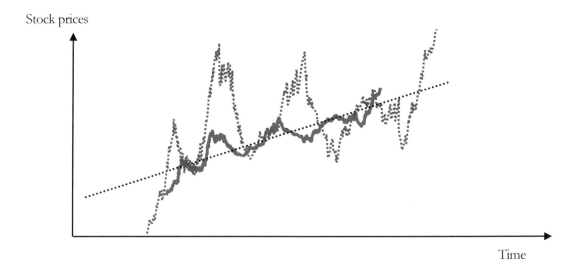

Figure 3.3 – Stock Price Fluctuations

Measuring the Skew of the Distribution—the Third Moment

The third moment measures a distribution's skewness, that is, how the distribution is pulled to one side or the other. Figure 3.4 illustrates a negative skew, or left skew, where the tail of the distribution points to the left. Figure 3.5 illustrates a positive skew, or right skew, where the tail of the distribution points to the right. The mean is always skewed toward the tail of the distribution, while the median remains constant. Another way of seeing this relationship is that the mean moves but the standard deviation, variance, or width may still remain constant. If the third moment is not considered, then looking only at the expected returns (e.g., median or mean) and risk (standard deviation), a positively skewed project might be incorrectly chosen! For example, if the horizontal axis represents the net revenues of a project, then clearly a left, or negatively, skewed distribution might be preferred because there is a higher probability of greater returns (Figure 3.4) as compared to a higher probability for lower-level returns (Figure 3.5). Thus, in a skewed distribution, the median is a better measure of returns, as the medians for both Figures 3.4 and 3.5 are identical, risks are identical, and, hence, a project with a negatively skewed distribution of net profits is a better choice. Failure to account for a project's distributional skewness may mean that the incorrect project could be chosen (e.g., two projects may have identical first and second moments, that is, they both have identical returns and risk profiles, but their distributional skews may be very different).

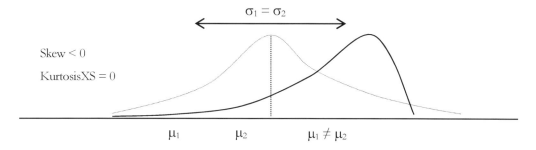

Figure 3.4 – Third Moment (Left Skew)

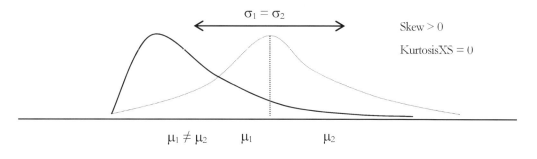

Figure 3.5 – Third Moment (Right Skew)

Measuring the Catastrophic Tail Events in a Distribution—the Fourth Moment

The fourth moment, or kurtosis, measures the peakedness of a distribution. Figure 3.6 illustrates this effect. The background (denoted by the dotted line) is a normal distribution with a kurtosis of 3.0, or an excess kurtosis (KurtosisXS) of 0.0. PEAT's results show the KurtosisXS value, using 0 as the normal level of kurtosis, which means that a negative KurtosisXS indicates flatter tails (platykurtic distributions such as the uniform distribution), while positive values indicate fatter tails (leptokurtic distributions such as the student's t or lognormal distributions). The distribution depicted by the bold line has a higher excess kurtosis, thus the area under the curve is thicker at the tails with less area in the central body. This condition has major impacts on risk analysis. As shown for the two distributions in Figure 3.6, the first three moments (mean, standard deviation, and skewness) can be identical, but the fourth moment (kurtosis) is different. This condition means that, although the returns and risks are identical, the probabilities of extreme and catastrophic events (potential large losses or large gains) occurring are higher for a high kurtosis distribution (e.g., stock market returns are leptokurtic, or have high kurtosis). Ignoring a project's kurtosis may be detrimental. Typically, a higher excess kurtosis value indicates that the downside risks are higher (e.g., the Value at Risk of a project might be significant).

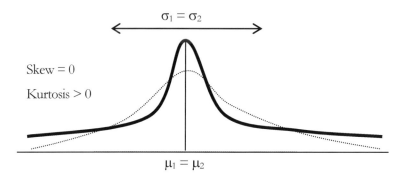

Figure 3.6 – Fourth Moment

The Functions of Moments

Ever wonder why these risk statistics are called "moments"? In mathematical vernacular, *moment* means raised to the power of some value. In other words, the third moment implies that in an equation, three is most probably the highest power. In fact, the following equations illustrate the mathematical functions and applications of some moments for a sample statistic. For example, notice that the highest power for the first moment average is one, the second moment standard deviation is two, the third moment skew is three, and the highest power for the fourth moment is four.

First Moment: Arithmetic Average or Simple Mean (Sample)

$$\bar{x} = \frac{\sum_{i=1}^{n} x_i}{n}$$ The Excel equivalent function is AVERAGE.

Second Moment: Standard Deviation (Sample)

$$s = \sqrt{\frac{\sum_{i=1}^{n} (x_i - \bar{x})^2}{n-1}}$$

The Excel equivalent function is STDEV for a sample standard deviation.

The Excel equivalent function is STDEVP for a population standard deviation.

Third Moment: Skew (Sample)

$$skew = \frac{n}{(n-1)(n-2)} \sum_{i=1}^{n} \frac{(x_i - \bar{x})^3}{s}$$

The Excel equivalent function is SKEW.

Fourth Moment: Kurtosis (Sample)

$$kurtosis = \frac{n(n+1)}{(n-1)(n-2)(n-3)} \sum_{i=1}^{n} \frac{(x_i - \bar{x})^4}{s} - \frac{3(n-1)^2}{(n-2)(n-3)}$$

The Excel equivalent function is KURT.

3.2 Understanding Probability Distributions for Monte Carlo Risk Simulation

This section demonstrates the power of Monte Carlo simulation, but to get started with simulation, one first needs to understand the concept of *probability distributions*. To begin to understand probability, consider this example: You want to look at the distribution of nonexempt wages within one department of a large company. First, you gather raw data—in this case, the wages of each nonexempt employee in the department. Second, you organize the data into a meaningful format and plot the data as a frequency distribution on a chart. To create a frequency distribution, you divide the wages into group intervals and list these intervals on the chart's horizontal axis. Then you list the number, or frequency, of employees in each interval on the chart's vertical axis. Now you can easily see the distribution of nonexempt wages within the department.

A glance at the chart illustrated in Figure 3.7 reveals that most of the employees (approximately 60 out of a total of 180) earn from $7.00 to $9.00 per hour.

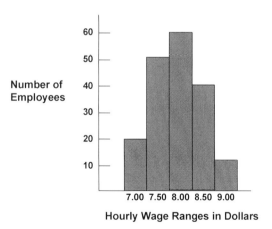

Figure 3.7 – Frequency Histogram I

You can chart this data as a probability distribution. A probability distribution shows the number of employees in each interval as a fraction of the total number of employees. To create a probability distribution, you divide the number of employees in each interval by the total number of employees and list the results on the chart's vertical axis.

The chart in Figure 3.8 shows you the number of employees in each wage group as a fraction of all employees; you can estimate the likelihood or probability that an employee drawn at random from the whole group earns a wage within a given interval. For example, assuming the same conditions exist at the time the sample was taken, the probability is 0.33 (a one in three chance) that an employee drawn at random from the whole group earns between $8.00 and $8.50 an hour.

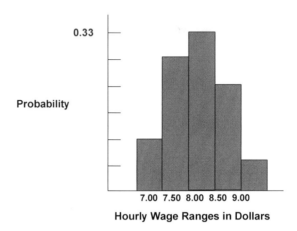

Figure 3.8 – Frequency Histogram II

Probability distributions are either discrete or continuous. *Discrete* probability distributions describe distinct values, usually integers, with no intermediate values and are shown as a series of vertical bars. A discrete distribution, for example, might describe the number of heads in four flips of a coin as 0, 1, 2, 3, or 4. *Continuous* distributions are actually mathematical abstractions because they assume the existence of every possible intermediate value between two numbers. That is, a continuous distribution assumes there is an infinite number of values between any two points in the distribution. However, in many situations, you can effectively use a continuous distribution to approximate a discrete distribution even though the continuous model does not necessarily describe the situation exactly.

Selecting the Best Probability Distribution

Plotting data is one guide to selecting a probability distribution. The following steps provide another process for selecting probability distributions that best describe the uncertain variables in your spreadsheets:

- Look at the variable in question. List everything you know about the conditions surrounding this variable. You might be able to gather valuable information about the uncertain variable from historical data. If historical data are not available, use your own judgment, based on experience, listing everything you know about the uncertain variable.

- Review the descriptions of the probability distributions.

- Select the distribution that characterizes this variable. A distribution characterizes a variable when the conditions of the distribution match those of the variable.

Monte Carlo Risk Simulation

Monte Carlo simulation in its simplest form is a random number generator that is useful for forecasting, estimation, and risk analysis. A simulation calculates numerous scenarios of a model by repeatedly picking values from a user-predefined *probability distribution* for the uncertain variables and using those values for the model. As all those scenarios produce associated results in a model, each scenario can have a *forecast*. Forecasts are events (usually with formulas or functions) that you define as important outputs of the model. These usually are events such as totals, net profit, or gross expenses.

Simplistically, think of the Monte Carlo simulation approach as repeatedly picking golf balls out of a large basket with replacement. The size and shape of the basket depend on the distributional ***input assumption*** (e.g., a normal distribution with a mean of 100 and a standard deviation of 10, versus a uniform distribution or a triangular distribution) where some baskets are deeper or more symmetrical than others, allowing certain balls to be pulled out more frequently than others. The number of balls pulled repeatedly depends on the number of ***trials*** simulated. For a large model with multiple related assumptions, imagine a very large basket wherein many smaller baskets reside. Each small basket has its own set of golf balls that are bouncing around. Sometimes these small baskets are linked with each other (if there is a ***correlation*** between the variables) and the golf balls are bouncing in tandem, while other times the balls are bouncing independent of one another. The balls that are picked each time from these interactions within the model (the large central basket) are tabulated and recorded, providing a ***forecast output*** result of the simulation.

With Monte Carlo Risk Simulation, PEAT generates random values for each assumption's probability distribution that are totally independent. In other words, the random value selected for one trial has no effect on the next random value generated. Use Monte Carlo sampling when you want to simulate real-world what-if scenarios for your spreadsheet model.

The two following sections provide a detailed listing of the different types of discrete and continuous probability distributions that can be used in Monte Carlo simulation.

3.3 PDF, CDF, and ICDF

This section briefly explains the probability density function (PDF) for continuous distributions, which is also called the probability mass function (PMF) for discrete distributions (we use these terms interchangeably), where given some distribution and its parameters, we can determine the probability of occurrence given some outcome x. In addition, the cumulative distribution function (CDF) can also be computed, which is the sum of the PDF values up to this x value. Finally, the inverse cumulative distribution function (ICDF) is used to compute the value x given the cumulative probability of occurrence.

In mathematics and Monte Carlo Risk Simulation, a probability density function (PDF) represents a ***continuous*** probability distribution in terms of integrals. If a probability distribution has a density of $f(x)$, then intuitively the infinitesimal interval of $[x, x + dx]$ has a probability of $f(x) \, dx$. The PDF, therefore, can be seen as a smoothed version of a probability histogram; that is, by providing an empirically large sample of a continuous random variable repeatedly, the histogram using very narrow ranges will resemble the random variable's PDF. The probability of the interval between $[a, b]$ is given by $\int_a^b f(x)dx$, which means that the total integral of the function f must be 1.0. **It is a common mistake to think of $f(a)$ as the probability of a.** This is incorrect. In fact, $f(a)$ can sometimes be larger than 1—consider a uniform distribution between 0.0 and 0.5. The random variable x within this distribution will have $f(x)$ greater than 1. The probability, in reality, is the function $f(x)dx$ discussed previously, where dx is an infinitesimal amount.

The cumulative distribution function (CDF) is denoted as $F(x) = P(X \leq x)$ indicating the probability of X taking on a less than or equal value to x. Every CDF is monotonically increasing, is continuous from the right, and at the limits, has the following properties: $\lim_{x \to -\infty} F(x) = 0$ and $\lim_{x \to +\infty} F(x) = 1$.

Further, the CDF is related to the PDF by $F(b) - F(a) = P(a \leq X \leq b) = \int_a^b f(x)dx$, where the PDF function f is the derivative of the CDF function F. In probability theory, a probability mass function, or PMF, gives the probability that a ***discrete*** random variable is exactly equal to some value. The PMF differs from the PDF in that the values of the latter, defined only for continuous random variables, are not probabilities; rather, its integral over a set of possible values of the random variable is a probability. A random variable is discrete if its probability distribution is discrete and can be characterized by a PMF. Therefore, X is a discrete random variable if $\sum_u P(X = u) = 1$ as u runs through all possible values of the random variable X.

3.4 Tips on Interpreting the Distributional Charts

The rest of this document focuses on the details on each of the 45 distributions available in PEAT, separated by discrete distributions and continuous distributions. Here are some tips to help decipher the characteristics of a distribution when looking at different PDF and CDF charts:

- For each distribution, a PDF chart will be shown—continuous distributions are shown as area charts (Figure 3.9) whereas discrete distributions are shown as bar charts (Figure 3.10).

- If the distribution can only take a single shape (e.g., normal distributions are always bell shaped, with the only difference being the central tendency measured by the mean and the spread measured by the standard deviation), then typically only one PDF area chart will be shown with an overlay PDF line chart (Figure 3.11) showing the effects of various parameters on the distribution.

- Multiple area charts and line charts will be shown (e.g., beta distribution) if the distribution can take on multiple shapes (e.g., the beta distribution is a uniform distribution when alpha = beta = 1; a parabolic distribution when alpha = beta = 2; a triangular distribution when alpha = 1 and beta = 2, or vice versa; a positively skewed distribution when alpha = 2 and beta = 5, and so forth). In this case, you will see multiple area charts and line charts (Figure 3.13).

- The CDF charts, or PEATs, are shown as line charts (Figure 3.12).

- The central tendency of a distribution (e.g., the mean of a normal distribution) is its central location (Figure 3.11).

- The starting point of the distribution is sometimes its minimum parameter (e.g., parabolic, triangular, uniform, arcsine, etc.) or its location parameter (e.g., the beta distribution's starting location is 0, but a beta 4 distribution's starting point is the location parameter; Figure 3.13's top left chart shows a beta 4 distribution with location = 10, its starting point on the x-axis).

- The ending point of the distribution is sometimes its maximum parameter (e.g., parabolic, triangular, uniform, arcsine, etc.) or its natural maximum multiplied by the factor parameter shifted by a location parameter (e.g., the original beta distribution has a minimum of 0 and maximum value of 1, but a beta 4 distribution with location = 10 and factor = 2 indicates that the shifted starting point is 10 and ending point is 11, and its width of 1 is multiplied by a factor of 2, which means that the beta 4 distribution now will have an ending value of 12, as shown in Figure 3.13).

- Interactions between parameters are sometimes evident. For example, in the beta 4 distribution, if the alpha = beta, the distribution is symmetrical, whereas it is more positively skewed the greater the difference between beta − alpha, and the more negatively skewed, the greater the difference between alpha − beta (Figure 3.13).

- Sometimes a distribution's PDF is shaped by two or three parameters called *shape* and *scale*. For instance, the Laplace distribution has two input parameters, alpha location and beta scale, where alpha indicates the central tendency of the distribution (like the mean in a normal distribution) and beta indicates the spread from the mean (like the standard deviation in a normal distribution).

- The narrower the PDF (Figure 3.9's normal distribution with a mean of 10 and standard deviation of 2), the steeper the CDF PEAT looks (Figure 3.12), and the smaller the width on the CDF curve.

- A 45-degree straight line CDF (an imaginary straight line connecting the starting and ending points of the CDF) indicates a uniform distribution; an PEAT CDF with equal amounts above and below the 45-degree straight line indicates a symmetrical and somewhat like a bell- or mound-shaped curve; a CDF completely curved above the 45-degree line indicates a positively skewed distribution, while a CDF completely curved below the 45-degree line indicates a negatively skewed distribution, as shown in the first four graphs in Figure 3.13.

- A CDF line that looks identical in shape but shifted to the right or left indicates the same distribution but shifted by some location, and a CDF line that starts from the same point but is pulled either to the left or right indicates a multiplicative effect on the distribution such as a factor multiplication, as shown in the last two graphs in Figure 3.13.

- An almost vertical CDF indicates a high kurtosis distribution with fat tails, and where the center of the distribution is pulled up (e.g., see the Cauchy distribution) versus a relatively flat CDF, a very wide and perhaps flat-tailed distribution is indicated.

- Some discrete distributions can be approximated by a continuous distribution if its number of trials is sufficiently large and its probability of success and failure are fairly symmetrical (e.g., see the binomial and negative binomial distributions). For instance, with a small number of trials and a low probability of success, the binomial distribution is positively skewed, whereas it approaches a symmetrical normal distribution when the number of trials is high and the probability of success is around 0.50.

- Many distributions are both flexible and interchangeable—refer to the details of each distribution in the next few sections—e.g., binomial is Bernoulli repeated multiple times; arcsine and parabolic are special cases of beta; Pascal is a shifted negative binomial; binomial and Poisson approach normal at the limit; chi-square is the squared sum of multiple normal; Erlang is a special case of gamma; exponential is the inverse of the Poisson but on a continuous basis; F is the ratio of two chi-squares; gamma is related to the lognormal, exponential, Pascal, Erlang, Poisson, and chi-square distributions; Laplace comprises two exponential distributions in one; the log of a lognormal approaches normal; the sum of multiple discrete uniforms approaches normal; Pearson V is the inverse of gamma; Pearson VI is the ratio of two gammas; PERT is a modified beta; a large degree of freedom T approaches normal; Rayleigh is a modified Weibull; and so forth.

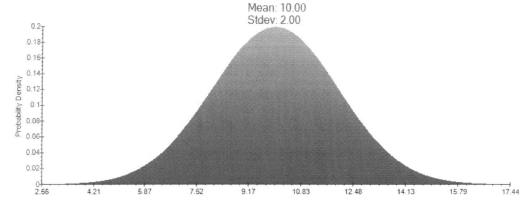

Figure 3.9 – Continuous PDF (Area Chart)

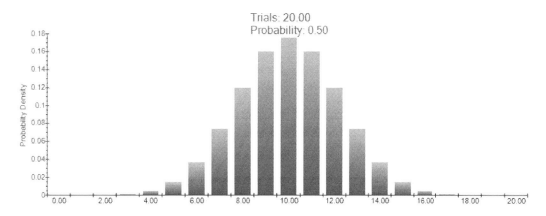

Figure 3.10 – Discrete PDF (Bar Chart)

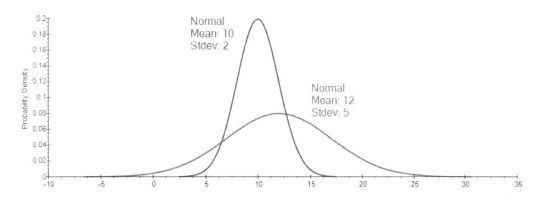

Figure 3.11 – Multiple Continuous PDF Overlay Charts

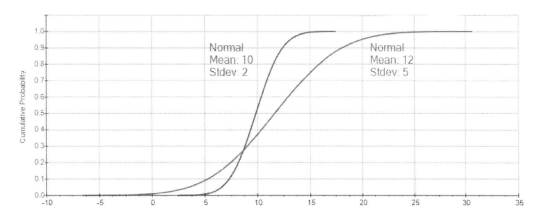

Figure 3.12 – CDF Overlay Charts

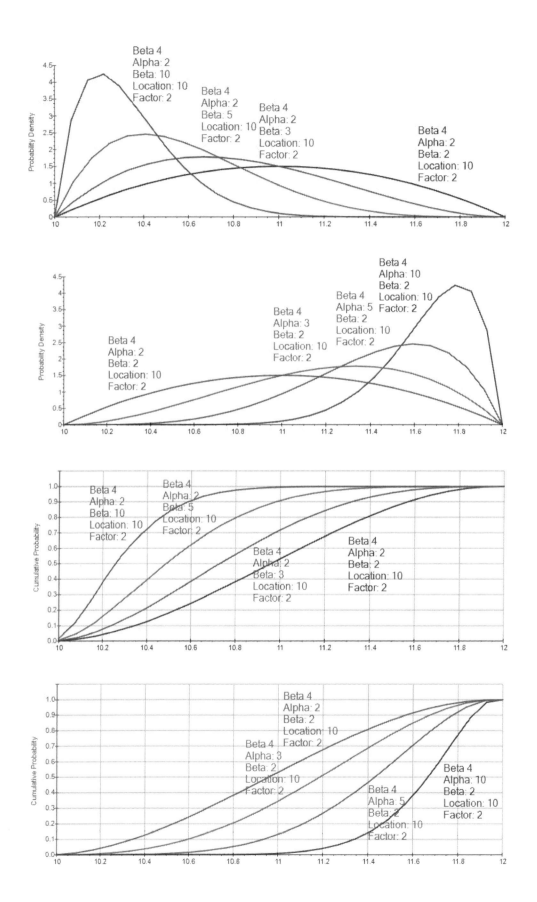

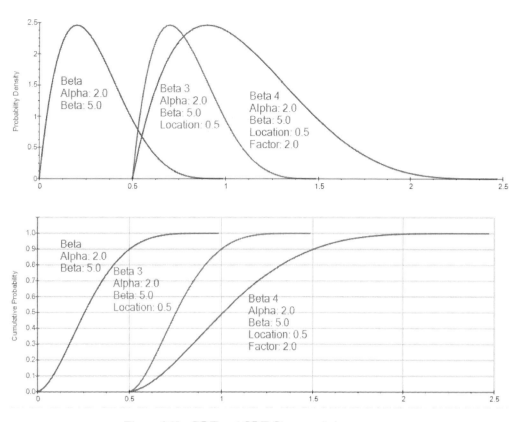

Figure 3.13 – PDF and CDF Characteristics

3.5 Three Most Commonly Used Distributions in PEAT

Normal Distribution

The normal distribution is the most important distribution in probability theory because it describes many natural phenomena, such as people's IQs or heights. Decision makers can use the normal distribution to describe uncertain variables such as the inflation rate or the future price of gasoline.

Conditions

The three conditions underlying the normal distribution are:

- Some value of the uncertain variable is the most likely (the mean of the distribution).

- The uncertain variable could as likely be above the mean as it could be below the mean (symmetrical about the mean).

- The uncertain variable is more likely to be in the vicinity of the mean than further away.

The mathematical constructs for the normal distribution are as follows:

$$f(x) = \frac{1}{\sqrt{2\pi}\sigma} e^{-\frac{(x-\mu)^2}{2\sigma^2}}$$

For all values of x and μ, while $\sigma > 0$

Mean $= \mu$

Standard Deviation $= \sigma$

Skewness $= 0$ (this applies to all inputs of mean and standard deviation)

Excess Kurtosis $= 0$ (this applies to all inputs of mean and standard deviation)

Mean (μ) and standard deviation (σ) are the distributional parameters.

Input requirements:

Standard deviation > 0 and can be any positive value.

Mean can take on any value.

Triangular Distribution

The triangular distribution describes a situation where you know the minimum, maximum, and most-likely values to occur. For example, you could describe the number of cars sold per week when past sales show the minimum, maximum, and usual number of cars sold.

Conditions

The three conditions underlying the triangular distribution are:

- The minimum number of items is fixed.

- The maximum number of items is fixed.

- The most-likely number of items falls between the minimum and maximum values, forming a triangular-shaped distribution, which shows that values near the minimum and maximum are less likely to occur than those near the most-likely value.

The mathematical constructs for the triangular distribution are as follows:

$$f(x) = \begin{cases} \dfrac{2(x - Min)}{(Max - Min)(Likely - min)} & \text{for } Min < x < Likely \\ \dfrac{2(Max - x)}{(Max - Min)(Max - Likely)} & \text{for } Likely < x < Max \end{cases}$$

$$Mean = \frac{1}{3}(Min + Likely + Max)$$

$$Standard\ Deviation = \sqrt{\frac{1}{18}(Min^2 + Likely^2 + Max^2 - Min\,Max - Min\,Likely - Max\,Likely)}$$

$$Skewness = \frac{\sqrt{2}(Min + Max - 2Likely)(2Min - Max - Likely)(Min - 2Max + Likely)}{5(Min^2 + Max^2 + Likely^2 - MinMax - MinLikely - MaxLikely)^{3/2}}$$

Excess Kurtosis $= -0.6$ *(this applies to all inputs of Min, Max, and Likely)*

Minimum value (*Min*), most-likely value (*Likely*), and maximum value (*Max*) are the distributional parameters.

Input requirements:

Min ≤ Most Likely ≤ Max and can take any value.

However, Min < Max and can take any value.

Uniform Distribution

With the uniform distribution, all values fall between the minimum and maximum and occur with equal likelihood.

Conditions

The three conditions underlying the uniform distribution are:

- The minimum value is fixed.

- The maximum value is fixed.

- All values between the minimum and maximum occur with equal likelihood.

The mathematical constructs for the uniform distribution are as follows:

$$f(x) = \frac{1}{Max - Min} \quad \text{for all values such that } Min < Max$$

$$Mean = \frac{Min + Max}{2}$$

$$Standard\ Deviation = \sqrt{\frac{(Max - Min)^2}{12}}$$

Skewness = 0 (this applies to all inputs of Min and Max)

Excess Kurtosis = −1.2 (this applies to all inputs of Min and Max)

Maximum value (*Max*) and minimum value (*Min*) are the distributional parameters.

Input requirements:

Min < Max and can take any value.

See *Modeling Risk*, Third Edition by Dr. Johnathan Mun (2015) for more details on the remaining 42 probability distributions.

3.6 Understanding and Interpreting PEAT's Risk Simulation Results

The PEAT, or Cumulative Distribution Function (CDF), is a very powerful and often-used visual representation of a distribution of data points. This section briefly reviews the salient points of the PEAT. We do this through the following visual examples, where we start with the four moments showing the Probability Density Function (PDF) or probability histogram shapes, and then move on to the corresponding CDF charts.

3.6.1 First Moment

Figure 3.14 shows three Normal distributions with different first moments (mean) but identical second moments (standard deviation). The resulting PDF charts would simply be a shift in the central tendency, or location, of the PDF. Figure 3.15 shows the corresponding CDFs. We see three identical PEATs, indicating the same distribution, but they are shifted from one another, indicating the mean or central tendencies differ.

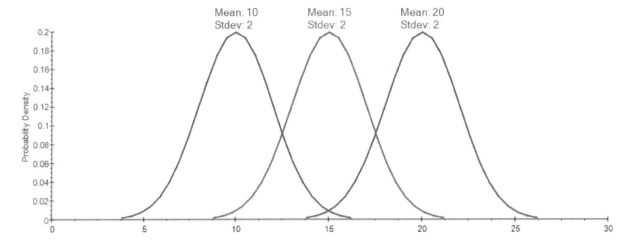

Figure 3.14 – PDFs of Three Normal Distributions (Different Means, Identical Standard Deviations)

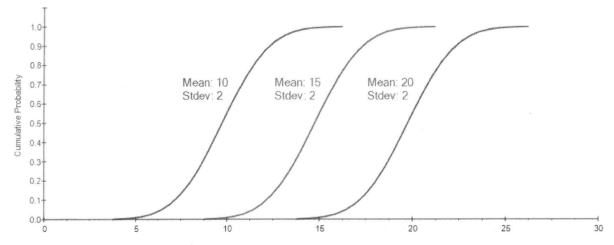

Figure 3.15 – CDFs of the Three Normal Distributions (Different Means, Identical Standard Deviations)

Figure 3.16 shows the basic characteristics of the CDF, where the vertical axis is the cumulative probability, going from 0% to 100%, and the x-axis shows the numerical values in the distribution. The center of the PEAT is the median or 50th percentile (A), and we can clearly see that the central tendency of the three curves are shifted away from one another, indicating a different median and median (and because the Normal distribution s symmetrical, the mean is exactly at the median). The equal areas above (B) and below (C) the 45-degree line indicates a symmetrical distribution, where we have equally likely outcomes above and below the median. Finally, the length from one end to another (D) measures the spread, or risk, and we see that these three curves have similar widths or lengths, indicating similar risk levels (identical standard deviations).

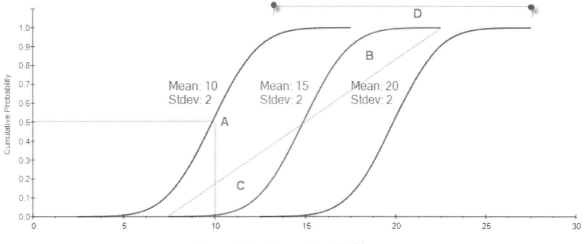

Figure 3.16 – Interpreting PEATs

3.6.2 Second Moment

Figure 3.17 shows the PDF of three Normal distributions with identical means (first moment) but different risks or spread (second moments). A wider PDF has a higher risk spread.

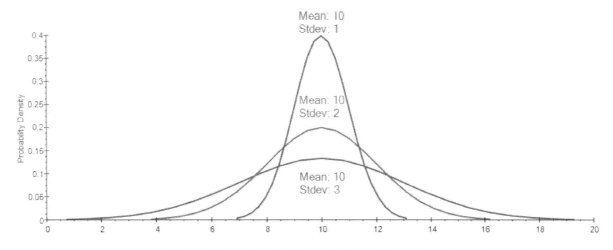

Figure 3.17 – PDFs of Three Normal Distributions (Identical Means, Different Standard Deviations)

Figure 3.18 shows the corresponding PEATs. We see that the steeper the slope of the PEAT, the less risk, or width, of the distribution. The longer or wider the PEAT, and the flatter the PEAT, the higher the standard deviation (second moment, measuring risk, dispersion, and range of possible outcomes).

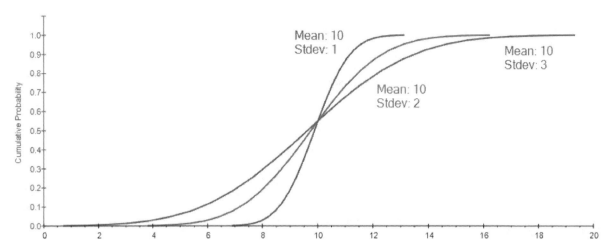

Figure 3.18 – CDFs of Three Normal Distributions (Identical Means, Different Standard Deviations)

3.6.3 Third Moment

Figure 3.19 shows the PDF of three Triangular distributions with identical Most Likely values (first moment) but different skews (third moments). The left or negative skew distirbution (red) has a longer tail pointing to the left or negative side, whereas the positive or right skew distribution (purple) has a longer tail pointing to the right or positive side. A symmetrical distribution (green) has equal tails on both sides.

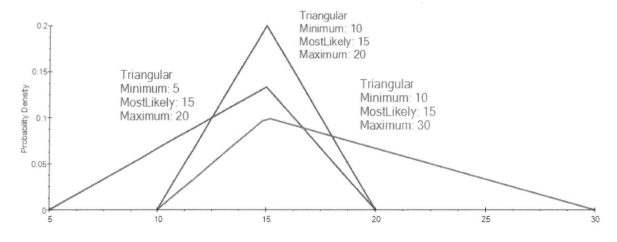

Figure 3.19 – PDFs of Three Triangular Distributions (Different Skew and Symmetry)

Figure 3.20 shows the corresponding PEATs. We see that when we draw a 45-degree line (starting from the minimum and ending at the maximum of the PEAT), the area above/below the 45-degree line provides an insight into the skewness of the distribution. We see that the negative skew distribution (red) has greater area below the 45-degree line than above, whereas the inverse is true for the positive skew (purple). The symmetrical distribution (green) has equal areas above and below the 45-degree line.

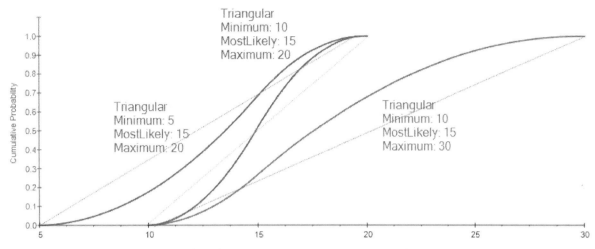

Figure 3.20 – CDFs of Three Triangular Distributions (Different Skew and Symmetry)

3.6.4 Fourth Moment

Figure 3.21 shows the PDF interpretation of the fourth moment of a distribution (or its kurtosis, measuring the extreme values in the tails). The T distribution with a higher degree of freedom (purple curve with the DF of 50) is closer to a Normal distribution, with zero excess kurtosis, whereas the fatter tailed distribution (green curve with the DF of 5) has a higher kurtosis (higher probailities of occurrence of extreme events in the tails).

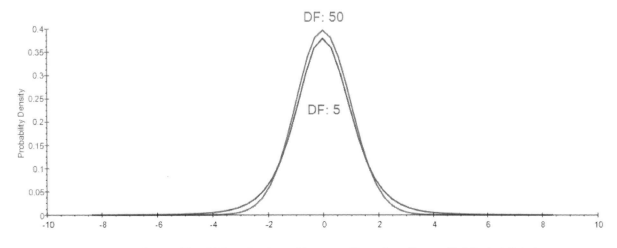

Figure 3.21 – PDFs of Two T-Distributions (Illustrates Kurtosis or Excess Tail Probabilities)

Figure 3.22 shows the corresponding CDF and we see that the distribution with the fatter tails (higher kurtosis), indicating higher probabilities of extreme events, will have longer tails at the extreme low and extreme high (green curve) as compared to another distribution with less kurtosis (purple curve).

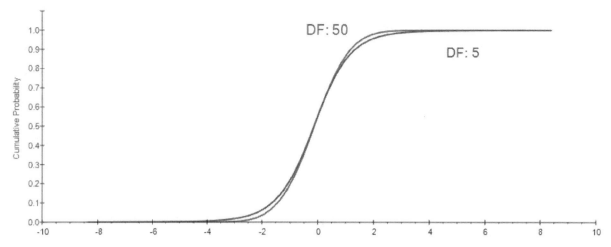

Figure 3.22 – CDFs of Two T-Distributions (Illustrates Kurtosis or Excess Tail Probabilities)

3.6.5 Multiple Moments: Shift, Spread, Skew, Kurtosis

Figure 3.23 shows three Beta distributions. The green PDF shows a wide dispersion with a lower central tendency and a positive skew and a high kurtosis. Figure 3.24's PEAT for this distribution (green curve) can be used to arrive at the same conclusions: the 50th percentile is on the left of the other two curves (indicating a lower median or central tendency), the width from minimum to maximum is the widest (indicating a higher standard deviation or risk spread), the area above the 45-degree line is greater than the area below (indicating a positive skew), and the right tail is longer than the other two distributions, indicating a higher kurtosis.

Using this approach, you can now very quickly compare and contrast different PEATs and their related moments.

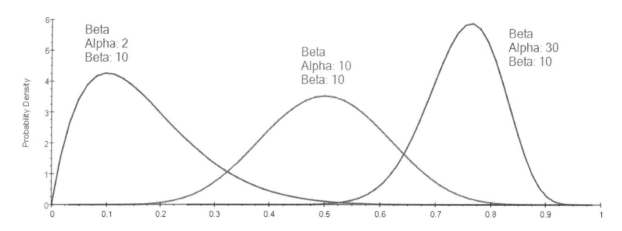

Figure 3.23 – PDFs of Three Different Beta Distributions

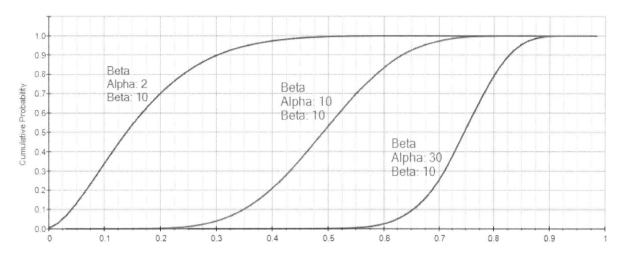

Figure 3.24 – CDFs of Three Different Beta Distributions

As a hint, you can click on the **Show Gridlines…** button to add gridlines on the PEATs or PDF curves, providing additional visual cues to the width and central tendencies of the curves.

4. TECHNICAL APPENDIX: PROJECT ECONOMICS ANALYSIS

The Project Economics Analysis Tool (PEAT) computes various project economics and financial results including Net Present Value (NPV), Internal Rate of Return (IRR), Modified Internal Rate of Return (MIRR), Profitability Index (PI), Return on Investment (ROI), Payback Period (PP), and Discounted Payback Period (DPP). This Appendix provides more details on these metrics as they pertain to project economics analysis (Figure 4.1).

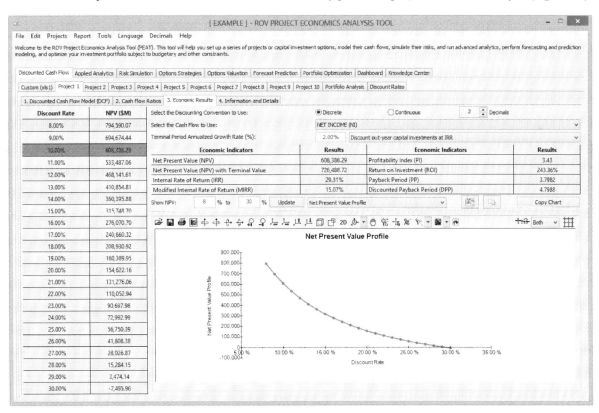

Figure 4.1 – Sample Project Economics Results

This section describes the main techniques (NPV, IRR, MIRR, PI, ROI, PP, and DPP) that are used in capital budgeting analysis. Each approach provides a different piece of information, so in this age of computers, managers often look at all of them when evaluating projects. However,

NPV is the best single measure, and almost all firms now use NPV. The key concepts covered are listed below:

- *Capital budgeting* is the process of analyzing potential projects. Capital budgeting decisions are probably the most important ones managers must make, which helps decision makers to decide if a company should replace worn out/damaged equipment, or replace or add to existing equipment to reduce cost; undergo expansion; or invest in a new project or equipment. At its most general, the capital budgeting process involves simply choosing the best project from among several alternatives.

- Once a potential capital budgeting project is identified, its evaluation usually requires the determination of project investment cost, project cash flow estimation, riskiness of the project, and cost of capital adjusting for riskiness of the project, as well as a determination of the key economic indicators (Figure 4.1).

- The *payback period* is defined as the number of years required to recover a project's cost. The regular *payback period method* ignores cash flows beyond the payback period, and it does not consider the time value of money. The payback does, however, provide an indication of a project's risk and liquidity, because it shows how long the invested capital will be "at risk."

- The *discounted payback* method is similar to the regular payback method except that it discounts cash flows at the project's cost of capital. It considers the time value of money, but it ignores cash flows beyond the payback period.

- The *net present value* (NPV) method discounts all cash flows at the project's cost of capital and then sums those cash flows. The project should be accepted if the NPV is positive.

- The *internal rate of return* (IRR) is defined as the discount rate that forces a project's NPV to equal zero. The project should be accepted if the IRR is greater than the cost of capital.

- The NPV and IRR methods make the same accept/reject decisions for independent projects, but if projects are mutually exclusive, ranking conflicts can arise. If conflicts arise, the NPV method should be used. The NPV and IRR methods are both superior to the payback method, but NPV is superior to IRR.

- The NPV method assumes that cash flows will be reinvested at the firm's cost of capital, while the IRR method assumes reinvestment at the project's IRR. Reinvestment at the cost of capital is generally a better assumption because it is closer to reality.

- The *modified IRR* (MIRR) method corrects some of the problems with the regular IRR. MIRR involves finding the terminal value (TV) of the cash inflows, compounded at the firm's cost of capital, and then determining the discount rate that forces the present value of the TV to equal the present value of the outflows.

- The *profitability index* (PI) shows the dollars of present value divided by the initial cost, so it measures relative profitability.

- Sophisticated managers consider all of the project evaluation measures because each measure provides a useful piece of information.

- *Payback measures liquidity, NPV measures direct dollar benefit, IRR measures percentage return with a safety margin built in, MIRR measures a percentage return considering a better reinvestment rate, and PI measures bang for the buck.*

- The post-audit is a key element of capital budgeting. By comparing actual results with predicted results and then determining why differences occurred, decision makers can improve both their operations and their forecasts of projects' outcomes.

- Small firms tend to use the payback method rather than a discounted cash flow method. This may be rational because (1) the cost of conducting a Discounted Cash Flow analysis may outweigh the benefits for the project being considered, (2) the firm's cost of capital cannot be estimated accurately, or (3) the small-business owner may be considering nonmonetary goals.

- If mutually exclusive projects have unequal lives, it may be necessary to adjust the analysis to put the projects on an equal-life basis. This can be done using the replacement chain (common life) approach, covered later in this module.

- A project's true value may be greater than the NPV based on its physical life if it can be terminated at the end of its economic life.

- Flotation costs and increased riskiness associated with unusually large expansion programs can cause the marginal cost of capital to rise as the size of the capital budget increases.

- Capital rationing occurs when management places a constraint on the size of the firm's capital budget during a particular period.

4.1 Net Present Value

The net present value (NPV) method is simple and powerful: *All future cash flows are discounted at the project's cost of capital and then summed.* Be aware that CF_0 is usually a negative number as this may be an initial capital investment in the project. Complications include differing life spans and different rankings using IRR. The general rule is if NPV > 0, accept the project; if NPV < 0, reject the project; if NPV = 0, you are indifferent (other qualitative variables need to be considered). The NPV is the sum of cash flows (CF) from time zero ($t = 0$) to the final cash flow period (N) discounted as some discount rate (k), which is typically the WACC:

$$NPV = CF_0 + \frac{CF_1}{(1+k)^1} + \frac{CF_2}{(1+k)^2} + ... + \frac{CF_N}{(1+k)^N} = \sum_{t=0}^{N} \frac{CF_t}{(1+k)^t}$$

$$NPV = CF_0 + \frac{CF_1}{(1+WACC)^1} + \frac{CF_2}{(1+WACC)^2} + ... + \frac{CF_N}{(1+WACC)^N} = \sum_{t=0}^{N} \frac{CF_t}{(1+WACC)^t}$$

NPV has a direct relationship between economic value added (EVA) and market value added (MVA). It is equal to the present value of the project's future EVA, and, hence, a positive NPV usually implies a positive EVA and MVA.

4.2 Internal Rate of Return

Internal rate of return (IRR) is the discount rate that equates the project's cost to the sum of the present cash flow of the project. That is, setting NPV = 0 and solving for k in the NPV equation, where k is now called *IRR*. In other words, where:

$$NPV = \sum_{t=0}^{N} \frac{CF_t}{(1+IRR)^t} = 0$$

Note that there may exist multiple IRRs when the cash flow stream is erratic. Also, the IRR and NPV rankings may be dissimilar. The general rule is that when IRR > required rate of return or hurdle rate or cost of capital, accept the project. That is, if the IRR exceeds the cost of capital required to finance and pay for the project, a surplus remains after paying for the project, which is passed on to the shareholders. The NPV and IRR methods make the same accept/reject decisions for *independent* projects, but if projects are *mutually exclusive*, ranking conflicts can arise. If conflicts arise, the NPV method should be used. The NPV and IRR methods are both superior to the payback, but NPV is superior to IRR. Conflicts may arise when the cash flow timing (most of the cash flows come in during the early years compared to later years in another project) and amounts (the cost of one project is significantly larger than another) are vastly different from one project to another. Finally, there sometimes can arise *multiple* IRR solutions in erratic cash flow streams such as large cash outflows occurring during or at the end of a project's life. In such situations, the NPV provides a more robust and accurate assessment of the project's value.

4.3 Modified Internal Rate of Return

The NPV method assumes that the project cash flows are reinvested at the cost of capital, whereas the IRR method assumes project cash flows are reinvested at the project's own IRR. The reinvestment rate at the cost of capital is the more correct approach in that this is the firm's opportunity cost of money (if funds were not available, then capital is raised at this cost).

The modified internal rate of return (MIRR) method is intended to overcome two IRR shortcomings by setting the cash flows to be reinvested at the cost of capital and not its own IRR, as well as preventing the occurrence of multiple IRRs, because only a single MIRR will exist for all cash flow scenarios. Also, NPV and MIRR will usually result in the same project selection when projects are of equal size (significant scale differences might still result in a conflict between MIRR and NPV ranking).

The MIRR is the discount rate that forces the present value of costs of cash outflows (COF) to be equal to the present value of the terminal value (the future value of cash inflows, or CIF, compounded at the project's cost of capital, k).

$$\sum_{t=0}^{n} \frac{COF_t}{(1+k)^t} = \sum_{t=0}^{n} \frac{CIF_t(1+k)^{n-t}}{(1+MIRR)^n}$$

$$\sum_{t=0}^{n} \frac{COF_t}{(1+WACC)^t} = \sum_{t=0}^{n} \frac{CIF_t(1+WACC)^{n-t}}{(1+MIRR)^n}$$

$$PV \ Costs = \frac{Terminal \ Value}{(1+MIRR)^n}$$

4.4 Profitability Index and Return on Investment

The *profitability index* (PI) is the ratio of the sum of the present value of cash flows to the initial cost of the project, which measures its *relative profitability*. A project is acceptable if PI > 1, and the higher the PI, the higher the project ranks. PI is mathematically very similar to return on investment (ROI). PI is a relative measure whereas ROI is an absolute measure. PI returns a ratio *(the ratio is an absolute value, ignoring the negative investment cost)* while ROI is usually described as a percentage.

$$PI = \frac{\sum_{t=1}^{n} \frac{CF_t}{(1+k)^t}}{CF_0} = \frac{Benefit}{Cost} = \frac{PV \ Cash \ Flows}{Initial \ Cost}$$

$$ROI = \frac{\sum_{t=1}^{n} \frac{CF_t}{(1+k)^t} - CF_0}{CF_0} = \frac{Benefit - Cost}{Cost} = PI - 1$$

Mathematically, NPV, IRR, MIRR, and PI should provide similar rankings although conflicts may sometimes arise, and all methods should be considered as each provides a different set of relevant information.

4.5 Payback Period

Simple but ineffective by itself, the payback period method calculates the time necessary to pay back the initial cost (i.e., a breakeven analysis). It does not take into account time valuation of money and it does not consider different life spans after the initial payback breakpoint and ignores the cost of capital. The payback period approach helps identify the project's *liquidity* in determining how long funds will be tied up in the project.

Payback = Year before full recovery + [unrecovered cost ÷ Cash Flow at time t]

4.5 Discounted Payback Period

The discounted payback period method is similar to the payback period method but the cash flows used are in present values. This solves the issue of cost of capital, but the disadvantage of ignoring cash flows beyond the payback period still remains.

> Discounted Payback = Year before full recovery + [unrecovered cost ÷ PV Cash Flow at time t]

4.6 Exercise: NPV, IRR, MIRR, PI, ROI, PP, DPP

Payback Period

Suppose you are to choose between two projects, A and B. Project A costs $442 but pays back $200 for the next 3 years, while B costs $718 and pays back $250, $575, and $100 for the next 3 years.

$$Payback\ A = 2 + [42 \div 200] = 2.21\ years$$

$$Payback\ B = 1 + [(718\text{-}250) \div 575] = 1.81\ years$$

PAYBACK PERIOD

Suppose you are to choose between two projects, A and B. Project A costs $442 but pays back $200 for the next 3 years while Project B costs $718 and pays back $250, $575 and $100 for the next 3 years:

Project A:	Time	0	1	2	3		Project B:	Time	0	1	2	3
	Cash Flow	($442)	$200	$200	$200			Cash Flow	($718)	$250	$575	$100

We compute the cumulative positive cash flow and find the year prior to payback, and then add the proportion of unpaid balance to the cash flow of the following year:

Project A:	Time	0	1	2	3		Project B:	Time	0	1	2	3
	Cash Flow	($442)	$200	$200	$200			Cash Flow	($718)	$250	$575	$100
	CUM +CF		$200	$400	$600			CUM +CF		$250	$825	$925

Project A:			Project B:	
Year prior to payback:	2		Year prior to payback:	1
Unpaid Amount:	($42)		Unpaid Amount:	($468)
Proportion of Following Year:	0.21		Proportion of Following Year:	0.81
Payback Period (Years):	**2.21**		**Payback Period (Years):**	**1.81**

Disadvantages of Payback Period

- *Neglects time value of money.* To solve this, use present values instead of cash flows, that is, use a discounted payback period instead. This means that in the example above, the $200, or $250, $575, and $100 cash flows are first discounted to present values. See the Discounted Payback Period example below.
- *Cash flows and length of time remaining are left out after the payback period.* As an example, suppose we have two new projects, X and Y with cash flows shown below. Both have identical payback periods but clearly, project Y is superior as it has additional cash flows. These cash flows post payback period are ignored.

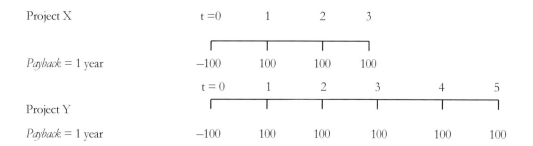

Discounted Payback Period

Suppose you are to choose between two projects, A and B. Project A costs $442 but pays back $200 for the next 3 years, while B costs $718 and pays back $250, $575, and $100 for the next 3 years. Further suppose that the WACC discount rate is 12%.

$$Discounted\ Payback\ A = 2 + [(442\text{-}338.0) \div 142.4] = 2.73\ years$$

$$Discounted\ Payback\ B = 2 + [(718\text{-}681.6) \div 71.2] = 2.51\ years$$

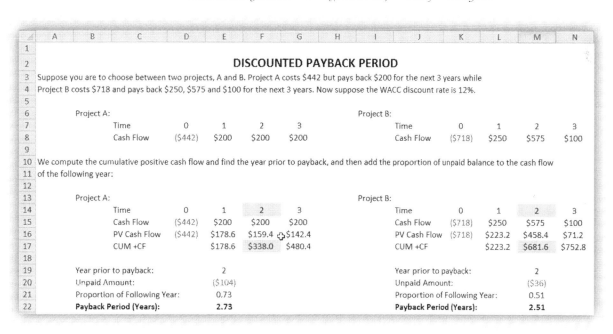

Net Present Value

Using the same projects A and B above, which project is better assuming a 12% WACC discount rate? Use the NPV method.

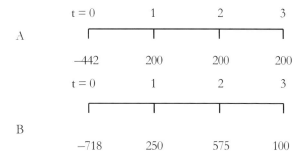

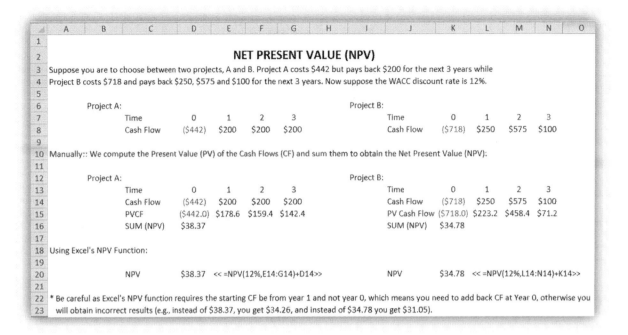

Comparing A and B, A has a higher NPV, therefore A should be chosen before B although both projects should be undertaken if there exists sufficient funds, otherwise, only undertake project A. Rank remains the same but NPV values differ using different discount rates.

Internal Rate of Return

Using the same scenario above, calculate the IRR for projects A and B assuming a 12% WACC discount rate (this will now be used as the hurdle rate). Should we accept both projects again and which project is better?

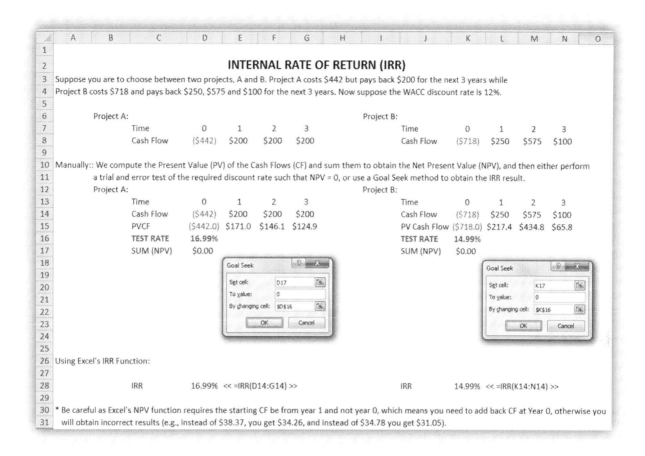

Choose Project A over B as it has a higher return (IRR) and IRR > k for both.

Multiple Internal Rate of Returns

When cash flows are both + and –, there may exist multiple IRRs. For instance, consider a project costing –$1.6M with returns of +$10M in the first year and a loss of –$10M in the second year. What is the project's IRR?

$$NPV = -1.6M + [10 \div (1+IRR)^1] - [10 \div (1+IRR)^2] \text{ yields } IRR = 25\% \text{ and } 400\%.$$

Try it! The moral of the story? Use all methods at one's disposal and see which makes more sense! In regular situations, they should all have similar results.

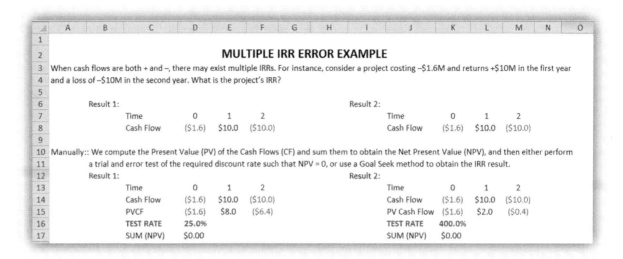

Modified IRR (MIRR)

The following example calculates the MIRR for the two projects A and B as specified previously.

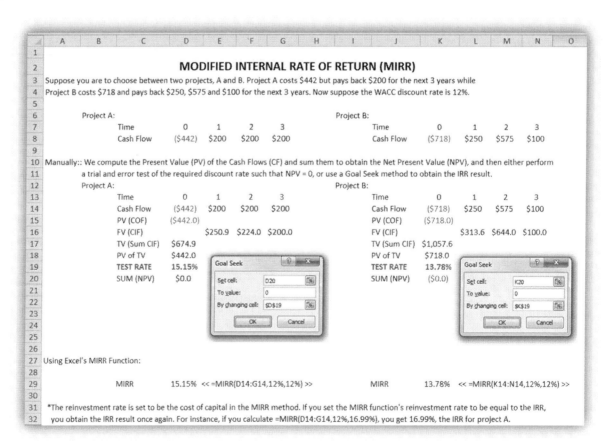

PROJECT ECONOMICS ANALYSIS TOOL (PEAT)

Profitability Index (PI) and Return on Investment (ROI)

The following example calculates the PI and ROI on Projects A and B as previously specified.

	A	B	C	D	E	F	G	H	I	J	K	L	M	N	O
1															
2			**PROFITABILITY INDEX (PI) AND RETURN ON INVESTMENT (ROI)**												
3		Suppose you are to choose between two projects, A and B. Project A costs $442 but pays back $200 for the next 3 years while													
4		Project B costs $718 and pays back $250, $575 and $100 for the next 3 years. Now suppose the WACC discount rate is 12%.													
5															
6		Project A:							Project B:						
7			Time	0	1	2	3			Time	0	1	2	3	
8			Cash Flow	($442)	$200	$200	$200			Cash Flow	($718)	$250	$575	$100	
9															
10		Manually:: We compute the Present Value (PV) of the Cash Flows (CF) for the negative CF (investment cost) and positive CF:													
11															
12		Project A:							Project B:						
13			Time	0	1	2	3			Time	0	1	2	3	
14			Cash Flow	($442)	$200	$200	$200			Cash Flow	($718)	$250	$575	$100	
15			PVCF	($442.0)	$178.6	$159.4	$142.4			PV Cash Flow	($718.0)	$223.2	$458.4	$71.2	
16			ABS(CF(0)) Cost	$442.0	<< =ABS(D15) >>					ABS(CF(0)) Cost	$718.0	<< =ABS(K15) >>			
17			SUM CF(i)	$480.4	<< =SUM(E15:G15) >>					SUM CF(i)	$752.8	<< =SUM(L15:N15) >>			
18															
19		Profitability Index (PI)		1.0868	<< =D17/D16 >>				Profitability Index (PI)		1.0484	<< =K17/K16 >>			
20		Return on Investment (ROI)		8.68%	<< =(D17-D16)/D16 >>				Return on Investment (ROI)		4.84%	<< =(K17-K16)/K16 >>			
21															
22		* We usually convert the initial investment cost (a negative value) into a positive absolute value to simplify the calculations, otherwise it is difficult to keep													
23		in mind which values are positive and which are negative. The *ROI* value is simply *PI - 1* in percent.													

5. TECHNICAL APPENDIX: FORECAST PREDICTION ANALYTICS

The Forecast Prediction module is a sophisticated Business Analytics and Business Statistics module with over 150 functionalities (Figure 5.1). Start by entering the data in Step 1 (copy and paste from Excel or other ODBC-compliant data source, manually type in data, or click on the EXAMPLE button to load a sample dataset complete with previously saved models). Then, choose the analysis to perform in Step 2 and, using the variables list provided, enter the desired variables to model given the chosen analysis (if you previously clicked EXAMPLE, you can double-click to use and run the saved models in Step 4 to see how variables are entered in Step 2, and use that as an example for your analysis). Click RUN in Step 3 when ready to obtain the Results, Charts, and Statistics of the analysis. You can also SAVE your model by giving it a name for future retrieval.

5.1 Quick Descriptions of Analytics

5.1.1 Descriptive Statistics

Almost all distributions can be described within four moments (some distributions require one moment, while others require two moments, etc.). Descriptive statistics quantitatively captures these moments. The first moment describes the location of a distribution (i.e., mean, median, and mode) and is interpreted as the expected value, expected returns, or the average value of occurrences.

The second moment measures a distribution's spread, or width, and is frequently described using measures such as Standard Deviations, Variances, Quartiles, and Inter-Quartile Ranges. Standard deviation is a popular measure indicating the average deviation of all data points from their mean. It is a popular measure as it is frequently associated with risk (higher standard deviations meaning a wider distribution, higher risk, or wider dispersion of data points around the mean value) and its units are identical to the units in the original data set.

Skewness is the third moment in a distribution. Skewness characterizes the degree of asymmetry of a distribution around its mean. Positive skewness indicates a distribution with an asymmetric tail extending toward more positive values. Negative skewness indicates a distribution with an asymmetric tail extending toward more negative values.

Kurtosis characterizes the relative peakedness or flatness of a distribution compared to the normal distribution. It is the fourth moment in a distribution. A positive kurtosis value indicates a relatively peaked distribution. A negative kurtosis indicates a relatively flat distribution. The kurtosis measured here has been centered to zero (certain other kurtosis measures are centered on 3.0). While both are equally valid, centering across zero makes the interpretation simpler. A high positive kurtosis indicates a peaked distribution around its center and leptokurtic or fat tails. This indicates a higher probability of extreme events (e.g., catastrophic events, terrorist attacks, stock market crashes) than is predicted in a normal distribution.

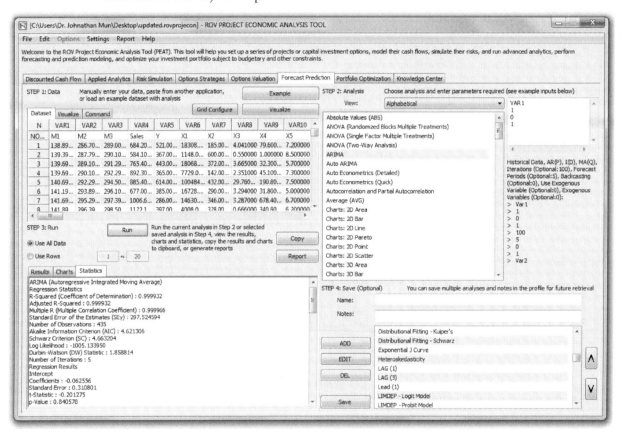

Figure 5.1 – Forecast Prediction Module

5.1.2 Correlation Matrix

The Correlation module lists the Pearson's product moment correlations (commonly referred to as the Pearson's R) between variable pairs. The correlation coefficient ranges between –1.0 and +1.0 inclusive. The sign indicates the direction of association between the variables, while the coefficient indicates the magnitude or strength of association. The Pearson's R only measures a linear relationship and is less effective in measuring nonlinear relationships.

A hypothesis t-test is performed on the Pearson's R and the p-values are reported. If the calculated p-value is less than or equal to the significance level used in the test, then reject the null hypothesis and conclude that there is a significant correlation between the two variables in question. Otherwise, the correlation is not statistically significant.

Finally, a Spearman Rank-Based Correlation is also included. The Spearman's R first ranks the raw data then performs the correlation calculation, which allows it to better capture nonlinear relationships. The Pearson's R is a parametric test and the underlying data is assumed to be normally distributed, hence, the t-test can be applied. However, the Spearman's R is a nonparametric test, where no underlying distributions are assumed, and, hence, the t-test cannot be applied.

5.1.3 Variance-Covariance Matrix

The Covariance measures the average of the products of deviations for each data point pair. Use covariance to determine the relationship between two variables. The covariance is related to the correlation in that the correlation is the covariance divided by the product of the two variables' standard deviation, standardizing the correlation measurement to be unitless and between -1 and $+1$.

Covariance is used when the units of the variables are similar, allowing for easy comparison of the magnitude of variability about their respective means. The covariance of the same variable is also known as the *variance*. The variance of a variable is the square of its standard deviation. This is why standardizing the variance through dividing it by the variable's standard deviation (twice) yields a correlation of 1.0, indicating that a variable is perfectly correlated to itself.

It must be stressed that a high covariance does not imply causation. Associations between variables in no way imply that the change of one variable causes another variable to change. Two variables that are moving independently of each other but in a related path may have a high covariance but their relationship might be spurious. In order to capture this relationship, use regression analysis instead.

5.1.4 Basic Statistics

The following basic statistical functions are also included in *PEAT's Forecast Statistics module* and their short definitions are listed below:

Absolute Values

Computes the absolute value of a number where it is the number without its sign.

Average

Computes the average or arithmetic mean of the rows of data for the selected variable.

Count

Computes how many numbers there are in the rows of data for the selected variable.

Difference

Computes the difference of the current period from the previous period.

Lag

Returns the value lagged some number of periods (the entire chronological data set is shifted down the number of lagged periods specified).

Lead

Returns the value leading by some number of periods (the entire chronological data set is shifted up the number of lead periods specified).

LN

Computes the natural logarithm.

Log

Computes the logarithmic value of some specified base.

Max

Computes the maximum of the rows of data for the selected variable.

Median

Computes the median of the rows of data for the selected variable.

Min

Computes the minimum of the rows of data for the selected variable.

Mode

Computes the mode or most frequently occurring of data points for the selected variable.

Power

Computes the result of a number raised to a specified power.

Rank Ascending

Ranks the rows of data for the selected variable in ascending order.

Rank Descending

Ranks the rows of data for the selected variable in descending order.

Relative LN Returns

Computes the natural logarithm of the relative returns from one period to another, where the relative return is computed as the current value divided by its previous value.

Relative Returns

Computes the relative return where the current value is divided by its previous value.

Semi-Standard Deviation (Lower)

Computes the sample standard deviation of data points below a specified value.

Semi-Standard Deviation (Upper)

Computes the sample standard deviation of data points above a specified value.

Standard Deviation (Population)

Computes the population standard deviation of the rows of data for the selected variable.

Standard Deviation (Sample)

Computes the sample standard deviation of the rows of data for the selected variable.

Variance (Population)

Computes the population variance of the rows of data for the selected variable.

Variance (Sample)

Computes the sample variance of the rows of data for the selected variable.

5.1.5 Hypothesis Tests: Parametric Models

One-Variable Testing for Means (T-Test)

This one-variable t-test of means is appropriate when the population standard deviation is not known but the sampling distribution is assumed to be approximately normal (the t-test is used when the sample size is less than 30). This t-test can be applied to three types of hypothesis tests to be examined—a two-tailed test, a right-tailed test, and a left-tailed test—based on the sample data set if the population mean is equal to, less than, or greater than the hypothesized mean.

If the calculated p-value is less than or equal to the significance level in the test, then reject the null hypothesis and conclude that the true population mean is not equal to (two-tailed test), less than (left-tailed test), or greater than (right-tailed test) the hypothesized mean based on the sample tested. Otherwise, the true population mean is statistically similar to the hypothesized mean.

One-Variable Testing for Means (Z-Test)

The one-variable Z-test is appropriate when the population standard deviation is known, and the sampling distribution is assumed to be approximately normal (this applies when the number of data points exceeds 30). This Z-test can be applied to three types of hypothesis tests to be examined—a two-tailed test, a right-tailed test, and a left-tailed test—based on the sample data set if the population mean is equal to, less than, or greater than the hypothesized mean.

If the calculated p-value is less than or equal to the significance level in the test, then reject the null hypothesis and conclude that the true population mean is not equal to (two-tailed test), less than (left-tailed test), or greater than (right-tailed test) the hypothesized mean based on the sample tested. Otherwise, the true population mean is statistically similar to the hypothesized mean.

One-Variable Testing for Proportions (Z-Test)

The one-variable Z-test for proportions is appropriate when the sampling distribution is assumed to be approximately normal (this applies when the number of data points exceeds 30, and when the number of data points, N, multiplied by the hypothesized population proportion mean, P, is greater than or equal to five, or $NP \geq 5$). The data used in the analysis have to be proportions and be between 0 and 1. This Z-test can be applied to three types of hypothesis tests to be examined—a two-tailed test, a right-tailed test, and a left-tailed test—based on the sample data set if the population mean is equal to, less than, or greater than the hypothesized mean.

If the calculated p-value is less than or equal to the significance level in the test, then reject the null hypothesis and conclude that the true population mean is not equal to (two-tailed test), less than (left-tailed test), or greater than (right-tailed test) the hypothesized mean based on the sample tested. Otherwise, the true population mean is statistically similar to the hypothesized mean.

Two Variables with Dependent Means (T-Test)

The two-variable dependent t-test is appropriate when the population standard deviation is not known but the sampling distribution is assumed to be approximately normal (the t-test is used when the sample size is less than 30). In addition, this test is specifically formulated for testing the same or similar samples before and after an event (e.g., measurements taken before a medical treatment are compared against those measurements taken after the treatment to see if there is a difference). This t-test can be applied to three types of hypothesis tests: a two-tailed test, a right-tailed test, and a left-tailed test.

Suppose that a new heart medication was administered to 100 patients (N = 100) and the heart rates before and after the medication was administered were measured. The two dependent variables t-test can be applied to determine if the new medication is effective by testing to see if there are statistically different "before and after" averages. The dependent variables test is used here because there is only a single sample collected (the same patients' heartbeats were measured before and after the new drug administration).

The two-tailed null hypothesis tests that the true population's mean of the difference between the two variables is zero, versus the alternate hypothesis that the difference is statistically different from zero. The right-tailed null hypothesis test is such that the differences in the population means (first mean less second mean) is statistically less than or equal to zero (which is identical to saying that mean of the first sample is less than or equal to the mean of the second sample). The alternative hypothesis is that the real populations' mean difference is statistically greater than zero when tested using the sample data set (which is identical to saying that the mean of the first sample is greater than the mean of the second sample). The left-tailed null hypothesis test is such that the differences in the population means (first mean less second mean) is statistically greater than or equal to zero (which is identical to saying that the mean of the first sample is greater than or equal to the mean of the second sample). The alternative hypothesis is that the real populations' mean difference is statistically less than zero when tested using the sample data set (which is identical to saying that the mean of the first sample is less than the mean of the second sample).

If the calculated p-value is less than or equal to the significance level in the test, then reject the null hypothesis and conclude that the true population difference of the population means is not equal to (two-tailed test), less than (left-tailed test), or greater than (right-tailed test) zero based on the sample tested. Otherwise, the true population mean is statistically similar to the hypothesized mean.

Two (Independent) Variables with Equal Variances (T-Test)

The two-variable t-test with equal variances is appropriate when the population standard deviation is not known but the sampling distribution is assumed to be approximately normal (the t-test is used when the sample size is less than 30). In addition, the two independent samples are assumed to have similar variances.

For illustration, suppose that a new engine design is tested against an existing engine design to see if there is a statistically significant different between the two. The t-test on two (independent) variables with equal variances can be applied. This test is used because there are two distinctly different samples collected here (new engine and existing engine) but the variances of both samples are assumed to be similar (the means may or may not be similar, but the fluctuations around the mean are assumed to be similar).

This t-test can be applied to three types of hypothesis tests: a two-tailed test, a right-tailed test, and a left-tailed test. A two-tailed hypothesis tests the null hypothesis, H_0, such that the populations' mean difference (HMD) between the two variables is statistically identical to the hypothesized mean differences. If HMD is set to zero, this is the same as saying that the first mean equals the second mean. The alternative hypothesis, H_a, is that the difference between the real population means is statistically different from the hypothesized mean differences when tested using the sample data set. If HMD is set to zero, this is the same as saying that the first mean does not equal the second mean.

A right-tailed hypothesis tests the null hypothesis, H_0, such that the population mean differences between the two variables is statistically less than or equal to the hypothesized mean differences. If HMD is set to zero, this is the same as saying that the first mean is less than or equals the second mean. The alternative hypothesis, H_a, is that the real difference between population means is statistically greater than the hypothesized mean differences when tested using the sample data set. If HMD is set to zero, this is the same as saying that the first mean is greater than the second mean.

A left-tailed hypothesis tests the null hypothesis, H_0, such that the differences between the population means of the two variables is statistically greater than or equal to the hypothesized mean differences. If HMD is set to zero, this is the same as saying that the first mean is greater than or equals the second mean. The alternative hypothesis, H_a, is that the real difference between population means is statistically less than the hypothesized mean difference when tested using the sample data set. If HMD is set to zero, this is the same as saying that the first mean is less than the second mean.

If the calculated p-value is less than or equal to the significance level in the test, then reject the null hypothesis and conclude that the true population difference of the population means is not equal to (two-tailed test), less than (left-tailed test), or greater than (right-tailed test) HMD based on the sample tested. Otherwise, the true difference of the population means is statistically similar to the HMD.

For data requirements, see the preceding section, Two Variables with Dependent Means (T-Test).

Two (Independent) Variables with Unequal Variances (T-Test)

The two-variable t-test with unequal variances (the population variance of sample 1 is expected to be different from the population variance of sample 2) is appropriate when the population standard deviation is not known but the sampling distribution is assumed to be approximately normal (the t-test is used when the sample size is less than 30). In addition, the two independent samples are assumed to have similar variances.

To illustrated, suppose that a new customer relationship management (CRM) process is being evaluated for its effectiveness, and the customer satisfaction rankings between two hotels (one with and the other without CRM implemented) are collected. The t-test on two (independent) variables with unequal variances can be applied. This test is used here because there are two distinctly different samples collected (customer survey results of two different hotels) and the variances of both samples are assumed to be dissimilar (due to the difference in geographical location, plus the demographics and psychographics of the customers are different on both properties).

This t-test can be applied to three types of hypothesis tests: a two-tailed test, a right-tailed test, and a left-tailed test. A two-tailed hypothesis tests the null hypothesis, H_0, such that the population mean differences between the two variables are statistically identical to the hypothesized mean differences. If HMD is set to zero, this is the same as saying that the first mean equals the second mean. The alternative hypothesis, H_a, is that the real difference between the population means is statistically different from the hypothesized mean differences when tested using the sample data set. If HMD is set to zero, this is the same as saying that the first mean does not equal the second mean.

A right-tailed hypothesis tests the null hypothesis, H_0, such that the difference between the two variables' population means is statistically less than or equal to the hypothesized mean differences. If HMD is set to zero, this is the same as saying that the first mean is less than or equals the second mean. The alternative hypothesis, H_a, is that the real populations' mean difference is statistically greater than the hypothesized mean differences when tested using the sample data set. If HMD is set to zero, this is the same as saying that the first mean is greater than the second mean.

A left-tailed hypothesis tests the null hypothesis, H_0, such that the difference between the two variables' population means is statistically greater than or equal to the hypothesized mean differences. If HMD is set to zero, this is the same as saying that the first mean is greater than or equals the second mean. The alternative hypothesis, H_a, is that the real difference between population means is statistically less than the hypothesized mean difference when tested using the sample data set. If HMD is set to zero, this is the same as saying that the first mean is less than the second mean.

If the calculated p-value is less than or equal to the significance level in the test, then reject the null hypothesis and conclude that the true population difference of the population means is not equal to (two-tailed test), less than (left-tailed test), or greater than (right-tailed test) the hypothesized mean based on the sample tested. Otherwise, the true difference of the population means is statistically similar to the hypothesized mean.

Two (Independent) Variables Testing for Means (Z-Test)

The two-variable Z-test is appropriate when the population standard deviations are known for the two samples, and the sampling distribution of each variable is assumed to be approximately normal (this applies when the number of data points of each variable exceeds 30).

To illustrate, suppose that a market survey was conducted on two different markets, the sample collected is large (N must exceed 30 for both variables), and the researcher is interested in testing whether there is a statistically significant difference between the two markets. Further suppose that such a market survey has been performed many times in the past and the population standard deviations are known. A two independent variables Z-test can be applied because the sample size exceeds 30 on each market and the population standard deviations are known.

This Z-test can be applied to three types of hypothesis tests: a two-tailed test, a right-tailed test, and a left-tailed test. A two-tailed hypothesis tests the null hypothesis, H_0, such that the difference between the two population means is statistically identical to the hypothesized mean. The alternative hypothesis, H_a, is that the real difference between the two population means is statistically different from the hypothesized mean when tested using the sample data set.

A right-tailed hypothesis tests the null hypothesis, H_0, such that the difference between the two population means is statistically less than or equal to the hypothesized mean. The alternative hypothesis, H_a, is that the real difference between the two population means is statistically greater than the hypothesized mean when tested using the sample data set.

A left-tailed hypothesis tests the null hypothesis, H_0, such that the difference between the two population means is statistically greater than or equal to the hypothesized mean. The alternative hypothesis, H_a, is that the real difference between the two population means is statistically less than the hypothesized mean when tested using the sample data set.

Two (Independent) Variables Testing for Proportions (Z-Test)

The two-variable Z-test on proportions is appropriate when the sampling distribution is assumed to be approximately normal (this applies when the number of data points of both samples exceeds 30). Further, the data should all be proportions and be between 0 and 1.

To illustrate, suppose that a brand research was conducted on two different headache pills, the sample collected is large (N must exceed 30 for both variables), and the researcher is interested in testing whether there is a statistically significant difference between the proportion of headache sufferers of both samples using the different headache medication. A two independent variables Z-test for proportions can be applied because the sample size exceeds 30 on each market, and the data collected are proportions.

This Z-test can be applied to three types of hypothesis tests: a two-tailed test, a right-tailed test, and a left-tailed test. A two-tailed hypothesis tests the null hypothesis, H_0, that the difference in the population proportion is statistically identical to the hypothesized difference (if the hypothesized difference is set to zero, the null hypothesis tests if the population proportions of the two samples are identical). The alternative hypothesis, H_a, is that the real difference in population proportions is statistically different from the hypothesized difference when tested using the sample data set.

A right-tailed hypothesis tests the null hypothesis, H_0, that the difference in the population proportion is statistically less than or equal to the hypothesized difference (if the hypothesized difference is set to zero, the null hypothesis tests if population proportion of sample 1 is equal to or less than the population proportion of sample 2). The alternative hypothesis, H_a, is that the real difference in population proportions is statistically greater than the hypothesized difference when tested using the sample data set.

A left-tailed hypothesis tests the null hypothesis, H_0, that the difference in the population proportion is statistically greater than or equal to the hypothesized difference (if the hypothesized difference is set to zero, the null hypothesis tests if population proportion of sample 1 is equal to or greater than the population proportion of sample 2). The alternative hypothesis, H_a, is that the real difference in population proportions is statistically less than the hypothesized difference when tested using the sample data set.

Two (Independent) Variables Testing for Variances (F-Test)

The two-variable F-test analyzes the variances from two samples (the population variance of sample 1 is tested with the population variance of sample 2 to see if they are equal) and is appropriate when the population standard deviation is not known but the sampling distribution is assumed to be approximately normal. The measurement of variation is a key issue in Six Sigma and quality control applications. In this illustration, suppose that the variation or variance around the units produced in a manufacturing process is compared to another process to determine which process is more variable and, hence, less predictable in quality.

This F-test can typically be applied to a single hypothesis test: a two-tailed test. A two-tailed hypothesis tests the null hypothesis, H_0, such that the population variance of the two variables is statistically identical. The alternative hypothesis, H_a, is that the population variances are statistically different from one another when tested using the sample data set.

If the calculated p-value is less than or equal to the significance level in the test, then reject the null hypothesis and conclude that the true population variances of the two variables are not statistically equal to one another. Otherwise, the true population variances are statistically similar to each other.

5.1.6 Nonparametric Analysis

The Basics of Nonparametric Methodologies

Nonparametric techniques make no assumptions about the specific shape or distribution from which the sample is drawn. This lack of assumptions makes it different from the other hypotheses tests such as ANOVA or t-tests (parametric tests) where the sample is assumed to be drawn from a population that is normally or approximately normally distributed. If normality is assumed, the power of the test is higher due to this normality restriction. However, if flexibility on distributional requirements is needed, then nonparametric techniques are superior. In general, nonparametric methodologies provide the following advantages over other parametric tests:

- Normality or approximate normality does not have to be assumed.
- Fewer assumptions about the population are required; that is, nonparametric tests do not require that the population assume any specific distribution.
- Smaller sample sizes can be analyzed.
- Samples with nominal and ordinal scales of measurement can be tested.
- Sample variances do not have to be equal, whereas equality is required in parametric tests.

However, several caveats are worthy of mention:

- Compared to parametric tests, nonparametric tests use data less efficiently.
- The power of the test is lower than that of the parametric tests.

Therefore, if all the required assumptions are satisfied, it is better to use parametric tests. However, in reality, it may be difficult to justify these distributional assumptions, or small sample sizes may exist, requiring the need for nonparametric tests. Thus, nonparametric tests should be used when the data are nominal or ordinal, or when the data are interval or ratio but the normality assumption is not met.

The following covers each of the nonparametric tests available for use in the software.

Chi-Square Goodness-of-Fit Test

The Chi-Square test for goodness of fit is used to determine whether a sample data set could have been drawn from a population having a specified probability distribution. The probability distribution tested here is the normal distribution. The null hypothesis (H_0) tested is such that the sample is randomly drawn from the normal distribution, versus the alternate hypothesis (H_a) that the sample is not from a normal distribution. If the calculated p-value is less than or equal to the alpha significance value, then reject the null hypothesis and accept the alternate hypothesis. Otherwise, if the p-value is higher than the alpha significance value, do not reject the null hypothesis.

For the Chi-Square goodness-of-fit test, create data tables such as the one below, and select the data in the blue area (e.g., select the data from D6 to E13, or data points 800 to 4). To extend the data set, just add more observations (rows).

	C	D	E
4	Chi-Square Goodness of Fit		
5	Category	Upper Limit	Frequency
6	700-800	800	36
7	800-900	900	96
8	900-1000	1000	78
9	1000-1100	1100	48
10	1100-1200	1200	25
11	1200-1300	1300	10
12	1300-1400	1400	3
13	1400-1500	1500	4

*For the Chi-Square Goodness of Fit Test, create data tables such as these, and select the data area in blue area (e.g., select the data from D6 to E13, or data points 800 to 4). To extend the data set, just add more observations (rows).

Chi-Square Test of Independence

The Chi-Square test for independence examines two variables to see if there is some statistical relationship between them. This test is not used to find the exact nature of the relationship between the two variables, but to simply test if the variables could be independent of each other. The null hypothesis (H_0) tested is such that the variables are independent of each other, versus the alternate hypothesis (H_a) that the variables are not independent of each other.

The Chi-Square test looks at a table of observed frequencies and a table of expected frequencies. The amount of disparity between these two tables is calculated and compared with the Chi-Square test statistic. The observed frequencies reflect the cross-classification for members of a single sample, and the table of expected frequencies is constructed under the assumption that the null hypothesis is true.

Chi-Square Population Variance Test

The Chi-Square test for population variance is used for hypothesis testing and confidence interval estimation for a population variance. The population variance of a sample is typically unknown, and, hence, the need for quantifying this confidence interval. The population is assumed to be normally distributed.

Friedman Test

The Friedman test is a form of nonparametric test, which makes no assumptions about the specific shape of the population from which the sample is drawn, allowing for smaller sample data sets to be analyzed. This method is the extension of the Wilcoxon Signed Rank test for paired samples. The corresponding parametric test is the Randomized Block Multiple Treatment

ANOVA, but unlike the ANOVA, the Friedman test does not require that the data set be randomly sampled from normally distributed populations with equal variances.

The Friedman test uses a two-tailed hypothesis test where the null hypothesis (H_0) is such that the population medians of each treatment are statistically identical to the rest of the group. That is, there is no effect among the different treatment groups. The alternative hypothesis (H_a) is such that the real population medians are statistically different from one another when tested using the sample data set. That is, the medians are statistically different, which means that there is a statistically significant effect among the different treatment groups. If the calculated p-value is less than or equal to the alpha significance value, then reject the null hypothesis and accept the alternate hypothesis. Otherwise, if the p-value is higher than the alpha significance value, do not reject the null hypothesis.

For the Friedman test, create data tables such as the one below, and select the data in the blue area (e.g., select the data from C22 to F32, or data points Treatment 1 to 80).

	B	C	D	E	F
22	Blocks	Treatment 1	Treatment 2	Treatment 3	Treatment 4
23	1	90	87	93	85
24	2	86	79	87	83
25	3	76	77	91	85
26	4	75	78	92	83
27	5	79	79	89	82
28	6	68	75	88	83
29	7	69	74	87	84
30	8	68	76	82	81
31	9	59	72	91	81
32	10	62	71	90	80
33					
34	*For the Friedman's Test, create data tables such as these, and select the data				
35	area in blue area (e.g., select the data from C22 to F32, or data points Treatment 1				
36	to 80). If selecting the headers, remember to select "Treat first row as headers." To				
37	extend the data set, just add more observations (rows).				

Kruskal-Wallis Test

The Kruskal-Wallis test is a form of nonparametric test, which makes no assumptions about the specific shape of the population from which the sample is drawn, allowing for smaller sample data sets to be analyzed. This method is the extension of the Wilcoxon Signed Rank test by comparing more than two independent samples. The corresponding parametric test is the One-Way ANOVA, but unlike the ANOVA, the Kruskal-Wallis does not require that the data set be randomly sampled from normally distributed populations with equal variances. The Kruskal-Wallis test is a two-tailed hypothesis test where the null hypothesis (H_0) is such that the population medians of each treatment are statistically identical to the rest of the group. That is, there is no effect among the different treatment groups. The alternative hypothesis (H_a) is such that the real population medians are statistically different from one another when tested using the sample data set. That is, the medians are statistically different, which means that there is a statistically significant effect among the different treatment groups. If the calculated p-value is less than or equal to the alpha significance value, then reject the null hypothesis and accept the alternate hypothesis. Otherwise, if the p-value is higher than the alpha significance value, do not reject the null hypothesis.

The benefit of the Kruskal-Wallis test is that it can be applied to ordinal, interval, and ratio data while ANOVA is only applicable for interval and ratio data. Also, the Friedman test can be run with fewer data points.

To illustrate, suppose that three different drug indications (T = 3) were developed and tested on 100 patients each (N = 100). The Kruskal-Wallis test can be applied to test if these three drugs are all equally effective statistically. If the calculated p-value is less than or equal to the significance level used in the test, then reject the null hypothesis and conclude that there is a significant difference among the different treatments. Otherwise, the treatments are all equally effective.

For the Kruskal-Wallis test, create data tables such as the one below, and select the data in the blue area (e.g., select the data from C40 to F50, or data points Treatment 1 to 80). To extend the data set, just add more observations (rows) or more treatment variables to compare (columns).

	B	C	D	E	F
39	One-Way ANOVA and Kruskal-Wallis Test				
40	Observations	Treatment 1	Treatment 2	Treatment 3	Treatment 4
41	1	90	87	93	85
42	2	86	79	87	83
43	3	76	77	91	85
44	4	75	78	92	83
45	5	79	79	89	82
46	6	68	75	88	83
47	7	69	74	87	84
48	8	68	76	82	81
49	9	59	72	91	81
50	10	62	71	90	80

Lilliefors Test

The Lilliefors test is a form of nonparametric test, which makes no assumptions about the specific shape of the population from which the sample is drawn, allowing for smaller sample data sets to be analyzed. This test evaluates the null hypothesis (H_0) of whether the data sample was drawn from a normally distributed population, versus an alternate hypothesis (H_a) that the data sample is not normally distributed. If the calculated p-value is less than or equal to the alpha significance value, then reject the null hypothesis and accept the alternate hypothesis. Otherwise, if the p-value is higher than the alpha significance value, do not reject the null hypothesis. This test relies on two cumulative frequencies: one derived from the sample data set and one from a theoretical distribution based on the mean and standard deviation of the sample data. An alternative to this test is the Chi-Square test for normality. The Chi-Square test requires more data points to run compared to the Lilliefors test.

Runs Test

The runs test is a form of nonparametric test, which makes no assumptions about the specific shape of the population from which the sample is drawn, allowing for smaller sample data sets to be analyzed. This test evaluates the randomness of a series of observations by analyzing the number of runs it contains. A run is a consecutive appearance of one or more observations that are similar. The null hypothesis (H_0) tested is whether the data sequence is random, versus the alternate hypothesis (H_a) that the data sequence is not random. If the calculated p-value is less than or equal to the alpha significance value, then reject the null hypothesis and accept the alternate hypothesis. Otherwise, if the p-value is higher than the alpha significance value, do not reject the null hypothesis.

Wilcoxon Signed-Rank Test (One Variable)

The single variable Wilcoxon Signed Rank test is a form of nonparametric test, which makes no assumptions about the specific shape of the population from which the sample is drawn, allowing for smaller sample data sets to be analyzed. This method looks at whether a sample data set could have been randomly drawn from a particular population whose median is being hypothesized. The corresponding parametric test is the one-sample t-test, which should be used if the underlying population is assumed to be normal, providing a higher power on the test. The Wilcoxon Signed Rank test can be applied to three types of hypothesis tests: a two-tailed test, a right-tailed test, and a left-tailed test. If the calculated Wilcoxon statistic is outside the critical limits for the specific significance level in the test, reject the null hypothesis and conclude that the true population median is not equal to (two-tailed test), less than (left-tailed test), or greater than (right-tailed test) the hypothesized median based on the sample tested. Otherwise, the true population median is statistically similar to the hypothesized median.

Wilcoxon Signed-Rank Test (Two Variables)

The Wilcoxon Signed Rank test for paired variables is a form of nonparametric test, which makes no assumptions about the specific shape of the population from which the sample is drawn, allowing for smaller sample data sets to be analyzed. This method looks at whether the median of the differences between the two paired variables are equal. This test is specifically formulated for testing the same or similar samples before and after an event (e.g., measurements taken before a medical treatment are compared against those measurements taken after the treatment to see if there is a difference). The corresponding parametric test is the two-sample t-test with dependent means, which should be used if the underlying population is assumed to be normal, providing a higher power on the test. The Wilcoxon Signed Rank test can be applied to three types of hypothesis tests: a two-tailed test, a right-tailed test, and a left-tailed test.

To illustrate, suppose that a new engine design is tested against an existing engine design to see if there is a statistically significant different between the two. The paired variable Wilcoxon Signed-Rank test can be applied. If the calculated Wilcoxon statistic is outside the critical limits for the specific significance level in the test, reject the null hypothesis and conclude that the difference between the true population medians is not equal to (two-tailed test), less than (left-tailed test), or greater than (right-tailed test) the hypothesized median difference based on the sample tested. Otherwise, the true population median is statistically similar to the hypothesized median.

5.1.7 ANOVA (Multivariate Hypothesis Tests)

Single Factor Multiple Treatments ANOVA

The one-way ANOVA for single factor with multiple treatments test is an extension of the two-variable t-test, looking at multiple variables simultaneously. The ANOVA is appropriate when the sampling distribution is assumed to be approximately normal. ANOVA can be applied to only the two-tailed hypothesis test. A two-tailed hypothesis tests the null hypothesis (H_0) such that the population means of each treatment is statistically identical to the rest of the group, which means that there is no effect among the different treatment groups. The alternative hypothesis (H_a) is such that the real population means are statistically different from one another when tested using the sample data set.

To illustrate, suppose that three different drug indications (T = 3) were developed and tested on 100 patients each (N = 100). The one-way ANOVA can be applied to test if these three drugs are all equally effective statistically. If the calculated p-value is less than or equal to the significance level used in the test, then reject the null hypothesis and conclude that there is a significant difference among the different treatments. Otherwise, the treatments are all equally effective.

Randomized Block Multiple Treatments ANOVA

The one-way randomized block ANOVA is appropriate when the sampling distribution is assumed to be approximately normal and when there exists a block variable for which ANOVA will control (block the effects of this variable by controlling it in the experiment). ANOVA can be applied to only the two-tailed hypothesis test. This analysis can test for the effects of both the treatments as well as the effectiveness of the control, or block, variable.

If the calculated p-value for the treatment is less than or equal to the significance level used in the test, then reject the null hypothesis and conclude that there is a significant difference among the different treatments. If the calculated p-value for the block variable is less than or equal to the significance level used in the test, then reject the null hypothesis and conclude that there is a significant difference among the different block variables.

To illustrate, suppose that three different headlamp designs (T = 3) were developed and tested on four groups of volunteer drivers grouped by their age (B = 4). The one-way randomized block ANOVA can be applied to test if these three headlamps are all equally effective statistically when tested using the volunteers' driving test grades. Otherwise, the treatments are all equally effective. This test can determine if the differences occur because of the treatment (that the type of headlamp will determine differences in driving test scores) or from the block, or controlled, variable (that age may yield different driving abilities).

Two-Way ANOVA

The two-way ANOVA is an extension of the single factor and randomized block ANOVA by simultaneously examining the effects of two factors on the dependent variable, along with the effects of interactions between the different levels of these two factors. Unlike the randomized block design, this model examines the interactions between different levels of the factors, or independent variables. In a two-factor experiment, interaction exists when the effect of a level for one factor depends on which level of the other factor is present.

There are three sets of null (H_0) and alternate (H_a) hypotheses to be tested in the two-way analysis of variance.

The first test is on the first independent variable, where the null hypothesis is that no level of the first factor has an effect on the dependent variable. The alternate hypothesis is that there is at least one level of the first factor having an effect on the dependent variable. If the calculated p-value is less than or equal to the alpha significance value, then reject the null hypothesis and accept the alternate hypothesis. Otherwise, if the p-value is higher than the alpha significance value, do not reject the null hypothesis.

The second test is on the second independent variable, where the null hypothesis is that no level of the second factor has an effect on the dependent variable. The alternate hypothesis is that there is at least one level of the second factor having an effect on the dependent variable. If the calculated p-value is less than or equal to the alpha significance value, then reject the null hypothesis and accept the alternate hypothesis. Otherwise, if the p-value is higher than the alpha significance value, do not reject the null hypothesis.

The third test is on the interaction of both the first and second independent variables, where the null hypothesis is that there are no interacting effects between levels of the first and second factors. The alternate hypothesis is that there is at least one combination of levels of the first and second factors having an effect on the dependent variable. If the calculated p-value is less than or equal to the alpha significance value, then reject the null hypothesis and accept the alternate hypothesis. Otherwise, if the p-value is higher than the alpha significance value, do not reject the null hypothesis.

For the *Two-Way ANOVA* module, create tables such as the one below, and select the data in the blue area (804 to 835). You can extend the data by adding rows of factors and columns of treatments. Note that the number of replications in the table above is 2 (i.e., two rows of observations per Factor A type). Of course, you can increase the number of replications as required. The number of replications has to be consistent if you wish to extend the data set.

		B	C	D	E	F
26				Two-Way ANOVA		
27				Factor B		
28						
29				*j* =1	*j* =2	*j* =3
30						
31		Factor A	*i* = 1	804	836	804
32				816	828	808
33			*i* = 2	819	844	807
34				813	836	819
35			*i* = 3	820	814	819
36				821	811	829
37			*i* = 4	806	811	827
38				805	806	835

5.1.8 Forecasting, Multiple Regression, and Econometrics

ARIMA (Autoregressive Integrated Moving Average)

One very powerful advanced times-series forecasting tool is the ARIMA or *Auto Regressive Integrated Moving Average* approach. ARIMA forecasting assembles three separate tools into a comprehensive model. The first tool segment is the autoregressive or "AR" term, which corresponds to the number of lagged value of the residual in the unconditional forecast model. In essence, the model captures the historical variation of actual data to a forecasting model and uses this variation, or residual, to create a better predicting model. The second tool segment is the integration order or the "I" term. This integration term corresponds to the number of differencing the time series to be forecasted goes through. This element accounts for any nonlinear growth rates existing in the data. The third tool segment is the moving average or "MA" term, which is essentially the moving average of lagged forecast errors. By incorporating this average of lagged forecast errors, the model, in essence, learns from its forecast errors or mistakes and corrects for them through a moving average calculation.

Auto ARIMA (Automatic Autoregressive Integrated Moving Average)

ARIMA is an advanced modeling technique used to model and forecast time-series data (data that have a time component to them, e.g., interest rates, inflation, sales revenues, gross domestic product).

The *ARIMA Auto Model* selection will analyze all combinations of ARIMA (p,d,q) for the most common values of 0, 1, and 2, and reports the relevant Akaike Information Criterion (AIC) and Schwarz Criterion (SC). The lowest AIC and SC model is then chosen and run. You can also add in exogenous variables into the model selection.

In addition, in order to forecast ARIMA models with exogenous variables, make sure that the exogenous variables have enough data points to cover the additional number of periods to forecast. Finally, be aware that due to the complexity of the models, this module may take several minutes to run. Please be patient.

Autoregressive Integrated Moving Average, or ARIMA(p,d,q), models are the extension of the AR model that uses three components for modeling the serial correlation in the time-series data. The first component is the autoregressive (AR) term. The AR(p) model uses the p lags of the time series in the equation. An AR(p) model has the form: $y_t = a_1 y_{t-1} + ... + a_p y_{t-p} + e_t$. The second component is the integration (d) order term. Each integration order corresponds to differencing the time series. I(1) means differencing the data once; I(d) means differencing the data d times. The third component is the moving average (MA) term. The MA(q) model uses the q lags of the forecast errors to improve the forecast. An MA(q) model has the form: $y_t = e_t + b_1 e_{t-1} + ... + b_q e_{t-q}$. Finally, an ARMA(p,q) model has the combined form: $y_t = a_1 y_{t-1} + ... + a_p y_{t-p} + e_t + b_1 e_{t-1} + ... + b_q e_{t-q}$.

Basic Multiple Regression

It is assumed that the user is familiar with regression analysis. If not, refer to Dr. Johnathan Mun's *Modeling Risk* (Third Edition, Wiley 2015), or this manual's Appendix 3: A Primer on Regression Analysis before continuing. Multiple Regression analysis is used to find a statistical and mathematical relationship between a single dependent variable and multiple independent variables. Regression is useful for determining the relationship as well as for forecasting.

To illustrate, suppose you want to determine if sales of a product can be attributed to an advertisement in a local paper. In this case, sales revenue is the dependent variable, Y (it is dependent on size of the advertisement and how frequently is appears a week), while advertisement size and frequency are the independent variables X1 and X2 (they are independent of sales). Interpreting the regression analysis is more complex (this may include hypothesis t-tests, F-tests, ANOVA, correlations, autocorrelations, etc.).

Basic Econometrics and Autoeconometrics

Econometrics refers to a branch of business analytics, modeling, and forecasting techniques for modeling the behavior or forecasting certain business, financial, economic, physical science, and other variables. Running the *Basic Econometrics* models is similar to regular regression analysis except that the dependent and independent variables are allowed to be modified before a regression is run. The report generated is the same as shown in the Multiple Regression section previously and the interpretations are identical to those described previously

Combinatorial Fuzzy Logic

In contrast, the term *fuzzy logic* is derived from fuzzy set theory to deal with reasoning that is approximate rather than accurate. As opposed to *crisp logic*, where binary sets have binary logic, fuzzy logic variables may have a truth value that ranges between 0 and 1 and is not constrained to the two truth values of classic propositional logic. This fuzzy weighting schema is used together with a combinatorial method to yield time-series forecast results. Note that neither neural networks nor fuzzy logic techniques have yet been established as valid and reliable methods in the business forecasting domain, on either a strategic, tactical, or operational level. Much research is still required in these advanced forecasting fields. Nonetheless, *PEAT's Forecast Statistics module* provides the fundamentals of these two techniques for the purposes of running time-series forecasts. We recommend that you do not use any of these techniques in isolation, but, rather, in combination with the other *ROV BizStats* forecasting methodologies to build more robust models.

GARCH Volatility Forecasts

The *Generalized Autoregressive Conditional Heteroskedasticity* (GARCH) *Model* is used to model historical and forecast future volatility levels of a marketable security (e.g., stock prices, commodity prices, oil prices, etc.). The data set has to be a time series of raw price levels. GARCH will first convert the prices into relative returns and then run an internal optimization to fit the historical data to a mean-reverting volatility term structure, while assuming that the volatility is heteroskedastic in nature (changes over time according to some econometric characteristics). The theoretical specifics of a GARCH model are outside the purview of this user manual.

Notes

The typical volatility forecast situation requires P = 1, Q = 1; Periodicity = number of periods per year (12 for monthly data, 52 for weekly data, 252 or 365 for daily data); Base = minimum of 1 and up to the periodicity value; and Forecast Periods = number of annualized volatility forecasts you wish to obtain. There are several GARCH models available in *PEAT's Forecast Statistics module*, including EGARCH, EGARCH-T, GARCH-M, GJR-GARCH, GJR-GARCH-T, IGARCH, and T-GARCH.

GARCH models are used mainly in analyzing financial time-series data to ascertain their conditional variances and volatilities. These volatilities are then used to value the options as usual, but the amount of historical data necessary for a good volatility estimate remains significant. Usually, several dozen—and even up to hundreds—of data points are required to obtain good GARCH estimates.

GARCH is a term that incorporates a family of models that can take on a variety of forms, known as GARCH(p,q), where p and q are positive integers that define the resulting GARCH model and its forecasts. In most cases for financial instruments, a GARCH(1,1) is sufficient and is most generally used. For instance, a GARCH (1,1) model takes the form of:

$$y_t = x_t \gamma + \varepsilon_t$$
$$\sigma_t^2 = \omega + \alpha \varepsilon_{t-1}^2 + \beta \sigma_{t-1}^2$$

where the first equation's dependent variable *(yt)* is a function of exogenous variables *(xt)* with an error term *(εt)*. The second equation estimates the variance (squared volatility σ_t^2) at time *t*, which depends on a historical mean *(ω)*; news about volatility from the previous period, measured as a lag of the squared residual from the mean equation *(ε_{t-1}^2)*; and volatility from the previous period *(σ_{t-1}^2)*. The exact modeling specification of a GARCH model is beyond the scope of this manual. Suffice it to say that detailed knowledge of econometric modeling (model specification tests, structural breaks, and error estimation) is required to run a GARCH model, making it less accessible to the general analyst. Another problem with GARCH models is that the model usually does not provide a good statistical fit. That is, it is impossible to predict the stock market and, of course, equally if not harder to predict a stock's volatility over time.

Note that the GARCH function has several inputs as follow:

- *Time-Series Data.* The time series of data in chronological order (e.g., stock prices). Typically, dozens of data points are required for a decent volatility forecast.
- *Periodicity.* A positive integer indicating the number of periods per year (e.g., 12 for monthly data, 252 for daily trading data, etc.), assuming you wish to annualize the volatility. For getting periodic volatility, enter 1.
- *Predictive Base.* The number of periods back (of the time-series data) to use as a base to forecast volatility. The higher this number, the longer the historical base is used to forecast future volatility.
- *Forecast Period.* A positive integer indicating how many future periods beyond the historical stock prices you wish to forecast.
- *Variance Targeting.* This variable is set as False by default (even if you do not enter anything here) but can be set as True. False means the omega variable is automatically optimized and computed. The suggestion is to leave this variable empty. If you wish to create mean-reverting volatility with variance targeting, set this variable as True.
- *P.* The number of previous lags on the mean equation.
- *Q.* The number of previous lags on the variance equation.

The accompanying table lists some of the GARCH specifications used in *PEAT* with two underlying distributional assumptions: one for normal distribution and the other for the t distribution.

	$z_t \sim$ Normal Distribution	$z_t \sim$ T Distribution
GARCH-M Variance in Mean Equation	$y_t = c + \lambda \sigma_t^2 + \varepsilon_t$ $\varepsilon_t = \sigma_t z_t$ $\sigma_t^2 = \omega + \alpha \varepsilon_{t-1}^2 + \beta \sigma_{t-1}^2$	$y_t = c + \lambda \sigma_t^2 + \varepsilon_t$ $\varepsilon_t = \sigma_t z_t$ $\sigma_t^2 = \omega + \alpha \varepsilon_{t-1}^2 + \beta \sigma_{t-1}^2$
GARCH-M Standard Deviation in Mean Equation	$y_t = c + \lambda \sigma_t + \varepsilon_t$ $\varepsilon_t = \sigma_t z_t$ $\sigma_t^2 = \omega + \alpha \varepsilon_{t-1}^2 + \beta \sigma_{t-1}^2$	$y_t = c + \lambda \sigma_t + \varepsilon_t$ $\varepsilon_t = \sigma_t z_t$ $\sigma_t^2 = \omega + \alpha \varepsilon_{t-1}^2 + \beta \sigma_{t-1}^2$
GARCH-M Log Variance in Mean Equation	$y_t = c + \lambda \ln(\sigma_t^2) + \varepsilon_t$ $\varepsilon_t = \sigma_t z_t$ $\sigma_t^2 = \omega + \alpha \varepsilon_{t-1}^2 + \beta \sigma_{t-1}^2$	$y_t = c + \lambda \ln(\sigma_t^2) + \varepsilon_t$ $\varepsilon_t = \sigma_t z_t$ $\sigma_t^2 = \omega + \alpha \varepsilon_{t-1}^2 + \beta \sigma_{t-1}^2$
GARCH	$y_t = x_t \gamma + \varepsilon_t$ $\sigma_t^2 = \omega + \alpha \varepsilon_{t-1}^2 + \beta \sigma_{t-1}^2$	$y_t = \varepsilon_t$ $\varepsilon_t = \sigma_t z_t$ $\sigma_t^2 = \omega + \alpha \varepsilon_{t-1}^2 + \beta \sigma_{t-1}^2$
EGARCH	$y_t = \varepsilon_t$ $\varepsilon_t = \sigma_t z_t$ $\ln\left(\sigma_t^2\right) = \omega + \beta \cdot \ln\left(\sigma_{t-1}^2\right) +$ $\alpha\left[\left|\dfrac{\varepsilon_{t-1}}{\sigma_{t-1}}\right| - E(|\varepsilon_t|)\right] + r\dfrac{\varepsilon_{t-1}}{\sigma_{t-1}}$ $E(|\varepsilon_t|) = \sqrt{\dfrac{2}{\pi}}$	$y_t = \varepsilon_t$ $\varepsilon_t = \sigma_t z_t$ $\ln\left(\sigma_t^2\right) = \omega + \beta \cdot \ln\left(\sigma_{t-1}^2\right) +$ $\alpha\left[\left|\dfrac{\varepsilon_{t-1}}{\sigma_{t-1}}\right| - E(|\varepsilon_t|)\right] + r\dfrac{\varepsilon_{t-1}}{\sigma_{t-1}}$ $E(|\varepsilon_t|) = \dfrac{2\sqrt{\nu-2}\ \Gamma((\nu+1)/2)}{(\nu-1)\Gamma(\nu/2)\sqrt{\pi}}$

GJR-GARCH	$y_t = \varepsilon_t$ $\varepsilon_t = \sigma_t z_t$ $\sigma_t^2 = \omega + \alpha \varepsilon_{t-1}^2 +$ $r\varepsilon_{t-1}^2 d_{t-1} + \beta \sigma_{t-1}^2$ $d_{t-1} = \begin{cases} 1 & \text{if } \varepsilon_{t-1} < 0 \\ 0 & \text{otherwise} \end{cases}$	$y_t = \varepsilon_t$ $\varepsilon_t = \sigma_t z_t$ $\sigma_t^2 = \omega + \alpha \varepsilon_{t-1}^2 +$ $r\varepsilon_{t-1}^2 d_{t-1} + \beta \sigma_{t-1}^2$ $d_{t-1} = \begin{cases} 1 & \text{if } \varepsilon_{t-1} < 0 \\ 0 & \text{otherwise} \end{cases}$

For the GARCH-M models, the conditional variance equations are the same in the six variations, but the mean questions are different and assumption on z_t can be either normal distribution or t distribution. The estimated parameters for GARCH-M with normal distribution are those five parameters in the mean and conditional variance equations. The estimated parameters for GARCH-M with the t distribution are those five parameters in the mean and conditional variance equations plus another parameter, the degrees of freedom for the t distribution. In contrast, for the GJR models, the mean equations are the same in the six variations and the differences are that the conditional variance equations and the assumption on z_t can be either a normal distribution or t distribution. The estimated parameters for EGARCH and GJR-GARCH with normal distribution are those four parameters in the conditional variance equation. The estimated parameters for GARCH, EARCH, and GJR-GARCH with t distribution are those parameters in the conditional variance equation plus the degrees of freedom for the t distribution. More technical details of GARCH methodologies fall outside of the scope of this manual.

J-Curve and S-Curve Forecasts

The J curve, or exponential growth curve, is one where the growth of the next period depends on the current period's level and the increase is exponential. This phenomenon means that over time, the values will increase significantly, from one period to another. This model is typically used in forecasting biological growth and chemical reactions over time.

The S curve, or logistic growth curve, starts off like a J curve, with exponential growth rates. Over time, the environment becomes saturated (e.g., market saturation, competition, overcrowding), the growth slows, and the forecast value eventually ends up at a saturation or maximum level. The S-curve model is typically used in forecasting market share or sales growth of a new product from market introduction until maturity and decline, population dynamics, growth of bacterial cultures, and other naturally occurring variables.

Markov Chains

A Markov chain exists when the probability of a future state depends on a previous state and when linked together forms a chain that reverts to a long-run steady state level. This Markov approach is typically used to forecast the market share of two competitors. The required inputs are the starting probability of a customer in the first store (the first state) returning to the same store in the next period versus the probability of switching to a competitor's store in the next state.

Neural Network Forecasting

The term Neural Network is often used to refer to a network or circuit of biological neurons, while modern usage of the term often refers to artificial neural networks comprising artificial neurons, or nodes, recreated in a software environment. Such networks attempt to mimic the neurons in the human brain in ways of thinking and identifying patterns and, in our situation, identifying patterns for the purposes of forecasting time-series data. Note that the number of hidden layers in the network is an input parameter and will need to be calibrated with your data. Typically, the more complicated the data pattern, the higher the number of hidden layers you would need and the longer it would take to compute. It is recommended that you start at 3 layers. The testing period is simply the number of data points used in the final calibration of the Neural Network model, and we recommend using at least the same number of periods you wish to forecast as the testing period.

Nonlinear Extrapolation

Extrapolation involves making statistical forecasts by using historical trends that are projected for a specified period of time into the future. It is only used for time-series forecasts. For cross-sectional or mixed panel data (time-series with cross-sectional data), multivariate regression is more appropriate. This methodology is useful when major changes are not expected; that is, causal factors are expected to remain constant or when the causal factors of a situation are not clearly understood. It also helps discourage the introduction of personal biases into the process. Extrapolation is fairly reliable, relatively simple, and inexpensive. However, extrapolation, which assumes that recent and historical trends will continue, produces large forecast errors if discontinuities occur within the projected time period; that is, pure extrapolation of time series assumes that all we need to know is contained in the historical values of the series being forecasted. If we assume that past behavior is a good predictor of future behavior, extrapolation is appealing. This makes it a useful approach when all that is needed are many short-term forecasts.

This methodology estimates the $f(x)$ function for any arbitrary x value, by interpolating a smooth nonlinear curve through all the x values and, using this smooth curve, extrapolates future x values beyond the historical data set. The methodology employs either the polynomial functional form or the rational functional form (a ratio of two polynomials). Typically, a polynomial functional form is sufficient for well-behaved data, however, rational functional forms are sometimes more accurate (especially with polar functions, i.e., functions with denominators approaching zero).

Principal Components Analysis

Principal Components Analysis is a way of identifying patterns in data and recasting the data in such a way as to highlight their similarities and differences. Patterns of data are very difficult to find in high dimensions when multiple variables exist, and higher dimensional graphs are very difficult to represent and interpret. Once the patterns in the data are found, they can be compressed, resulting in a reduction of the number of dimensions. This reduction of data dimensions does not mean much loss of information. Instead, similar levels of information can now be obtained by fewer variables.

The analysis provides the Eigenvalues and Eigenvectors of the data set. The Eigenvector with the highest Eigenvalue is the principle component of the data set. Ranking the Eigenvalues from highest to lowest provides the components in order of statistical significance. If the Eigenvalues are small, you do not lose much information. It is up to you to decide how many components to ignore based on their Eigenvalues. The proportions and cumulative proportions tell you how much of the variation in the data set can be explained by incorporating that component. Finally, the data is then transformed to account for only the number of components you decide to keep.

Spline (Cubic Spline Interpolation and Extrapolation)

Sometimes there are missing values in a time-series data set. For instance, interest rates for years 1 to 3 may exist, followed by years 5 to 8, and then year 10. Spline curves can be used to interpolate the missing years' interest rate values based on the data that exist. Spline curves can also be used to forecast or extrapolate values of future time periods beyond the time period of available data. The data can be linear or nonlinear. The Known X values represent the values on the x-axis of a chart (in our example, this is Years of the known interest rates, and, usually, the x-axis are the values that are known in advance such as time or years) and the Known Y values represent the values on the y-axis (in our case, the known Interest Rates). The y-axis variable is typically the variable you wish to interpolate missing values from or extrapolate the values into the future.

Stepwise Regression

One powerful automated approach to regression analysis is Stepwise Regression. Based on its namesake, the regression process proceeds in multiple steps. There are several ways to set up these stepwise algorithms, including the correlation approach, forward method, backward method, and the forward and backward method (these methods are all available in *ROV BizStats*).

In the correlation method, the dependent variable (Y) is correlated to all the independent variables (X), and a regression is run, starting with the X variable with the highest absolute correlation value. Then subsequent X variables are added until the p-values indicate that the new X variable is no longer statistically significant. This approach is quick and simple but does not account for interactions among variables, and an X variable, when added, will statistically overshadow other variables.

In the forward method, we first correlate Y with all X variables, run a regression for Y on the highest absolute value correlation of X, and obtain the fitting errors. Then, correlate these errors with the remaining X variables and choose the highest absolute value correlation among this remaining set and run another regression. Repeat the process until the p-value for the latest X variable coefficient is no longer statistically significant then stop the process.

In the backward method, run a regression with Y on all X variables and, reviewing each variable's p-value, systematically eliminate the variable with the largest p-value. Then run a regression again, repeating each time until all p-values are statistically significant.

In the forward and backward method, apply the forward method to obtain three X variables, and then apply the backward approach to see if one of them needs to be eliminated because it is statistically insignificant. Repeat the forward method, and then the backward method until all remaining X variables are considered.

The Stepwise Regression is an automatic search process iterating through all the independent variables, and it models the variables that are statistically significant in explaining the variations in the dependent variable. Stepwise Regression is very powerful when there are many independent variables and a large combination of models can be built. To illustrate, suppose you want to determine if sales of a product can be attributed to an advertisement in a local paper. In this case, sales revenue is the dependent variable Y, while the independent variables X1 to X5 are the size of the advertisement, cost of the ad, number of readers, day of the week, and how frequently it appears a week. Stepwise Regression will automatically iterate through these X variables to find those that are statistically significant in the regression model. Interpreting the regression analysis is more complex (this may include hypothesis t-tests, F-tests, ANOVA, correlations, autocorrelations, etc.).

5.1.9 Forecasting with Time-Series Decomposition

It is assumed that the user is familiar with basic time-series analysis methodologies. If not, refer to Dr. Johnathan Mun's *Modeling Risk* (Third Edition, Wiley 2015), or this manual's Appendix 2: A Primer on Time-Series Methodologies before continuing. Forecasting is the act of predicting the future whether it is based on historical data or speculation about the future when no history exists. When historical data exist, a quantitative or statistical approach is best, but if no historical data exist, then a qualitative or judgmental approach is usually the only recourse. The figure below lists the eight most common time-series models, segregated by seasonality and trend. For instance, if the data variable has no trend or seasonality, then a single moving-average model or a single exponential-smoothing model would suffice. However, if seasonality exists but no discernible trend is present, either a seasonal additive or seasonal multiplicative model would be better, and so forth. The following subsections explore these models in more detail through computational examples.

	NO SEASONALITY	WITH SEASONALITY
WITHOUT TREND	Single Moving Average	Seasonal Additive
WITHOUT TREND	Single Exponential Smoothing	Seasonal Multiplicative
WITH TREND	Double Moving Average	Holt–Winters Additive
WITH TREND	Double Exponential Smoothing	Holt–Winters Multiplicative

The best-fitting test for the moving average forecast uses the Root Mean Squared Errors (RMSE). The RMSE calculates the square root of the average squared deviations of the fitted values versus the actual data points.

Mean Squared Error (MSE) is an absolute error measure that squares the errors (the difference between the actual historical data and the forecast-fitted data predicted by the model) to keep the positive and negative errors from canceling each other out. This measure also tends to exaggerate large errors by weighting the large errors more heavily than smaller errors by squaring them, which can help when comparing different time-series models. Root Mean Square Error (RMSE) is the square root of MSE and is the most popular error measure, also known as the quadratic loss function. RMSE can be defined as the average of the absolute values of the forecast errors and is highly appropriate when the cost of the forecast errors is proportional to the absolute size of the forecast error. The RMSE is used as the selection criteria for the best-fitting time-series model.

Mean Absolute Deviation (MAD) is an error statistic that averages the distance (absolute value of the difference between the actual historical data and the forecast-fitted data predicted by the model) between each pair of actual and fitted forecast data points and is most appropriate when the cost of forecast errors is proportional to the absolute size of the forecast errors.

Mean Absolute Percentage Error (MAPE) is a relative error statistic measured as an average percent error of the historical data points and is most appropriate when the cost of the forecast error is more closely related to the percentage error than the numerical size of the error. Finally, an associated measure is the Theil's U statistic, which measures the naivety of the model's forecast. That is, if the Theil's U statistic is less than 1.0, then the forecast method used provides an estimate that is statistically better than guessing.

Single Moving Average

The single moving average is applicable when time-series data with no trend and seasonality exist. This model is not appropriate when used to predict cross-sectional data. The single moving average simply uses an average of the actual historical data to project future outcomes. This average is applied consistently moving forward, hence the term *moving average*. The value of the moving average for a specific length is simply the summation of actual historical data arranged and indexed in a time sequence. The software finds the optimal moving average lag automatically through an optimization process that minimizes the forecast errors.

Single Exponential Smoothing

The single exponential smoothing approach is used when no discernible trend or seasonality exists in the time-series data. This model is not appropriate when used to predict cross-sectional data. This method weights past data with exponentially decreasing weights going into the past; that is, the more recent the data value, the greater its weight. This weighting largely overcomes the limitations of moving averages or percentage-change models. The weight used is termed the *alpha* measure. The software finds the optimal alpha parameter automatically through an optimization process that minimizes the forecast errors.

Double Moving Average

The double moving average method will smooth out past data by performing a moving average on a subset of data that represents a moving average of an original set of data. That is, a second moving average is performed on the first moving average. The second moving average application captures the trending effect of the data. The results are then weighted and forecasts are created. The software finds the optimal moving average lag automatically through an optimization process that minimizes the forecast errors.

Double Exponential Smoothing

The double exponential smoothing method is used when the data exhibit a trend but no seasonality. This model is not appropriate when used to predict cross-sectional data. Double exponential smoothing applies single exponential smoothing twice, once to the original data and then to the resulting single exponential smoothing data. An alpha weighting parameter is used on the first or single exponential smoothing (*SES*), while a beta weighting parameter is used on the second or double exponential smoothing (*DES*). This approach is useful when the historical data series is not stationary. The software finds the optimal alpha and beta parameters automatically through an optimization process that minimizes the forecast errors.

Seasonal Additive

If the time-series data has no appreciable trend but exhibits seasonality, then the additive seasonality and multiplicative seasonality methods apply. The additive seasonality model breaks the historical data into a level (*L*), or base-case, component as measured by the alpha parameter, and a seasonality (*S*) component measured by the gamma parameter. The resulting forecast value is simply the addition of this base-case level to the seasonality value. The software finds the optimal alpha and gamma parameters automatically through an optimization process that minimizes the forecast errors.

Seasonal Multiplicative

If the time-series data has no appreciable trend but exhibits seasonality, then the additive seasonality and multiplicative seasonality methods apply. The multiplicative seasonality model breaks the historical data into a level (*L*), or base-case, component as measured by the alpha parameter, and a seasonality (*S*) component measured by the gamma parameter. The resulting forecast value is simply the multiplication of this base-case level by the seasonality value. The software finds the optimal alpha and gamma parameters automatically through an optimization process that minimizes the forecast errors.

Holt-Winter's Seasonal Additive

When both seasonality and trend exist, more advanced models are required to decompose the data into their base elements: a base-case level (*L*) weighted by the alpha parameter; a trend component (*b*) weighted by the beta parameter; and a seasonality component (*S*) weighted by the gamma parameter. Several methods exist, but the two most common are the Holt-Winter's additive seasonality and Holt-Winter's multiplicative seasonality methods. In the Holt-Winter's additive model, the base-case level, seasonality, and trend are added together to obtain the forecast fit.

Holt-Winter's Seasonal Multiplicative

When both seasonality and trend exist, more advanced models are required to decompose the data into their base elements: a base-case level (L) weighted by the alpha parameter; a trend component (b) weighted by the beta parameter; and a seasonality component (S) weighted by the gamma parameter. Several methods exist, but the two most common are the Holt-Winter's additive seasonality and Holt-Winter's multiplicative seasonality methods. In the Holt-Winter's multiplicative model, the base-case level and trend are added together and multiplied by the seasonality factor to obtain the forecast fit.

Trendlines

Trendlines can be used to determine if a set of time-series data follows any appreciable trend. Trends can be linear or nonlinear (such as exponential, logarithmic, moving average, polynomial, or power). In forecasting models, the process usually includes removing the effects of accumulating data sets from seasonality and trend to show only the absolute changes in values and to allow potential cyclical patterns to be identified after removing the general drift, tendency, twists, bends, and effects of seasonal cycles of a set of time-series data. For example, a detrended data set may be necessary to see a more accurate account of a company's sales in a given year by shifting the entire data set from a slope to a flat surface to better expose the underlying cycles and fluctuations.

Volatility: Log Returns Approach

There are several ways to estimate the volatility used in forecasting and option valuation models. The most common approach is the Logarithmic Returns Approach. This method is used mainly for computing the volatility on liquid and tradable assets, such as stocks in financial options. However, sometimes it is used for other traded assets, such as the price of oil or electricity. This method cannot be used when negative cash flows or prices occur, which means it is used only on positive data, making it most appropriate for computing the volatility of traded assets. The approach is simply to take the annualized standard deviation of the logarithmic relative returns of the time-series data as the proxy for volatility. See the section on GARCH models for more advanced volatility computations.

Yield Curves: Bliss and Nelson-Siegel Methods

The Bliss interpolation model is used for generating the term structure of interest rates and yield curve estimation. Econometric modeling techniques are required to calibrate the values of several input parameters in this model. The Bliss approach modifies the Nelson-Siegel method by adding an additional generalized parameter. Virtually any yield curve shape can be interpolated using these two models, which are widely used at banks around the world. In contrast, the Nelson-Siegel model is run with four curve estimation parameters. If properly modeled, it can be made to fit almost any yield curve shape. Calibrating the inputs in these models requires facility with econometric modeling and error optimization techniques. Typically, if some interest rates exist, a better approach is to use a spline interpolation method such as cubic spline and so forth.

5.1.10 Forecasting with Stochastic Processes

The Basics of Forecasting with Stochastic Processes

A stochastic process is nothing but a mathematically defined equation that can create a series of outcomes over time, outcomes that are not deterministic in nature. That is, it does not follow any simple discernible rule such as price will increase X percent every year or revenues will increase by this factor of X plus Y percent. A stochastic process is, by definition, nondeterministic, and one can plug numbers into a stochastic process equation and obtain different results every time. For instance, the path of a stock price is stochastic in nature, and one cannot reliably predict the stock price path with any certainty. However, the price evolution over time is enveloped in a process that generates these prices. The process is fixed and predetermined, but the outcomes are not. Hence, by stochastic simulation, we create multiple pathways of prices, obtain a statistical sampling of these simulations, and make inferences on the potential pathways that the actual price may undertake given the nature and parameters of the stochastic process used to generate the time series.

Random Walk: Brownian Motion

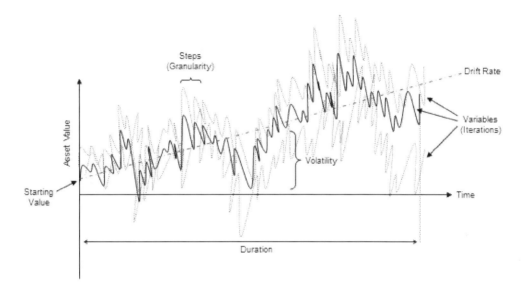

Assume a process X, where $X = [X_t : t \geq 0]$ if and only if X_t is continuous, where the starting point is $X_0 = 0$, where X is normally distributed with mean zero and variance one or $X \in N(0,1)$, and where each increment in time is independent of each other previous increment and is itself normally distributed with mean zero and variance t, such that $X_{t+a} - X_t \in N(0,t)$. Then, the process $dX = \alpha X \, dt + \sigma X \, dZ$ follows a Geometric Brownian Motion, where α is a drift parameter, σ the volatility measure, and $dZ = \varepsilon_t \sqrt{\Delta t}$ such that $\ln\left[\dfrac{dX}{X}\right] \in N(\mu, \sigma)$ or X and dX are lognormally distributed. If at time zero, $X(0) = 0$, then the expected value of the process X at any time t is such that $E[X(t)] = X_0 e^{\alpha t}$ and the variance of the process X at time t is $V[X(t)] = X_0^2 e^{2\alpha t}(e^{\sigma^2 t} - 1)$. In the continuous case where there is a drift parameter α, the expected value then becomes $E\left[\int_0^\infty X(t)e^{-rt} \, dt\right] = \int_0^\infty X_0 e^{-(r-\alpha)t} \, dt = \dfrac{X_0}{(r-\alpha)}$.

Jump-Diffusion

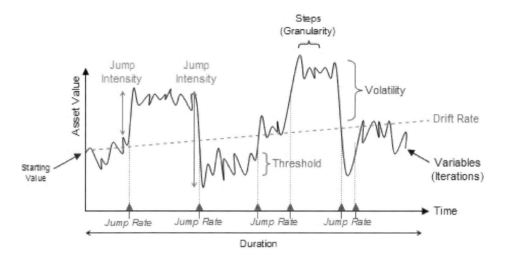

Start-up ventures and research and development initiatives usually follow a jump-diffusion process. Business operations may be status quo for a few months or years, and then a product or initiative becomes highly successful and takes off. An initial public offering of equities is a textbook example of this. Assuming that the probability of the jumps follows a Poisson distribution, we have a process $dX = f(X,t)dt + g(X,t)dq$, where the functions f and g are known and where the probability process is $dq = \begin{cases} 0 & with\ P(X) = 1 - \lambda dt \\ \mu & with\ P(X) = Xdt \end{cases}$.

Mean-Reversion

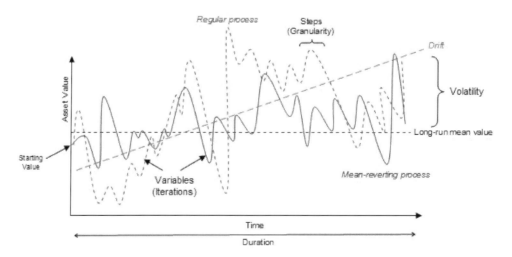

If a stochastic process has a long-run attractor such as a long-run production cost or long-run steady state inflationary price level, then a mean-reversion process is more likely. The process reverts to a long-run average such that the expected value is $E[X_t] = \overline{X} + (X_0 - \overline{X})e^{-\eta t}$ and the variance is $V[X_t - \overline{X}] = \dfrac{\sigma^2}{2\eta(1 - e^{-2\eta t})}$. The special circumstance that becomes useful is that in the limiting case when the time change becomes instantaneous or when $dt \rightarrow 0$, we have the condition where $X_t - X_{t-1} = \bar{X}(1 - e^{-\eta}) + X_{t-1}(e^{-\eta} - 1) + \varepsilon_t$, which is the first order autoregressive process, and η can be tested econometrically in a unit root context.

5.1.11 Analytical Models

Autocorrelation

Autocorrelation can be defined as the correlation of a data set to itself in the past. It is the correlation between observations of a time series separated by specified time units. Certain time-series data follow an autocorrelated series as future outcomes rely heavily on past outcomes (e.g., revenues or sales that follow a weekly, monthly, quarterly, or annual seasonal cycle; inflation and interest rates that follow some economic or business cycle, etc.). The term *autocorrelation* describes a relationship or correlation between values of the same data series at different time periods. The term *lag* defines the offset when comparing a data series with itself. For autocorrelation, lag refers to the offset of data that you choose when correlating a data series with itself. In *PEAT's Forecast Statistics module*, the autocorrelation function is calculated, together with the Q-statistic and relevant p-values. If the p-values are below the tested significance level, then the null hypothesis (H_0) of no autocorrelation is rejected, and it is concluded that there is autocorrelation that that particular lag.

Control Charts

Sometimes the specification limits are not set; instead, statistical control limits are computed based on the actual data collected (e.g., the number of defects in a manufacturing line). For instance, in Figure 8.1, we see 20 sample experiments or samples taken at various times of a manufacturing process. The number of samples taken varied over time, and the number of defective parts were also gathered. The upper control limit (UCL) and lower control limit (LCL) are computed, as are the central line (CL) and other sigma levels. The resulting chart is called a *control chart*, and if the process is out of control, the actual defect line will be outside of the UCL and LCL lines. Typically, when the LCL is a negative value, we set the floor as zero, as illustrated in Figure 8.1. In the interpretation of a control chart, by adding in the ± 1 and 2 sigma lines, we can divide the control charts into several areas or zones, as illustrated in Figure 8.2. The following are rules of thumb that typically apply to control charts to determine if the process is out of control:

- If one point is beyond Area A
- If two out of three consecutive points are in Area A or beyond
- If four out of five consecutive points are in Area B or beyond
- If eight consecutive points are in Area C or beyond

Additionally, a potential structural shift can be detected if any one of the following occurs:

- At least 10 out of 11 sequential points are on one side of the CL
- At least 12 out of 14 sequential points are on one side of the CL
- At least 14 out of 17 sequential points are on one side of the CL
- At least 16 out of 20 sequential points are on one side of the CL

Subgroup	Defective Units	Sample Size	Defect Proportion	LCL	CL	UCL
1	5	25	20.00%	0.00%	24.76%	53.71%
2	3	23	13.04%	0.00%	24.76%	53.71%
3	4	19	21.05%	0.00%	24.76%	53.71%
4	2	18	11.11%	0.00%	24.76%	53.71%
5	6	19	31.58%	0.00%	24.76%	53.71%
6	12	20	60.00%	0.00%	24.76%	53.71%
7	5	17	29.41%	0.00%	24.76%	53.71%
8	6	25	24.00%	0.00%	24.76%	53.71%
9	4	26	15.38%	0.00%	24.76%	53.71%
10	3	24	12.50%	0.00%	24.76%	53.71%
11	5	21	23.81%	0.00%	24.76%	53.71%
12	4	26	15.38%	0.00%	24.76%	53.71%
13	5	25	20.00%	0.00%	24.76%	53.71%
14	1	19	5.26%	0.00%	24.76%	53.71%
15	11	20	55.00%	0.00%	24.76%	53.71%
16	5	19	26.32%	0.00%	24.76%	53.71%
17	6	18	33.33%	0.00%	24.76%	53.71%
18	6	18	33.33%	0.00%	24.76%	53.71%
19	4	16	25.00%	0.00%	24.76%	53.71%
20	5	14	35.71%	0.00%	24.76%	53.71%

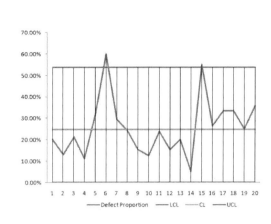

Figure 8.1 – Example quality control p-chart

X-Bar Chart — Used when the variable has raw data values and there are multiple measurements in a sample experiment, multiple experiments are run, and the average of the collected data is of interest.

R-Bar Chart — Used when the variable has raw data values and there are multiple measurements in a sample experiment, multiple experiments are run, and the range of the collected data is of interest.

XMR Chart — Used when the variable has raw data values and is a single measurement taken in each sample experiment, multiple experiments are run, and the actual value of the collected data is of interest.

P Chart — Used when the variable of interest is an attribute (e.g., defective or nondefective) and the data collected are in proportions of defects (or number of defects in a specific sample), there are multiple measurements in a sample experiment, multiple experiments are run with differing numbers of samples collected in each, and the average proportion of defects of the collected data is of interest.

NP Chart — Used when the variable of interest is an attribute (e.g., defective or nondefective) and the data collected are in proportions of defects (or number of defects in a specific sample), there are multiple measurements in a sample experiment, multiple experiments are run with a constant number of samples in each, and the average proportion of defects of the collected data is of interest.

C Chart — Used when the variable of interest is an attribute (e.g., defective or nondefective) and the data collected are in total number of defects (actual count in units), there are multiple measurements in a sample experiment, multiple experiments are run with the same number of samples collected in each, and the average number of defects of the collected data is of interest.

U Chart — Used when the variable of interest is an attribute (e.g., defective or nondefective) and the data collected are in total number of defects (actual count in units), there are multiple measurements in a sample experiment, multiple experiments are run with differing numbers of samples collected in each, and the average number of defects of the collected data is of interest.

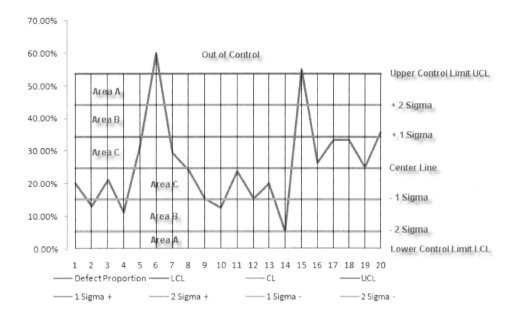

Figure 8.2 – Interpreting control charts

Deseasonalization

The data deseasonalization method removes any seasonal components in your original data. In forecasting models, the process usually includes removing the effects of accumulating data sets from seasonality and trend to show only the absolute changes in values and to allow potential cyclical patterns to be identified after removing the general drift, tendency, twists, bends, and effects of seasonal cycles of a set of time-series data. Many time-series data exhibit seasonality where certain events repeat themselves after some time period or seasonality period (e.g., ski resorts' revenues are higher in winter than in summer, and this predictable cycle will repeat itself every winter). Seasonality periods represent how many periods would have to pass before the cycle repeats itself (e.g., 24 hours in a day, 12 months in a year, 4 quarters in a year, 60 minutes in an hour, etc.). For deseasonalized and detrended data, a seasonal index greater than 1 indicates a high period or peak within the seasonal cycle, and a value below 1 indicates a dip in the cycle.

Distributional Fitting

Another powerful simulation tool is distributional fitting or determining which distribution to use for a particular input variable in a model and what the relevant distributional parameters are. If no historical data exist, then the analyst must make assumptions about the variables in question. One approach is to use the Delphi method where a group of experts is tasked with estimating the behavior of each variable. For instance, a group of mechanical engineers can be tasked with evaluating the extreme possibilities of a spring coil's diameter through rigorous experimentation or guesstimates. These values can be used as the variable's input parameters (e.g., uniform distribution with extreme values between 0.5 and 1.2). When testing is not possible (e.g., market share and revenue growth rate), management can still make estimates of potential outcomes and provide the best-case, most-likely case, and worst-case scenarios. However, if reliable historical data are available, distributional fitting can be accomplished. Assuming that historical patterns hold and that history tends to repeat itself, then historical data can be used to find the best-fitting distribution with their relevant parameters to better define the variables to be simulated.

Heteroskedasticity

A common violation in regression, econometric modeling, and some time-series forecast methods is heteroskedasticity. Heteroskedasticity is defined as the variance of the forecast errors increasing over time. If pictured graphically, the width of the vertical data fluctuations increases or fans out over time. In this example, the data points have been changed to exaggerate the effect. However, in most time-series analysis, checking for heteroskedasticity is a much more difficult task. The coefficient of determination, or R-squared, in a multiple regression analysis drops significantly when heteroskedasticity exists. As is, the current regression model is insufficient and incomplete.

If the variance of the dependent variable is not constant, then the error's variance will not be constant. The most common form of such heteroskedasticity in the dependent variable is that the variance of the dependent variable may increase as the mean of the dependent variable increases for data with positive independent and dependent variables.

Unless the heteroskedasticity of the dependent variable is pronounced, its effect will not be severe: the least-squares estimates will still be unbiased, and the estimates of the slope and intercept will either be normally distributed if the errors are normally distributed, or at least normally distributed asymptotically (as the number of data points becomes large) if the errors are not normally distributed. The estimate for the variance of the slope and overall variance will be inaccurate, but the inaccuracy is not likely to be substantial if the independent-variable values are symmetric about their mean.

Heteroskedasticity of the dependent variable is usually detected informally by examining the X-Y scatter plot of the data before performing the regression. If both nonlinearity and unequal variances are present, employing a transformation of the dependent variable may have the effect of simultaneously improving the linearity and promoting equality of the variances. Otherwise, a weighted least-squares linear regression may be the preferred method of dealing with nonconstant variance of the dependent variable.

Maximum Likelihood Models on Logit, Probit, and Tobit

Limited Dependent Variables describe the situation where the dependent variable contains data that are limited in scope and range, such as binary responses (0 or 1), truncated, ordered, or censored data. For instance, given a set of independent variables (e.g., age, income, education level of credit card or mortgage loan holders), we can model the probability of default using maximum likelihood estimation (MLE). The response or dependent variable Y is binary, that is, it can have only two possible outcomes that we denote as 1 and 0 (e.g., Y may represent presence/absence of a certain condition, defaulted/not defaulted on previous loans, success/failure of some device, answer yes/no on a survey, etc.) and we also have a vector of independent variable regressors X, which are assumed to influence the outcome Y. A typical ordinary least squares regression approach is invalid because the regression errors are heteroskedastic and non-normal, and the resulting estimated probability estimates will return nonsensical values of above 1 or below 0. MLE analysis handles these problems using an iterative optimization routine to maximize a log likelihood function when the dependent variables are limited.

A Logit or Logistic regression is used for predicting the probability of occurrence of an event by fitting data to a logistic curve. It is a generalized linear model used for binomial regression, and like many forms of regression analysis, it makes use of several predictor variables that may be either numerical or categorical. MLE applied in a binary multivariate logistic analysis is used to model dependent variables to determine the expected probability of success of belonging to a certain group. The estimated coefficients for the Logit model are the logarithmic odds ratios and cannot be interpreted directly as probabilities. A quick computation is first required and the approach is simple.

Specifically, the Logit model is specified as *Estimated Y = LN[P$_i$/(1–P$_i$)]* or, conversely, *P$_i$ = EXP(Estimated Y)/(1+EXP(Estimated Y))*, and the coefficients *β$_i$* are the log odds ratios. So, taking the antilog, or *EXP(β$_i$)*, we obtain the odds ratio of *P$_i$/(1–P$_i$)*. This means that with an increase in a unit of *β$_i$* the log odds ratio increases by this amount. Finally, the rate of change in the probability is *dP/dX = β$_i$P$_i$(1–P$_i$)*. The Standard Error measures how accurate the predicted Coefficients are, and the t-Statistics are the ratios of each predicted Coefficient to its Standard Error and are used in the typical regression hypothesis test of the significance of each estimated parameter. To estimate the probability of success of belonging to a certain group (e.g., predicting if a smoker will develop chest complications given the amount smoked per year), simply compute the *Estimated Y* value using the MLE coefficients. For example, if the model is *Y = 1.1 + 0.005 (Cigarettes)*, then someone smoking 100 packs per year has an *Estimated Y* of *1.1 + 0.005(100) = 1.6*. Next, compute the inverse antilog of the odds ratio: *EXP(Estimated Y)/[1 + EXP(Estimated Y)] = EXP(1.6)/(1+ EXP(1.6)) = 0.8320*. So, such a person has an *83.20%* chance of developing some chest complications in his or her lifetime.

A Probit model (sometimes also known as a Normit model) is a popular alternative specification for a binary response model, which employs a Probit function estimated using maximum likelihood estimation and is called Probit regression. The Probit and Logistic regression models tend to produce very similar predictions where the parameter estimates in a logistic regression tend to be 1.6 to 1.8 times higher than they are in a corresponding Probit model. The choice of using a Probit or Logit is entirely up to convenience, and the main distinction is that the logistic distribution has a higher kurtosis (fatter tails) to account for extreme values. For example, suppose that house ownership is the decision to be modeled, and this response variable is binary (home purchase or no home purchase) and depends on a series of independent variables *X$_i$* such as income, age, and so forth, such that *I$_i$ = β$_0$ + β$_1$X$_1$ +...+ β$_n$X$_n$*, where the larger the value of *I$_i$*, the higher the probability of home ownership. For each family, a critical *I** threshold exists, where if exceeded, the house is purchased, otherwise, no home is purchased, and the outcome probability (*P*) is assumed to be normally distributed such that *P$_i$ = CDF(I)* using a standard normal cumulative distribution function (*CDF*). Therefore, use the estimated coefficients exactly like those of a regression model and using the *Estimated Y* value, apply a standard normal distribution (you can use Excel's *NORMSDIST* function or *PEAT's* Distributional Analysis tool by selecting Normal distribution and setting the mean to be *0* and standard deviation to be *1*). Finally, to obtain a Probit or probability unit measure, set *I$_i$ + 5* (this is because whenever the probability *P$_i$ < 0.5*, the estimated *I$_i$* is negative, due to the fact that the normal distribution is symmetrical around a mean of zero).

The Tobit model (Censored Tobit) is an econometric and biometric modeling method used to describe the relationship between a non-negative dependent variable *Y$_i$* and one or more independent variables *X$_i$*. A Tobit model is an econometric model in which the dependent variable is censored; that is, the dependent variable is censored because values below zero are not observed. The Tobit model assumes that there is a latent unobservable variable *Y**. This variable is linearly dependent on the *X$_i$* variables via a vector of *β$_i$* coefficients that determine their interrelationships. In addition, there is a normally distributed error term, *U$_i$*, to capture random influences on this relationship. The observable variable *Y$_i$* is defined to be equal to the latent variables whenever the latent variables are above zero and *Y$_i$* is assumed to be zero otherwise. That is, *Y$_i$ = Y** if *Y* > 0* and *Y$_i$ = 0* if *Y* = 0*. If the relationship parameter *β$_i$* is estimated by using ordinary least squares regression of the observed *Y$_i$* on *X$_i$*, the resulting regression estimators are inconsistent and yield downward-biased slope coefficients and an upward-biased intercept. Only MLE would be consistent for a Tobit model. In the Tobit model, there is an ancillary statistic called sigma, which is equivalent to the standard error of estimate in a standard ordinary least squares regression, and the estimated coefficients are used the same way as a regression analysis.

Multicollinearity

Multicollinearity exists when there is a linear relationship between the independent variables in a regression analysis. When this occurs, the regression equation cannot be estimated at all. In near-collinearity situations, the estimated regression equation will be biased and provide inaccurate results. This situation is especially true when a stepwise regression approach is used, where the statistically significant independent variables will be thrown out of the regression mix earlier than expected, resulting in a regression equation that is neither efficient nor accurate.

As an example, suppose the following multiple regression analysis exists, where

$$Y_i = \beta_1 + \beta_2 X_{2,i} + \beta_3 X_{3,i} + \varepsilon_i$$

then the estimated slopes can be calculated through

$$\hat{\beta}_2 = \frac{\sum Y_i X_{2,i} \sum X_{3,i}^2 - \sum Y_i X_{3,i} \sum X_{2,i} X_{3,i}}{\sum X_{2,i}^2 \sum X_{3,i}^2 - \left(\sum X_{2,i} X_{3,i}\right)^2}$$

$$\hat{\beta}_3 = \frac{\sum Y_i X_{3,i} \sum X_{2,i}^2 - \sum Y_i X_{2,i} \sum X_{2,i} X_{3,i}}{\sum X_{2,i}^2 \sum X_{3,i}^2 - \left(\sum X_{2,i} X_{3,i}\right)^2}$$

Now suppose that there is perfect multicollinearity, that is, there exists a perfect linear relationship between X_2 and X_3, such that $X_{3,i} = \lambda X_{2,i}$ for all positive values of λ. Substituting this linear relationship into the slope calculations for β_2, the result is indeterminate. In other words, we have

$$\hat{\beta}_2 = \frac{\sum Y_i X_{2,i} \sum \lambda^2 X_{2,i}^2 - \sum Y_i \lambda X_{2,i} \sum \lambda X_{2,i}^2}{\sum X_{2,i}^2 \sum \lambda^2 X_{2,i}^2 - \left(\sum \lambda X_{2,i}^2\right)^2} = \frac{0}{0}$$

The same calculation and results apply to β_3, which means that the multiple regression analysis breaks down and cannot be estimated given a perfect collinearity condition. One quick test of the presence of multicollinearity in a multiple regression equation is that the R-squared value is relatively high while the t-statistics are relatively low. Another quick test is to create a correlation matrix between the independent variables. A high cross-correlation indicates a potential for autocorrelation. The rule of thumb is that a correlation with an absolute value greater than 0.75 is indicative of severe multicollinearity. Another test for multicollinearity is the use of the variance inflation factor (VIF), obtained by regressing each independent variable to all the other independent variables, obtaining the R-squared value, and calculating the VIF of that variable by estimating:

$$VIF_i = \frac{1}{(1 - R_i^2)}$$

A high VIF value indicates a high R-squared near unity. As a rule of thumb, a VIF value greater than 10 is usually indicative of destructive multicollinearity.

Partial Autocorrelation

Autocorrelation can be defined as the correlation of a data set to itself in the past. It is the correlation between observations of a time series separated by specified time units. Certain time-series data follow an autocorrelated series as future outcomes rely heavily on past outcomes (e.g., revenues or sales that follow a weekly, monthly, quarterly, or annual seasonal cycle; inflation and interest rates that follow some economic or business cycle, etc.). Partial Autocorrelations (PAC), in contrast, are used to measure the degree of association between each data point at a particular time Y_t and a time lag Y_{t-k} when the cumulative effects of all other time lags (1, 2, 3, ..., k–1) have been removed. The term *lag* defines the offset when comparing a data series with itself. In this module, the Partial Autocorrelation function is calculated, together with the Q-statistic and relevant p-values. If the p-values are below the tested significance level, then the null hypothesis (H_0) of no autocorrelation is rejected and it is concluded that there is autocorrelation that that particular lag.

Segmentation Clustering

Segmentation clustering takes the original data set and runs some internal algorithms (a combination or k-means hierarchical clustering and other method of moments in order to find the best-fitting groups or natural statistical clusters) to statistically divide, or segment, the original data set into multiple groups. This technique is valuable in a variety of settings including marketing (such as market segmentation of customers into various customer relationship management groups), physical sciences, engineering, and others.

Seasonality Test

Many time-series data exhibit seasonality where certain events repeat themselves after some time period or seasonality period (e.g., ski resorts' revenues are higher in winter than in summer, and this predictable cycle will repeat itself every winter). Seasonality periods represent how many periods would have to pass before the cycle repeats itself (e.g., 24 hours in a day, 12 months in a year, 4 quarters in a year, 60 minutes in an hour, etc.). For deseasonalized and detrended data, a seasonal index greater than 1 indicates a high period or peak within the seasonal cycle, and a value below 1 indicates a dip in the cycle. Enter in the maximum seasonality period to test. That is, if you enter 6, the tool will test the following seasonality periods: 1, 2, 3, 4, 5, and 6. Period 1, of course, implies no seasonality in the data. Review the report generated for more details on the methodology, application, and resulting charts and seasonality test results. The best seasonality periodicity is listed first (ranked by the lowest RMSE error measure), and all the relevant error measurements are included for comparison: root mean squared error (RMSE), mean squared error (MSE), mean absolute deviation (MAD), and mean absolute percentage error (MAPE).

Structural Break

A structural break tests whether the coefficients in different data sets are equal, and this test is most commonly used in time-series analysis to test for the presence of a structural break. A time-series data set can be divided into two subsets. Structural break analysis is used to test each subset individually and on one another and on the entire data set to statistically determine if, indeed, there is a break starting at a particular time period. The structural break test is often used to determine whether the independent variables have different impacts on different subgroups of the population, such as to test if a new marketing campaign, activity, major event, acquisition, divestiture, and so forth have an impact on the time-series data. Suppose, for example, a data set has 100 time-series data points. You can set various breakpoints to test, for instance, data points 10, 30, and 51. (This means that three structural break tests will be performed: data points 1–9 compared with 10–100; data points 1–29 compared with 30–100; and 1–50 compared with 51–100 to see if there is a break in the underlying structure at the start of data points 10, 30, and 51.). A one-tailed hypothesis test is performed on the null hypothesis (H_0) such that the two data subsets are statistically similar to one another, that is, there is no statistically significant structural break. The alternative hypothesis (H_a) is that the two data subsets are statistically different from one another, indicating a possible structural break. If the calculated p-values are less than or equal to 0.01, 0.05, or 0.10, then the hypothesis is rejected, which implies that the two data subsets are statistically significantly different at the 1%, 5%, and 10% significance levels. High p-values indicate that there is no statistically significant structural break.

SECTION II
PEAT VISUAL GUIDES

GETTING STARTED VISUAL GUIDES

PEAT VISUAL GUIDE

VOLUME 1:
Installation and Licensing

RealOptions Valuation

1. Download and install PEAT

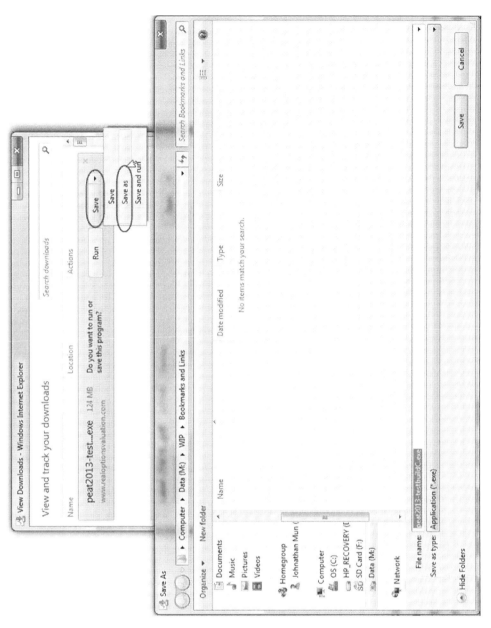

FYI. The download link might change with a newer version in the near future but all the instructions attached herein remains the same... FYI. The installation download file is approximately 480MB. If your downloaded file is significantly smaller in size, the download was probably incomplete (in that case, delete the file and try the download again).

1. Start PEAT (double click on the ROV PEAT desktop icon)
2. Select any module and click LOAD EXAMPLE

Real Options Valuation

Project Economics Analysis Tool

© Copyright 2012-2014 Real Options Valuation, Inc.

Applying Integrated Risk Management methodologies (Monte Carlo risk simulation, strategic real options, stochastic forecasting, business analytics, and portfolio optimization) to project and portfolio economics and financial analysis.

Load Example   New   Open   Exit

English

Note that you may not have access to all the modules as shown because some are company-specific proprietary modules developed for various multinationals.

Corporate Investments - Stochastic DCF Analysis

Enterprise Risk Management (ERM) - Risk Register

Corporate Investments - Buy vs. Lease

Project Management - Dynamic Schedule and Cost Analysis

Public Sector Analysis - Knowledge Value Added

ROV Compiled Models

Oil and Gas Economics - Investment Decision Analysis

Customized Encrypted Models

Saudi Aramco – FPD Standard Economic Model

Saudi Aramco – FPD Standard Economic Model
Saudi Aramco - FPD Expanded Economic Model
Saudi Aramco – CFPD Standard Corporate Finance Projects
Saudi Aramco - JV Expanded Joint Venture Valuation
Saudi Aramco - Corporate Planning Portfolio Management
Northrop Grumman – IR&D Model
Northrop Grumman - S-Curve Analysis
Arco Oil and Gas Co. - Economics of Oil Field Reserves
Arco Oil and Gas Co. - Remaining Oil Recovery Analysis
Arco Oil and Gas Co. - Oil Well Type Curves
Health Economics Analysis Tool (HEAT)
ROV HQDM Rapid Economic Justification (REJ)
Goals Analytics

Real Options Valuation

1. Click HELP | INSTALL LICENSE

2. E-mail admin@realoptionsvaluation.com your Hardware Fingerprint and we will send you your Name and License Key. In the meantime, you may use the temporary Name and Key below for a 14-day trial

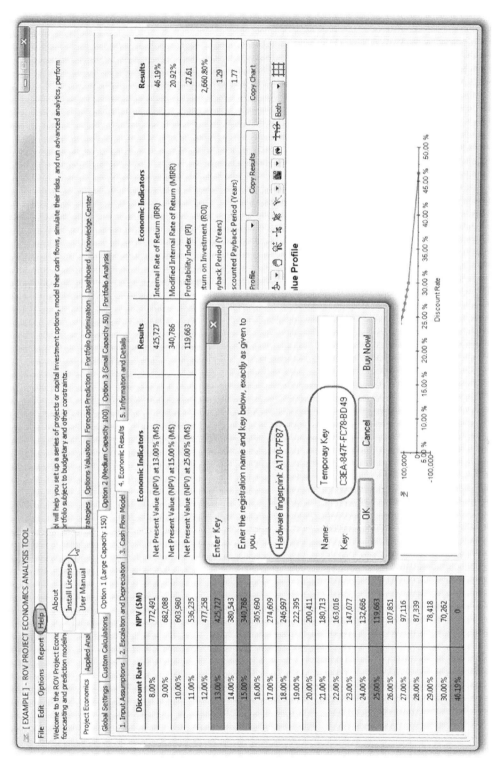

FYI. Enter the Name and Key exactly as specified. If you are receiving a permanent license, you only need to do this one time.

PEAT VISUAL GUIDE

VOLUME 2:

Quick Getting Started with Discounted Cash Flow Module and Integrated Risk Management

RealOptions Valuation

Instructions

- This is a quick getting started guide, not a detailed user manual. See the user manual and related books for more technical information.

- Text in RED is instructions, text in BLUE is notes for your information only.

- This visual guide showcases the Discounted Cash Flow module and summarizes how the following methods are implemented and run in PEAT using an example model:

  - DCF Metrics (Net Present Value, Internal Rate of Return, Modified Internal Rate of Return, Profitability Index, Return on Investment, Payback Period, and Discounted Payback Period), for individual projects/options and within a Portfolio

  - Analytics (Tornado Analysis for identifying critical success factors, and Scenario Analysis for identifying hot spots)

  - Risk Simulations (running tens of thousands of simulation trials to determine probabilistic risk metrics, comparing dynamic sensitivities of inputs, and comparing risk metrics and returns across multiple projects)

  - Real Options Strategies (visual representation of strategies with decision trees and strategy trees)

  - Real Options Valuation (computes the values of each individual real options path)

  - Portfolio Optimization (budget allocation and optimal project selection subject to budget and other strategic constraints)

  - Management Dashboards (create multiple results dashboards for management)

  - Knowledge and Training Center (quick lessons on using PEAT, project economics basics, and getting started videos)

1. Start PEAT and Select "Corporate Investments – Stochastic Discount Cash Flow (DCF) Analysis"
2. Click "Load Example"

Project Economics Analysis Tool

© Copyright 2012-2014 Real Options Valuation, Inc.

Applying Integrated Risk Management methodologies (Monte Carlo risk simulation, strategic real options, stochastic forecasting, business analytics, and portfolio optimization) to project and portfolio economics and financial analysis.

New   Open   Exit

Load Example

English

Real Options Valuation

- ● Corporate Investments - Stochastic DCF Analysis
- ○ Enterprise Risk Management (ERM) - Risk Register
- ○ Corporate Investments - Buy vs. Lease
- ○ Project Management - Dynamic Schedule and Cost Analysis
- ○ Public Sector Analysis - Knowledge Value Added
- ○ ROV Compiled Models
- ○ Oil and Gas Economics - Investment Decision Analysis
- ○ Customized Encrypted Models
- Saudi Aramco – FPD Standard Economic Model

Click on "Load Example" to follow along and walk through this Visual Guide...

Go to "DCF | Project 1 | DCF" to see the sample model data loaded and ready to go

[EXAMPLE] - ROV PROJECT ECONOMICS ANALYSIS TOOL

File   Edit   Projects   Report   Tools   Language   Decimals   Help

Welcome to the ROV Project Economics Analysis Tool (PEAT). This tool will help you set up a series of projects or capital investment options, model their cash flows, simulate their risks, and run advanced analytics, perform forecasting and prediction modeling, and optimize your investment portfolio subject to budgetary and other constraints.

Discounted Cash Flow | Applied Analytics | Risk Simulation | Options Valuation | Options Strategies | Forecast Prediction | Portfolio Optimization | Dashboard | Knowledge Center

Custom (xls1) | Project 1 | Project 2 | Project 3 | Project 4 | Project 5 | Project 6 | Project 7 | Project 8 | Project 9 | Project 10 | Portfolio Analysis | Discount Rates

1. Discounted Cash Flow Model (DCF) | 2. Cash Flow Ratios | 3. Economic Results | 4. Information and Details

DCF Starting Year: 2016   DCF Ending Year: 2043   Discount Rate (%): 10.00%   Marginal Tax Rate (%): 28.50%

Revenues: 1 Rows   Direct Costs: 4 Rows   Indirect Expenses: 6 Rows   Allow Negative Taxes   View Full Grid

Year	2016	2017	2018	2019	2020	2021	2022	2023	2024	2025	2026
Revenues	1,742.50	11,737.14	225,850.12	225,850.12	225,850.12	225,850.12	225,850.12	225,850.12	225,850.12	225,850.12	225,850.12
Sales Revenue - Global Sales	1,742.50	11,737.14	225,850.12	225,850.12	225,850.12	225,850.12	225,850.12	225,850.12	225,850.12	225,850.12	225,850.12
Direct Costs	1,141.09	1,141.09	26,392.75	26,392.75	26,392.75	26,456.81	27,888.82	27,888.82	27,888.82	27,888.82	27,888.82
Direct R&D	1,110.26	1,110.26	24,896.68	24,896.68	24,896.68	24,896.68	24,896.68	24,896.68	24,896.68	24,896.68	24,896.68
Manufacturing	18.50	18.50	414.95	414.95	414.95	453.38	829.89	829.89	829.89	829.89	829.89
Fabrication	12.33	12.33	25.62	25.62	25.62	51.25	51.25	51.25	51.25	51.25	51.25
Direct COGS	0.00	0.00	1,055.50	1,055.50	1,055.50	1,055.50	2,111.00	2,111.00	2,111.00	2,111.00	2,111.00
Gross Profit (Operating Income)	601.41	10,596.05	199,457.37	199,457.37	199,457.37	199,393.31	197,961.30	197,961.30	197,961.30	197,961.30	197,961.30
Indirect Expenses (General & Administrative)	799.42	3,073.28	9,212.61	9,212.61	9,212.61	9,212.61	9,212.61	10,877.49	9,567.71	9,567.71	12,187.27
Sales and Administrative	0.00	31.00	703.00	703.00	703.00	703.00	703.00	703.00	703.00	703.00	703.00
Marketing and Advertising	0.00	0.00	0.00	0.00	0.00	0.00	0.00	0.00	0.00	0.00	0.00
Operations	0.00	0.00	1,248.07	1,248.07	1,248.07	1,248.07	1,248.07	1,248.07	1,248.07	1,248.07	1,248.07
Maintenance	799.42	2,997.82	4,758.48	4,758.48	4,758.48	4,758.48	4,758.48	6,423.36	5,113.58	5,113.58	7,733.14
Foreign Transactions	0.00	0.00	1,506.00	1,506.00	1,506.00	1,506.00	1,506.00	1,506.00	1,506.00	1,506.00	1,506.00
Channel Partners	0.00	44.46	997.06	997.06	997.06	997.06	997.06	997.06	997.06	997.06	997.06
EBITDA: Earnings Before Interest, Taxes, Depreciation, and Amortization	-198.01	7,522.77	190,244.76	190,244.76	190,244.76	190,180.70	188,748.69	187,083.81	188,393.59	188,393.59	185,774.03
Depreciation	0.00	9,874.00	39,827.00	39,074.00	38,161.00	37,206.00	36,172.00	35,223.00	34,478.00	33,835.00	33,103.00
Amortization	0.00	0.00	0.00	0.00	0.00	0.00	0.00	0.00	0.00	0.00	0.00
EBIT: Earnings Before Interest and Taxes	-198.01	-2,351.23	150,417.76	151,170.76	152,083.76	152,974.70	152,576.69	151,860.81	153,915.59	154,558.59	152,671.03
Interest	0.00	6,779.32	25,892.66	22,767.15	19,224.35	15,842.53	13,062.00	12,303.79	11,571.22	8,977.41	5,886.42
EBT: Earnings Before Taxes	-198.01	-9,130.55	124,525.10	128,403.61	132,859.41	137,132.17	139,514.69	139,557.02	142,344.37	145,581.18	146,784.61

In your own model, simply enter the required inputs (input boxes) or Copy | Paste from Excel or another data source. You can add/reduce the number of rows to show for each category, and Copy grid icon to paste into Excel/Word/PowerPoint, or click on the Excel icon to extract the model to a worksheet.

Go to "DCF | Project 1 | Cash Flow Ratios" and see the sample inputs and results

[EXAMPLE] - ROV PROJECT ECONOMICS ANALYSIS TOOL

File Edit Projects Report Tools Language Decimals Help

Welcome to the ROV Project Economics Analysis Tool (PEAT). This tool will help you set up a series of projects or capital investment options, model their cash flows, simulate their risks, and run advanced analytics, perform forecasting and prediction modeling, and optimize your investment portfolio subject to budgetary and other constraints.

Tabs: Discounted Cash Flow | Applied Analytics | Risk Simulation | Options Strategies | Options Valuation | Forecast Prediction | Portfolio Optimization | Dashboard | Knowledge Center

Custom (xls1) | Project 1 | Project 2 | Project 3 | Project 4 | Project 5 | Project 6 | Project 7 | Project 8 | Project 9 | Project 10 | Portfolio Analysis | Discount Rates

1. Discounted Cash Flow Model (DCF) | 2. Cash Flow Ratios | 3. Economic Results | 4. Information and Details

Current Asset	32,806.00	
Accounts Receivables	4,016.00	
Total Assets	146,901.00	

Current Liabilities	18,370.00	
Shares Outstanding	1,132,357,090.00	
Total Debt	58,001.00	

Long-Term Operating Assets	114,095.00	
Stock Price Per Share	27.00	
Total Net Operating Capital	128,531.00	

Total Inventories	676.61
Common Equity	70,530.00

Show Earnings and Cash Flow Values

View Full Grid

Year	2016	2017	2018	2019	2020	2021	2022	2023	2024	2025	2026	2027	2028	2
EARNINGS BEFORE INT, TAX, DEP, AMORT (EBITDA)	-198.01	7,522.77	190,244.76	190,244.76	190,244.76	190,180.70	188,748.69	187,083.81	188,393.59	188,393.59	185,774.03	188,329.53	186,897.52	188,
EARNINGS BEFORE INTEREST AND TAXES (EBIT)	-198.01	-2,351.23	150,417.76	151,170.76	152,083.76	152,974.70	152,576.69	151,860.81	153,915.59	154,558.59	152,671.03	155,992.53	155,278.52	157,
NET INCOME (NI)	-141.58	-6,528.34	89,035.45	91,808.58	94,994.48	98,049.50	99,753.00	99,783.27	101,776.22	104,090.54	104,951.00	109,153.87	110,519.10	112,
NET OPERATING PROFIT AFTER TAXES (NOPAT)	-141.58	-1,681.13	107,548.70	108,087.09	108,739.89	109,376.91	109,092.33	108,580.48	110,049.65	110,509.39	109,159.79	111,534.66	111,024.14	112,
NET CASH FLOW (NCF)	-141.58	3,345.66	128,862.45	130,882.58	133,155.48	135,255.50	135,925.00	135,006.27	136,254.22	137,925.54	138,054.00	141,490.87	142,138.10	143,
OPERATING CASH FLOW (OCF)	-141.58	8,192.87	147,375.70	147,161.09	146,900.89	146,582.91	145,264.33	143,803.48	144,527.65	144,344.39	142,262.79	143,871.66	142,643.14	143,
FREE CASH FLOW (FCF)	-141.58	8,192.87	147,375.70	147,161.09	146,900.89	146,582.91	145,264.33	143,803.48	144,527.65	144,344.39	142,262.79	143,871.66	142,643.14	143,
RETURN ON INVESTED CAPITAL (ROIC)	-0.11%	-1.31%	83.68%	84.09%	84.60%	85.10%	84.88%	84.48%	85.62%	85.98%	84.93%	86.78%	86.38%	87
ECONOMIC VALUE ADDED (EVA)	-12,994.68	-14,534.23	94,695.60	95,233.99	95,886.79	96,523.81	96,239.23	95,727.38	97,196.55	97,656.29	96,306.69	98,681.56	98,171.04	99,
TIMES INTEREST EARNED (TIE)		-0.35	5.81	6.64	7.91	9.66	11.68	12.34	13.30	17.22	25.94	46.85	219.83	24
NET PROFIT MARGIN (NPM)	-8.12%	-55.62%	39.42%	40.65%	42.06%	43.41%	44.17%	44.18%	45.06%	46.09%	46.47%	48.33%	48.93%	48
OPERATING PROFIT MARGIN (OPM)	-8.12%	-14.32%	47.62%	47.86%	48.15%	48.43%	48.30%	48.08%	48.73%	48.93%	48.33%	49.36%	49.16%	48
EARNINGS PER SHARE (EPS)	-0.00	-0.00	0.00	0.00	0.00	0.00	0.00	0.00	0.00	0.00	0.00	0.00	0.00	0.00

Balance Sheet Ratios

CURRENT RATIO (CR)	1.79
QUICK RATIO (QR)	1.75
NET OPERATING WORKING CAPITAL (NOWC)	14,436.00
NET OPERATING CAPITAL (NOC)	128,531.00
MARKET VALUE ADDED (MVA)	30,573,570,900.00

BOOK VALUE PER SHARE (BV)	0.00
DEBT TO ASSET RATIO	39.48%
MARKET TO BOOK RATIO (MB)	433,484.21
EQUITY MULTIPLIER (EM)	2.08
DEBT TO EQUITY RATIO (DE)	0.82

You can click on the droplist to view results in dollars or in relative percentages, View Full Grid, or Copy grid icon to paste into another software like Excel...

Go to "DCF | Project 1 | Economic Results" and see the computed results.
No other actions are required other than playing with some droplists...

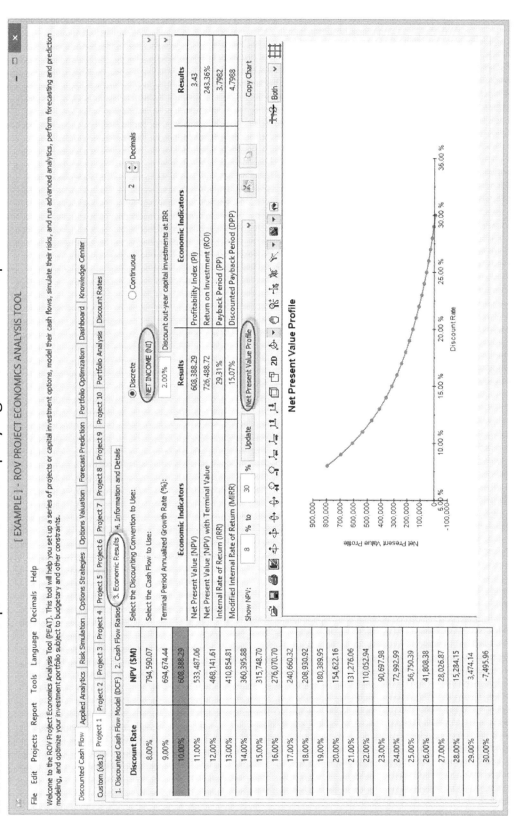

You can compute the project economic and financial metrics using different cash flows by choosing the relevant droplist items. You can also change the type of chart to display from the chart droplist as well as change the look and feel of the chart as required...

Go to "DCF | Project 1 | Information and Details"

You can enter in the project specific details as required, and replicate this on other projects as required... Categories can be customized and you can also link external files that may be relevant to this project using the Link File button... When you are done with this Project, note that you can continue to view other projects or proceed to the next step... As information, you can DUPLICATE, ADD, DELETE project tabs as required from the Projects menu...

Go to "DCF | Portfolio Analysis" and play with some of the checklists and droplists...

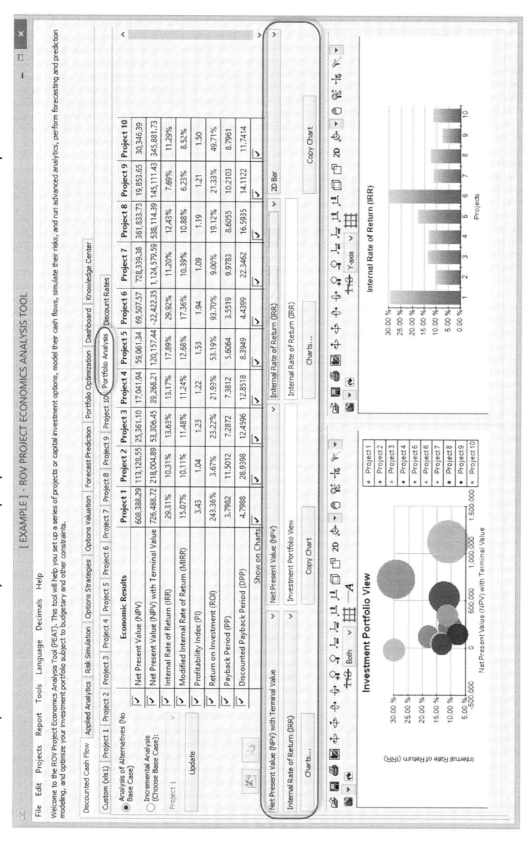

All projects are summarized in this tab as a Portfolio. You can now compare all single point results of the main project economic metrics, modify and view different charts, copy the results and charts to Excel or PowerPoint, and change details as well as the look and feel of the charts as required...

OPTIONAL STEP: Go to "DCF | Custom Calculations" and play with the worksheet and its functions, as well as perform some Live Excel Links

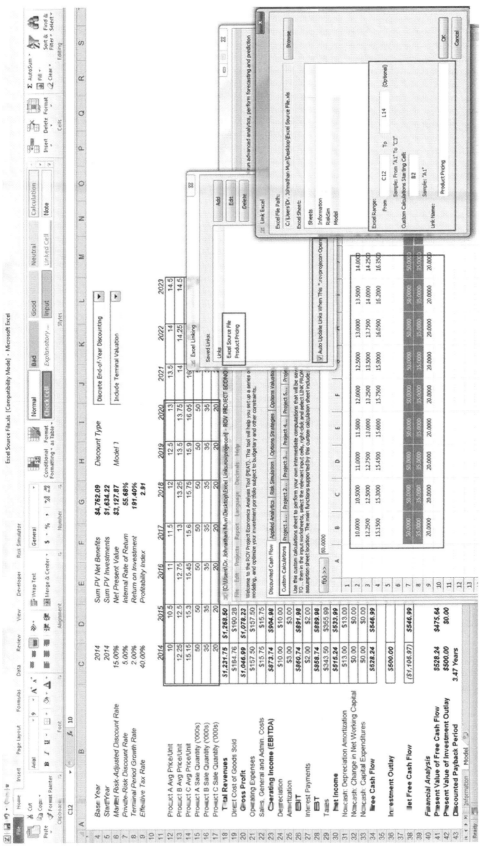

Custom Calculations tab's Excel button allows you to add/edit/delete Live Links from Excel to this tab. You can add multiple links from multiple workbooks and worksheets into this single tab. Reopening the file will auto update the data if you check the Auto Update option. From Custom Worksheet, you can now link to other tabs within PEAT. Right-click on the Custom tab to add new or delete/rename existing custom tabs.

OPTIONAL STEP: Go to "DCF | Custom Calculations" enable links from/to other tabs, name cells for use in later tabs like Tornado and Simulation, set input simulation assumptions, etc.

You can NAME cells in the Custom tab for use later in the Tornado, Scenario, and Simulation tabs. You can also right-click to set simulation input assumptions in the Custom tab.

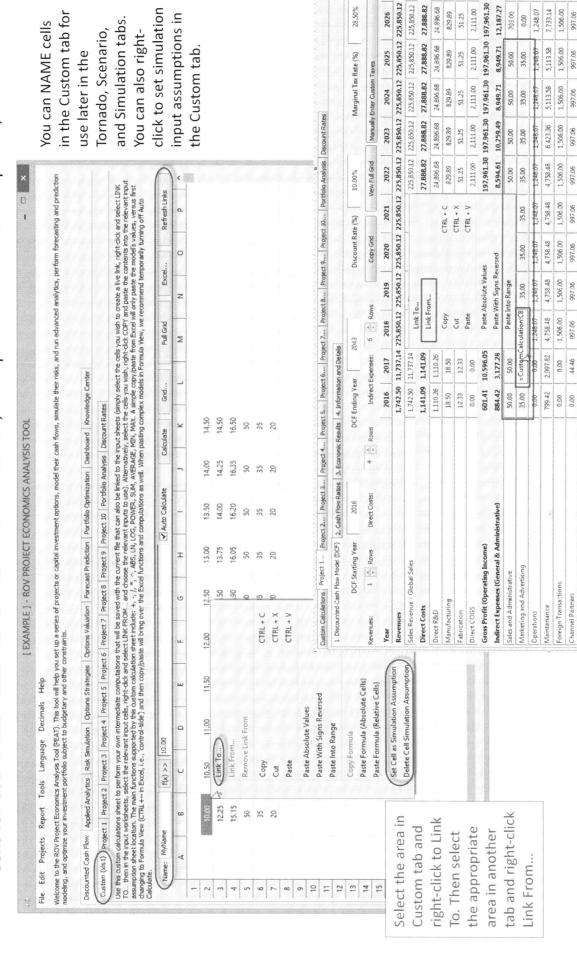

Select the area in Custom tab and right-click to Link To. Then select the appropriate area in another tab and right-click Link From...

Go to "Discounted Cash Flow | Discount Rates" and load an example to run

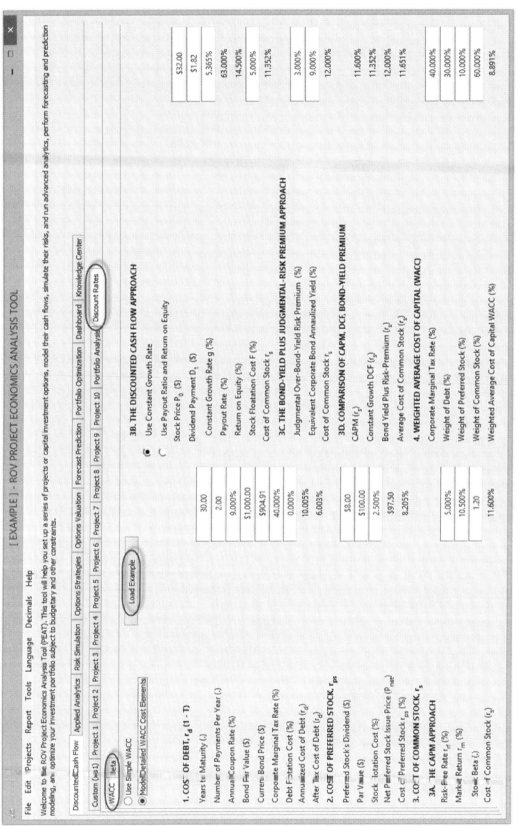

You can compute the weighted average cost of capital (WACC) and CAPM Beta estimates here. Load example data to get started or enter your assumptions to compute WACC. You can also paste stock prices and stock returns to compute a market-based Beta coefficient.

Go to "Applied Analytics | Static Tornado" and play with some of the checklists...

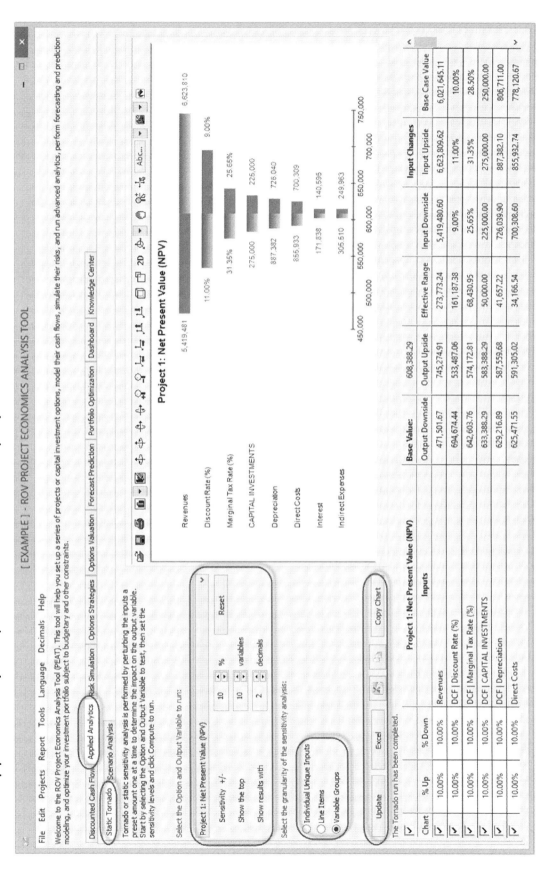

You can view the Tornado analysis (critical success factors) of each Project's economic metrics, copy the chart and sensitivity results, change the look and feel of the charts, and re-run the analysis based on your sensitivity settings etc.

Go to "Applied Analytics | Scenario Analysis | Scenario Input Settings"
Double click on a saved scenario model to view its settings or to make and save your own scenario model...

You can create and save multiple Scenario Analyses by selecting the Option droplist, checking up to two inputs, modifying the ranges to test, choosing color settings if required, entering a name, and "Save As" the scenario model... when done, proceed to the next step to view the results. You can Edit a saved model as well.

Go to "Applied Analytics | Scenario Analysis | Scenario Output Tables"
Select a saved scenario model from the droplist to run

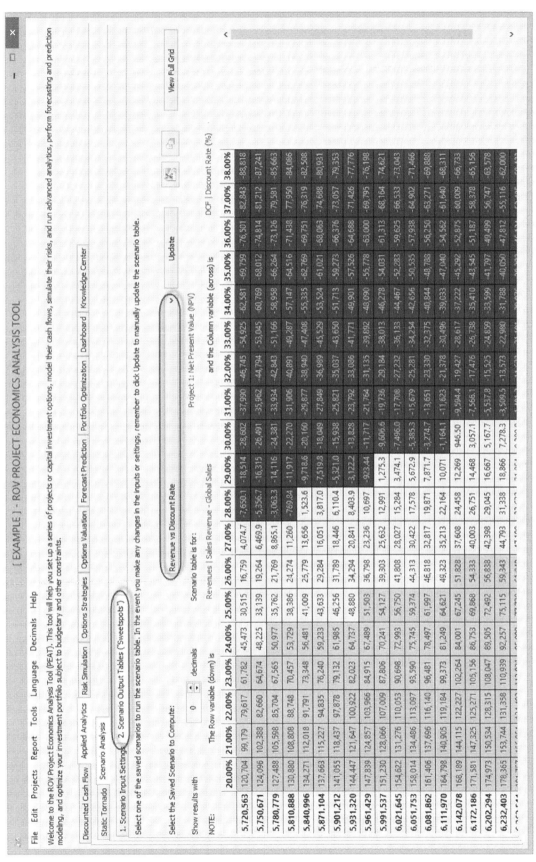

You can view all your saved scenario models here by selecting them from the droplist, complete with color codes. You can copy the results grid as required for pasting into PowerPoint or generate an Excel report...

Go to "Risk Simulation | Set Input Assumptions"
Double click on a saved simulation model to run (e.g., All Simulations Model)

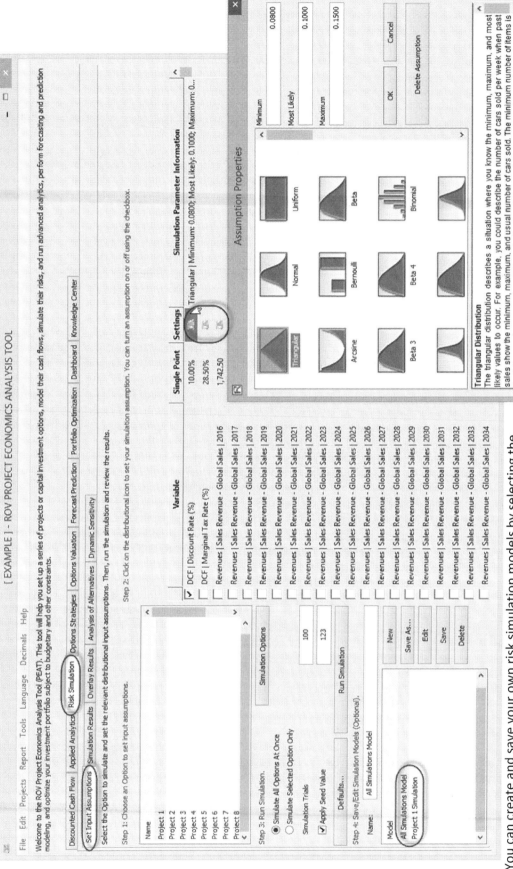

You can create and save your own risk simulation models by selecting the Option/Project, then checking the boxes of the input variables you wish to set assumptions on, clicking on the distribution icons to enter the distributional inputs, and saving the model...

Go to "Risk Simulation | Simulation Results"
Type in some sample Percentiles to obtain Confidence Levels or vice versa...

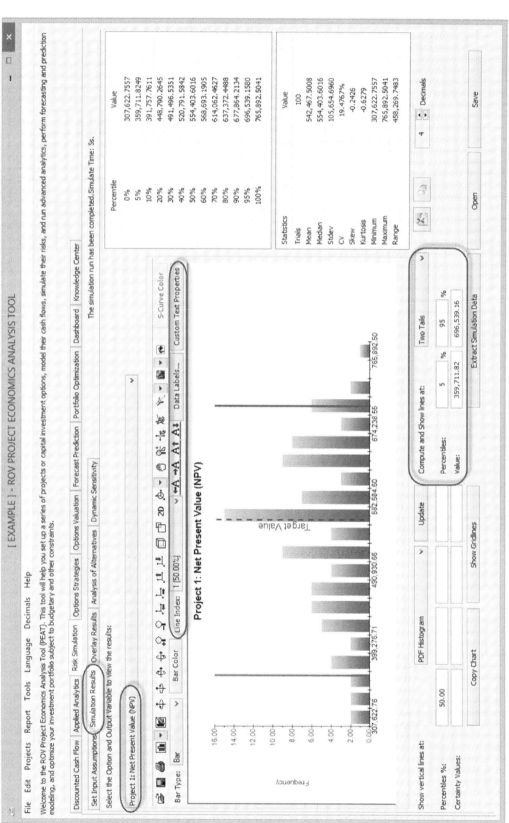

The risk simulated results and respective statistics are shown in this tab. You can select the distribution tails (left, right, two-tails), type in confidence levels and obtain percentiles, or enter in percentiles to calculate the confidence values, edit/modify/copy the charts and extract the simulated results, etc.

Go to "Risk Simulation | Overlay Results"
Select one or more output results and the chart type

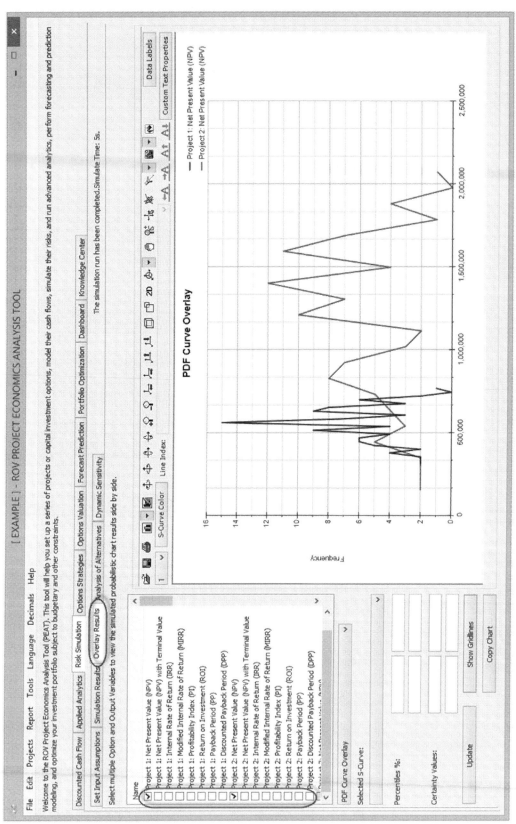

You can "overlay" multiple risk simulated results over one another using this tool... Risk Simulation must first be run in order for this tab to be populated. You can add chart-specific percentiles and certainty lines as well as modify the chart's look and feel or copy the chart for pasting into Excel or PowerPoint.

Go to "Risk Simulation | Analysis of Alternatives"

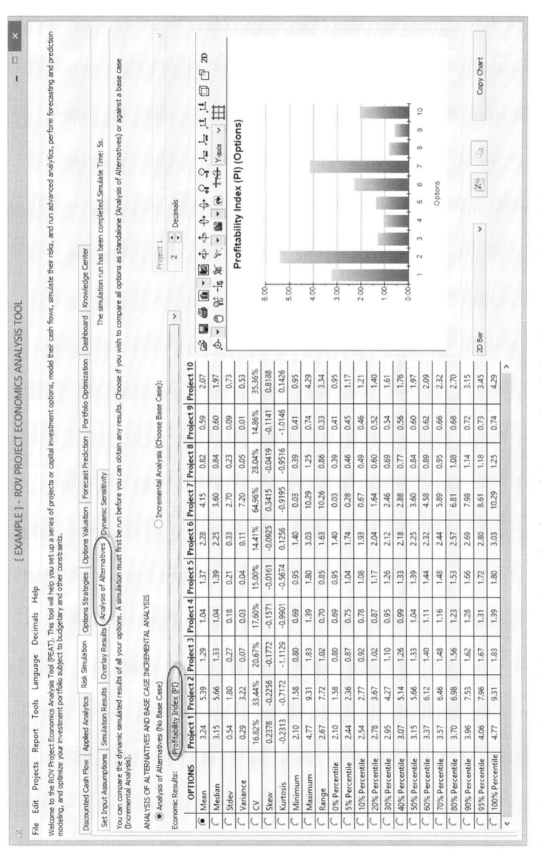

Similarly, you can view each Project or Option's risk simulation results side by side as an Analysis of Alternative or as Incremental Analysis (please be aware that some statistics may not be appropriate to use for incremental analysis due to the nature of simulations).

Go to "Risk Simulation | Dynamic Sensitivity" and select any output from the droplist

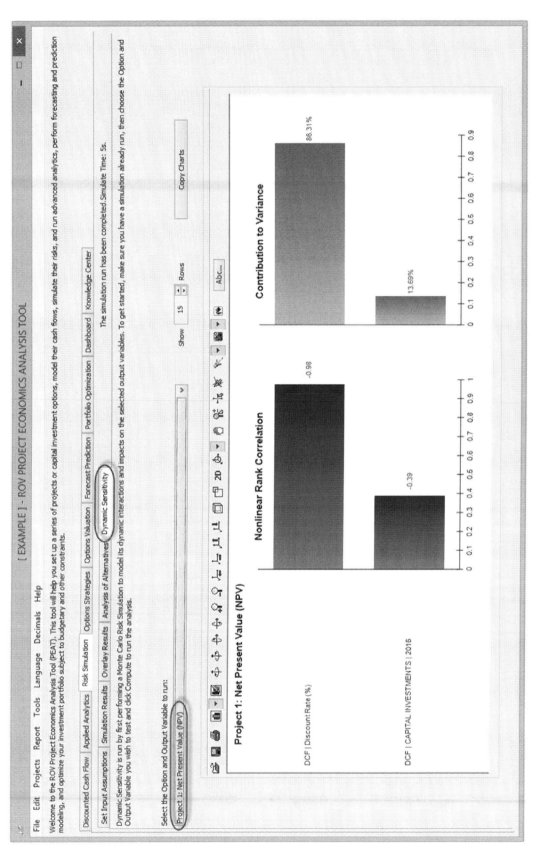

Tornado shows a static sensitivity whereas a Dynamic Sensitivity shows the impacts of each probabilistic input assumption on the risk simulated outcome where all inputs are changed simultaneously. The nonlinear rank correlation and contribution to variance charts are shown.

Go to "Options Strategies"

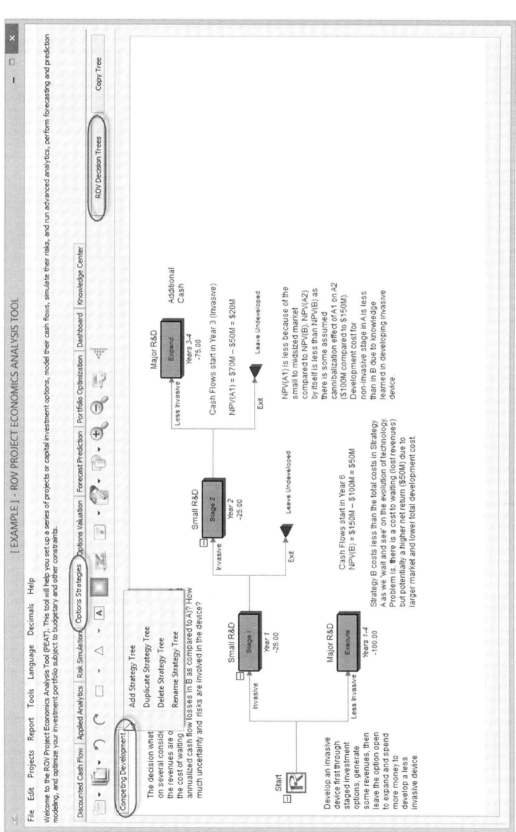

You can select any example model from the File icon (first icon), create your own strategy trees, or run example/create your own decision tree model. The last saved strategy tree model that is viewed will be opened the next time the PEAT profile is opened, assuming the corresponding strategy tree file has not changed its name or location. Right click on the Strategy Tree subtab to add, duplicate, delete or rename existing tree tabs. You can also run the ROV Decision Tree for stochastic simulations on decision trees.

Go to "Options Valuation" and double click on any of the saved models to run them

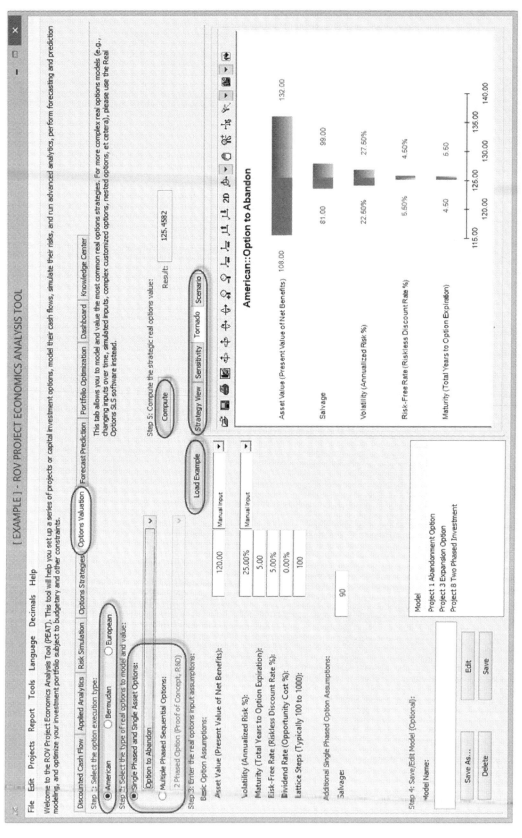

The most commonly used real options models are preset for you in this tab. Start by selecting the option type and enter your inputs, click on Load Example to view a sample set of inputs as a guideline, or click on several available droplists to link to the relevant project's values. Save the options model for later retrieval. You can also view a sample strategy tree of the selected option type, and view the sensitivity, tornado, and scenario analysis of the selected option.

Real Options Valuation

Go to "Options Valuation," run a model, and go to the "Sensitivity" subtab

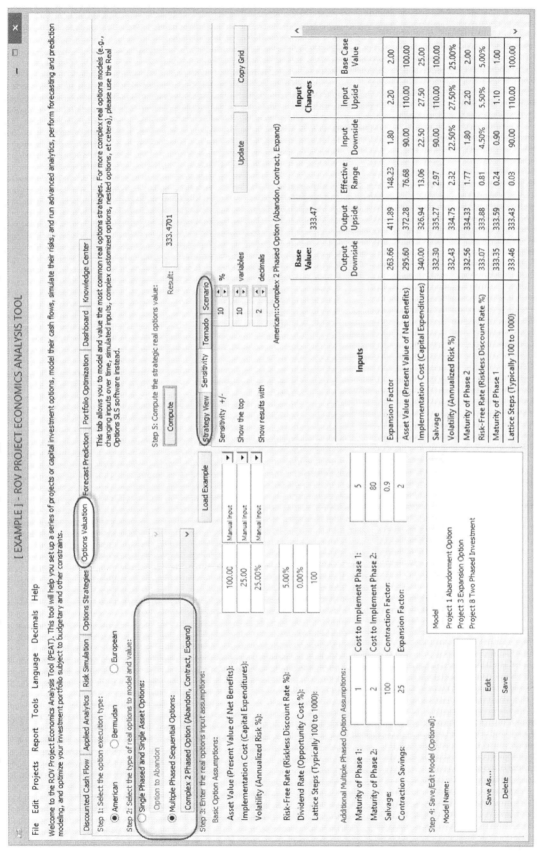

Double click on any saved model to run it. You can then view the model's sensitivity, tornado, or scenario analysis results.

Go to "Forecast Prediction" and double click on any saved model to run

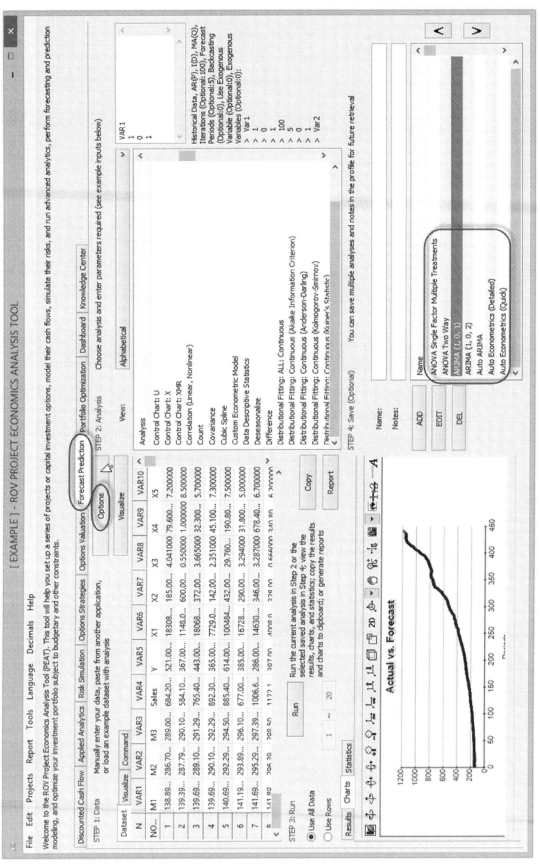

This tab has over 150 modeling and forecast methods available to run on your data. Follow the "Steps" and instructions to set up and save/retrieve your forecast model. Click on "Options" to open/load some example data and models or to save your forecast model as its own profile, or to recover an existing set of data/models.

Go to "Portfolio Optimization | Optimization Settings" and double click on a saved model to run

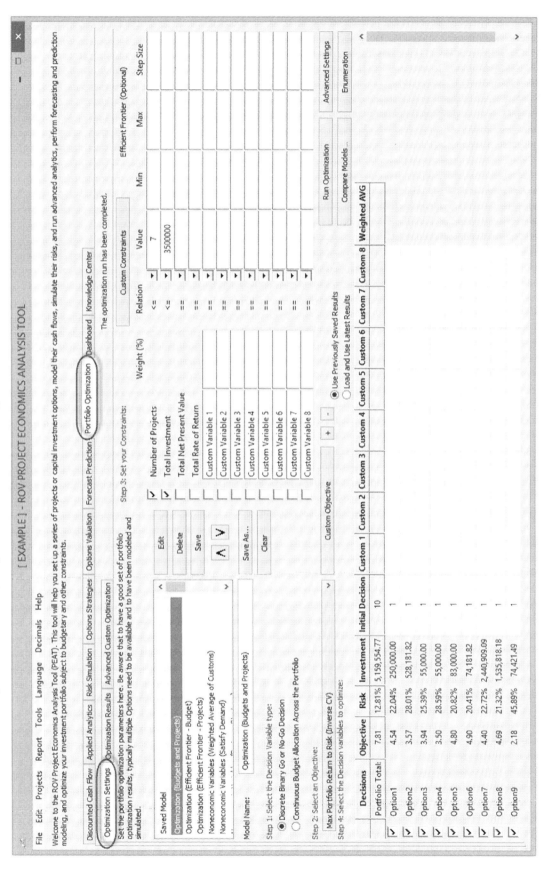

Double click on any saved model to run it or create your own portfolio optimization models here. You have to first set up the model's Decision Variables, Objective, and Constraints. You can set variable constraints with a range to run an investment efficient frontier analysis.

Go to "Portfolio Optimization | Optimization Results"

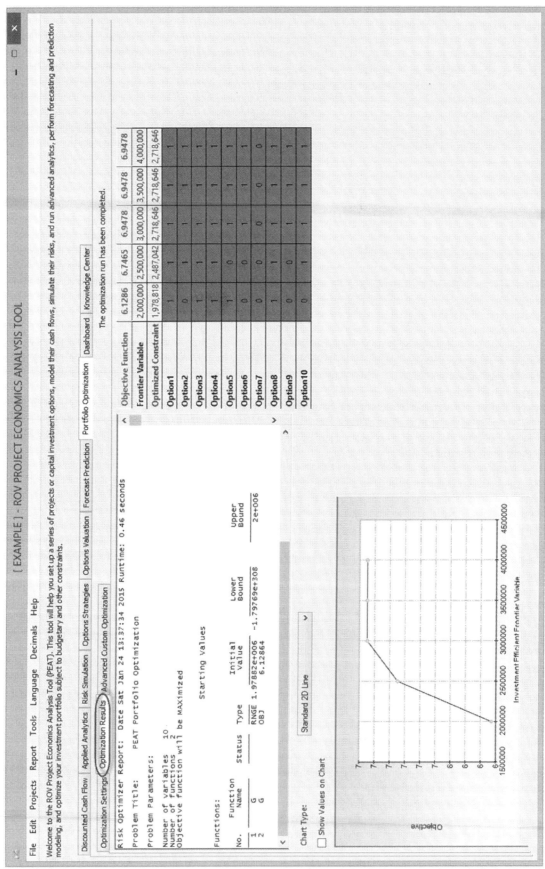

Double clicking on any saved optimization model in the previous Optimization Settings tab will run the optimization model and automatically bring you to this results tab.

Go to "Portfolio Optimization | Optimization Settings" and click Compare Models, then select
the five Noneconomic Variables to run and compare...

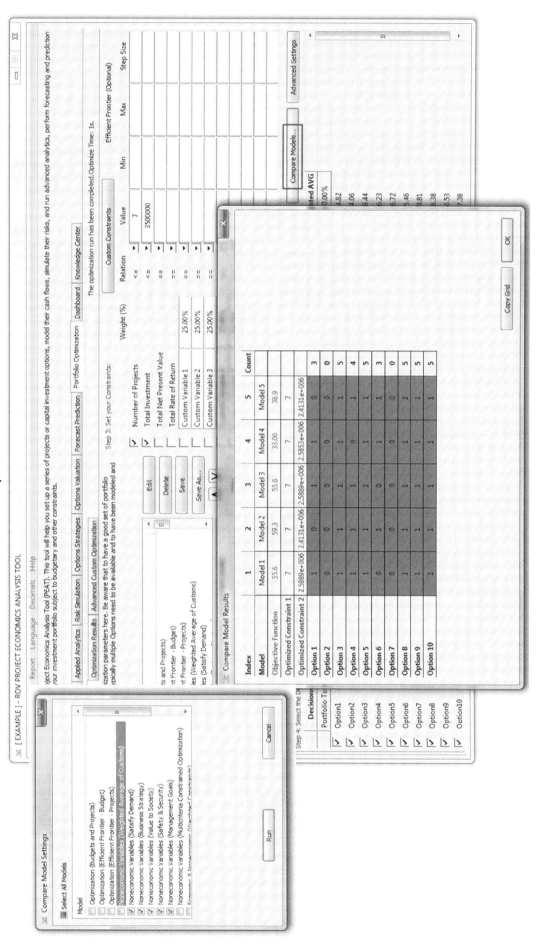

All selected models will run and you can see the results "sliced-and-diced" in various points of view, and the results will be returned
as an optimized matrix of decisions...

OPTIONAL: Go to "Portfolio Optimization | Advanced Custom Optimization"

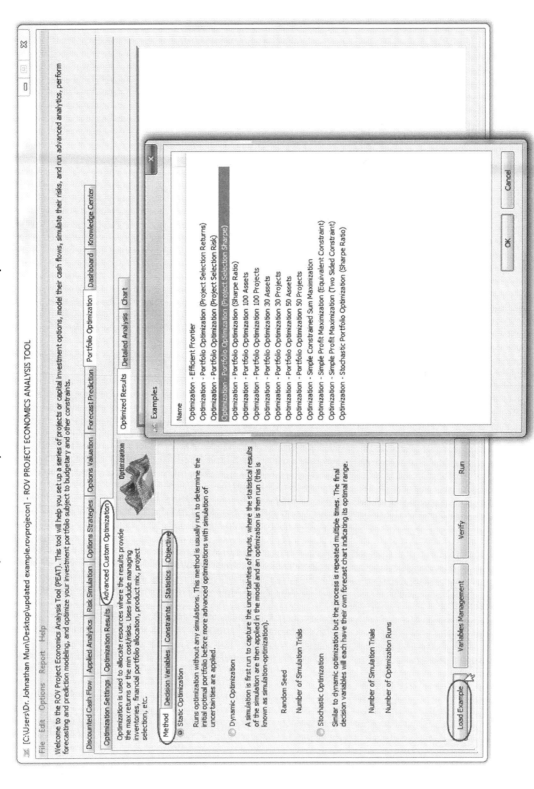

You can create, save, and run your own optimization models in this tab or run some previously saved example models. You have to first set up the model's Decision Variables using the Variables Management tool, then set the Objective and Constraints. You can set variable constraints with a range to run an investment efficient frontier analysis.

Go to "Dashboard" to review the settings and click "View Dashboards" when done

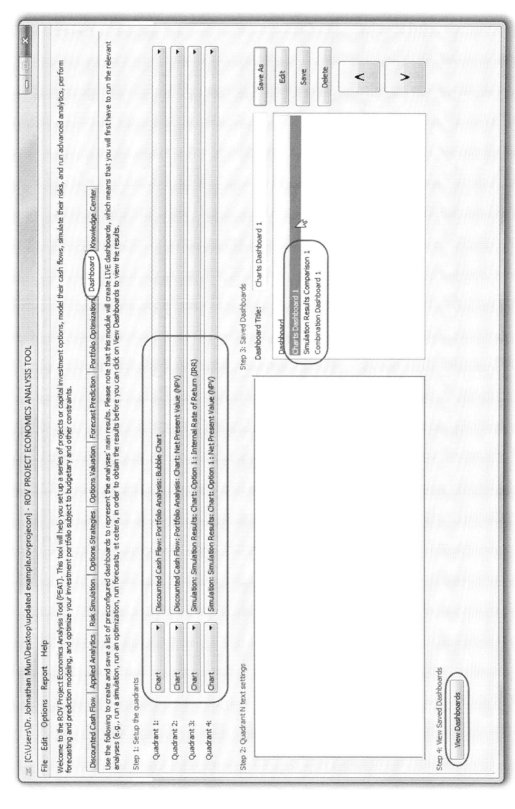

You can create and save multiple management dashboards here. Each dashboard can have four quadrants with any combinations of charts, results data grid, forecast or optimization results, or custom text. Please be aware that you must first run at least one RISK SIMULATION, OPTIMIZATION, and FORECAST model each before the dashboard will show any data/results. If you do not run anything, there will be no results to show. Click View Dashboard when done.

In the "View Dashboards" mode, select any one of the saved dashboards from the droplist

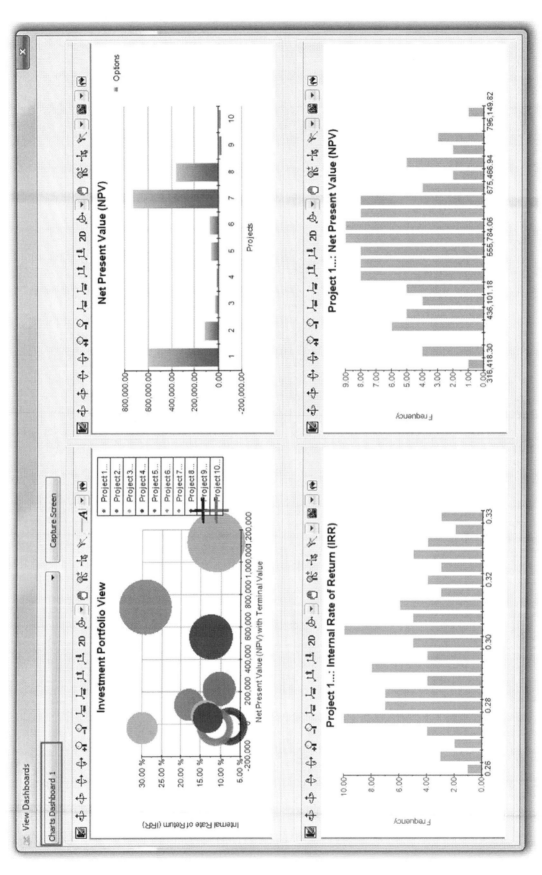

You can retrieve any of the saved dashboards from the droplist, and these dashboards will be populated only if the appropriate models have been run...

Go to "Knowledge Center | Step-by-Step Procedures" and step through the training material

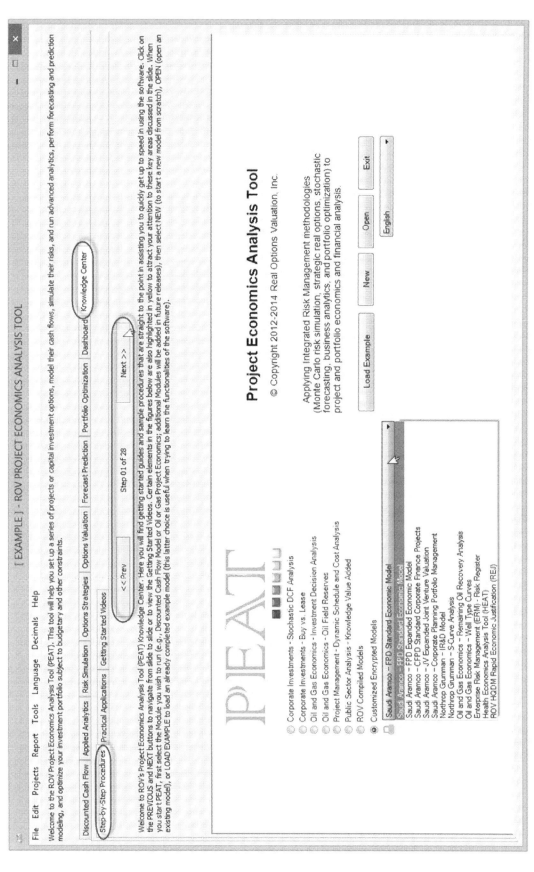

You can also learn the basics of PEAT through the knowledge center's procedures illustrations. Step back and forth from slide to slide while reviewing the text. You can create your own custom training materials for your staff and company's personnel, if you wish, by following some simple instructions in the user manual.

Go to "Knowledge Center | Basic Project Economics Lessons"

[EXAMPLE] - ROV PROJECT ECONOMICS ANALYSIS TOOL

File   Edit   Projects   Report   Tools   Language   Decimals   Help

Welcome to the ROV Project Economics Analysis Tool (PEAT). This tool will help you set up a series of projects or capital investment options, model their cash flows, simulate their risks, and run advanced analytics, perform forecasting and prediction modeling, and optimize your investment portfolio subject to budgetary and other constraints.

Discounted Cash Flow | Applied Analytics | Risk Simulation | Options Strategies | Options Valuation | Forecast Prediction | Portfolio Optimization | Dashboard | Knowledge Center

Step-by-Step Procedures | Practical Applications | Getting Started Videos

<< Prev   Lesson 05 of 20   Next >>

Lesson 05. The NPV method assumes that the project cash flows are reinvested at the cost of capital, whereas the IRR method assumes project cash flows are reinvested at the project's own IRR. The reinvestment rate at the cost of capital is the more correct approach in that this is the firm's opportunity cost of money. The Modified Internal Rate of Return (MIRR) method is intended to overcome two IRR shortcomings by setting the cash flows to be reinvested at the cost of capital and not its own IRR, as well as preventing the occurrence of multiple IRRs, because only a single MIRR will exist for all cash flow scenarios. Also, NPV and MIRR will usually result in the same project selection when projects are of equal size (significant scale differences might still result in a conflict between MIRR and NPV ranking). The MIRR is the discount rate that forces the present value of costs of cash outflows (COF) to be equal to the present value of the terminal value (the future value of cash inflows, or CIF, compounded at the project's cost of capital, k).

$$\sum_{t=0}^{n} \frac{COF_t}{(1+k)^t} = \sum_{t=0}^{n} \frac{CIF_t(1+k)^{n-t}}{(1+MIRR)^n}$$

$$\sum_{t=0}^{n} \frac{COF_t}{(1+WACC)^t} = \sum_{t=0}^{n} \frac{CIF_t(1+WACC)^{n-t}}{(1+MIRR)^n}$$

$$PV\ Costs = \frac{Terminal\,Value}{(1+MIRR)^n}$$

You can also learn the basics of the project economics and financial analytics that PEAT uses through the knowledge center's basic project economics lessons. Step back and forth as usual. You can also create your own custom training materials for your staff and company's personnel for this subtab.

Go to "Knowledge Center | Getting Started Videos" and click on the video icon to start watching

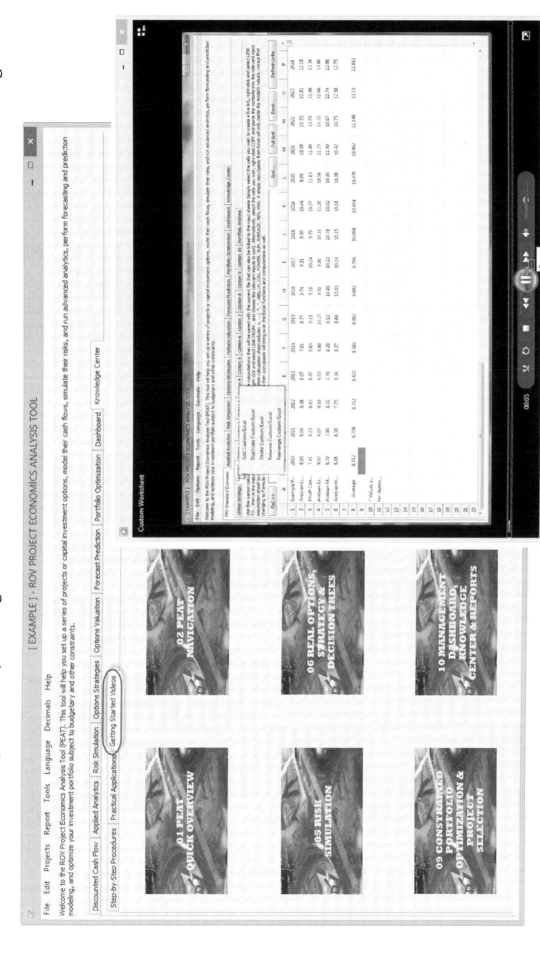

Some basic videos are also available as part of the PEAT tool to get you up to speed quickly on using the software application. Again, you can create and embed your own corporate training videos if required.

Click on the menus and explore...

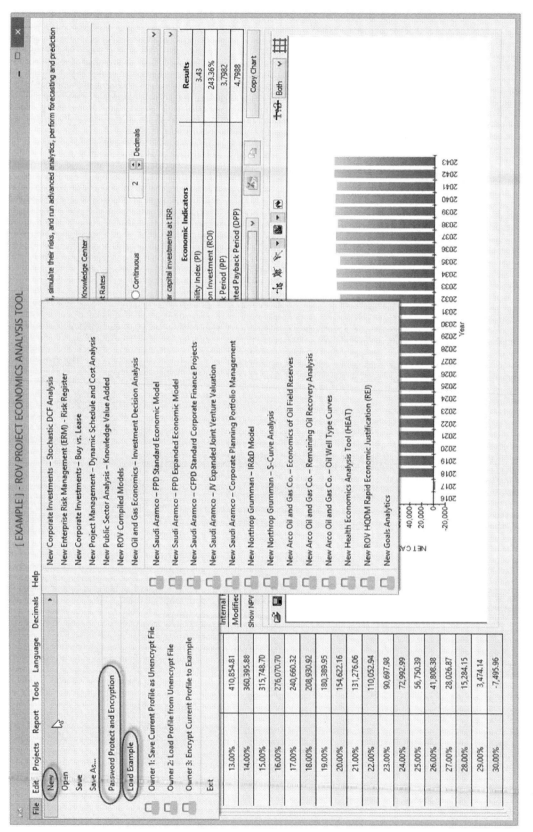

Do not forget to click on some of the menus to explore additional settings that are available such as performing data and model encryption, load example files, start new or open existing models, change international settings (foreign languages and decimal settings), as well as add/delete/rename/duplicate/rearrange Projects and Options.

Click on the "Report | Report Settings" menu

After completing and running your models (i.e., having completed and run any or all of the appropriate tabs: project economics, advanced analytics, risk simulations, forecasting, real options, and optimization), you can generate a report in Excel. A quick hint here is that once you click "Run Report" please make sure to be "hands-off" the computer until the report is complete.

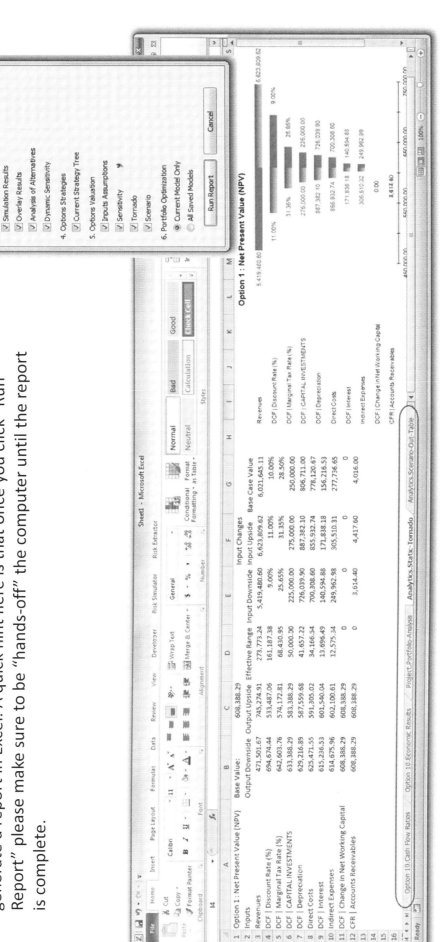

PEAT VISUAL GUIDE

VOLUME 3:

Quick Getting Started with Oil and Gas
Module and Integrated Risk Management

RealOptions
Valuation

Instructions

- This is a quick getting started guide, not a detailed user manual. See the user manual and related books for more technical information.

- Text in RED is instructions, text in BLUE is notes for your information only.

- This visual guide showcases the Oil and Gas module and summarizes how the following methods are implemented and run in PEAT using an example model:

  - DCF Metrics (Net Present Value, Internal Rate of Return, Modified Internal Rate of Return, Profitability Index, Return on Investment, Payback Period, and Discounted Payback Period) for individual projects/options and within a Portfolio

  - Analytics (Tornado Analysis for identifying critical success factors, and Scenario Analysis for identifying hot spots)

  - Risk Simulations (running tens of thousands of simulation trials to determine probabilistic risk metrics, comparing dynamic sensitivities of inputs, and comparing risk metrics and returns across multiple projects)

  - Real Options Strategies (visual representation of strategies with decision trees and strategy trees)

  - Real Options Valuation (computes the values of each individual real options path)

  - Portfolio Optimization (budget allocation and optimal project selection subject to budget and other strategic constraints)

  - Management Dashboards (create multiple results dashboards for management)

  - Knowledge and Training Center (quick lessons on using PEAT, project economics basics, and getting started videos)

1. Start PEAT and Select "Oil and Gas Project Economics"
2. Click "Load Example"

Project Economics Analysis Tool

© Copyright 2012-2013 Real Options Valuation, Inc.

Applying Integrated Risk Management methodologies (Monte Carlo risk simulation, strategic real options, stochastic forecasting, business analytics, and portfolio optimization) to project and portfolio economics and financial analysis.

New | Open | Exit

○ Discounted Cash Flow Model
● Oil and Gas Project Economics
○ Lease vs. Buy
○ Knowledge Value Added (Comparable IRM Analysis)

Load Example

Additional customized "Modules" will be added over time. Click on "Load Example" to follow along and walk through this Visual Guide...

Go to "Project Economics | Global Settings | Global Assumptions"

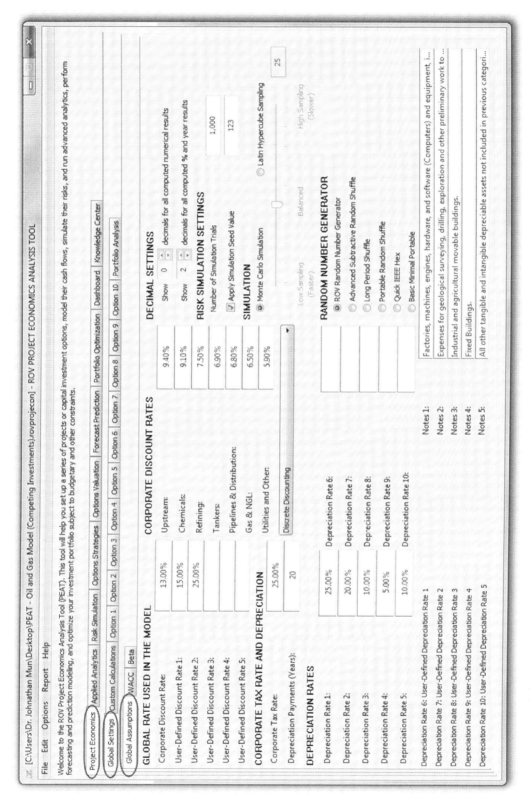

In your own model, simply enter the required inputs (input boxes) or Copy | Paste from Excel or another data source. Feel free to explore the WACC and Beta tabs as well.

Go to "Project Economics | Custom Calculations"

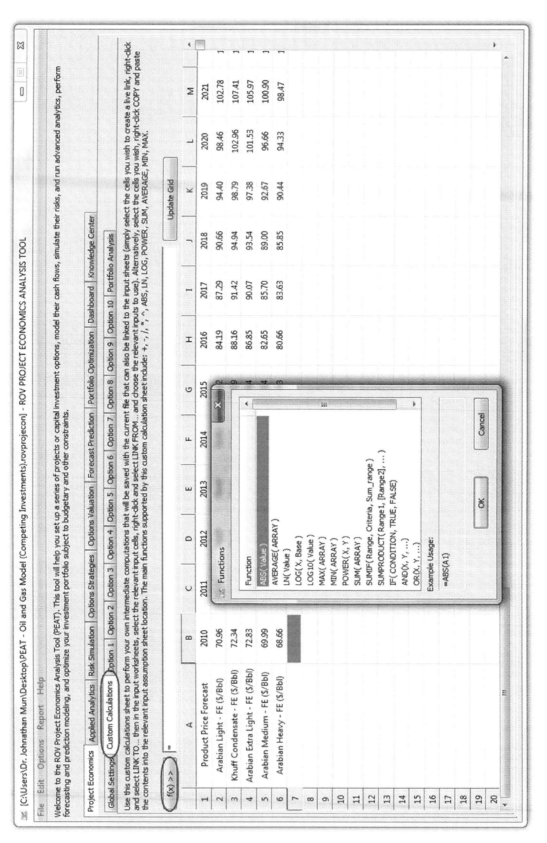

This is an optional location where you can enter your own information and data, and use basic equations or the FX insert function to create your own model.

Go to "Project Economics | Option 1 | Input Assumptions"

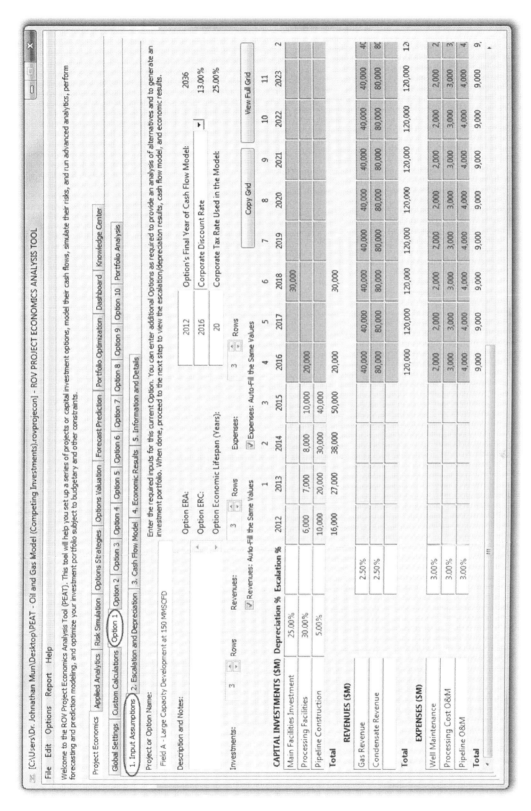

In your own model, simply enter the required inputs (input boxes) or Copy | Paste from Excel or another data source. Try the right click Paste method and explore the various data paste options available. You can also add/reduce the number of rows to show for each category, and Copy Grid to paste into Excel/Word/PowerPoint, etc.

Go to "Project Economics | Option 1 | Escalation and Depreciation"

File   Edit   Options   Report   Help

[C:\Users\Dr. Johnathan Mun\Desktop\PEAT - Oil and Gas Model (Competing Investments).rovprojecon] - ROV PROJECT ECONOMICS ANALYSIS TOOL

Welcome to the ROV Project Economics Analysis Tool (PEAT). This tool will help you set up a series of projects or capital investment options, model their cash flows, simulate their risks, and run advanced analytics, perform forecasting and prediction modeling, and optimize your investment portfolio subject to budgetary and other constraints.

Tabs: Project Economics | Applied Analytics | Risk Simulation | Option 1 | Option 2 | Option 3 | Option 4 | Option 5 | Option 6 | Option 7 | Option 8 | Option 9 | Option 10 | Portfolio Analysis

Global Settings | Custom Calculations | Options Strategies | Options Valuation | Forecast Prediction | Portfolio Optimization | Dashboard | Knowledge Center

1. Input Assumptions | 2. Escalation and Depreciation | 3. Cash Flow Model | 4. Economic Results | 5. Information and Details

	Depreciation	Escalation	2012	2013 (1)	2014 (2)	2015 (3)	2016 (4)	2017 (5)	2018 (6)	2019 (7)	2020 (8)	2021 (9)	2022 (10)	2023 (11)	2024 (12)	2025 (13)	2026 (14)
CAPITAL INVESTMENTS ($M)																	
Main Facilities Investment	25.00%								30,000								
Processing Facilities	30.00%		6,000	7,000	8,000	10,000	20,000										
Pipeline Construction	5.00%		10,000	20,000	30,000	40,000	20,000		30,000								
Total			16,000	27,000	38,000	50,000	20,000		30,000								
ESCALATED CAPITAL INVESTMENTS ($M)		Escalation															
ESCALATED (Main Facilities Investment)									30,000								
ESCALATED (Processing Facilities)			6,000	7,000	8,000	10,000	20,000										
ESCALATED (Pipeline Construction)			10,000	20,000	30,000	40,000	20,000		30,000								
Total			16,000	27,000	38,000	50,000	20,000		30,000								
DEPRECIATED CAPITAL INVESTMENTS ($M)	Depreciation																
DEPRECIATED (Main Facilities Investment)	25.00%									-7,500	-5,625	-4,219	-3,164	-2,373	-1,780	-1,335	-1,001
DEPRECIATED (Processing Facilities)	30.00%							-15,300	-10,710	-7,497	-5,248	-3,674	-2,571	-1,800	-1,260	-882	-617
DEPRECIATED (Pipeline Construction)	5.00%							-5,000	-4,750	-4,513	-4,287	-4,073	-3,869	-3,675	-3,492	-3,317	-3,151
Total								-20,300	-15,460	-19,510	-15,160	-11,966	-9,604	-7,848	-6,532	-5,554	-4,769
REVENUES ($M)		Escalation															
Gas Revenue		2.50%					40,000	40,000	40,000	40,000	40,000	40,000	40,000	40,000	40,000	40,000	40,000
Condensate Revenue		2.50%					80,000	80,000	80,000	80,000	80,000	80,000	80,000	80,000	80,000	80,000	80,000

Copy Grid   View Full Grid

This tab shows computed intermediate values...

Go to "Project Economics | Option 1 | Cash Flow Model"

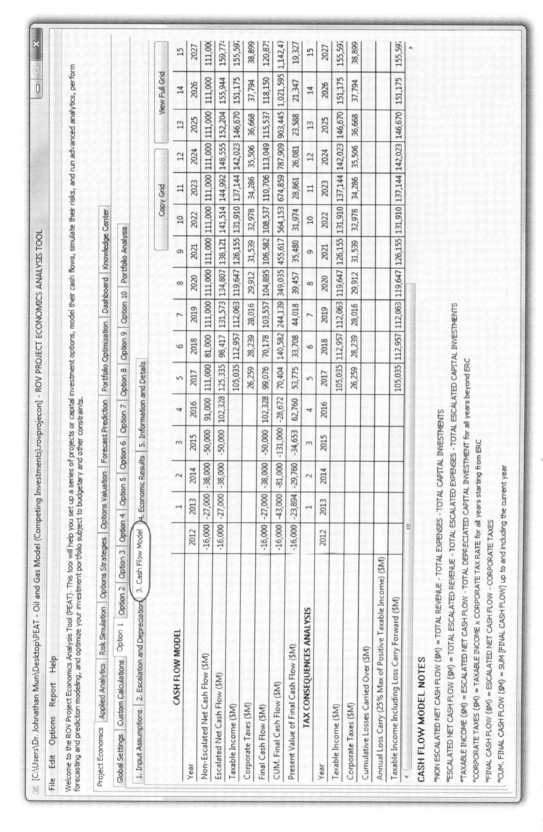

This tab shows computed cash flow values for the life of the project...

Go to "Project Economics| Option 1 | Economic Results" to see the computed results

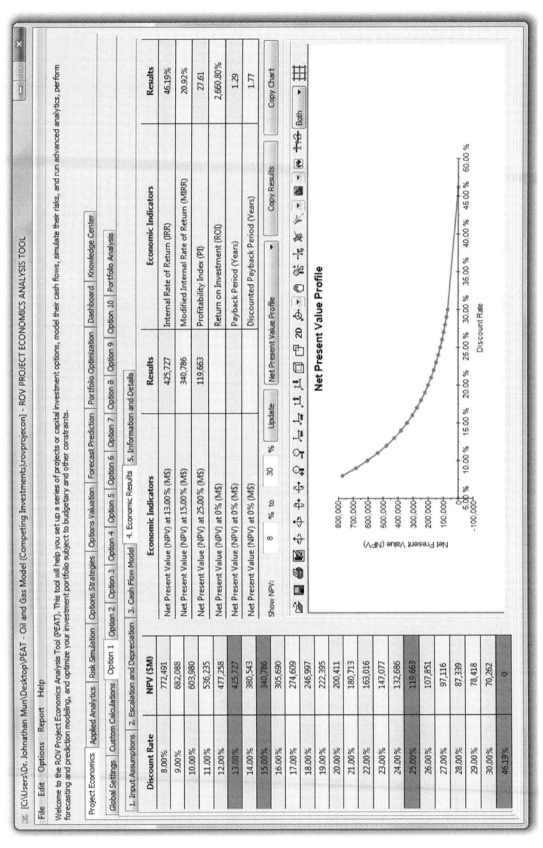

The project economic and financial metrics are automatically computed for you. You can also change the type of chart to display from the chart droplist as well as change the look and feel of the chart as required...

Go to "Project Economics | Option 1 | Information and Details"

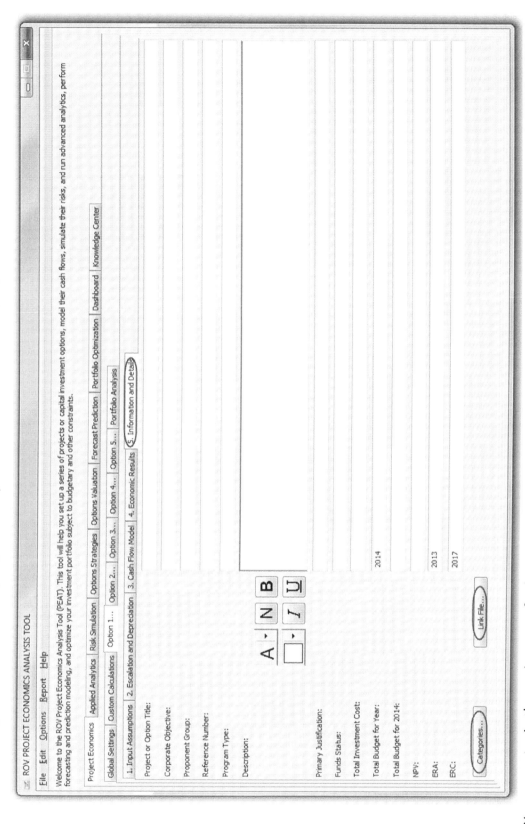

You can enter in the project specific details as required, and replicate this on other projects as required... Categories can be customized and you can also link external files that may be relevant to this project using the Link File button... When you are done with this Project, note that you can continue to view other projects or proceed to the next step... As information, you can DUPLICATE, ADD, DELETE the Option tabs as required without any limit...

Go to "Project Economics | Portfolio Analysis" and play with some of the checklists and droplists...

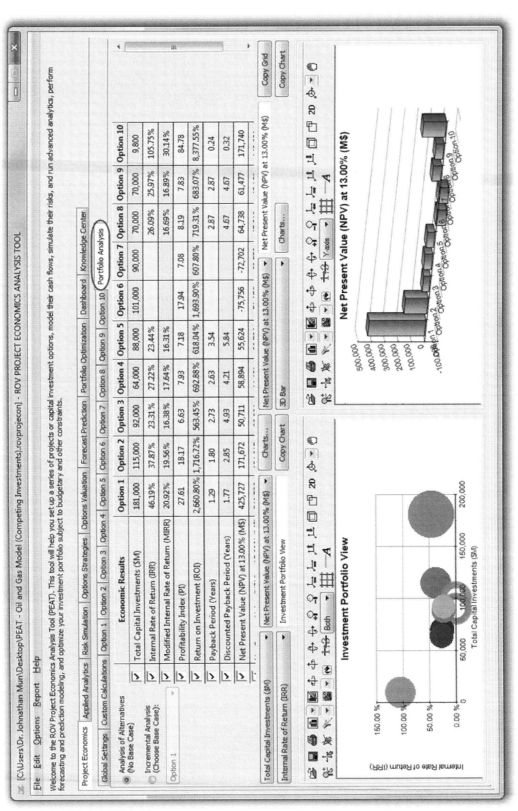

All projects and options are summarized in this tab as a Portfolio. You can now compare all single point results of the main project economic metrics, modify and view different charts, copy the results and charts to Excel or PowerPoint, and change details as well as the look and feel of the charts as required...

Go to "Applied Analytics | Static Tornado" and play with some of the droplists...

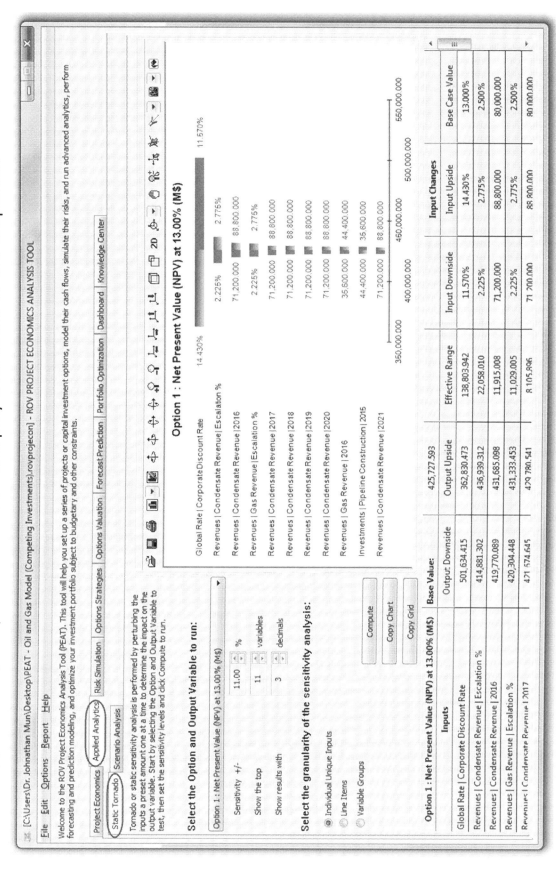

You can view the Tornado analysis (critical success factors) of each Project's economic metrics, copy the chart and sensitivity results, change the look and feel of the charts, and re-run the analysis based on your sensitivity settings etc.

Go to "Applied Analytics | Scenario Analysis | Scenario Input Settings"
Double click on a saved scenario (bottom right) to edit or make and save your own scenario models...

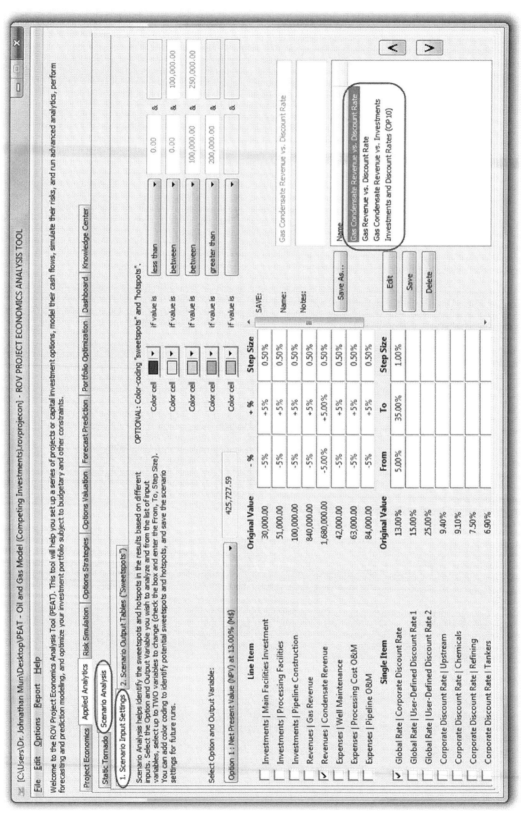

You can create and save multiple Scenario Analyses by selecting the Option droplist, checking up to two inputs, modifying the ranges to test, choosing color settings if required, entering a name, and "Save As" the scenario model... when done, proceed to the next step to view the results. You can Edit a saved model as well.

Real Options Valuation

Go to "Applied Analytics | Scenario Analysis | Scenario Output Tables"
Select a saved scenario model from the droplist to run

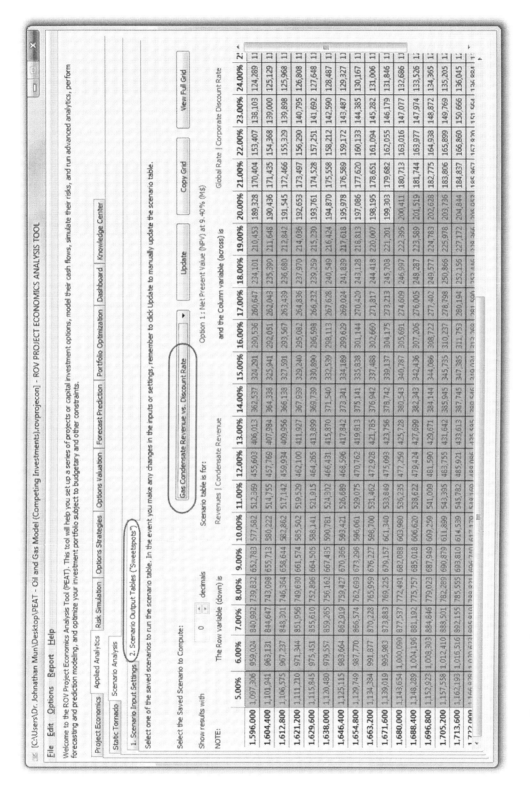

You can view all your saved scenario models here by selecting them from the droplist, complete with color codes. You can copy the results grid as required for pasting into PowerPoint or Excel...

Go to "Risk Simulation | Set Input Assumptions"
Double click on a saved simulation model to run (e.g., All Options Simulation)

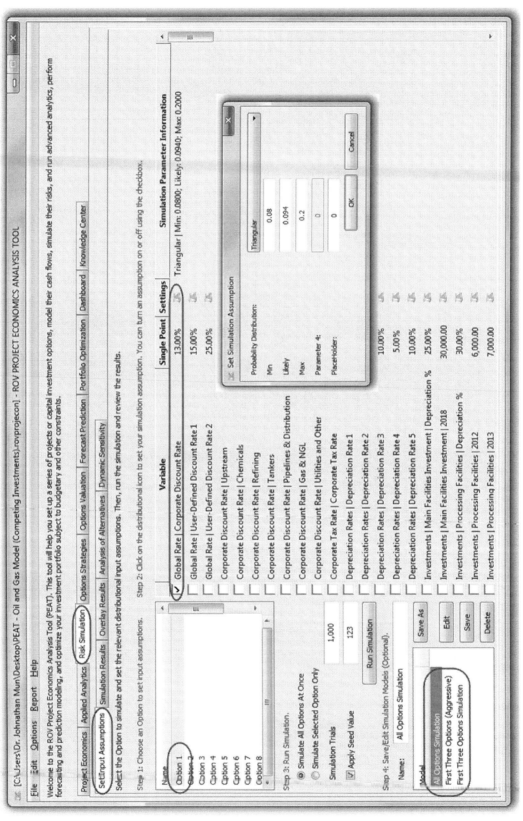

You can create and save your own risk simulation models by selecting the Option/Project, then clicking on the checkboxes of the input variables you wish to set assumptions on, entering the distributional inputs, and saving the model...

Go to "Risk Simulation | Simulation Results"
Type in some sample Percentiles to obtain Confidence Levels or vice versa...

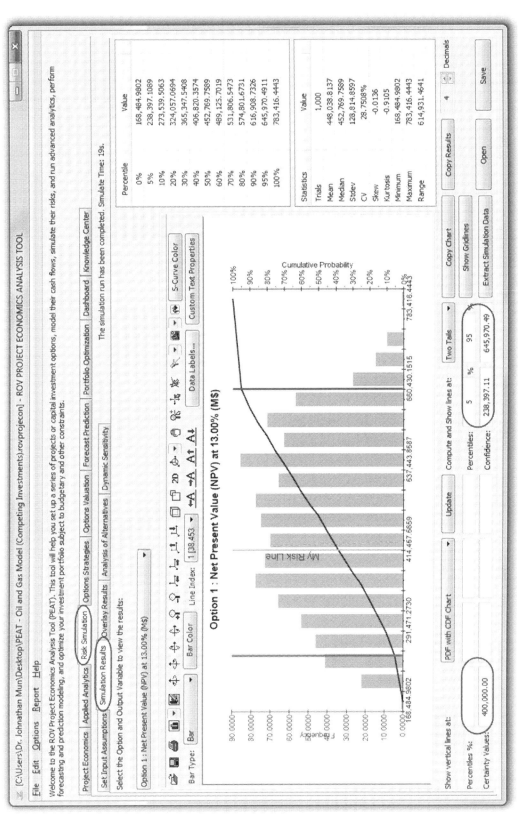

The risk simulated results and respective statistics are shown in this tab. You can select the distribution tails (left, right, two-tails), type in confidence levels and obtain percentiles, or enter in percentiles to calculate the confidence values, edit/modify/copy the charts and extract the simulated results, etc.

Go to "Risk Simulation | Overlay Results"
Select one or more output results and the chart type

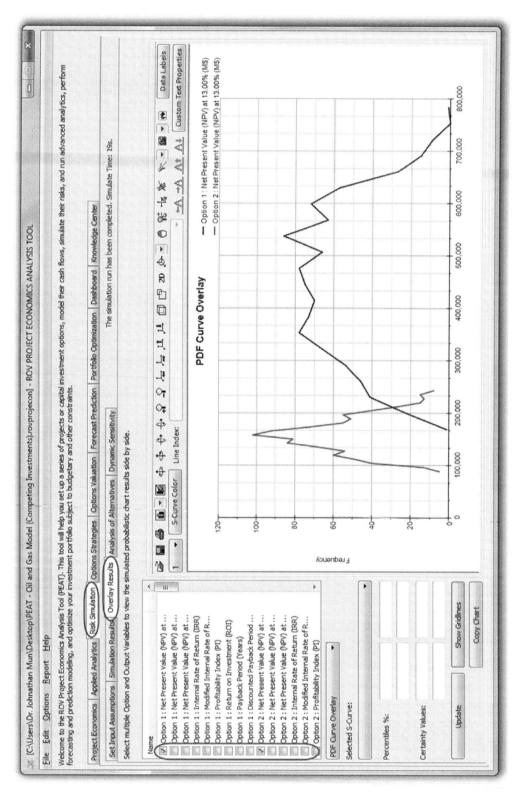

You can "overlay" multiple risk simulated results over one another using this tool... Risk Simulation must first be run in order for this tab to be populated. You can add chart-specific percentiles and certainty lines as well as modify the chart's look and feel or copy the chart for pasting into Excel or PowerPoint.

Go to "Risk Simulation | Analysis of Alternatives"

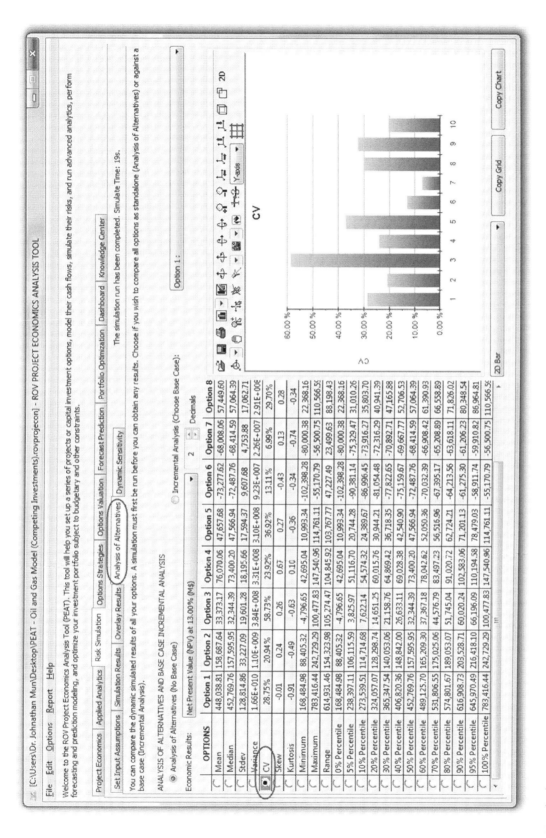

Similarly, you can view each Project or Option's risk simulation results side by side as an Analysis of Alternative or as Incremental Analysis (please be aware that some statistics may not be appropriate to use for incremental analysis due to the nature of simulations).

Go to "Risk Simulation | Dynamic Sensitivity" and select any output from the droplist

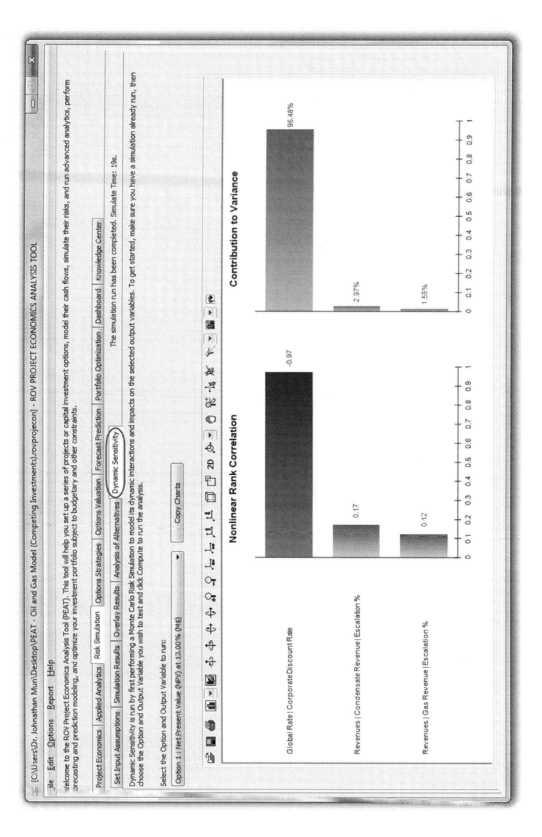

Tornado shows a static sensitivity whereas a Dynamic Sensitivity shows the impacts of each probabilistic input assumption on the risk simulated outcome where all inputs are changed simultaneously.

Go to "Options Strategies"

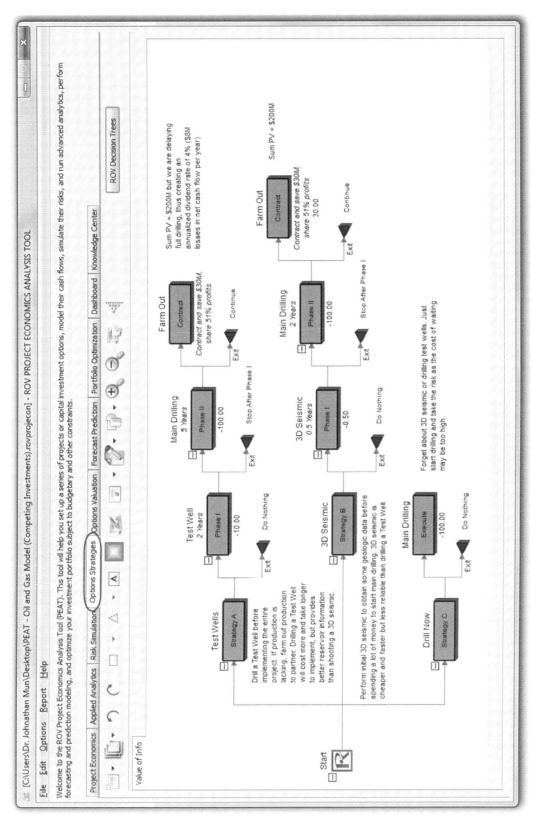

You can select any example model from the File icon, create your own strategy trees, or run example/create your own decision tree model. The last saved strategy tree model that is viewed will be opened the next time the PEAT profile is opened, assuming the corresponding strategy tree file has not changed its name or location.

Go to "Options Valuation" and double click on any of the saved models to run them

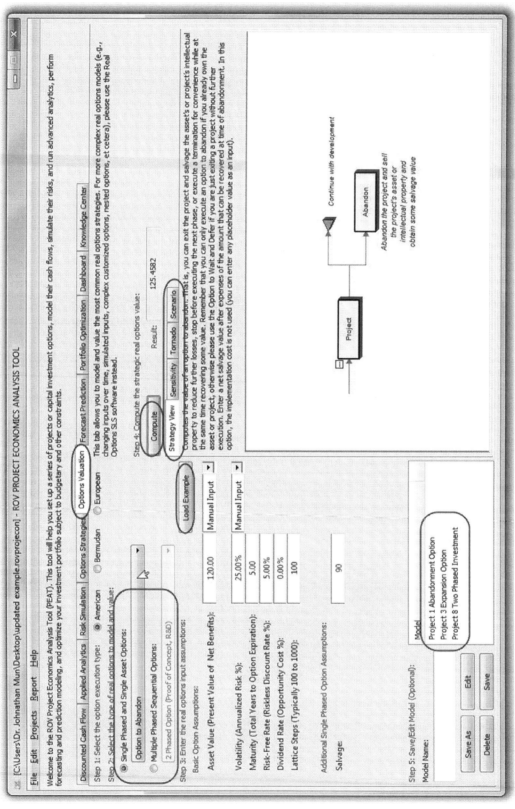

The most commonly used real options models are preset for you in this tab. Start by selecting the option type and enter your inputs, click on Load Example to view a sample set of inputs as a guideline, or click on several available droplists to link to the relevant project's values. Save the options model for later retrieval. You can also view a sample strategy tree of the selected option type, and view the sensitivity, tornado, and scenario analysis of the selected option.

Go to "Options Valuation," run a model, and go to the "Sensitivity" subtab

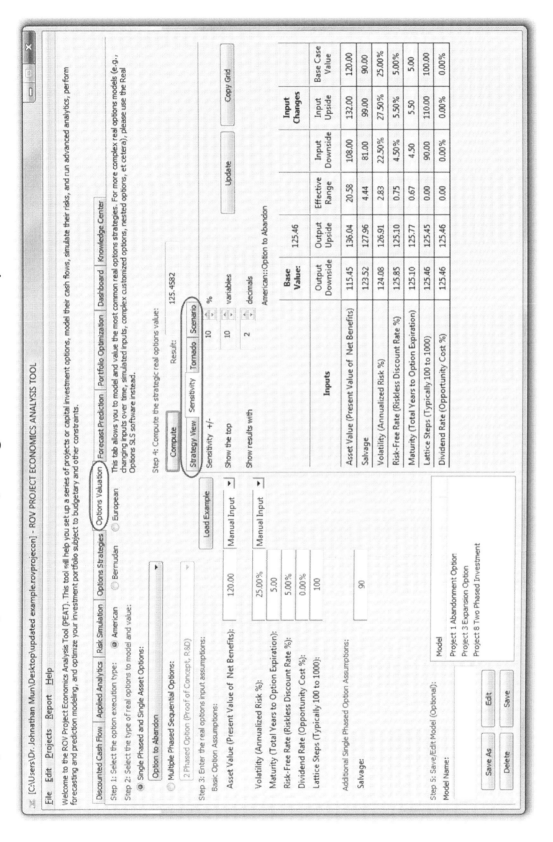

Double click on any saved model to run it. You can then view the model's sensitivity, tornado, or scenario analysis results.

Go to "Forecast Prediction" and double click on any saved model to run

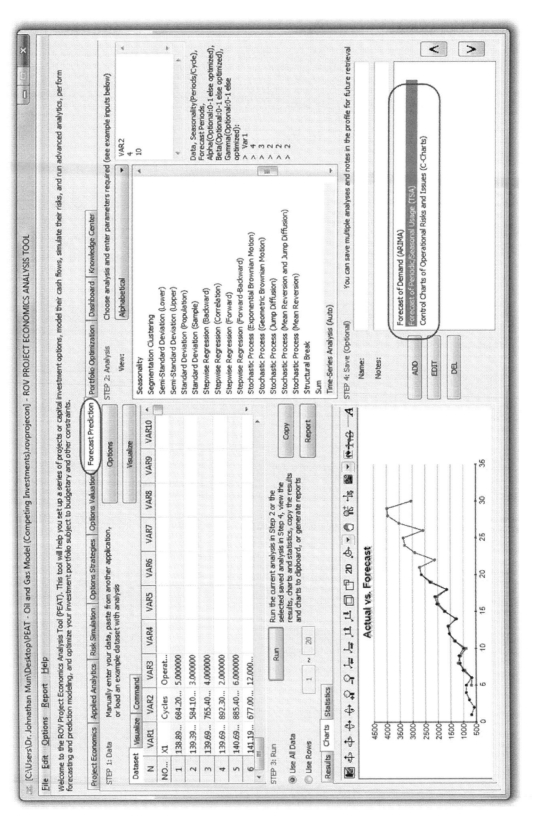

This tab has over 150 modeling and forecast methods available to run on your data. Follow the "Steps" and instructions to set up and save/retrieve your forecast model. Click on "Options" to open/load some example data and models or to save your forecast model as its own profile, or to recover an existing set of data/models.

Go to "Portfolio Optimization | Optimization Settings" and double click on a saved model to run

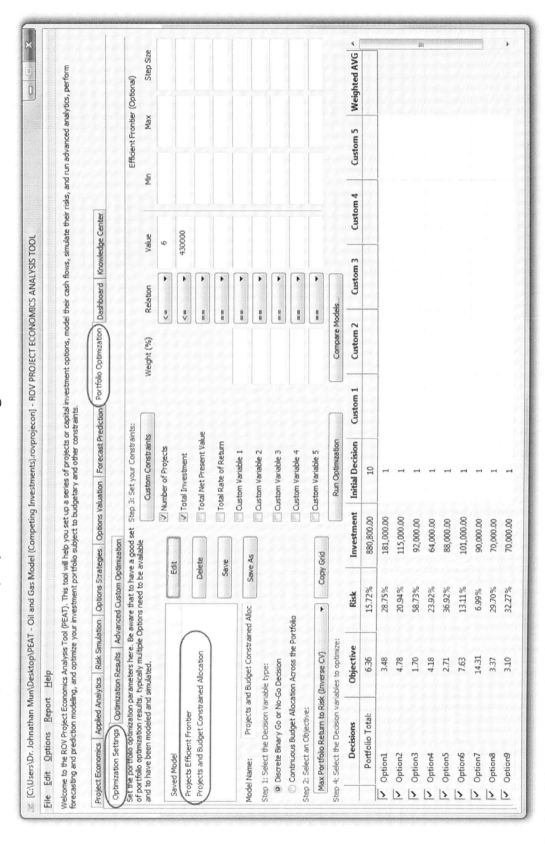

Double click on any saved model to run it or create your own portfolio optimization models here. You have to first set up the model's Decision Variables, Objective, and Constraints. You can set variable constraints with a range to run an investment efficient frontier analysis.

Go to "Portfolio Optimization | Optimization Results"

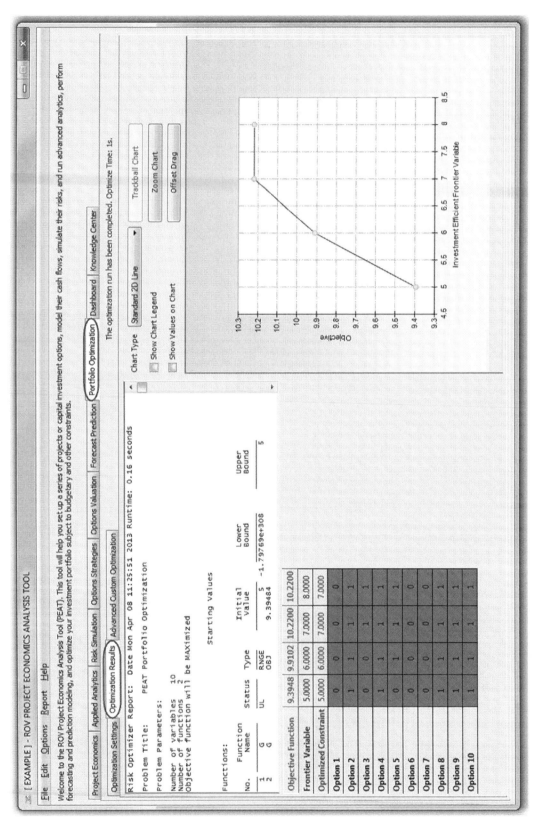

Double clicking on any saved optimization model in the previous Optimization Settings tab will run the optimization model and automatically bring you to this results tab.

Go to "Portfolio Optimization | Advanced Custom Optimization"

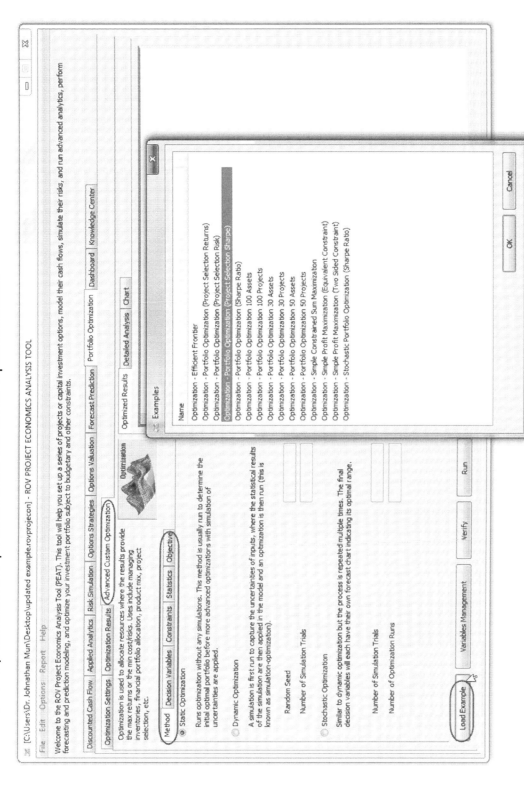

You can "create, save, and run your own optimization models" in this tab or run some previously saved example models. You have to first set up the model's Decision Variables using the Variables Management tool, then set the Objective and Constraints. You can set variable constraints with a range to run an investment efficient frontier analysis.

Go to "Dashboard" to review the settings and click "View Dashboards" when done

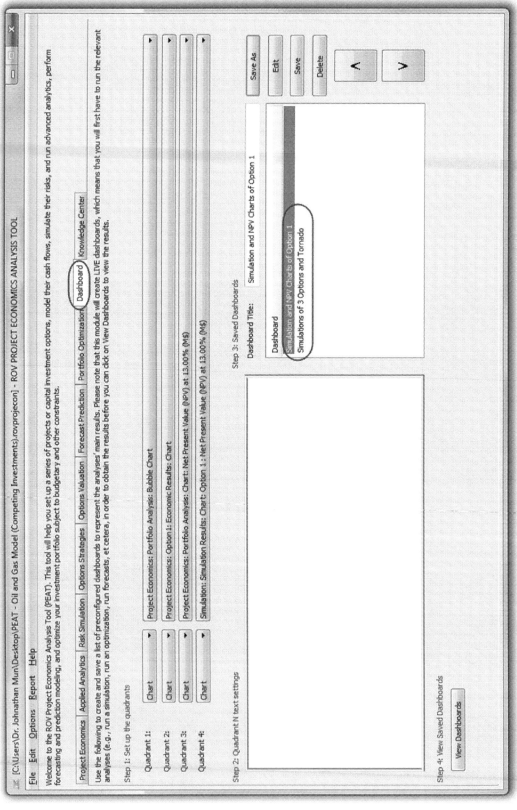

You can create and save multiple management dashboards here. Each dashboard can have four quadrants with any combinations of charts, results data grid, forecast or optimization results, or custom text. Please be aware that you must first run at least one RISK SIMULATION, OPTIMIZATION, and FORECAST model each before the dashboard will show any data/results. If you do not run anything, there will be no results to show!

In the "View Dashboards" mode, select any one of the saved dashboards from the droplist

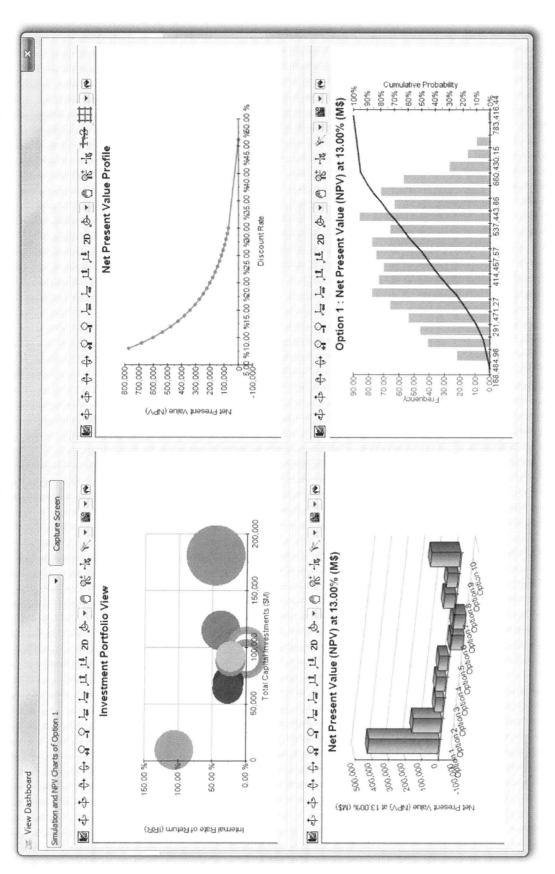

You can retrieve any of the saved dashboards and these dashboards will be populated only if the appropriate models have been run...

Go to "Knowledge Center | Step-by-Step Procedures" and step through the training material

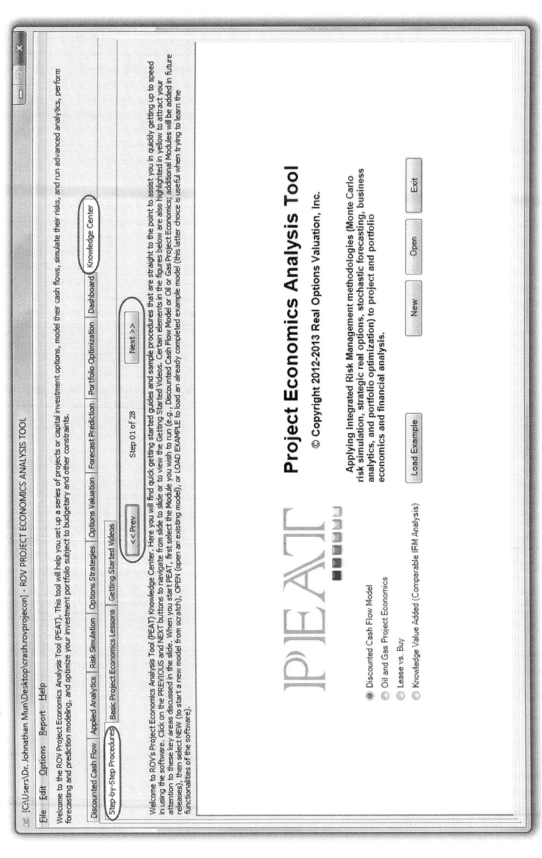

You can also learn the basics of PEAT through the knowledge center's procedures illustrations. Step back and forth from slide to slide while reviewing the text. You can create your own custom training materials for your staff and company's personnel, if you wish, by following some simple instructions in the user manual.

Go to "Knowledge Center | Basic Project Economics Lessons"

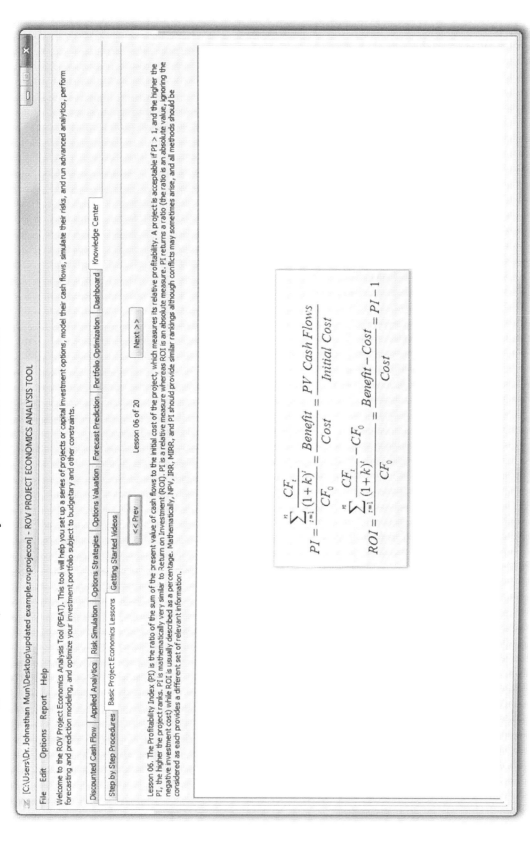

Go to "Knowledge Center | Getting Started Videos" and click on the video icon to start watching

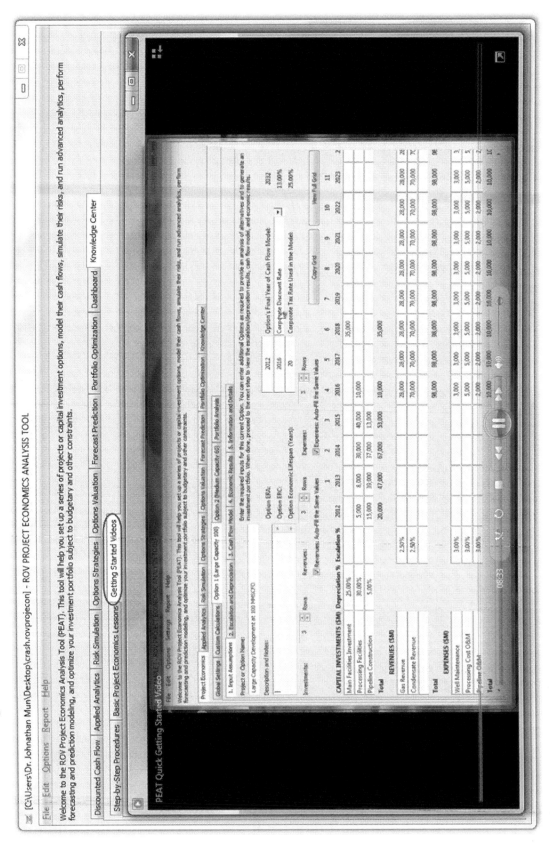

Some basic videos are also available as part of the PEAT tool to get you up to speed quickly on using the software application. Again, you can create and embed your own corporate training videos if required.

Click on the menus and explore…

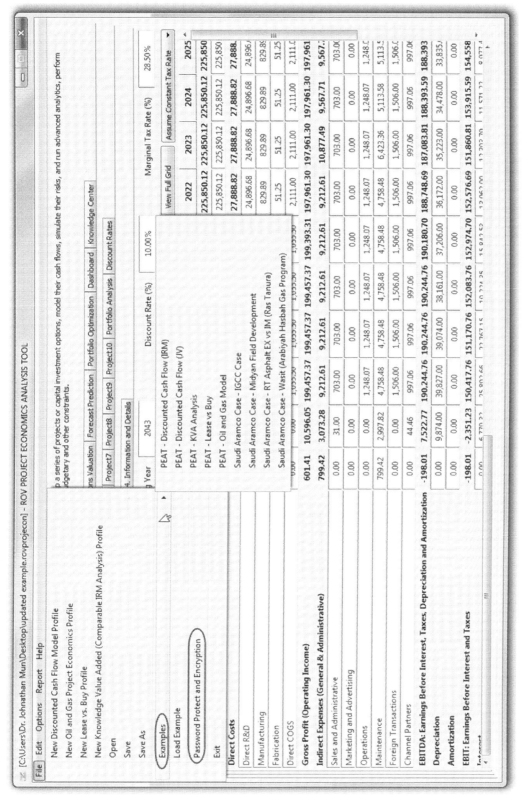

Do not forget to click on some of the menus to explore additional settings that are available such as performing data and model encryption, load example files, start new or open existing models, change international settings (foreign languages and decimal settings), as well as add/delete/rename/duplicate/rearrange Projects and Options.

Click on the "Report | Report Settings" menu

After completing and running your models (i.e., having completed and run any or all of the appropriate tabs: project economics, advanced analytics, risk simulations, forecasting, real options, and optimization), you can generate a report in Excel. A quick hint here is that once you click "Run Report" please make sure to be "hands-off" the computer until the report is complete.

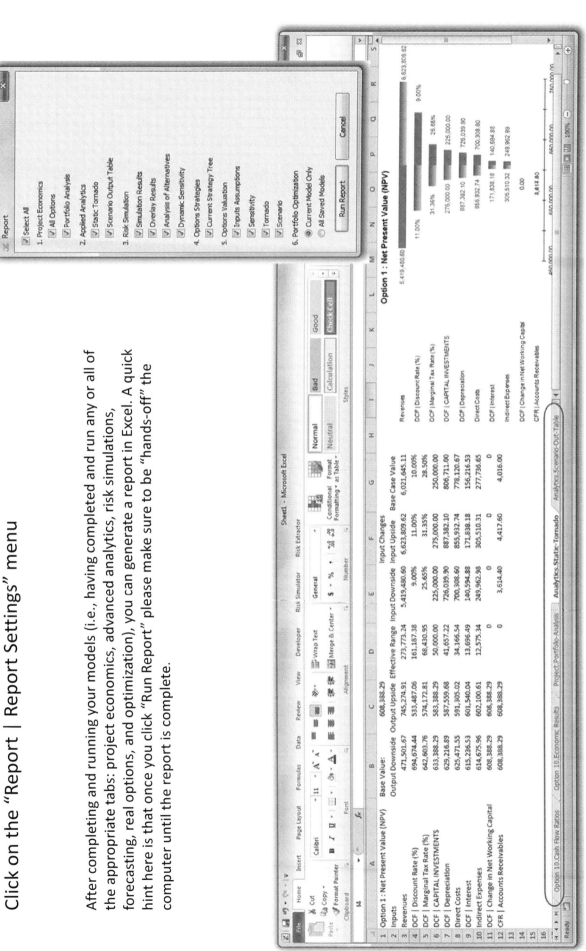

PEAT VISUAL GUIDE

VOLUME 4:
Quick Getting Started with Multiple Ways of SAVING & COPYING

Real Options Valuation

Saving a *.ROVPROJECON File: All inputs, models, and settings are saved in one file.

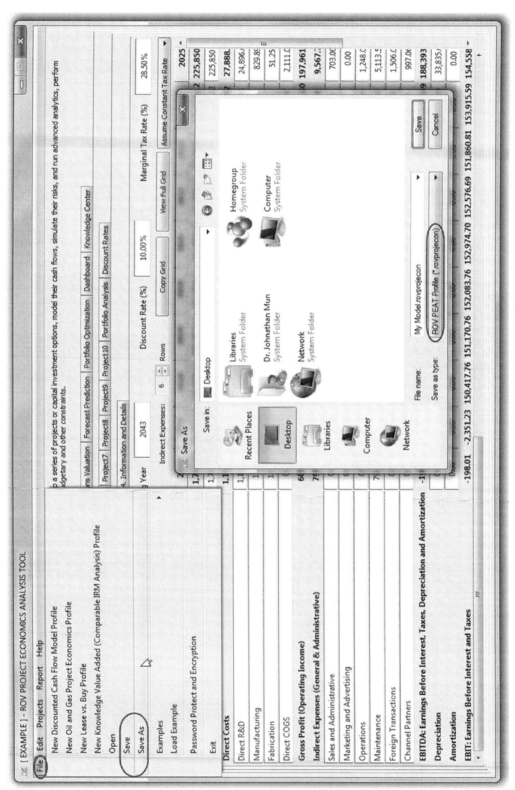

All of your data, inputs, password encryption, settings, droplist selections, chart edits, radio button selections, saved simulation models, saved forecast models, saved optimization models, and saved dashboard settings for each and every project can be saved as a single *.rovprojecon file. This file can be opened by anyone with PEAT.

Opening a Saved *.ROVPROJECON File: You will need to re-run the saved analytics.

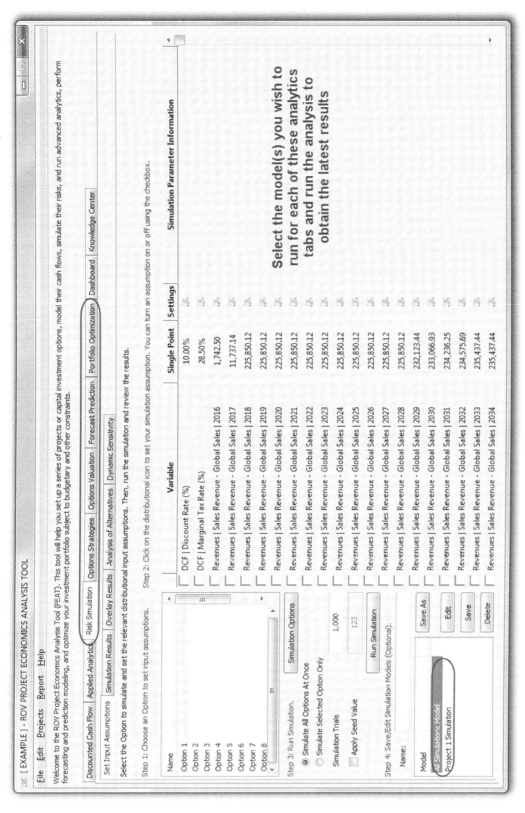

The *.rovprojecon file opens with all your saved input data, settings, models, and assumptions, but you will need to run the analysis again as results are not saved in the *.rovprojecon file. This is because we do not know if you have made any changes after the file is opened or if you modified the file outside of PEAT.

SAVING SIMULATED RESULTS

Archiving Simulation Results with *.ROVPROJECONSIMULTION File: Saves and archives all the results in Risk Simulation subtabs.

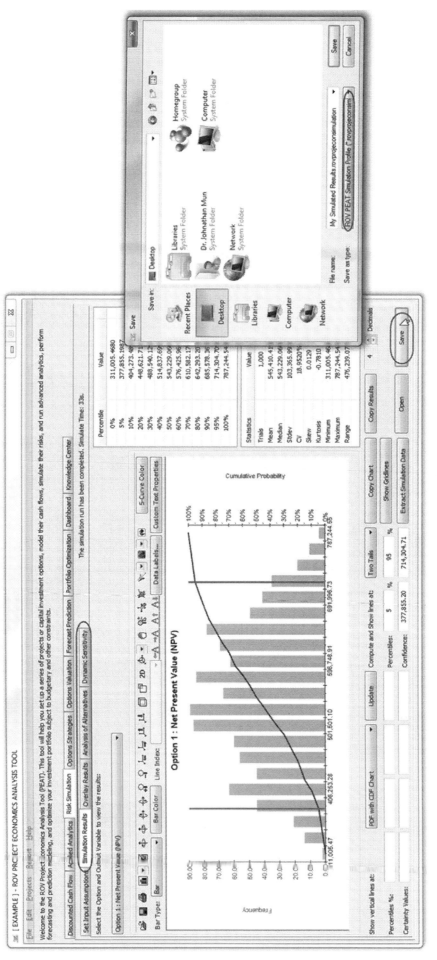

After running a simulation, creating overlay charts, looking at analysis of alternatives, and editing dynamic sensitivity charts, you can save these simulated results by clicking on the SAVE button in the Simulation Results tab. The results will be saved as an *.rovprojeconsimulation file and can be opened later by clicking on the OPEN button in this Simulation Results tab. This is a handy tool for archiving results or saving results from different versions of the model.

SAVING
SIMULATED
RAW DATA

Extracting Simulation Data: Perform your own analysis, upload to a database, or create your own charts and analytics.

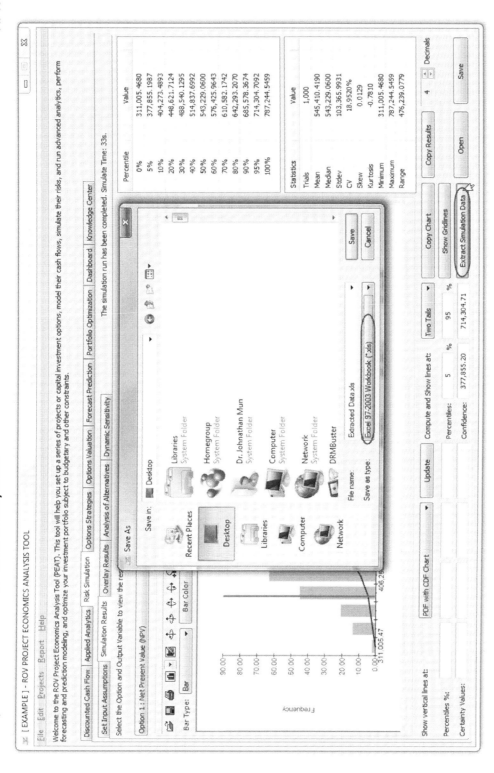

After running a simulation, you can extract the simulation data points by clicking on the EXTRACT SIMULATION DATA button in the Simulation Results tab. The simulated results for the selected chart will be extracted to an Excel file.

SAVING
CHARTS &
RESULTS

Saving and Copying Charts and Results: Copy and paste results and charts
into Word, Excel, or PowerPoint.

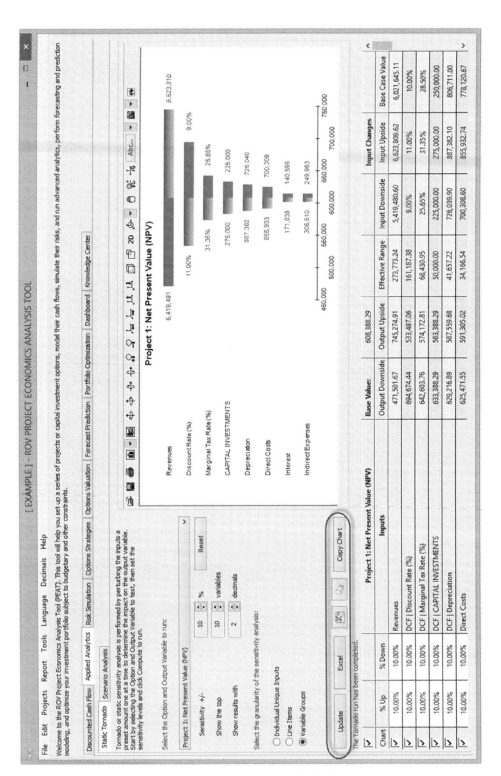

After running an analysis, you can click on Copy Chart or Excel button/icon to paste these items into Excel as live
editable charts and data tables.

Saving and Editing a Model: You can save multiple models with different inputs and settings in most of the analysis tabs.

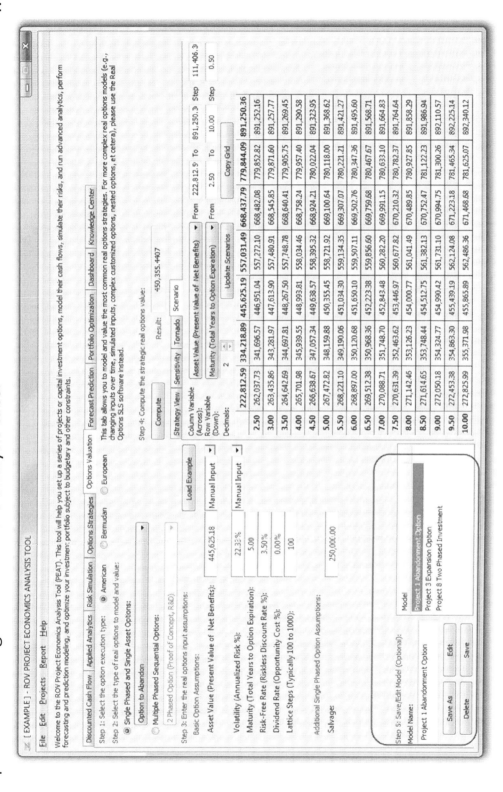

After setting up models with your custom inputs and settings, you can SAVE them for later retrievals and runs. You can save multiple models for each analysis tab, and these models can be retrieved, edited, duplicated, and run later. All analysis models in each tab are automatically saved in the *.rovprojecon file once you click on File | Save on the menu.

SAVING OPTIMIZATIONS

Saving and Editing Optimizations: You can save and edit multiple optimization models, each with its unique settings and inputs.

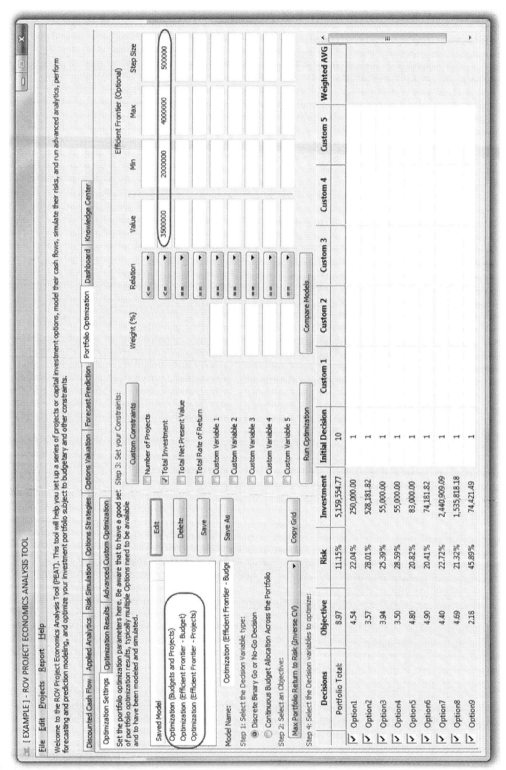

Each saved optimization model can have its own settings and custom inputs.

Real Options Valuation

Saving and Editing Dashboards: You can save and edit multiple dashboards only after the relevant analyses are run.

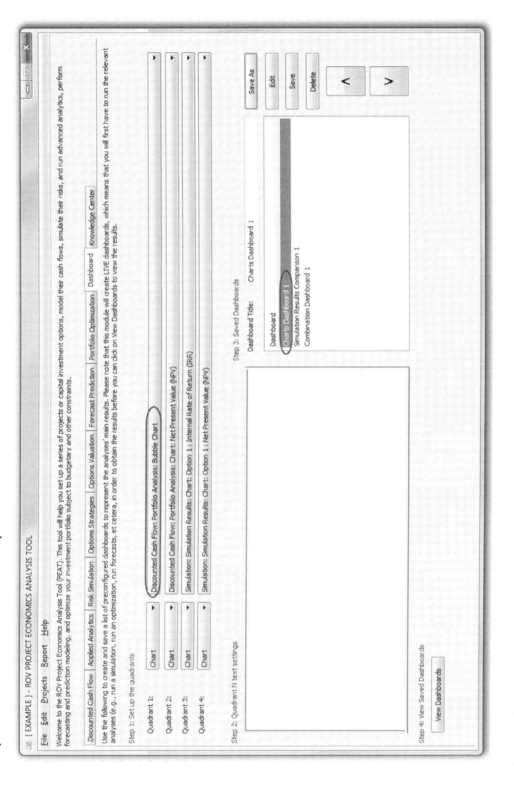

In order to edit or save Dashboards with specific analysis results, you need to first run the relevant analyses. That is, the droplist will not have simulation results available if you do not first run a simulation.

PEAT VISUAL GUIDE

VOLUME 5:

Quick Getting Started with Leasing Analysis and KVA Analysis

Real Options Valuation

Instructions

- This is a quick getting started guide, not a detailed user manual. See the user manual and related books for more technical information.

- Text in RED is instructions, text in BLUE is notes for your information only.

- This visual guide showcases the KVA Analysis module and summarizes how the methods are implemented and run in PEAT using an example model

- The LEASING module in PEAT allows you to compare a Lease versus Buy decision on machinery and equipment, and looks at the analysis from both the points of view of a Lessee (the party who leases the equipment for use) versus a Lessor (the party who owns the equipment and lends it to another company for a fee).

1. Start PEAT and Select "Lease vs. Buy"
2. Click "Load Example"

Project Economics Analysis Tool

© Copyright 2012-2013 Real Options Valuation, Inc.

Applying Integrated Risk Management methodologies (Monte Carlo risk simulation, strategic real options, stochastic forecasting, business analytics, and portfolio optimization) to project and portfolio economics and financial analysis.

PEAT

○ Corporate Investments - Stochastic DCF Analysis
◉ Corporate Investments - Buy vs. Lease
○ Oil and Gas Economics - Investment Decision Analysis
○ Oil and Gas Economics - Oil Field Reserves
○ Project Management - Dynamic Schedule and Cost Analysis
◉ Public Sector Analysis - Knowledge Value Added
○ Customized Encrypted Models

Saudi Aramco ~ FPD Standard Economic Model ▸

Load Example

English ▸

New   Open   Exit

Additional customized "Modules" will be added over time. Click on "Load Example" to follow along and walk through this Visual Guide...

Go to "Lease vs. Buy | Sample Leasing | Lessee" to see the sample model

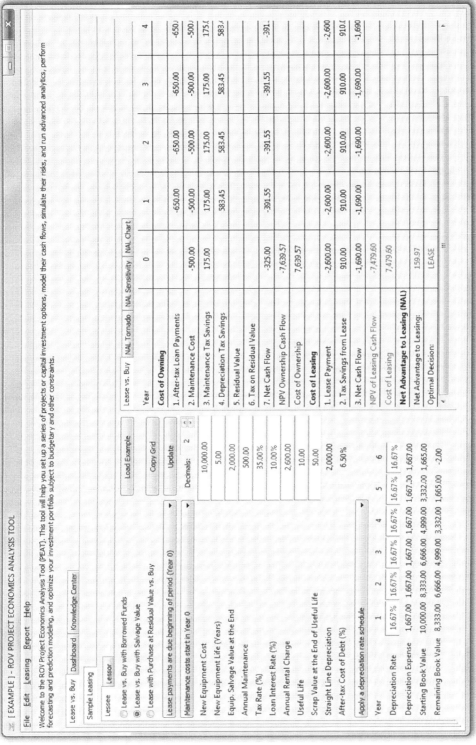

In your own model, simply enter the required inputs (input boxes), or Copy | Paste from Excel or another data source. Make sure to start with the Lessee subtab and choose one of the three options that fits your situation the most. Do not forget to select the relevant items from the droplists and remember to click UPDATE to update your calculations based on any updated inputs or settings. The model also allows for a straight line depreciation as well as your own custom depreciation schedule (e.g., MACRS accelerated depreciation, sum of year digits, etc.) and the sum of the depreciation percent has to equal 100% and the depreciation schedule needs to have one additional year beyond the life of the new equipment.

Real Options Valuation

Go to "NAL Tornado"

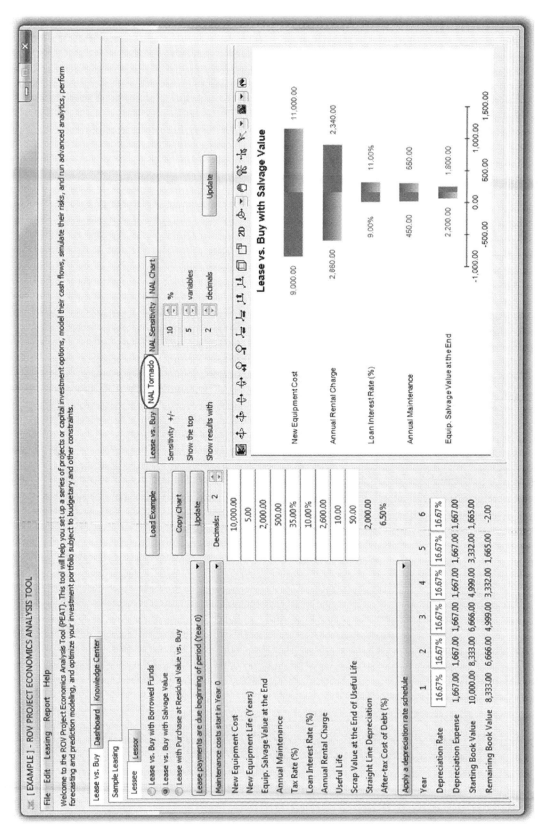

The NAL or Net Advantage to Leasing model comes equipped with a Tornado analysis, Sensitivity table, and Chart. As usual, if you edit any of the inputs and change any settings, remember to click the UPDATE button to obtain the most recent analyses results.

Go to "NAL Sensitivity"

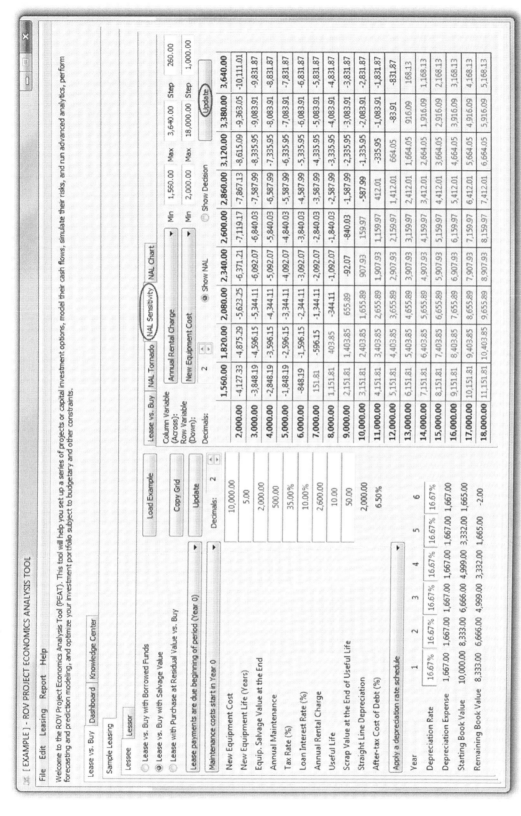

Select up to two input variables in the model and enter their ranges to generate a sensitivity table, or simply choose the variables of interest and use the auto default ranges. You can also show the results as NAL or Net Advantage to Leasing, which means a positive value implies Leasing is better than Buying (Green), and a negative value implies that Buying is better than Leasing (Blue).

Real Options Valuation

Go to "NAL Sensitivity"

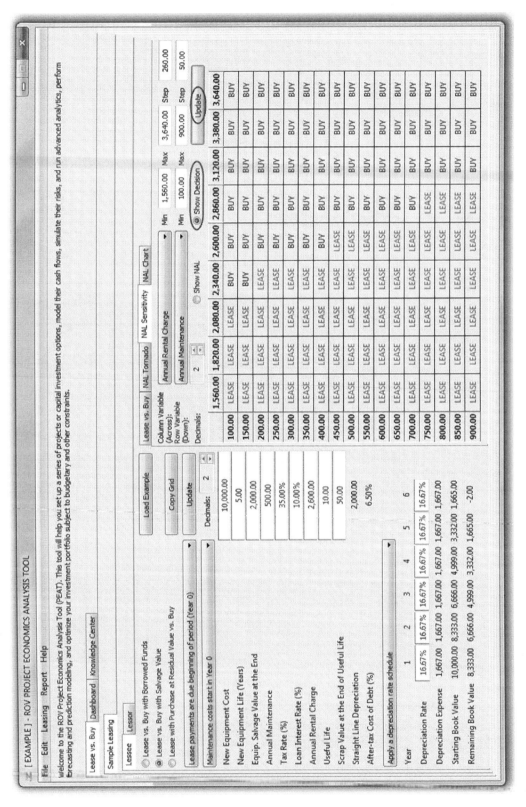

Alternatively, click on the Show Decision radio button and the values will be changed to decision nodes of Lease versus Buy, whichever is more advantageous based on the NAL analysis.

Go to "NAL Chart"

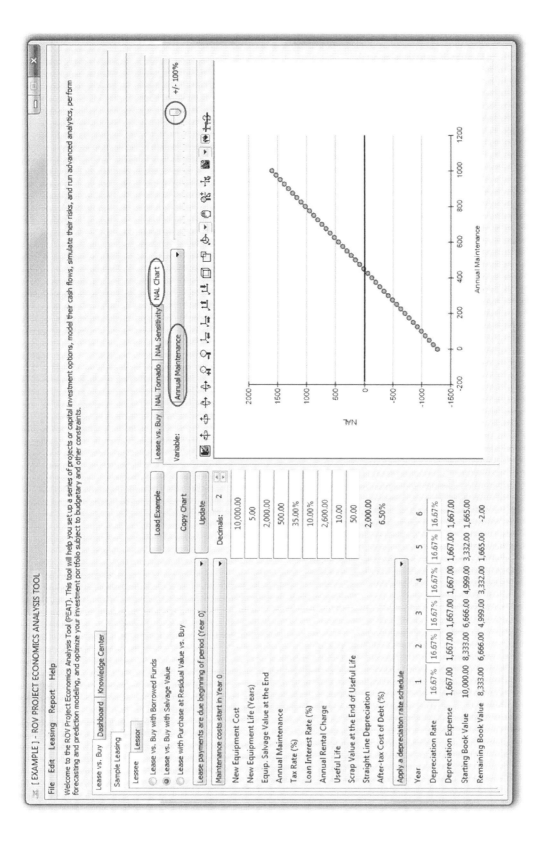

The NAL chart shows the NAL values and the zero threshold (i.e., positive NAL means Leasing is a better alternative than Buying). The chart provides a more visual representation of the sensitivity table seen previously.

PEAT VISUAL GUIDE

VOLUME 6:
Data Requirements and Inputs

Real Options Valuation

Manual Direct Data Input

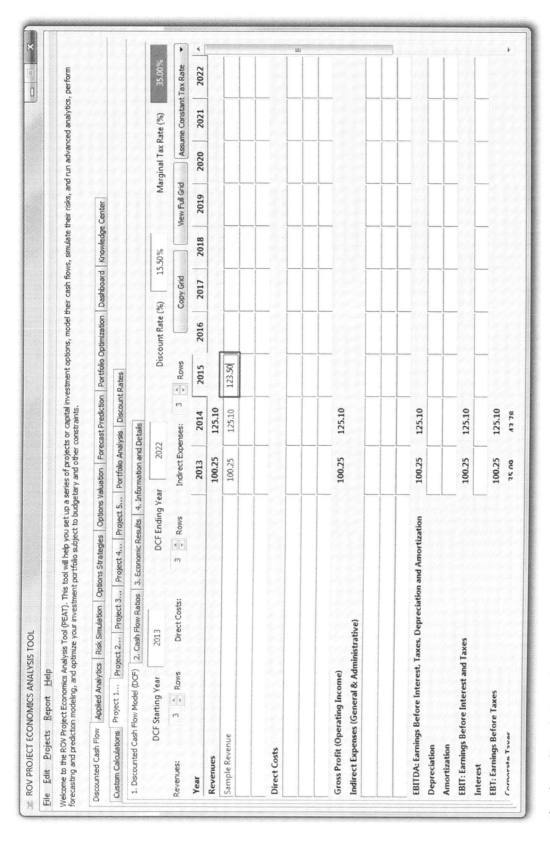

Enter the data directly into the input cells. To edit or re-enter inputs, you can select the input cell and double-click to enter/edit data or click on the F2 button to access the cell to edit.

COPY/PASTE from Excel

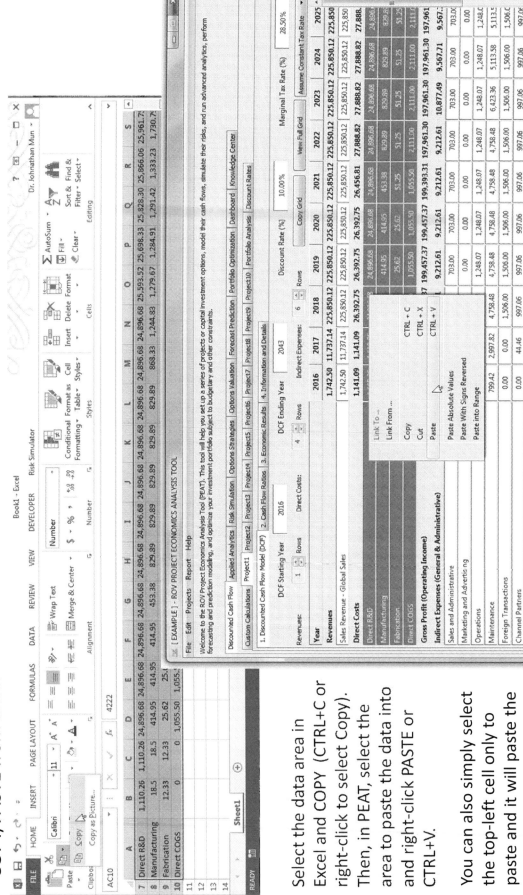

Select the data area in Excel and COPY (CTRL+C or right-click to select Copy). Then, in PEAT, select the area to paste the data into and right-click PASTE or CTRL+V.

You can also simply select the top-left cell only to paste and it will paste the entire grid.

Types of PASTE, Special (Right-Click on PEAT)

Link To …	
Link From …	
Copy	CTRL + C
Cut	CTRL + X
Paste	CTRL + V
Paste Absolute Values	
Paste With Signs Reversed	
Paste into Range	

PASTE. Pastes the selected data into the range "as is."

PASTE WITH ABSOLUTE VALUES. Pastes the numerical data and converts all values into positive values.

PASTE WITH SIGNS REVERSED. Pastes the numerical data and converts all negative values into positive values and vice versa.

PASTE INTO RANGE. Pastes the copied single value into the entire range that you have selected.

PASTE WITH ABSOLUTE VALUES and PASTE WITH SIGNS REVERSED may come in handy depending on the model convention you use in Excel. For instance, see the two similar models below. We know that Income = Revenue – Expenses. However, one can enter expenses as $50 and simply take the revenue number minus this expense number to obtain the income. Therefore, in Type A below, we enter expenses as a positive value. This is the typical convention used in most Excel financial models and also the same convention used in PEAT. Conversely, Type B has expenses listed as a negative number, and, therefore, Income in this case is simply the sum of revenue and expenses seeing that expenses is already negative. This is a less common approach but nonetheless valid because we show an outgoing amount (expenses) as a negative cash flow. So, imagine if you have a large model with such expense data and wish to copy/paste into PEAT. In such a case, PASTE WITH ABSOLUTE VALUES will come in handy indeed.

In the less common Type B convention, if there are reversions in expense charges (that is, you get paid back some overpaid expenses), these values might be shown as positive, and this is where PASTE WITH SIGNS REVERSED comes in handy as well.

	Type A	Type B
Revenue	100	100
Expenses	50	-50
Income	50	50

Excel Cell Formatting

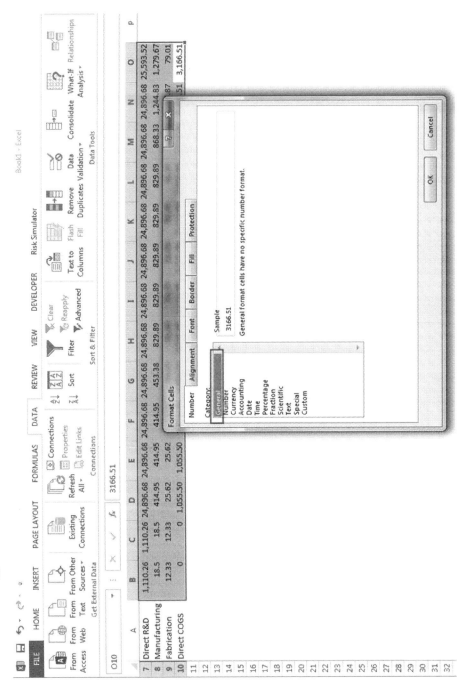

In most situations, you can copy and paste directly from Excel. However, some Excel spreadsheets may contain weird or custom formatting on the data. If you cannot paste directly from such spreadsheets, you need to first change the cell formatting. This can be done quickly. Select the Excel data you wish to copy, then click CTRL+1 or right-click and select Format Cells. Then change to the GENERAL setting. This will guarantee a smooth copy/paste experience.

Live Excel Links

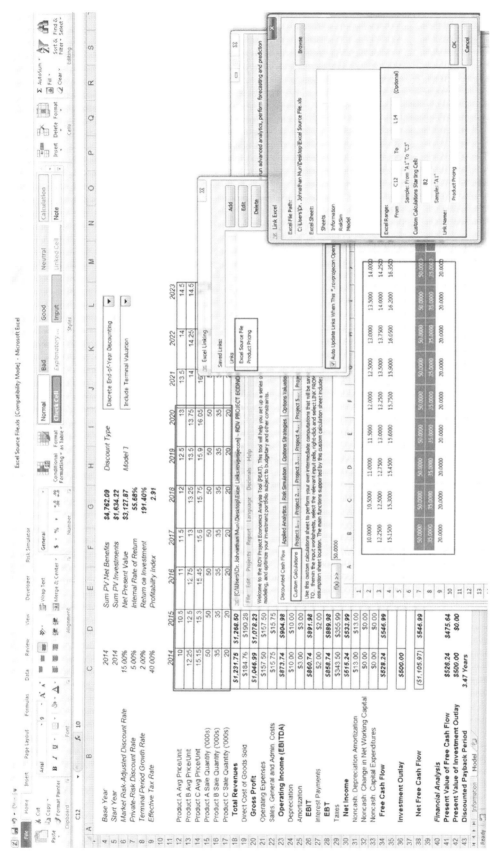

Custom Calculations tab's Excel button allows you to add/edit/delete Live Links from Excel to this tab. You can add multiple links from multiple workbooks and worksheets into this single tab. Reopening the file will auto update the data if you check the Auto Update option. From Custom Worksheet, you can now link to other tabs within PEAT.

Linking Custom Calculations to Other Tabs via Live Excel Links

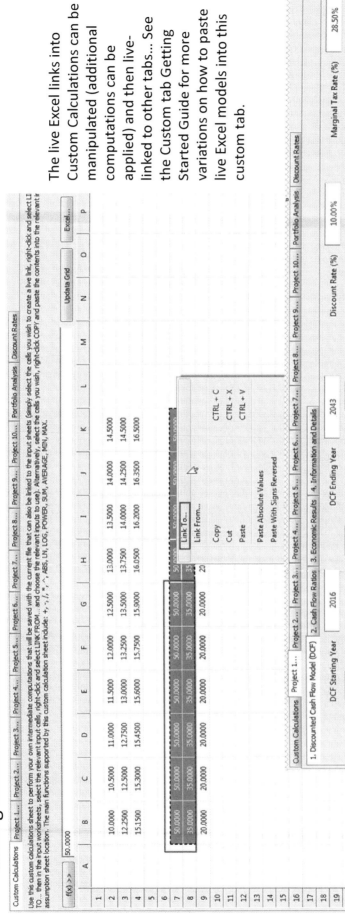

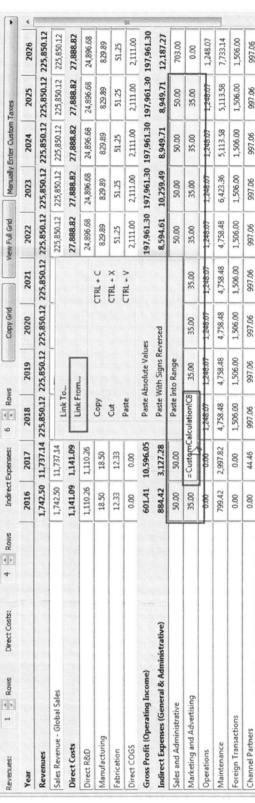

The live Excel links into Custom Calculations can be manipulated (additional computations can be applied) and then live-linked to other tabs... See the Custom tab Getting Started Guide for more variations on how to paste live Excel models into this custom tab.

Select the area in Custom tab and right-click to Link To. Then select the appropriate area in another tab and right-click Link From...

Error Capture

Intelligent logic has been built into the tool such that any bad data or invalid input assumptions are captured and disallowed at the point of input. This helps prevent any user errors and input errors in the model.

Different error captures exist. For example, ending periods have to be greater than starting periods, or positive values are required for certain inputs, or only numerical values are allowed (no alphanumerical inputs are allowed).

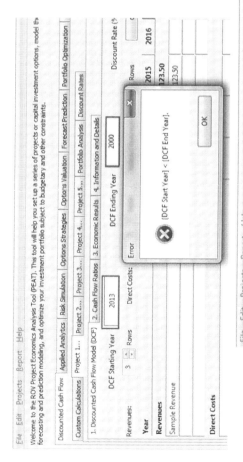

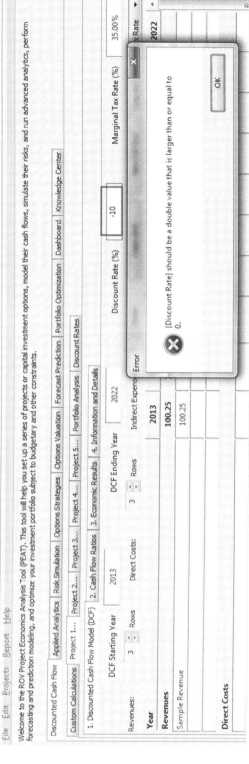

Error Capture

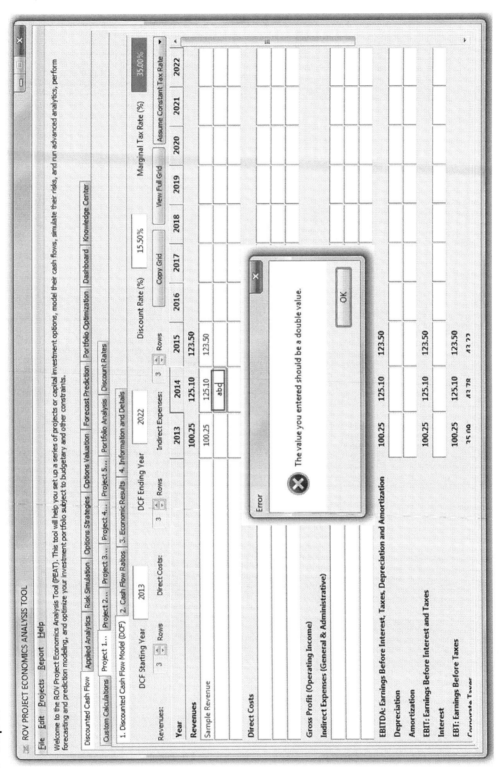

If a bad input data point is detected, you will be informed and the input cell will be cleared. This prevents the error from accidentally existing in the model despite the warning messages.

Empty Inputs, Inconsequential Inputs, and Notes

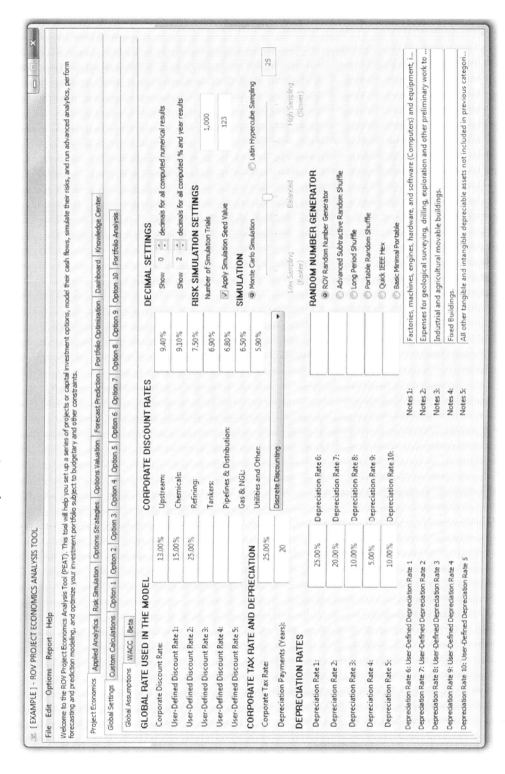

Sometimes there are inconsequential inputs and notes that can be kept blank or you can enter your inputs but they may not be used. These vary depending on the customized model that is developed within PEAT.

Droplists, Number of Rows, Fill Across, and Color Coding

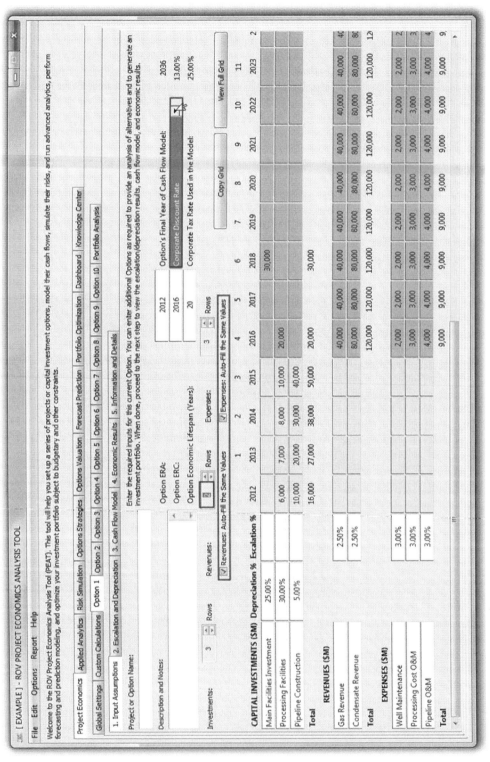

Watch out for droplists and make sure you select the relevant assumptions, although the default droplist item is the most frequently used in most cases. You can also add or remove rows as required, but make sure not to remove rows that are populated with important or required data. Finally, sometimes color coding exists in data input cells and computed results for a quick visual identification of different time segments (e.g., ERA vs. ERC time periods are color coded differently in the example above).

Number of Rows, Data Type, Model Compute

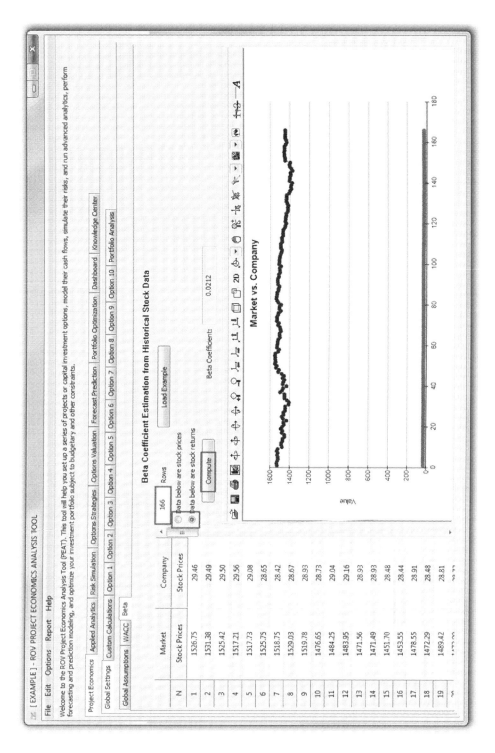

Be careful with number of rows. For instance, if you Load Example with 166 rows and then use it as a template whereupon you paste your own data, say 150 rows, the bottom 16 rows are old data and will skew your results. So, be careful. Also, when you see a Compute button, always use it to update the calculations.

PEAT VISUAL GUIDE

VOLUME 7:
Tips & Tricks

Real Options Valuation

Instructions

This is a quick getting started guide on tips and tricks for using PEAT.

- Running and Editing Saved Models
- Customizing Charts
- Copying Charts and Data Grids
- Applied Analytics, Scenario Hotspots, Tornado Analysis
- Risk Simulation, Assumptions, Charts
- Options Strategies and Options Valuation
- Forecast Prediction, Loading Example Models, Recovering Saved Models
- Optimization's Efficient Frontier and Custom Constraints (mutually exclusive projects)
- Editing XML Profiles and ROVPROJECON Files
- Data Encryption and Password Protection
- Running and Viewing Dashboards
- Report Generation

COPY/PASTE from Excel

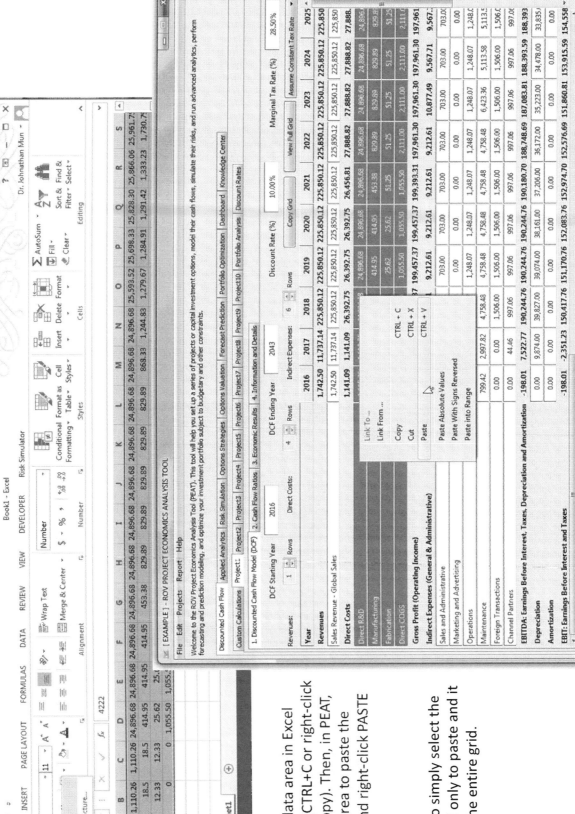

Select the data area in Excel and COPY (CTRL+C or right-click to select Copy). Then, in PEAT, select the area to paste the data into and right-click PASTE or CTRL+V.

You can also simply select the top-left cell only to paste and it will paste the entire grid.

Real Options Valuation

Types of PASTE, Special (Right-Click in PEAT)

Link To …	
Link From …	
Copy	CTRL + C
Cut	CTRL + X
Paste	CTRL + V
Paste Absolute Values	
Paste With Signs Reversed	
Paste into Range	

PASTE. Pastes the selected data into the range "as is."

PASTE WITH ABSOLUTE VALUES. Pastes the numerical data and converts all values into positive values.

PASTE WITH SIGNS REVERSED. Pastes the numerical data and converts all negative values into positive values and vice versa.

PASTE INTO RANGE. Pastes the copied single value into the entire range that you have selected.

PASTE WITH ABSOLUTE VALUES and PASTE WITH SIGNS REVERSED may come in handy depending on the model convention you use in Excel. For instance, see the two similar models below. We know that Income = Revenue − Expenses. However, one can enter expenses as $50 and simply take the revenue number minus this expense number to obtain the income. Therefore, in Type A below, we enter expenses as a positive value. This is the typical convention used in most Excel financial models and also the same convention used in PEAT. Conversely, Type B has expenses listed as a negative number, and, therefore, Income in this case is simply the sum of revenue and expenses seeing that expenses is already negative. This is a less common approach but nonetheless valid because we show an outgoing amount (expenses) as a negative cash flow. So, imagine if you have a large model with such expense data and wish to copy/paste into PEAT. In such a case, PASTE WITH ABSOLUTE VALUES will come in handy indeed.

	Type A	Type B
Revenue	100	100
Expenses	50	-50
Income	50	50

In the less common Type B convention, if there are reversions in expense charges (that is, you get paid back some overpaid expenses), these values might be shown as positive, and this is where PASTE WITH SIGNS REVERSED comes in handy as well.

Live Excel Links

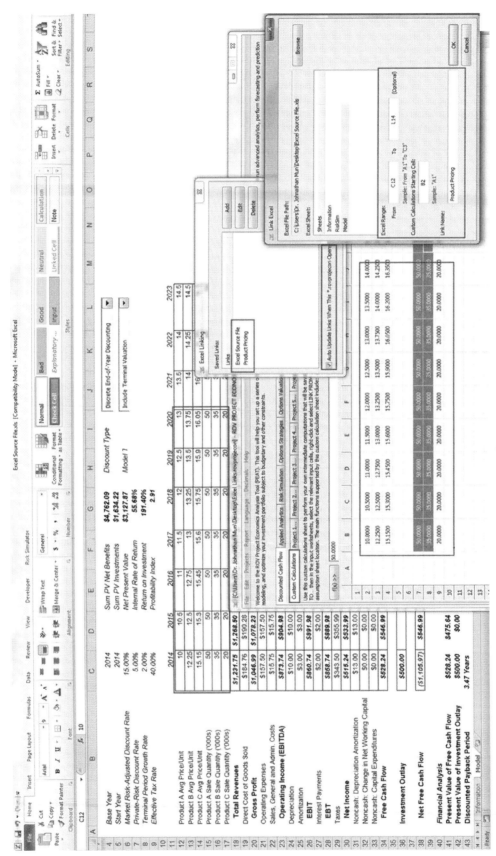

Custom Calculations tab's Excel button allows you to add/edit/delete Live Links from Excel to this tab. You can add multiple links from multiple workbooks and worksheets into this single tab. Reopening the file will auto update the data if you check the Auto Update option. From Custom Worksheet, you can now link to other tabs within PEAT. Right-click on the Custom tab to add new or delete/rename existing custom tabs.

Linking Custom Calculations to Other Tabs via Live Links, Naming Cells, and Setting Risk Simulation Assumptions on Custom Tab's Cells

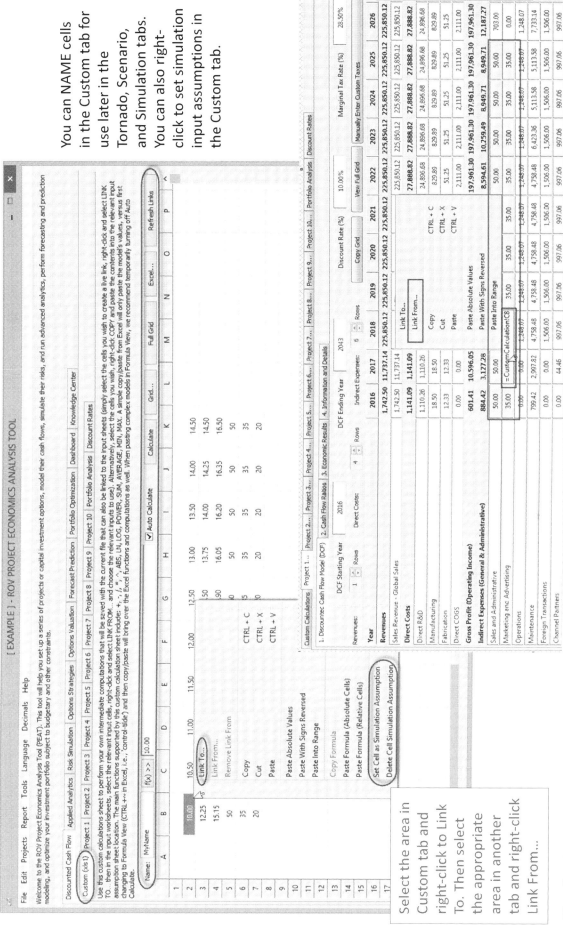

You can NAME cells in the Custom tab for use later in the Tornado, Scenario, and Simulation tabs. You can also right-click to set simulation input assumptions in the Custom tab.

Select the area in Custom tab and right-click to Link To. Then select the appropriate area in another tab and right-click Link From...

Excel Cell Formatting

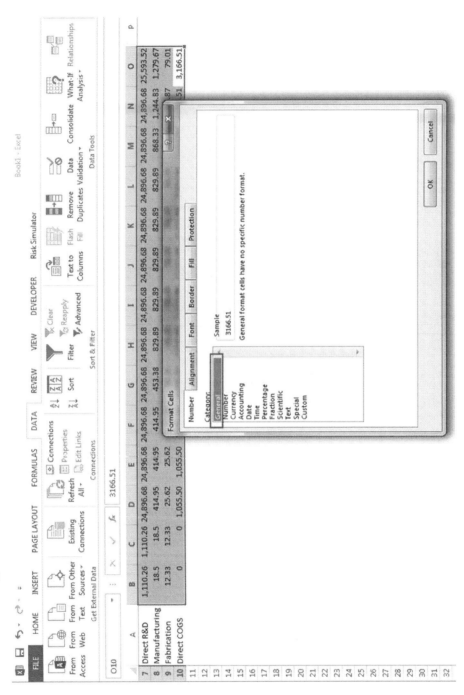

In most situations, you can copy and paste directly from Excel. However, some Excel spreadsheets may contain weird or custom formatting on the data. If you cannot paste directly from such spreadsheets, you need to first change the cell formatting. This can be done quickly. Select the Excel data you wish to copy, then click CTRL+1 or right-click and select Format Cells. Then change to the GENERAL setting. This will guarantee a smooth copy/paste experience.

Error Capture

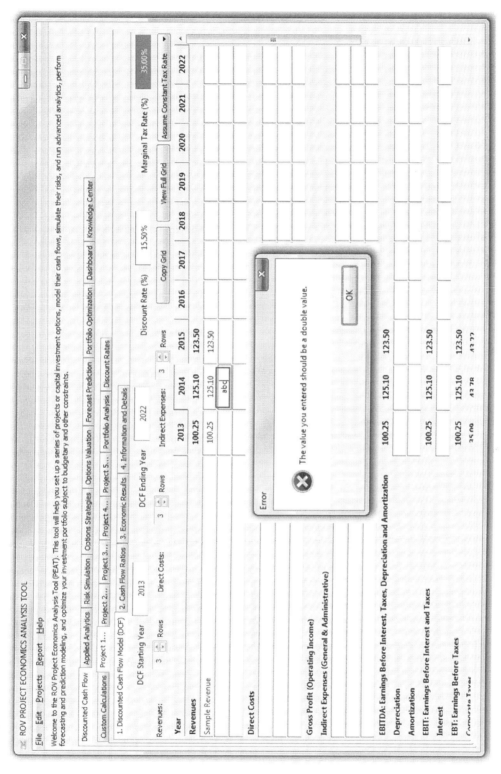

If a bad input data point is detected, you will be informed and the input cell will be cleared. This prevents the error from accidentally existing in the model despite the warning messages.

Droplists, Number of Rows, Fill Across, and Color Coding

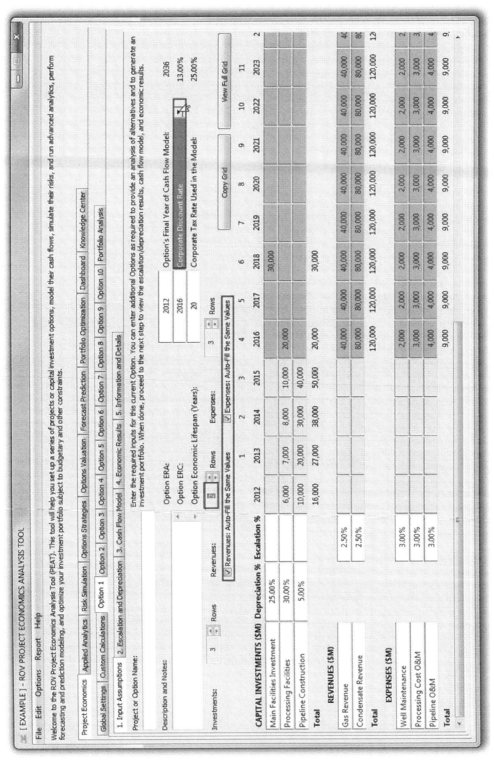

Watch out for droplists and make sure you select the relevant assumptions, although the default droplist item is the most frequently used in most cases. You can also add or remove rows as required, but make sure not to remove rows that are populated with important or required data. Finally, sometimes color coding exists in data input cells and computed results for a quick visual identification of different time segments (e.g., ERA vs. ERC time periods are color coded differently in the example above).

Real Options Valuation

TIP. Double-click to run saved models. Click once and select Edit to change settings

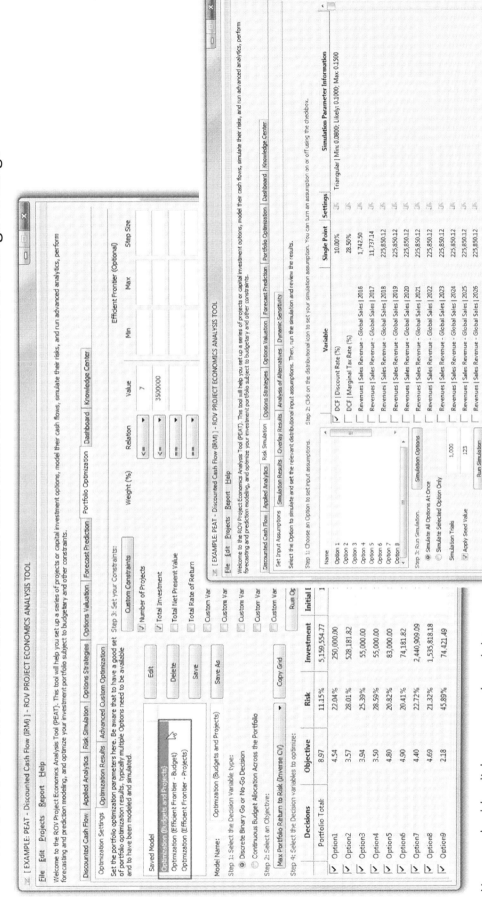

You can double-click on a saved model to run it or click once to select and then Run. To edit an existing model, click once to select then Edit. When done, remember to Save.

TIP. Applied Analytics and Tornado Analysis
[APPLIED ANALYTICS | TORNADO ANALYSIS]

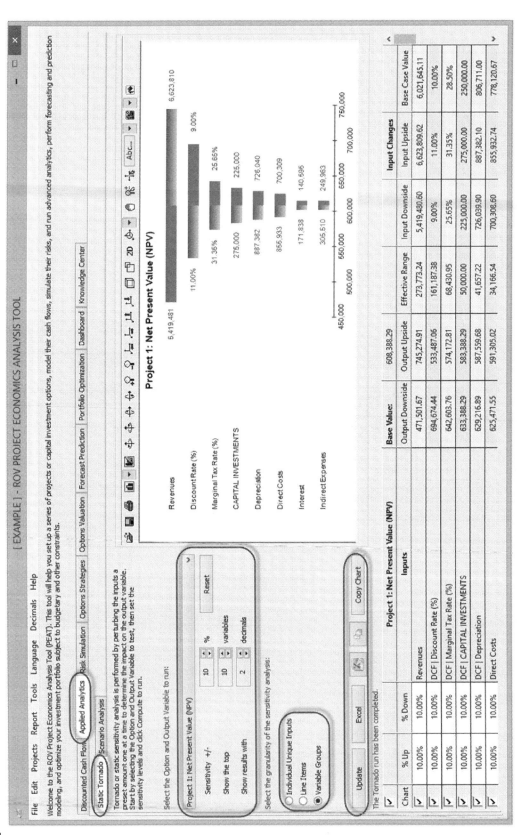

Do not forget to select the output variable on which to run a tornado analysis. Change the decimal settings and number of variables to show in order to change the look and feel of the chart.

TIP. Applied Analytics and Scenario Analysis
[APPLIED ANALYTICS | SCENARIO ANALYSIS]

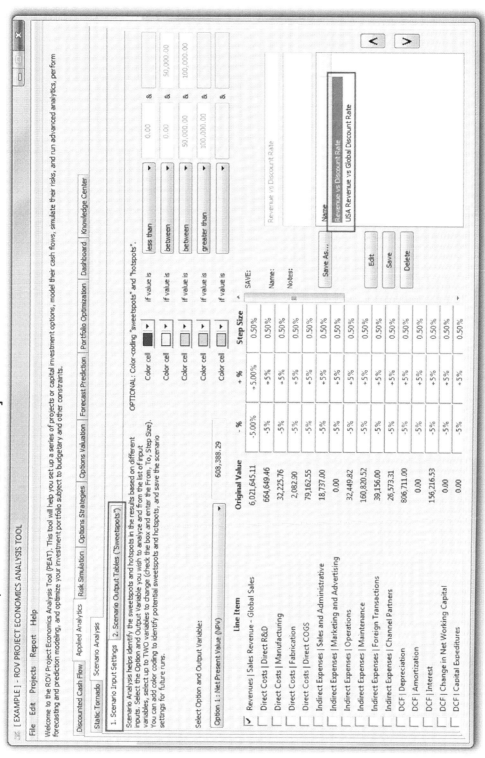

Do not forget that Scenario Analysis has two tabs: Settings and Output Tables. You cannot see the output tables or scenario results unless you first set up and save a scenario model, then proceed to the output tables results tab. Do not forget to select from the droplist the saved model you wish to run. Double-clicking on a saved model only allows you to edit it instead of running it.

TIP. Follow the steps to set up Risk Simulation assumptions one at a time

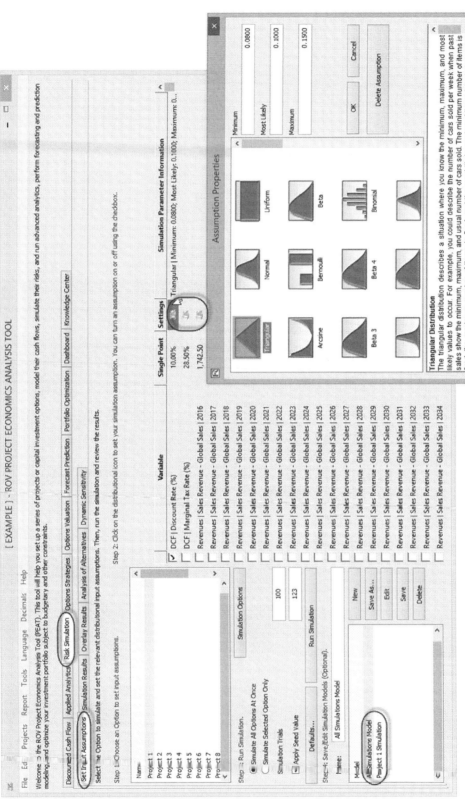

Risk Simulation assumptions can only be set up one at a time. Follow the steps outlined in the software. Select the Option/Project; decide if one option/project or all options/projects are to be simulated at once; and set up the input assumptions (click on the green assumptions icon, and the droplist shows 50 distributions, with the most commonly used ones listed first). Continue to set assumptions on other Options/Projects and Save the model when done. The saved model will include all the assumptions set in all the options/projects.

TIP. After running a simulation, you can review the simulation statistics and charts, as well as customize the look and feel of these charts

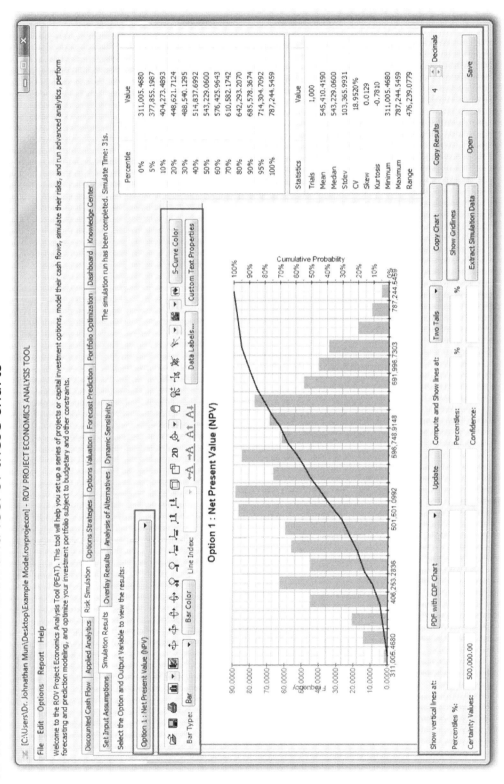

There are many things that can be done in the charts. All the modifications can be done using the droplists as well as icons and buttons usually directly above or below the charts. Try out some of these yourself.

TIP. You can add custom lines and text in the Simulation Charts

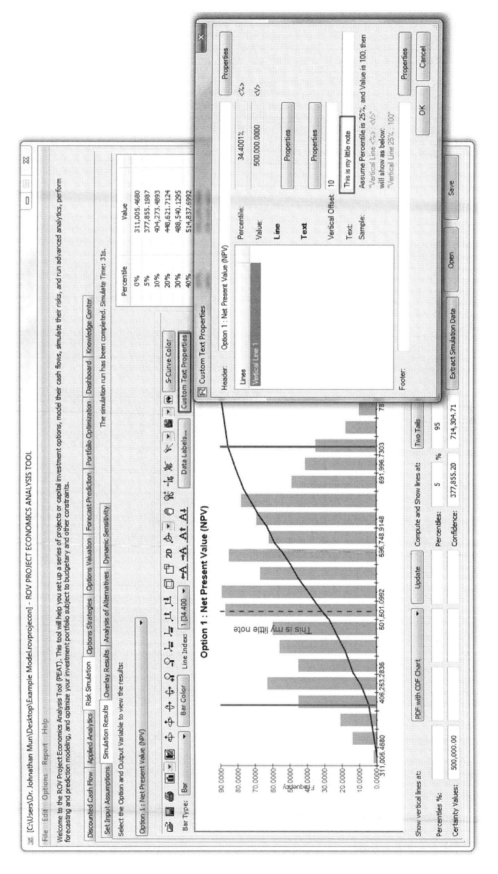

If you elect to show vertical lines (bottom-left section of the forecast charts) in the simulation forecast charts, you can then modify these custom lines' properties and add custom text to accompany these lines.

TIP. Copy and pasting charts
[COPY CHART]

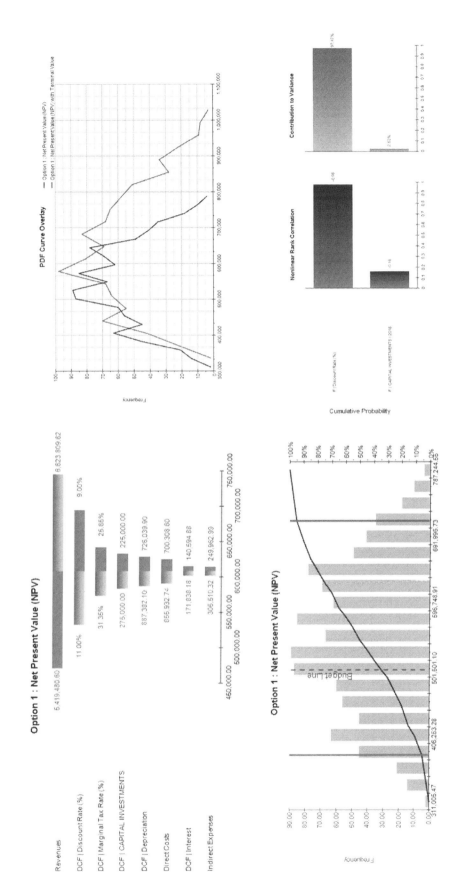

All the charts you see in PEAT can be copied and pasted into PowerPoint, Word, Excel, or other software applications. Simply modify the charts to how you want them to look and click on the Copy Chart button, then proceed to paste into another software of your choice. Some sample charts are pasted into this PowerPoint presentation to illustrate how they would look. You can resize and reposition as required.

TIP. Pasting results grids
[COPY GRID]

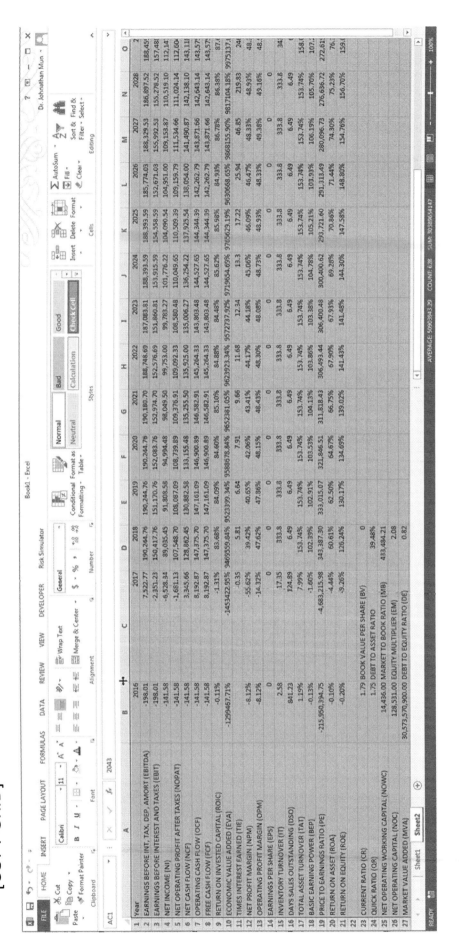

If you need the results in Excel, simply run the relevant PEAT models and when appropriate and available, click the Copy Grid, open Excel, and paste into Excel. The number of decimals and format settings (e.g., %, % or $) will be pasted "as is" from the PEAT results grid, so remember to make any changes in the grid first (e.g., adding or reducing the number of decimals) before you copy and paste the data grid. You can then format the Excel worksheet as you see fit (e.g., colors, font size/type, column width).

TIP. Pasting strategy trees
[OPTIONS STRATEGY | FIRST MENU ICON]

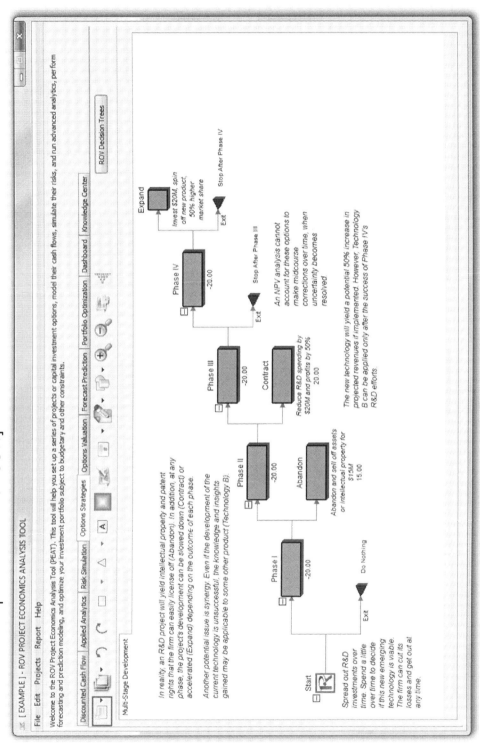

Use the first icon menu item to open saved example Options Strategy trees, to create a new Options Strategy tree, or to capture the figures in the Options Strategy tree view and paste them into PowerPoint or Word. See the user manual or saved example models on various shapes, branches, sizes, colors, fonts, nodes, and properties that can be set and modified in these Options Strategy trees.

TIP. Options Valuation
[OPTIONS VALUATION]

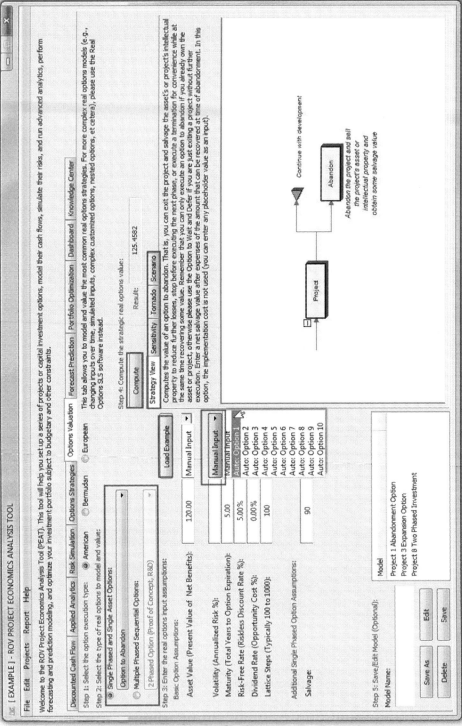

You can Load Example data and models in Options Valuation or enter your own inputs and use the droplist to auto compute some of the inputs. Some inputs will not be available unless you first run risk simulation (e.g., volatility inputs). Do not forget to view the Sensitivity, Tornado, and Scenario tabs after computing the model. Double-click on a saved model to load and run.

TIP. Forecast Prediction: Loading examples and recovering your saved models

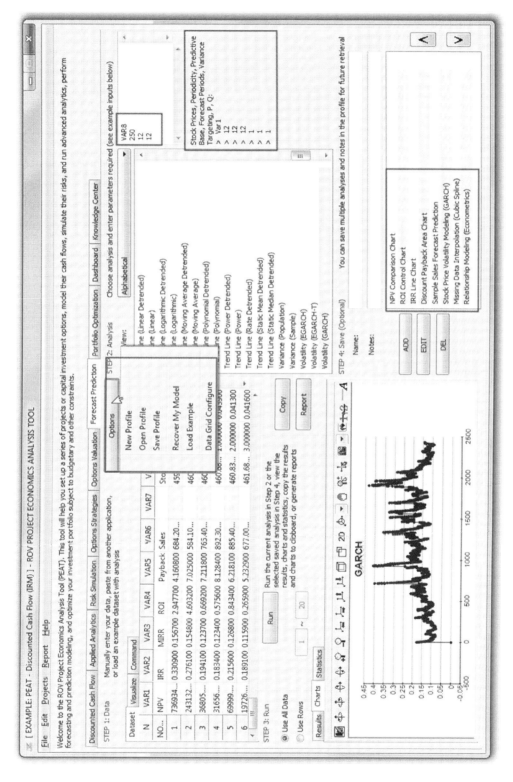

The Forecast Prediction module has over 150 models you can use. Click on Options | Load Example to see some sample data and saved models. You can use these saved models as templates on how to run and set up some of the available models. Click on Options | Recover My Example to recover your data and saved models.

Real Options Valuation

TIP. Portfolio Optimization: Remember to run a simulation before running an optimization

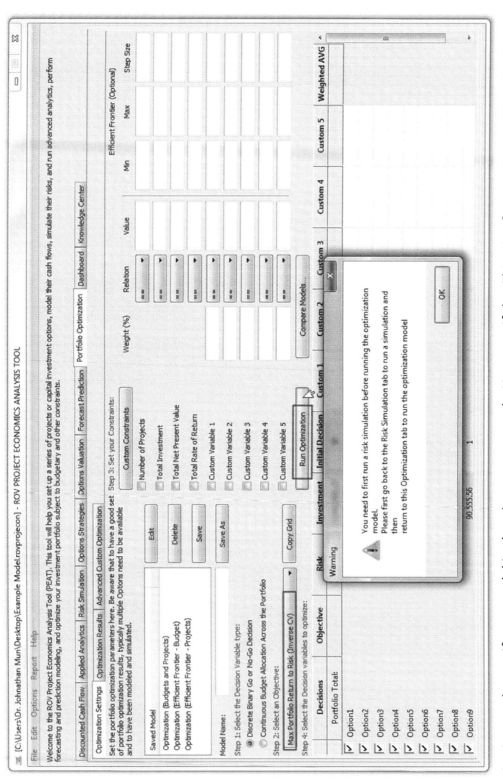

Optimization can be run if your model is already set up correctly. However, if the Objective function in Step 2 is "Max Return to Risk" or "Min Risk," then a simulation will first need to be run before an optimization can be run. This is because risk is computed through the simulation model. When in doubt, it is always safer to first run a simulation (takes only a few seconds).

TIP. Portfolio Optimization: Markowitz Investment Efficient Frontier

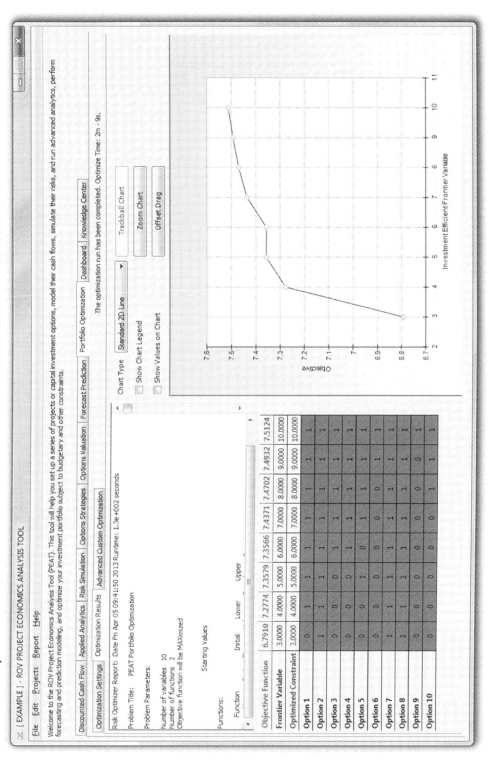

An investment efficient frontier can be set up by adding the Min, Max, Step Size inputs within the Optimization Settings tab, which, when run, will generate the results as shown above, as a matrix of decision variables and an efficient frontier chart (the x-axis is labeled Frontier Variable). Be careful that other charts generated that may look like a curve may not be efficient frontiers if you have not set up these min, max, steps, as these charts are simply optimization iteration charts, showing the progress of the objective function over various iterations. Color coding helps to identify which projects should be added based on different constraints.

TIP. Portfolio Optimization: Setting mutually exclusive projects as constraints [PORTFOLIO OPTIMIZATION | CUSTOM CONSTRAINTS | ADD]

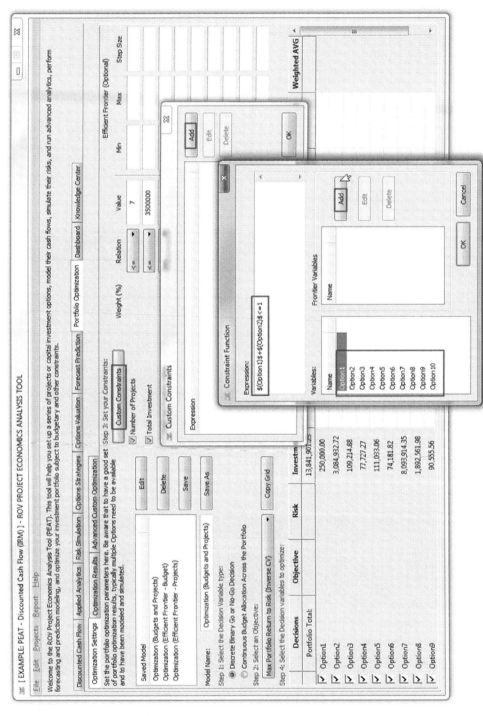

If two or more projects are mutually exclusive (i.e., only one project can be selected at a time within a batch of projects), then you can set Custom Constraints and set the SUM to be less than or equal to one. You can double-click on the Option/Project name to add the variable to the Expression box and use the relevant mathematical expressions (see example above).

TIP. ROVPROJECON Files

All your data, saved models, settings, simulations, optimizations, real options, scenarios, and analyses are saved as a single * .rovprojecon file. This file is actually an XML file type and can be read by PEAT. It is usually an optimized small file (except when you have significant amounts of data). Expert users can open and edit these files directly (e.g., drag and drop the *.rovprojecon file into Notepad or other XML editors) but for most users, we recommend using PEAT to make any edits as any errors introduced into this file will corrupt it and render it unusable.

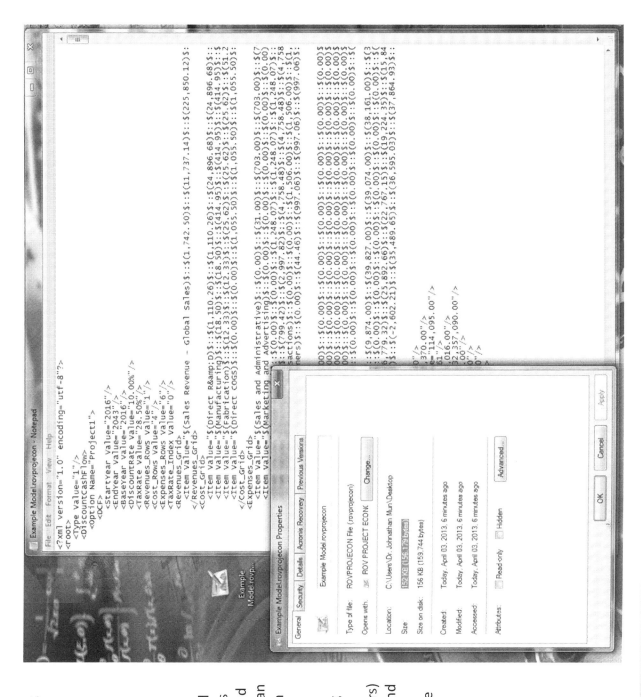

TIP. Advanced Data Encryption [FILE | PASSWORD ENCRYPT]

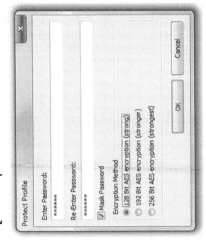

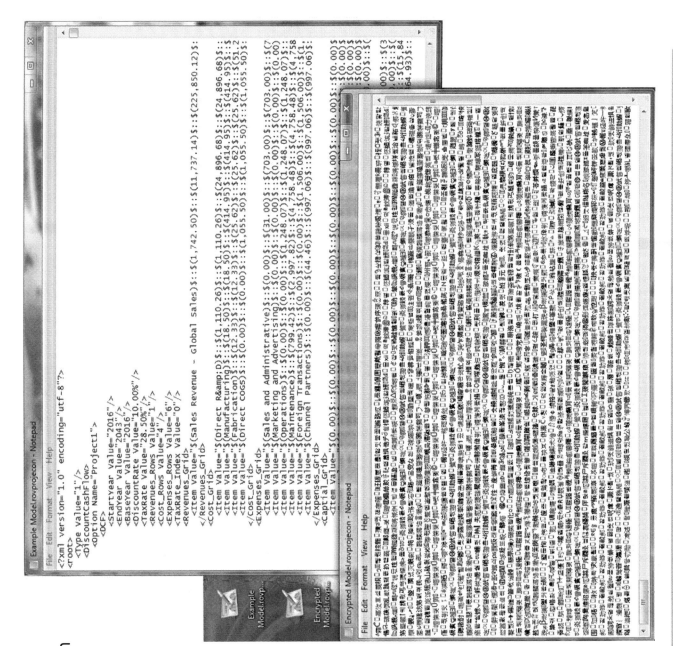

You can encrypt the *.rovprojecon file and provide it a password. Opening the file in an XML editor will show unreadable and undecipherable encrypted codes (military strength 256 bit encryption). Any attempt to open the file in PEAT will fail unless you have the correct password. This allows you to keep your data and models safe, but do not forget your passwords otherwise you would not be able to open the models yourself!

TIP. Dashboard: Remember to first run simulations and other models

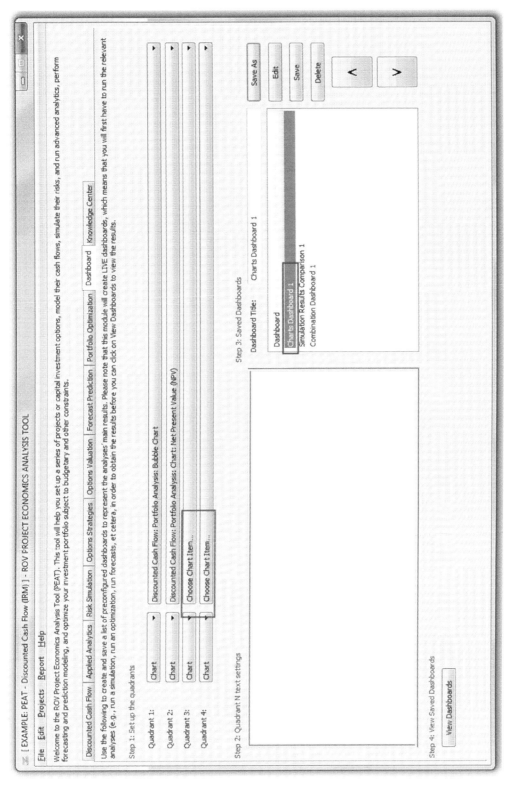

If you have previously saved or are currently creating some new dashboards, certain items may not be available on the droplist unless the relevant analyses are first run prior to coming to the Dashboard tab. For instance, simulation results charts are available for selection only after a risk simulation has been run.

TIP. Running a report
[REPORT | REPORT CONFIGURATION]

Before you run a report, make sure you have run the appropriate simulations, optimizations, real options, and other analyses you want reported. Otherwise, the report for these models may return empty sheets.

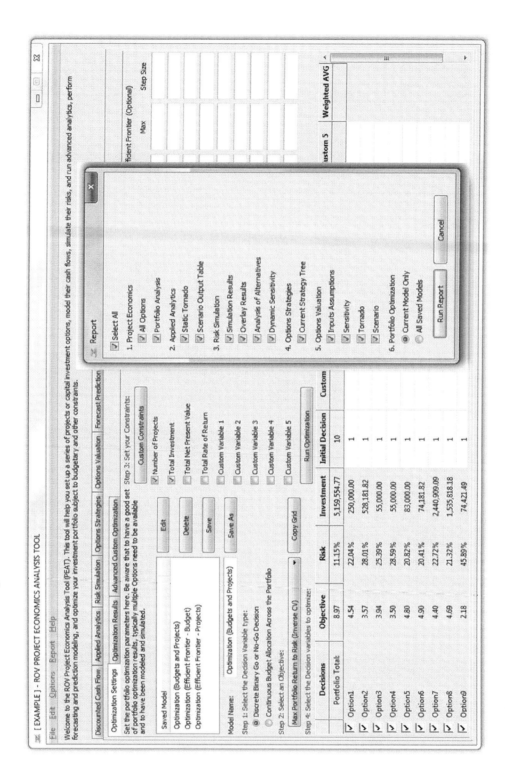

Give the software control of your computer! Right after you click Run Report, please keep your hands off the mouse and keyboard! The software needs to have control of your computer to generate reports, otherwise it will "compete" with you for control and lose...

MOST COMMONLY USED DISTRIBUTIONS

NORMAL
Continuous bell curve, a.k.a. Gaussian distribution, infinite tails on both ends, requires mean and standard deviation as inputs. Symmetrical with zero skew and zero excess kurtosis. Examples: stock returns, height, weight, IQ (most are truncated normal with limits).

BINOMIAL
Discrete events with two mutually exclusive and independent outcomes with fixed probability of success at each successive trial. Symmetrical and approaches normal distribution with high number of trials. Example: tossing a coin multiple times.

TRIANGULAR
Looks like a triangle, continuous values, tails end at min and max with most likely as its peak. Can be skewed or symmetrical, with negative excess kurtosis (truncated tails). Examples: sales forecasts, subject matter estimates, management assumptions.

POISSON
Discrete events occurring independently with the same average rate of repetition, and measured in time or space (area). Examples: sales forecasts, subject matter estimates, management assumptions. Approaches normal with high average rates.

UNIFORM
Flat continuous area with equal probability of occurrence at any point between the minimum and maximum. Symmetrical with zero skew and negative excess kurtosis (fixed end points). Examples: business forecasts and economic forecasts.

CUSTOM
Empirically-fitted discrete distribution when little data is available or when other theoretical distributions fail. Suitable for Delphi methods, can be multimodal and irregular. Examples: subject matter estimates, management assumptions, and qualitative estimates that are converted numerically.

LESS COMMONLY USED BUT IMPORTANT DISTRIBUTIONS

BERNOULLI
Single discrete trial version of Binomial (e.g., simulating success or failure of projects).

GUMBEL
Tail-end extreme value simulations of continuous outcomes (e.g., market crashes).

BETA 4
Highly flexible continuous distribution capable of taking on multiple shapes and scales.

LOGNORMAL
Variables with continuous non-negative and non-zero values (e.g., stock prices).

DISCRETE UNIFORM
Range of discrete events with equal probability of occurrence (e.g., rolling a six-sided die).

STUDENT'S T
Continuous NORMAL with fat tails or higher probability of extremes (e.g., risky returns).

EXPONENTIAL 2
High probably of low values, low probability of continuous high values (e.g., wait time).

WEIBULL 3
Continuous mean time before failure and reliability estimates (e.g., MTBF of an engine).

LEAST COMMONLY USED DISTRIBUTIONS

Arcsine, Beta, Beta 3, Cauchy, Chi-square, Cosine, Double Log, Erlang, Exponential, F, Fréchet, Gamma, Geometric, Gumbel Min, Gumbel Max, Hypergeometric, Laplace, Logistic, Lognormal 3, Negative Binomial, Parabolic, Generalized Pareto, Pareto, Pascal, Pearson V, Pearson VI, PERT, Power, Power 3, Rayleigh, Standard Normal, Standard-T, Weibull

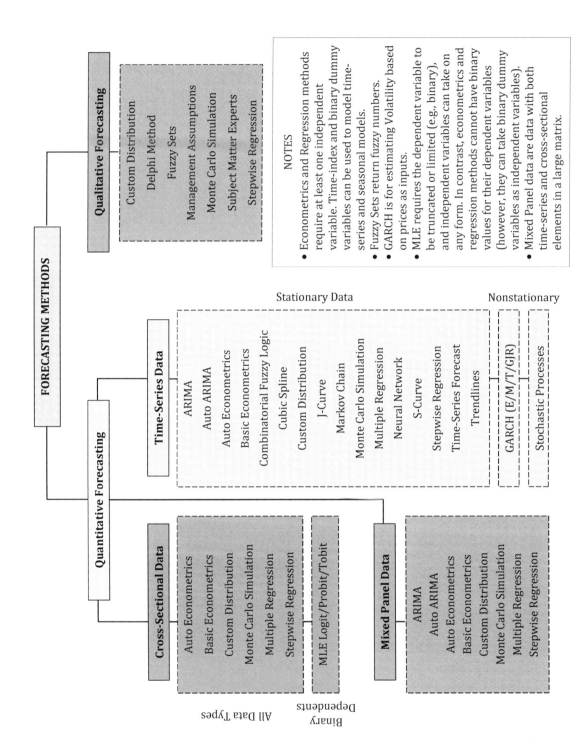

FORECASTING METHODS

Qualitative Forecasting
- Custom Distribution
- Delphi Method
- Fuzzy Sets
- Management Assumptions
- Monte Carlo Simulation
- Subject Matter Experts
- Stepwise Regression

Quantitative Forecasting

Cross-Sectional Data

All Data Types
- Auto Econometrics
- Basic Econometrics
- Custom Distribution
- Monte Carlo Simulation
- Multiple Regression
- Stepwise Regression

Binary Dependents
- MLE Logit/Probit/Tobit

Time-Series Data

Stationary Data
- ARIMA
- Auto ARIMA
- Auto Econometrics
- Basic Econometrics
- Combinatorial Fuzzy Logic
- Cubic Spline
- Custom Distribution
- J-Curve
- Markov Chain
- Monte Carlo Simulation
- Multiple Regression
- Neural Network
- S-Curve
- Stepwise Regression
- Time-Series Forecast
- Trendlines

Nonstationary
- GARCH (E/M/T/GJR)
- Stochastic Processes

Mixed Panel Data
- ARIMA
- Auto ARIMA
- Auto Econometrics
- Basic Econometrics
- Custom Distribution
- Monte Carlo Simulation
- Multiple Regression
- Stepwise Regression

NOTES
- Econometrics and Regression methods require at least one independent variable. Time-index and binary dummy variables can be used to model time-series and seasonal models.
- Fuzzy Sets return fuzzy numbers.
- GARCH is for estimating Volatility based on prices as inputs.
- MLE requires the dependent variable to be truncated or limited (e.g., binary), and independent variables can take on any form. In contrast, econometrics and regression methods cannot have binary values for their dependent variables (however, they can take binary dummy variables as independent variables).
- Mixed Panel data are data with both time-series and cross-sectional elements in a large matrix.

Real Options Valuation

OPTIMIZATION METHODS

STATIC
Runs optimization by iteratively changing the decision variables based on their allowed ranges to maximize or minimize the objective, while satisfying the constraints and restrictions imposed in the model.

DYNAMIC
Runs a Monte Carlo risk simulation, and the selected statistic (e.g., mean, Value at Risk, or percentile) is inserted into the model before optimization is run. This statistic accounts for uncertainties and variability in the inputs and model.

STOCHASTIC
Replicates dynamic optimization multiple times (i.e., simulate thousands of trials, statistics used in lieu of single-point-estimates, optimization run with multiple iterations, and the process is repeated multiple times). Distributions of decision variables are the result.

OPTIMIZATION INPUTS

OBJECTIVE
The outcome that is to be minimized (e.g., cost, schedule, error) or maximized (e.g., net income, profitability).

CONSTRAINT
Limitations or restrictions in the model (e.g., resource, budget, schedule, management constraints, risk).

DECISION
Variables or decisions you have control over (e.g., go or no-go decisions, % budget portfolio allocations).

ASSUMPTION
Uncertain variables to be simulated in dynamic and stochastic optimization (e.g., returns, demand).

EFFICIENT FRONTIER

Running multiple optimizations where each successive run perturbs and changes the constraints by some set amount to maximize or minimize the objective outcome while still satisfying the constraints and restrictions. The outcome is a set of multiple points that are the most optimal and efficient, and, when connected by a line, constitutes the efficient investment frontier, representing the best-bang-for-the-buck, where given the requisite constraints and restrictions, each point along the frontier is a portfolio of the best that can be achieved given the set of decision variables. The steep part of the frontier indicates it is better to pursue the higher constraint portfolio whereas, conversely, flat frontiers indicate diminishing marginal returns, and any additional resources provided to the portfolio will not significantly increase its overall portfolio objective.

STRATEGIC REAL OPTIONS

ABANDONMENT

Exit and salvage or sell the assets to cut losses, stop before executing the next phase after completing the current phase, contractual Termination for Convenience. To have an abandonment option, the holder must first own the asset.

BARRIER

The option comes in-the-money or out-of-the-money if the underlying asset value exceeds or does not exceed some pre-specified fixed or fluctuating contractual barrier. This option typically has lower value to the holder than a similarly specified option without the barriers. Combinations of single, double, upper, lower, knock-in, and knock-out barriers can be constructed.

CONTRACTION

Outsourcing, alliances, co-marketing, subcontractors, joint ventures, foreign partnerships, and other strategic relationships whereby cost is reduced and part of the asset's profits is shared with the partner. To have a contraction option, the holder must first own the asset.

EXPANSION

Platform technologies, mergers and acquisitions (new technologies, market, clients, or vertical solution), reusability and scalability, pre-investments, and pre-building facilities (faster and cheaper to pre-invest now then restart development in the future). To have an expansion option, the holder must first own the asset.

SEQUENTIAL

Stage-gate implementation of high-risk project development, prototyping, drug development phases, technology demonstration, contracts with multiple stages with the option to exit at any time, built-in flexibility to execute different courses of action at specific stages of development, milestones, R&D, and phased investments over time.

SIMULTANEOUS

Multiple assets or investments are executed simultaneously to reduce risks that one of these assets or projects fails. This is the same computation as a combination into a single asset for an option to wait and defer or execute. The result for Simultaneous options is typically less than Sequential options given the same parameters and asset valuation.

SWITCHING

Switching among multiple vendors, modular designs, multiple inputs or raw materials. This option allows production risk mitigation through multiple vendors and a strong industrial base, and takes advantage of market-based cost fluctuations. Negatively correlated assets tend to generate greater option values (portfolio diversification effects).

EXECUTION TYPES

American Options: Any time up to and including maturity date.
Asian Options: Backward-looking, time-specific.
Bermudan Options: Any time except during blackouts and vesting.
European Options: One time at maturity only. American ≥ Bermudan ≥ European except for plain-vanilla call options with zero dividends, where all values are identical.

WAIT & DEFER/EXECUTE

Proof of concept to better determine the costs, profitability, and schedule risks of a project. Holding on to the opportunity with contract in place while reducing large-scale implementation risks, low rate initial production, R&D, prototyping, and right of first refusal. Ability to wait and see for valuable information to arrive before deciding to execute the option if optimal.

Abandonment, Contraction, Expansion, and Switching options imply that the option holder currently owns the asset and, therefore, can sell it (abandon), reduce output and save on expenses (contract), expand upon it (expand), or change it out to an alternative (switch). Further, Switching options imply that the option holder can sequentially switch back and forth the underlying assets with some predetermined switching cost. Abandonment, Barrier, Contraction, Expansion, and Wait & Defer options typically have a single underlying asset, and can be executed in a single phase or multiple-phased Sequential option. Sequential options usually imply multiple phases (more than one) and a single underlying asset, and can be combined with the other types of real options. Finally, Switching and Simultaneous options imply more than one underlying asset exists and can be executed in a single phase at once or executed over time in a multiple-phased Sequential option.

Real Options Valuation

PEAT VISUAL GUIDE

VOLUME 8:
Custom Tab and Excel Links

Real Options Valuation

Instructions

This is a quick getting started guide on tips and tricks for using PEAT's Custom Worksheet.

- **Creating Multiple Custom Sheets: Duplicating, Deleting, Adding, Renaming Custom Sheets**
  - The custom worksheet is a math scratch area for your preliminary calculations
  - You can replicate your Excel models (multiple worksheets or multiple Excel workbooks) in this custom worksheet so that all the preliminary calculations linked to your project will be stored in one convenient place
  - You can insert multiple custom worksheets as required, and you can then edit, duplicate, rename, rearrange these worksheets

- **Replicating Excel Worksheets in Custom Worksheets without Equations (Numbers Only)**
  - Duplicating Excel worksheet models in PEAT (values only)

- **Replicating Excel Worksheets in Custom Worksheets with Live Equations (Computes/Updates)**
  - Duplicating Excel worksheet models in PEAT with live equations and links in the model

- **Supported Functions and Math Operators in Custom Sheets**
  - See the list of functions currently supported in the custom worksheets (more to come....)

- **Linking from Custom Worksheets to PEAT Models**
  - How to link from Custom worksheets to the actual PEAT models

- **Linking from Excel Files and Updating Excel Source Files**
  - How to link to a source Excel model and update these links when PEAT starts. This allows you to keep all the calculations and models in Excel and link the critical outputs and components into PEAT. If the Excel model is updated, the PEAT Custom worksheet will be updated as well.

- **Right-Click Shortcuts, Tips, Caveats, and Future Enhancements**

The CUSTOM worksheet tab can be used as a computational work area

[EXAMPLE] - ROV PROJECT ECONOMICS ANALYSIS TOOL

File   Edit   Options   Report   Tools   Language   Decimals   Help

Welcome to the ROV Project Economics Analysis Tool (PEAT). This tool will help you set up a series of projects or capital investment options, model their cash flows, simulate their risks, and run advanced analytics, perform forecasting and prediction modeling, and optimize your investment portfolio subject to budgetary and other constraints.

FPD Standard Economic | Applied Analytics | Risk Simulation | Options Strategies | Options Valuation | Forecast Prediction | Portfolio Optimization | Dashboard | Knowledge Center

Global Settings | Custom1 | Option 1 | Option 2 | Option 3 | Option 4 | Option 5 | Option 6 | Option 7 | Option 8 | Option 9 | Option 10 | Portfolio Analysis

Add Custom/Excel
Duplicate Custom/Excel
Delete Custom/Excel
Rename Custom/Excel
Rearrange Custom/Excel

Use this custom calculation
TO... then in the input work
assumption sheet location
changing to Formula View
Calculate.

...putations that will be saved with the current file that can also be linked to the input sheets (simply select the cells you wish to create a live link, right-click and select LINK
...ck and select LINK FROM... and choose the relevant inputs to use). Alternatively, select the cells you wish, right-click COPY and paste the contents into the relevant input
calculation sheet include: +, -, /, *, ^, ABS, LN, LOG, POWER, SUM, AVERAGE, MIN, MAX. A simple copy/paste from Excel will only paste the model's values, versus first
...copy/paste will bring over the Excel functions and computations as well. When pasting complex models in Formula View, we recommend temporarily turning off Auto

☑ Auto Calculate   Calculate   Grid...   Full Grid   Excel...   Refresh Links

Name:

	A	B	C	D	E	F	G	H	I	J	K	L	M	N	O
		2010	2011	2012	2013	2014	2015	2016	2017	2018	2019	2020	2021	2022	2023
1	Example Product Price Forecast														
2	Arabian Light - FE ($/Bbl)	8.66	9.04	9.38	8.07	7.91	8.77	9.74	9.31	9.30	10.44	9.99	10.49	11.55	12.81
3	Khuff Condensate - FE ($/Bbl)	7.41	9.23	8.82	8.97	8.63	9.15	9.18	10.24	9.79	10.37	11.13	11.40	11.55	11.98
4	Arabian Extra Light - FE ($/Bbl)	9.02	9.07	9.10	9.03	8.80	10.27	9.51	9.06	10.31	11.26	10.58	11.25	11.22	11.66
5	Arabian Medium - FE ($/Bbl)	8.79	7.90	8.51	7.70	9.20	8.13	10.00	10.22	10.79	10.02	10.30	11.40	10.67	11.74
6	Arabian Heavy - FE ($/Bbl)	8.68	8.30	7.75	8.34	8.37	8.69	10.03	10.14	10.15	10.18	10.38	10.42	10.75	12.56
7															
8	Average	8.512	8.708	8.712	8.422	8.582	9.002	9.692	9.794	10.068	10.454	10.476	10.992	11.148	12.15
9															
10	* Values above are														
11	for illustration only														

You can replicate your Excel models (multiple worksheets or multiple Excel workbooks) in this custom worksheet so that all the preliminary calculations linked to your project will be stored in one convenient place

Right-click on the CUSTOM tab to Add additional tabs, Delete existing tabs, Duplicate, Rename, and Rearrange Custom tabs...

Note that you can have multiple Custom tabs and rename them as you wish, each tab also has an internal name such as xls1, xls2, and so forth. These internal names are used in the software's internal algorithms as well as when you cross link cells (linking across different Custom tabs)...

You can Copy existing calculations/worksheets in Excel and Paste into the Custom tab

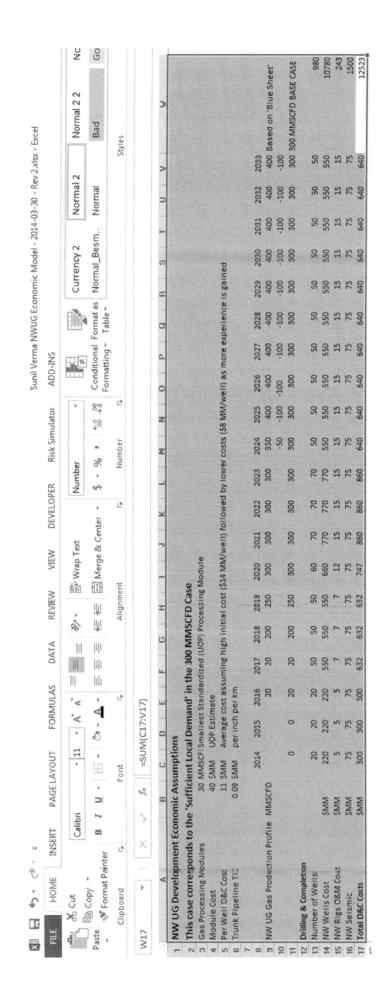

Simply select the cells/area in the Excel model/worksheet you wish to copy, then CTRL+C or right-click Copy or click on the Copy icon...

You can paste your Excel values and text into PEAT

[EXAMPLE 1 - ROV PROJECT ECONOMICS ANALYSIS TOOL]

File   Edit   Options   Report   Tools   Language   Decimals   Help

Welcome to the ROV Project Economics Analysis Tool (PEAT). This tool will help you set up a series of projects or capital investment options, model their cash flows, simulate their risks, and run advanced analytics, perform forecasting and prediction modeling, and optimize your investment portfolio subject to budgetary and other constraints.

FPD Standard Economic | Applied Analytics | Risk Simulation | Option 1 | Option 2 | Option 3 | Option 4 | Option 5 | Option 6 | Option 7 | Option 8 | Option 9 | Option 10 | Portfolio Analysis

Global Settings | Custom1 | Custom (xls2) | Options Strategies | Options Valuation | Forecast Prediction | Portfolio Optimization | Dashboard | Knowledge Center

Use this custom calculations sheet to perform your own intermediate computations that will be saved with the current file that can also be linked to the input sheets (simply select the cells you wish to create a live link, right-click and select LINK TO... then in the input worksheets, select the relevant input cells, right-click and select LINK FROM... and choose the relevant inputs to use). Alternatively, select the cells you wish, right-click COPY and paste the contents into the relevant input assumption sheet location. The main functions supported by this custom calculation sheet include: +, -, /, *, ^, ABS, LN, LOG, POWER, SUM, AVERAGE, MIN, MAX. A simple copy/paste from Excel will only paste the model's values, versus first changing to Formula View (CTRL+~ in Excel, i.e., control-tilde) and then copy/paste will bring over the Excel functions and computations as well. When pasting complex models in Formula View, we recommend temporarily turning off Auto Calculate.

Name: [300]   f(x) >> [300]   ☑ Auto Calculate   Calculate   Grid...   Full Grid   Excel...   Refresh Links

You can resize the column width.
Notice that the pasted results are values only.

	A	B	C	D	E	F	G	H	I
1	NW UG Development Economic Assumptions								
2	This case corresponds to the 'Sufficient Local Demand' in the 300 MMSCFD Case								
3	Gas Processing Modules	30	MMSCFD	Smallest					
4	Module Cost	40	MM						
5	Per Well D&C Cost	11	MM	Average cost assuming high initia...					
6	Trunk Pipeline TIC	0.09	MM	per inch per km					
7									
8	NW UG Gas Production Profile	MMSCFD	2014	2015	2016	2017	2018	2019	2020
9			0	0	20	20	200	250	300
10									
11									
12	Drilling & Completion								
13	Number of Wells		20	20	20	50	50	50	60
14	NW Wells Cost	MM	220	220	220	550	550	550	660
15	NW Rigs O&M Cost	MM	5	5	5	7	7	7	12
16	NW Seismic	MM	75	75	75	75	75	75	75
17	Total D&C Costs	MM	300	300	300	632	632	632	747
18									
19									
20									
21									

Then, select a cell in the Custom worksheet and hit CTRL+V or right-click PASTE to paste into the Custom worksheet... Note that only the LABEL/TEXT and VALUES will be pasted... Colors and formatting will not be included. If you wish to also paste a live model with equations, see the next few slides for details

You can also paste the MODEL with computations from Excel into the Custom worksheet PEAT

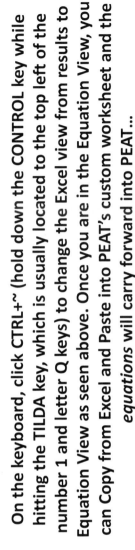

Suni Verma NWUG Economic Model - 2014-03-30 - Rev 2.xlsx - Excel

W17 =SUM(C17:V17)

	Unit	2014	2015	2016	2017	2018	2019	2020	2021	2022	
NW UG Development Economic Assumptions											
This case corresponds to the "Sufficient Local Demand"											
Gas Processing Modules	30	MMSCFD	Smallest Stand								
Module Cost	40	$MM	UOP Estimate								
Per Well D&C Cost	11	$MM	Average cost as								
Trunk Pipeline Tie	=90000/1000000	$MM	per inch per km								
NW UG Gas Production Profile	MMSCFD										
						200	250	300	300	300	
		=+C9+C10	=+D9+D10	=+E9+E10	=+F9+F10	=+G9+G10	=+H9+H10	=+I9+I10	=+J9+J10	=+K9+K10	
Drilling & Completion											
Number of Wells		20	20	20	20	50	50	60	70	70	
NW Wells Cost	$MM	=C13*B5	=D13*B5	=E13*B5	=F13*B5	=G13*B5	=H13*B5	=I13*B5	=J13*B5	=K13*B5	
NW Rigs O&M Cost	$MM	5	5	5	7	7	7	12	15	15	
NW Seismic	$MM	75	75	75	75	75	75	75	75	75	
Total D&C Costs	$MM	=SUM(C14:C16)	=SUM(D14:O16)	=SUM(E14:E16)	=SUM(F14:F16)	=SUM(G14:G16)	=SUM(H14:H16)	=SUM(I14:I16)	=SUM(J14:J16)	=SUM(K14:K16)	

On the keyboard, click CTRL+~ (hold down the CONTROL key while hitting the TILDA key, which is usually located to the top left of the number 1 and letter Q keys) to change the Excel view from results to Equation View as seen above. Once you are in the Equation View, you can Copy from Excel and Paste into PEAT's custom worksheet and the *equations* will carry forward into PEAT...

Be careful with the specific cell locations where you copy and paste. For example, if you copy cells A1:C10 in Excel, make sure to paste it into the same cell locations in the Custom tab so that the equations, links, and their computations will be preserved.

Real Options Valuation

Equations will be pasted into the Custom worksheet and be updated/calculated as live links

[EXAMPLE] - ROV PROJECT ECONOMICS ANALYSIS TOOL

File   Edit   Options   Report   Tools   Language   Decimals   Help

Welcome to the ROV Project Economics Analysis Tool (PEAT). This tool will help you set up a series of projects or capital investment options, model their cash flows, simulate their risks, and run advanced analytics, perform forecasting and prediction modeling, and optimize your investment portfolio subject to budgetary and other constraints.

FPD Standard Economic | Applied Analytics | Risk Simulation | Options Strategies | Forecast Prediction | Options Valuation | Portfolio Optimization | Dashboard | Knowledge Center

Global Settings | Custom1 | Custom (xls2) | Option 1 | Option 2 | Option 3 | Option 4 | Option 5 | Option 6 | Option 7 | Option 8 | Option 9 | Option 10 | Portfolio Analysis

Use this custom calculations sheet to perform your own intermediate computations that will be saved with the current file that can also be linked to the input sheets (simply select the cells you wish to create a live link, right-click and select LINK TO... then in the input worksheets, select the relevant input cells, right-click and select LINK FROM... and choose the relevant inputs to use). Alternatively, select the cells you wish, right-click COPY and paste the contents into the relevant input assumption sheet location. The main functions supported by this custom calculation sheet include: +, -, /, *, ^, ABS, LN, LOG, POWER, SUM, AVERAGE, MIN, MAX. A simple copy/paste from Excel will only paste the model's values, versus first changing to Formula View (CTRL+~ in Excel, i.e., control-tilde) and then copy/paste will bring over the Excel functions and computations as well. When pasting complex models in Formula View, we recommend temporarily turning off Auto Calculate.

Name: f(x) >   =SUM(D14:D16)

☑ Auto Calculate   Calculate   Grid...   Full Grid   Excel...   Refresh Links

	A	B	C	D	E	F	G	H	I	J	K
1	NW UG Development Economic Assumptions										
2	This case corresponds to the 'Sufficient Local Demand' in the 300 MMSCFD Case										
3	Gas Processing Modules	30	MMSCFD	Smallest Stand...							
4	Module Cost	40	MM	UOP Estimate							
5	Per Well D&C Cost	11	MM	Average cost a...							
6	Trunk Pipeline TIC	0.09	MM	per inch per km							
7											
8				2014	2015						
9	NW UG Gas Production Profile	MMSCFD		0	0	2016	2017	2018	2019	2020	2021	2022
10						20	20	200	250	300	300	300
11						20	20	200	250	300	300	300
12	Drilling & Completion										
13	Number of Wells		MM	20	20	20	50	50	50	60	70	70
14	NW Wells Cost		MM	220	220	220	550	550	550	660	770	770
15	NW Rigs O&M Cost		MM	5	5	5	7	7	7	12	15	15
16	NW Seismic		MM	75	75	75	75	75	75	75	75	75
17	Total D&C Costs		MM	300	=SUM(D14:D16)	300	632	632	632	747	860	860
18											
19											
20											
21											

See highlights above for the sample Equation View paste job. Please note that PEAT Custom worksheet now supports the main basic functions which are sufficient for most users. TIP: Turn off Auto Calculate before pasting a large model and turn it back on afterwards, for faster performance.

Supported Math and Functions in PEAT's Custom Worksheet: ABS, AVERAGE, CONCATENATE, LEFT, LEN, LN, LOG, LOG10, MAX, MIN, POWER, RIGHT, ROUND, SUM, SUMIF, SUMPRODUCT, IF, AND, OR, +, -, /, *, <

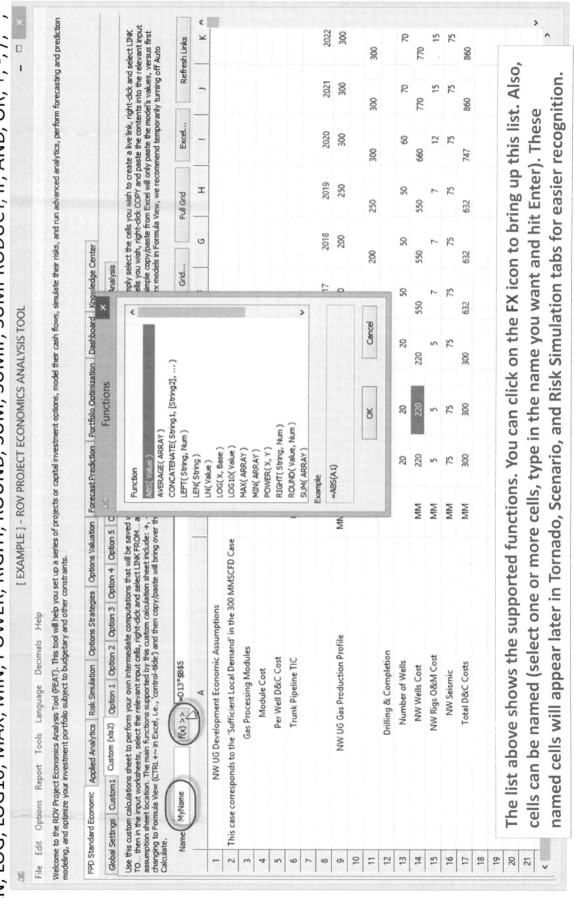

The list above shows the supported functions. You can click on the FX icon to bring up this list. Also, cells can be named (select one or more cells, type in the name you want and hit Enter). These named cells will appear later in Tornado, Scenario, and Risk Simulation tabs for easier recognition.

Linking from Custom Worksheets to PEAT Models: Step 1 is Link To

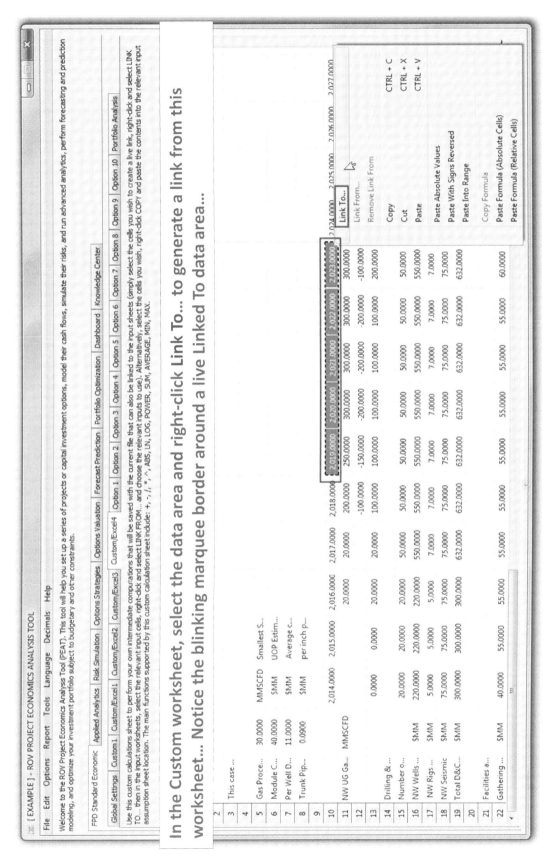

In the Custom worksheet, select the data area and right-click Link To... to generate a link from this worksheet... Notice the blinking marquee border around a live Linked To data area...

Linking from Custom Worksheets to PEAT Models: Step 2 is Link From

Select the cells/location you wish to link the data into and right-click then select Link From... You can also Remove Link later if required. Notice the Yellow highlights indicating a live link. Changing the values in the Custom worksheet will change the values here...

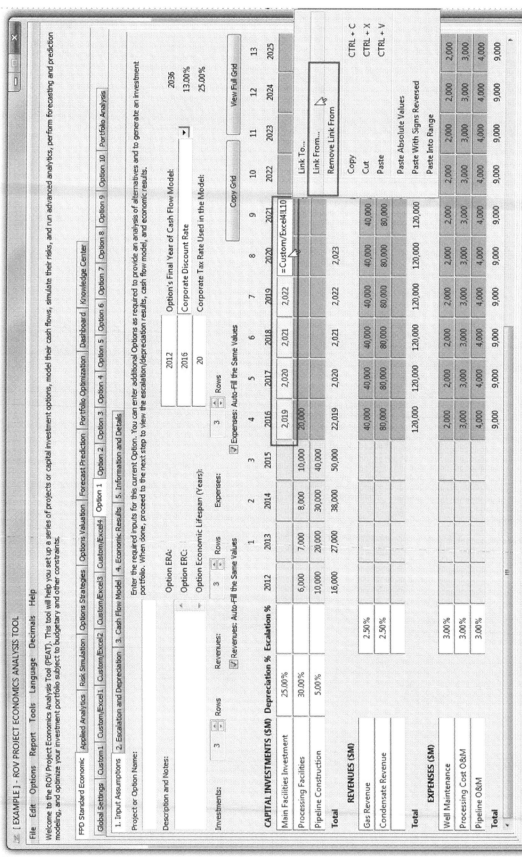

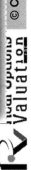

Linking from Excel Files and Updating Excel Source Files

In the Custom worksheet, click Excel [1] to Add [2] a new Excel link (or to Edit/Delete existing links). Then Browse to the Excel File [3] you need, select the Excel Worksheet [4] and Excel Cell Range [5] to link from, and enter the Starting Cell in the Custom worksheet to link to. Enter a Name and Notes for easy reference in the event you have multiple links (you can link multiple Excel workbook files and Excel worksheets) into one or more Custom worksheets...

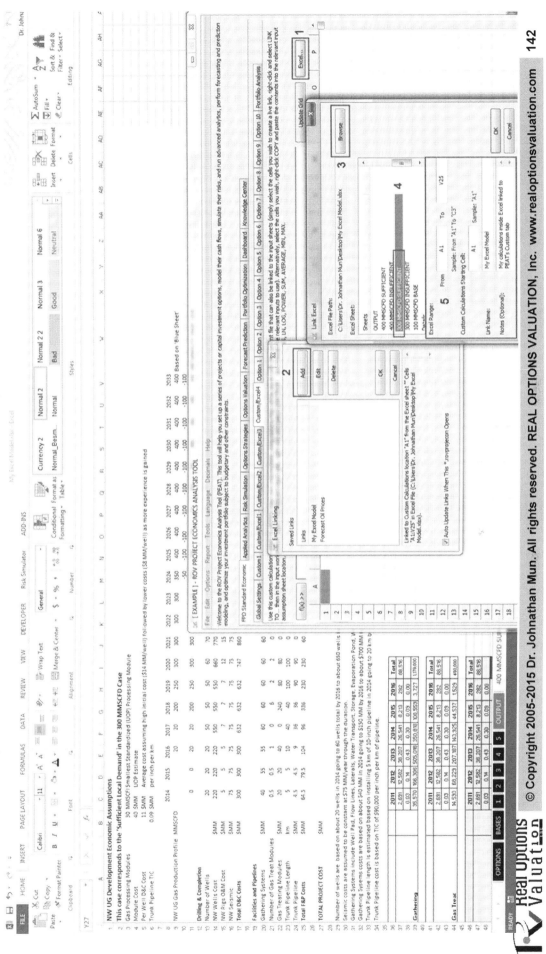

Right-Click Shortcuts and Tips: Paste and Setting Cells as Simulation Assumptions

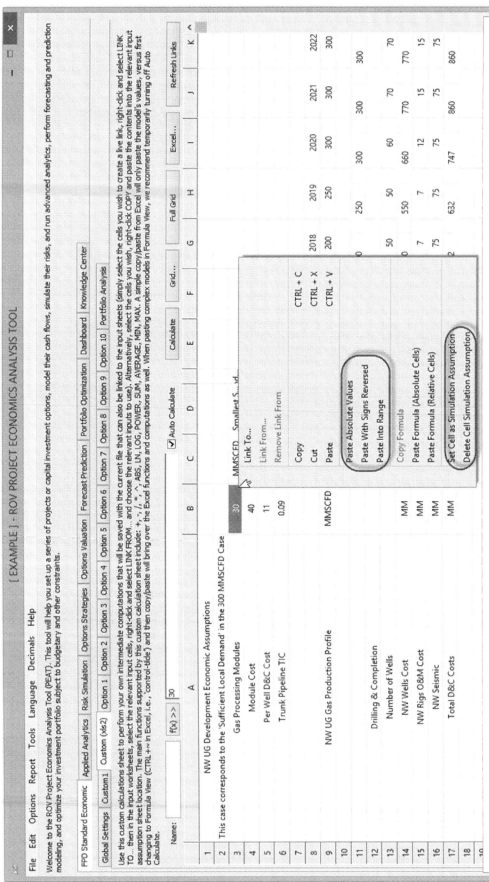

You can Copy Formula and then Paste the Formula with Relative versus Absolute cell addressing. This is the same as $ cell addressing in Excel. You can also paste data with Signs Reversed (e.g., expenses with -100 values will be pasted as 100 with signs reversed) or paste its Absolute Values regardless of signs. You can also select cells with basic input values and set them as Simulation Assumptions. These cells will turn green and show up later in the Risk Simulation | Set Input Assumptions tab.

Additional Tips

The following are reminders, tips, and caveats for using the PEAT Custom worksheet:

- Use the Up/Down/Left/Right arrows on the keyboard to navigate the data grid

- Use F2 or double click on a cell to access the contents of the cell for editing

- Click on the top left corner of the data grid to select all cells at once

- You can increase/decrease the column width as required

- You can click on and select multiple rows or columns at once

- Do not change the source Excel file name or folder location if you are performing a live link from Excel

- By default the Live Links from source Excel files are updated every time the *.rovprojecon file opens (this checkbox is default selected when you click on the Excel button in the Custom worksheet)

- Live Excel links when updating, will locate the same file name in the absolute folder path (e.g., c:\your folder\subfolder name\filename.xlsx) first and if the file does not exist, it will locate the same file name in the relative folder path where your *.rovprojecon file is stored. The latter comes in handy when you have to e-mail the model file as well as the Excel source file to another individual, and s/he may save the files in a different subdirectory/location/path but as long as both files reside in the same subfolder, the links will still update and work.

- The best way to update any externally linked Excel files is to SAVE and restart the *rovprojecon file.

- Manually inputted cells (black font) can be overridden easily by simply typing over the cell's values (type over the cell, double click, or F2 to access and edit the cell). Linked cells (blue font) are intentionally created to prevent accidental overrides (you cannot simply type over existing cell values) and you can only intentionally override Excel linked cells by selecting the cell and editing its contents in the Formula bar.

PEAT VISUAL GUIDE

VOLUME 9: SPEAR
Sales Performance Evaluation
Analysis and Reporting

"Getting Started"

RealOptions Valuation

Instructions

This is a quick Getting Started guide of tips and tricks for using the SPEAR Goals Analytics module.

SPEAR – Sales Performance Evaluation Analysis and Reporting is a suite of programs designed to offer insight into current Sales productivity and forecasts for success per periods of interest.

– The software has sophisticated computations packaged within easy-to-use templates that allow sales analysts to concentrate on the information identified in the graphs and spreadsheets.

– The first step in the use of SPEAR is the transfer of data on the sales performance of the Departments/Teams/Individuals of interest. This set-up exercise is described in the following slides.

– Information presented within the SPEAR graphics can be exported for presentation and/or specifically selected for further in-depth analysis.

Global Settings is the initial screen for information import including the aspects of sales performance that are of interest.

A. DEFAULT SETTINGS – Select either Individual, Teams, Departments or Corporate.

    A2. Select Default Date, Time – This is the reporting period of interest.

    A3. Select the Default KPI – The performance measures can be chosen (any number) but must sum to 100%.

    A4. Select the Performance Integers for review. Any or all as shown.

B. The database as received from the external source can be Excel; can use Copy/Paste to apply. Set the number of rows required. Load a list of the sales organization, Individual, Team and Department.

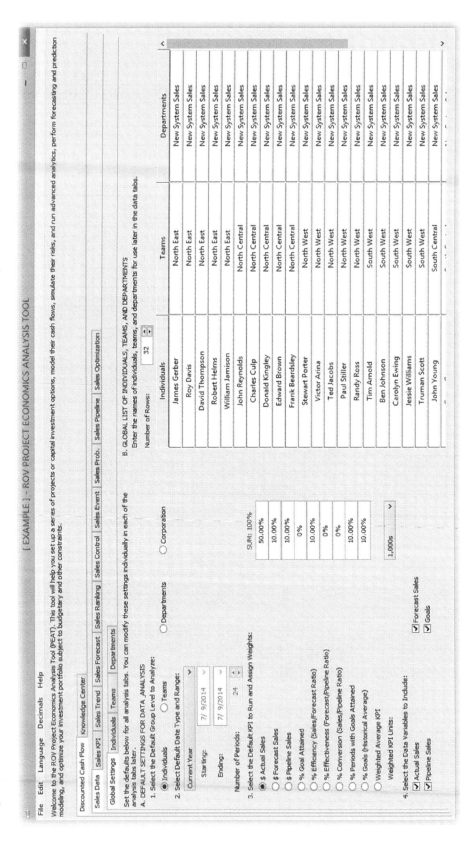

Sales Data/Individuals must be loaded from an external source as a separate step from the initial load of the sales Individuals/Teams/Departments.

1. Name the dataset to be loaded.
2. Load the dataset from an external source using Excel and Copy/Paste.
3. Select the variable types to be reviewed.
4. The data grid views will allow display the information by Individual or data element.
5. Select the period of interest. The data load can be for multiple periods.

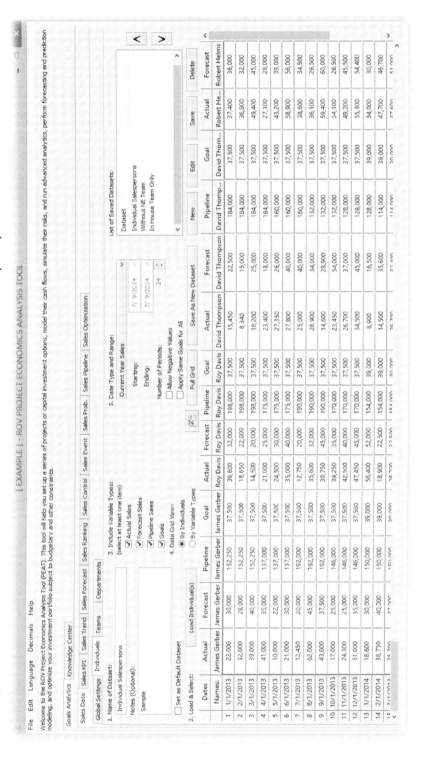

Sale Data/Teams is the same data loaded but summarized at the Teams level.

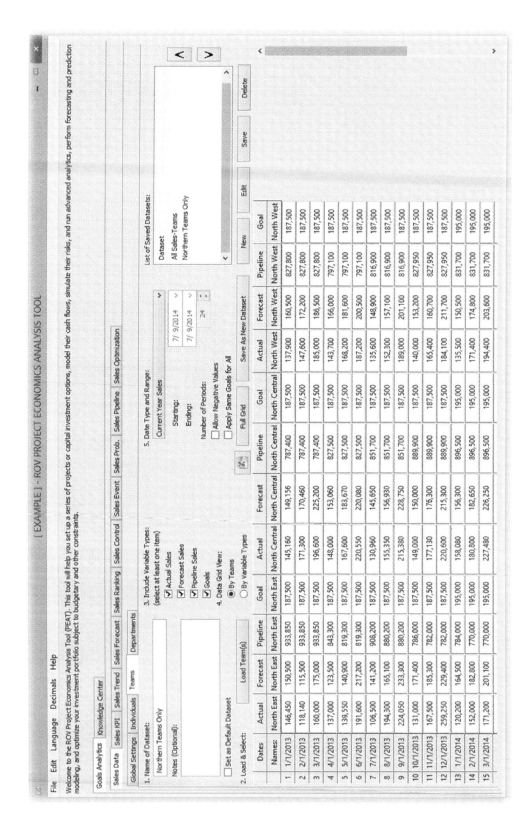

Sales Data/Departments is the same data as originally loaded but summarized at the Department level.

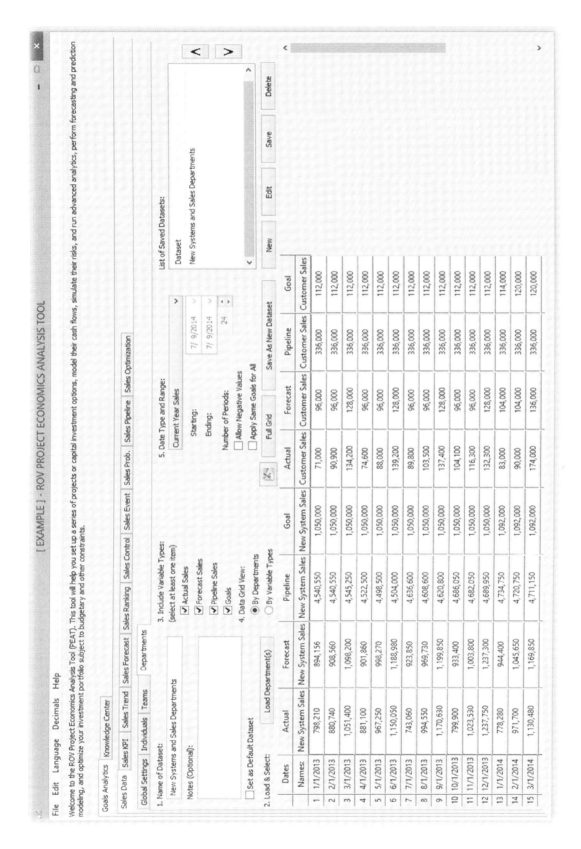

Real Options
Valuation

Sales KPI is the initial level of analysis. The data for actual sales is compared with the loaded calculation from the Sales Data tab.

1. Select the Analysis level.
2. Select the KPI components and the analysis by Individual or Summary.
3. Select the Period of review.
4. Select the Ranking element (example: date sequence).
5. Use the Name and Notes sections for identification of the data set version.

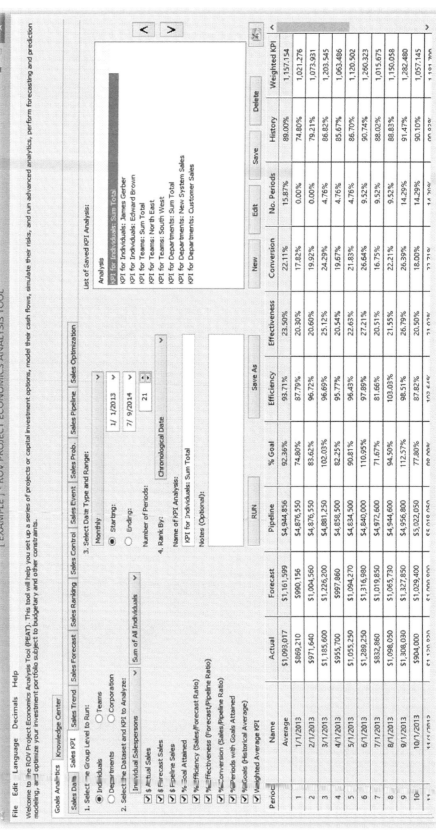

Sales Trend is the third tab and is used for describing the movement of actual results per period.

1. Select the Analysis level.
2. Select the Dataset as identified in the Sales Data input process and Summary level.
3. Select the Period of review
4. Select the KPI factor; choose one.
5. The analysis is graphed for review.

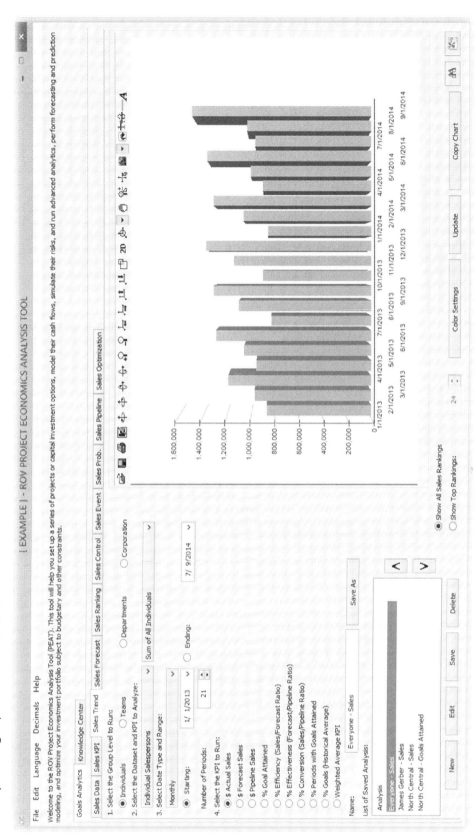

Sales Forecast/Time Series Chart is the analysis that provides a forward view of probable outcome based on historic success (also selectable for graph formats for Trendline and Time Series Forecast).

1. Select the Analysis Level.
2. Select the dataset for review as identified in the Sale Data input process and Summary level.
3. Select the Period of review. 4. Select the particular KPI for analysis.
5. Select the "Trendline", which is the number of periods consolidated.
6. Select the "Forecast Model" from the choices of Trendline, Time Series and Time Series Forecast.

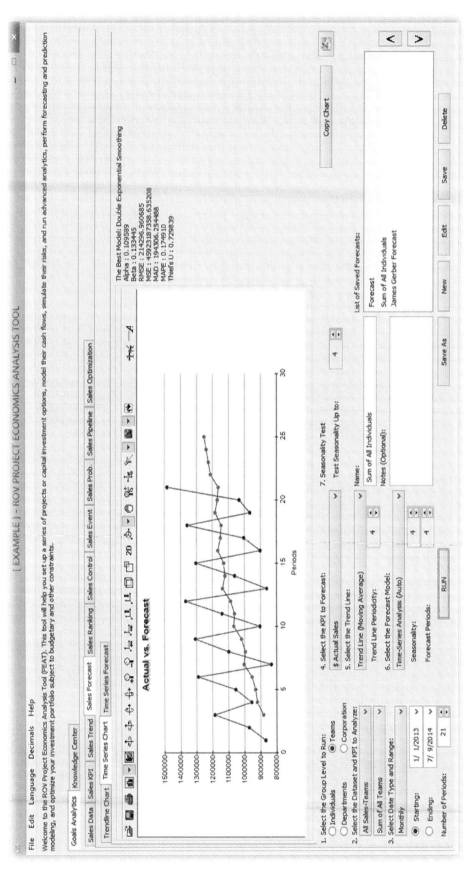

Sales Ranking is the analysis that provides for a sequencing of entities based on results.

1. Select the Analysis level.
2. Select the Dataset for review from among those saved and labeled.
3. Select the period of review.
4. Select the ranking criteria from the dropdown list.
5. Select the "Bubble Chart" setting for presentation. This labels the x and y axis

Rankings are displayed per the charts and list formats.

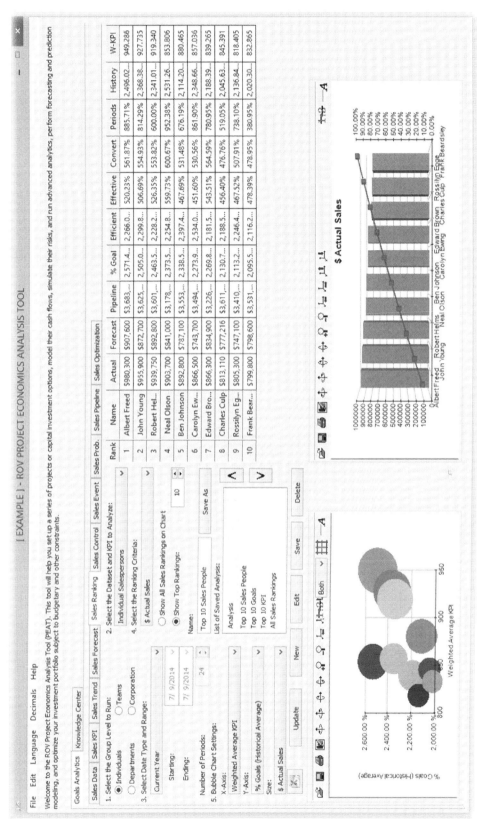

Sales Control is the analysis that provides a graph view of sales performance variations per periods.

1. Select the Analysis level.
2. Select the dataset, sales individual(s) and KPI component to review.
3. Select the period of review and/or the number of periods reviewed together.

Information charted shows the swings in sales performance per period and rates changes per statistical limits.

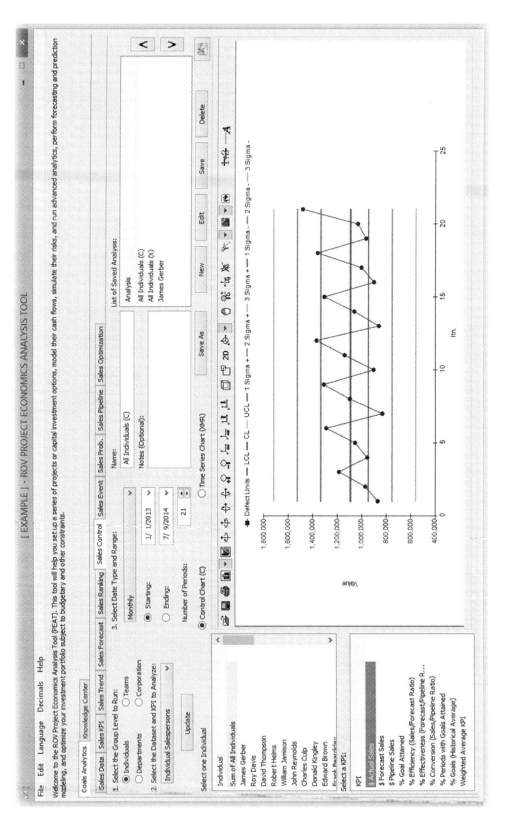

Real Options
Valuation

Sales Event is the analysis that provides a valuation of specific supportive functions intended to increase sales performance.

1. At least 2 variables must be entered in the chart (first set the rows that will be included in the variable database).
2. Select the Period of review.
3. Select one scenario that best defines the relationship of the data.
4. Select the 2 variables that will be compared.

The information significance is presented in the lower window.

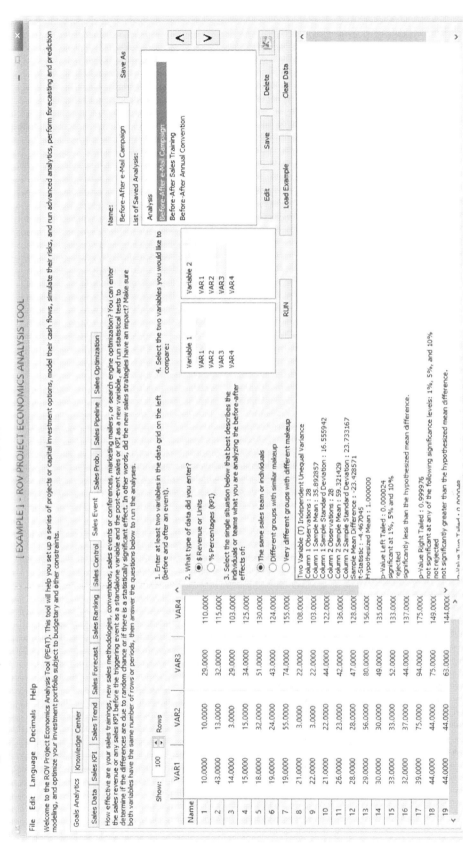

Sales Probability is the analysis that calculates probability for reaching particular thresholds of success.

1. The elements on the left of the screen allow for entry of the assumptions.
2. The list produced will rate the probability of success.
3. The charts describe the probability against monetary thresholds.

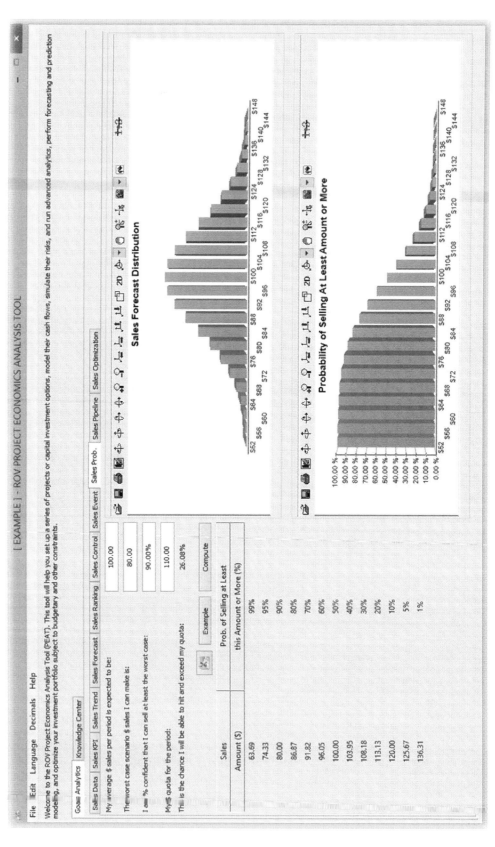

Sales Pipeline is the analysis of the value and movement of the backlog of prospects feeding the sales process. The Pipeline Data tab is the setup function for initiating the review.

1. Data must be imported from an external source using Excel Copy/Paste functions.
2. The data can be edited once entered to maintain currency, i.e. Close status.

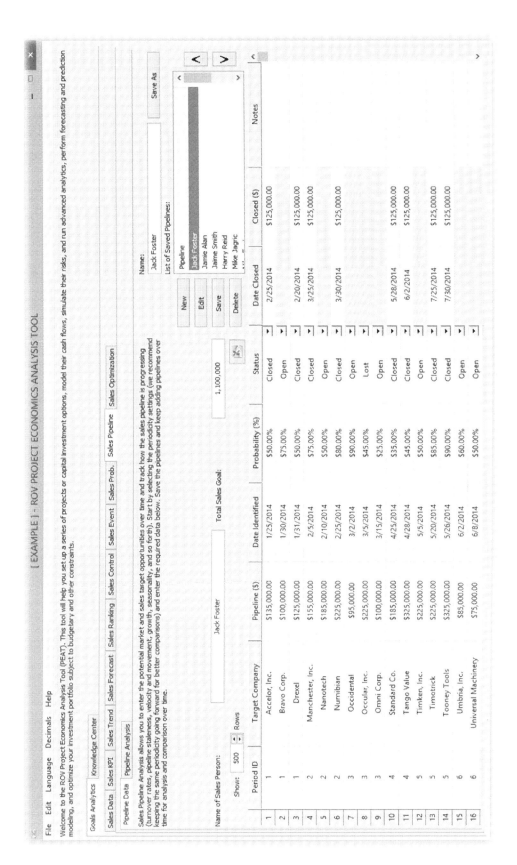

Real Options Valuation

Sales Pipeline/Pipeline Analysis is the function of calculating critical performance factors to rate the value and currency of the pipeline per sales entity.

1. Select the Individual(s) to review.
2. Select the period to review.
3. Select the type of chart to graph.
4. The models produced can be saved for future review.

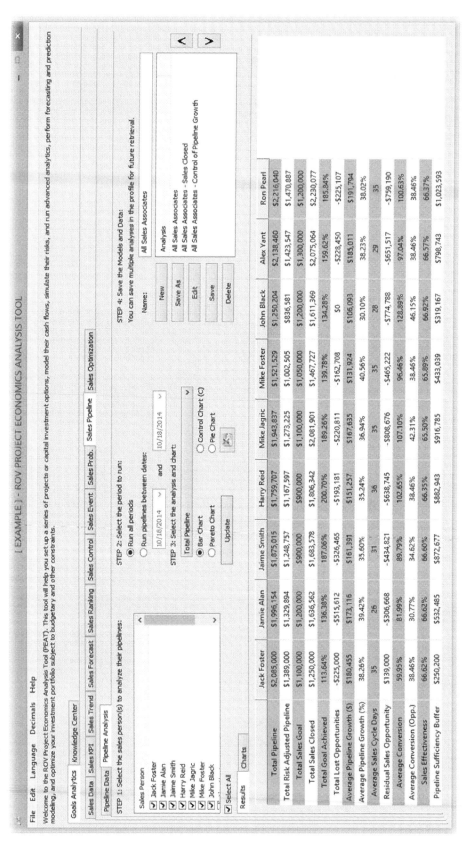

[EXAMPLE] - ROV PROJECT ECONOMICS ANALYSIS TOOL

	Jack Foster	Jamie Alan	Jaime Smith	Harry Reid	Mike Jagric	Mike Foster	John Black	Alex Vant	Ron Pearl
Total Pipeline	$2,085,000	$1,996,154	$1,875,015	$1,759,707	$1,943,837	$1,521,529	$1,250,204	$2,138,460	$2,216,040
Total Risk Adjusted Pipeline	$1,389,000	$1,329,894	$1,248,757	$1,167,597	$1,273,225	$1,002,505	$836,581	$1,423,547	$1,470,887
Total Sales Goal	$1,100,000	$1,200,000	$900,000	$900,000	$1,100,000	$1,050,000	$1,200,000	$1,300,000	$1,200,000
Total Sales Closed	$1,250,000	$1,636,562	$1,683,578	$1,806,342	$2,081,901	$1,467,727	$1,611,369	$2,075,064	$2,230,077
Total Goal Achieved	113.64%	136.38%	187.06%	200.70%	189.26%	139.78%	134.28%	159.62%	185.94%
Total Lost Opportunities	-$225,000	-$515,612	-$326,465	-$193,181	-$220,811	-$162,708	$0	-$228,450	-$225,107
Average Pipeline Growth ($)	$180,455	$173,116	$161,393	$151,257	$167,635	$131,924	$106,093	$185,011	$191,794
Average Pipeline Growth (%)	38.26%	39.42%	35.60%	35.24%	36.94%	40.56%	30.10%	38.23%	38.02%
Average Sales Cycle Days	35	26	31	36	35	35	28	29	35
Residual Sales Opportunity	$139,000	-$306,668	-$434,821	-$638,745	-$808,676	-$465,222	-$774,788	-$651,517	-$759,190
Average Conversion	59.95%	81.99%	89.79%	102.65%	107.10%	96.46%	128.89%	97.04%	100.63%
Average Conversion (Opp.)	38.46%	30.77%	34.62%	38.46%	42.31%	38.46%	46.15%	38.46%	38.46%
Sales Effectiveness	66.62%	66.62%	66.60%	66.35%	65.50%	65.89%	66.92%	66.57%	66.37%
Pipeline Sufficiency Buffer	$250,200	$532,485	$872,677	$882,943	$916,785	$433,039	$319,167	$798,743	$1,023,593

Sales Pipeline/Pipeline Analysis provides charting to rate the value of various sales entities Pipelines and display by rank.

1. Select the particular Individuals to review.

2. Select the period to review.

3. Select the chart format to display.

4. The models created can be saved for future review.

The chart displayed shows the Pipelines in order of value and labeled per sales entity.

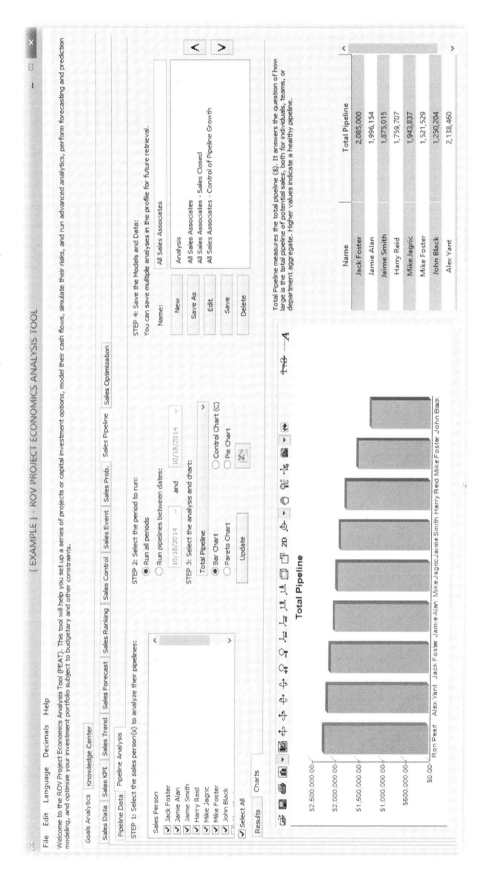

Sales Optimization/Standard Analysis is the function providing scenarios for maximization of staff and plans.

1. Inputs are requested to define thresholds as maximum and minimum sales potential.
2. Calculations are made on Sales potential as a forecast and probability of sales success.
3. Simulations provide a ranking of staffing levels to meet success goals.

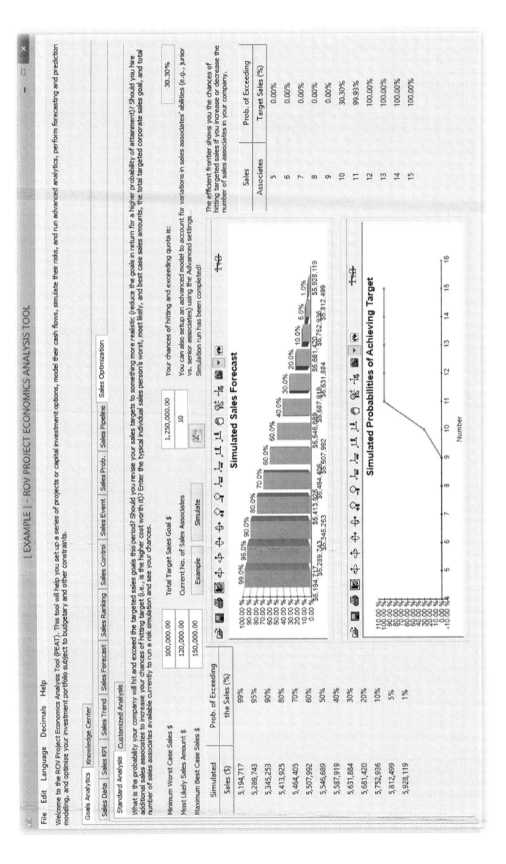

Real Options Valuation

Sales Optimization/Customized Analysis is the functions for allowing the setting of factors per sales entity.

1. The type of distribution (charting) is selected.
2. Data can be entered or "copied" from an external data source.
3. Randomization of the simulation model is created with the selection of these 2 inputs.
4. The model can be named and saved for future review.

Pressing the "Simulate" button will initiate the run and display the results.

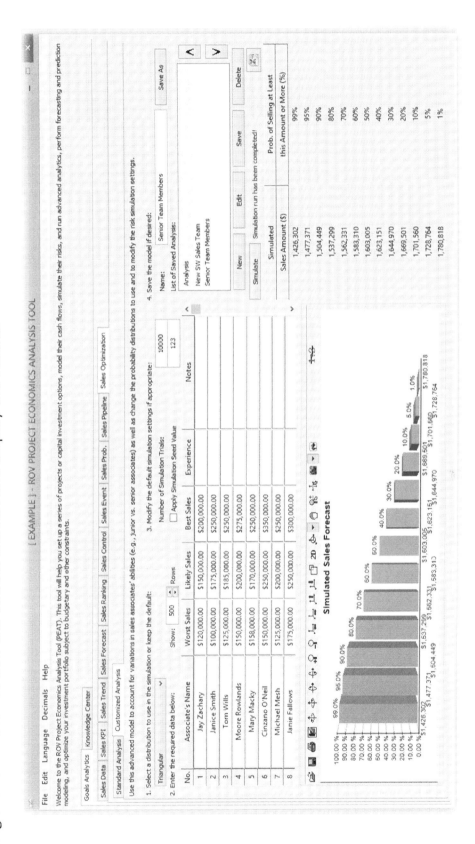

Real Options Valuation

PEAT'S ENTERPRISE RISK MANAGEMENT & RISK REGISTERS:

Key Features and Functions

Real Options Valuation

PEAT's Enterprise Risk Management: Risk Register

- Risk KRI. Global Settings of Risk Indicator Categories (1-5 or 1-10) with Customizable Color Coding of KRI (Key Risk Indicators) via a Risk Matrix that is customizable (colors, labels, and parameters are all customizable)

- Risk Division. Creation of multiple Divisions within the Company, such that the company can manage multiple risk profiles for each division

- Risk Taxonomy (G.O.P.A.D.). Creation and assignment of G.O.P.A.D. categories (geographic, operations, products, activity or process, and department) such that analysts can slide-and-dice the company's risk profile from multiple points of view, select from and create queries of specific G.O.P.A.D. to analyze, etc.

- Risk Categories. Creation of customized Risk Categories or use our library of predefined risk categories

- Risk Managers. Creation of persons in charge of certain risks, complete with contact information

- Risk Mapping. Creation and Linking of Risk Categories to one or more G.O.P.A.D.s and on to one or more Divisions. This allows the analyst the ability to view how a certain risk permeates through the organization as well as how a specific risk element may touch multiple departments, divisions, processes, and so forth.

- Risk Events. Allows simple data entry of risk events by dates, categories, counts, and generates comparative reports (month to month and year over year).

Real Options
Valuation

PEAT's Enterprise Risk Management: Risk Register

- Risk Registers. Creation of *multiple* Risk Registers where each Risk Register has *multiple* Risk Elements consisting of Causes of Risk, Consequences of Risk, Risk Mitigation Response, Risk Manager Assignments, Risk Category, Risk Status, Likelihood, Impact, Key Risk Indicators (KRI), Risk Dates (Creation, Edit, and Due Dates), Total $ Risk Levels, Residual $ Risk Levels, Mitigation Cost, as well as Multiple Risk Controls for each Risk Element with their respective % Weights and % Mitigation Completed.

- Risk Dashboards. Creation of the following customized Risk Dashboard views complete with reports, data grids, charts, and visuals, where analysts can select from a specific G.O.P.A.D., Division, Risk Category, or Risk Dates:

  - Risk Elements (viewing KRIs and Pareto charts)
  - Risk Maps (risk heat maps of KRI counts)
  - Risk Groups (risk accumulation by G.O.P.A.D.)
  - Risk Exposure (risk dials and dashboards of the selected category versus the entire Company)
  - Risk Taxonomy (top-down view to drill-down and see the structure of the corporation and its risk associations, versus a bottom-up view of how a specific risk permeates throughout the corporation)
  - Risk Inventory (running SQL queries to obtain the customized risk profiles and risk reports by Division, G.O.P.A.D., Risk Category, Risk Dates, and so forth)
  - Risk Probability (computing PDF and CDF of the probability of a discrete risk event occurring or continuous risk amounts based on historical experience)

Real Options Valuation

PEAT's Enterprise Risk Management: Risk Register

- Risk Engagements. Creation of *multiple* Risk Engagement projects where each of the following subsections has *multiple* Risk Elements:

  – Pre-Engagement Risks
  – Engagement Risks
  – Lessons Learned (Post-Engagement)

- Risk Diagrams. Custom creation of your own Risk Diagrams with ready-made templates on Bowtie Hazard Diagrams, Cause and Effect Ishikawa Fishbone Diagrams, Drill Down Diagrams, Influence Diagrams, Mind Maps, and Node Diagrams. Users can create multiple custom risk diagrams using this tool.

- Risk Controls. Determine if a specific risk event is in-control or out-of-control... For instance, if the number of risk events such as a plant accident spikes within a certain time period, was that set of events considered expected under statistically normal circumstances or an outlier requiring more detailed analysis?

- Risk Forecasts. Using historical risk data, analysts can now apply predictive modeling to forecast future states of risk, as well as Risk Tracking, Time Series Risk Forecasts, PDF/CDF Likelihood of Occurrence, Snapshots per period and over time

- Risk Mitigation. Determine if a specific risk mitigation strategy or technique is working, at least statistically speaking... Collect data from before and after a risk mitigation strategy is implemented and determine if there is a statistically significant difference between the two...

Real Options
Valuation

PEAT's Enterprise Risk Management: Risk Register

- Risk Sensitivity. Tornado Analysis helps identify the critical success factors or which risk element contributes the most to the bottom line risk profile of the company (or risk segment) by statically perturbing each of the risk element's financial risk levels

- Risk Scenarios. Scenario Analysis helps create multiple risk scenarios of your current or total risk amounts of individual risk elements to determine the impact on the corporate risk profile and create scenario heat maps

- Risk Simulation.

    – Simulation Assumptions. Run Monte Carlo Risk Simulations on your risk elements thousands to hundreds of thousands of times to generate probabilistic distributions and quantitative risk profiles

    – Simulation Results. Results from the Monte Carlo Risk Simulation run thousands to hundreds of thousands of times are presented as probability distributions and statistical moments, percentiles, and confidence intervals

    – Overlay Results. Overlay multiple risk profiles side by side to determine their respective impacts and uncertainty effects on the corporate risk profile

    – Analysis of Alternatives. Compare the simulated results of various risk profiles

    – Dynamic Sensitivity. Identify the contribution to variance and uncertainty of each risk element to the corporate, division or G.O.P.A.D. total as well as rank and identify the critical success factors or which risk element contributes the most to the bottom line risk profile when simulated in a dynamic setting

- Risk Reports. Auto generating Reports and extraction to Excel capabilities, as well as Pareto Charts, Risk Inventory, Risk Profiles by Division and G.O.P.A.D.

Real Options Valuation

PEAT's Enterprise Risk Management: Risk Register

- Risk Training. Knowledge Center slides, training materials, and videos are all fully customizable, including the following sections:

  - Step-by-Step Procedures
  - Basic Project Economics Lessons
  - Getting Started Videos

- Risk Security. Data Encryption and Foreign System Support. The software comes with a 256-bit encryption protocols to encrypt your Risk Database and supports foreign decimal settings (e.g., USA settings for one thousand dollars and fifty cents is $1,000.50 versus a Latin American peso of P1.000,50 with interchangeable decimal and thousand separators)

- User Manuals, Quick Getting Started Guides, and White Papers. The Help menu provides multiple Visual Guides, Whitepapers, and User Manuals to quickly get you started using the software.

- Additional Advanced Modules and Foreign Language Support. Multiple advanced analytical and decision analysis models accompany the PEAT software and complements the existing ERM module, including the Corporate Investment module, Project Management (Cost and Schedule Risk), and other relevant applications. The software also comes with multiple foreign language user interface.

ROV Risk Register software has two elements: a WEB module and a DESKTOP module. The Web module handles data inputs from multiple end-users and creates basic tables, as well as being able to extract/export to an Excel template; the data in this template is then used or copy/pasted into the Desktop module for additional advanced analytics. The Desktop module can also handle additional analysis and data inputs that the Web element cannot, and it can also Import the data from the Web module at the click of a button.

ROV Risk Register has a sophisticated Database management system to handle multiple RISK REGISTERS (individual risk elements), which then comprise diverse RISK CATEGORIES that make up different GEOGRAPHY / OPERATIONS / PRODUCT LINE / ACTIVITY OR PROCESS / DEPARTMENT (G.O.P.A.D.), where all of which rolls up to various DIVISIONS that ultimately form the CORPORATE level. Association of each of these entities with their respective Risks can maintain the alignment necessary for efficient execution of risk mitigation plans at all levels. This allows users to "slice and dice" their risk data and view results from various points of view (e.g., risks pertaining to a specific geography, department, manufacturing process, product line, risk category, etc.)

RISK REGISTER elements may be attached to one or more RISK CATEGORIES, and each RISK CATEGORY can belong to one or more G.O.P.A.D.'s, but these must roll up into various DIVISIONS and then up to the CORPORATION once.

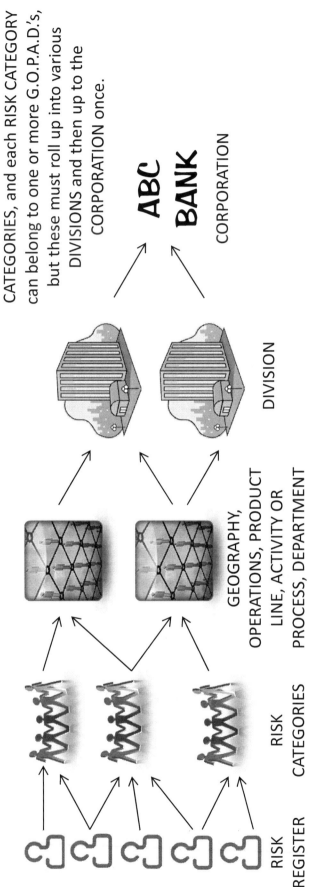

RISK REGISTER

RISK CATEGORIES

GEOGRAPHY, OPERATIONS, PRODUCT LINE, ACTIVITY OR PROCESS, DEPARTMENT

DIVISION

ABC BANK
CORPORATION

Real Options Valuation

The Risk Register segment includes risk items that users enter (information such as the name of the risk, short descriptions, who is in charge, risk mitigation techniques, date entered, required resolution date, etc.) and links to the relevant Risk Categories. Below is a simple example illustration. The Web module handles data collection from multiple users logged in and extracts to an Excel file. Our PEAT-based Desktop module will take care of everything else. As additional explanation and overview, this module is used to capture and model QUALITATIVE risks (e.g., how many thefts a year, chances of a fire at the power plant, etc.) and each risk item or element is given a number (1–5 integer scale or 1–10 integer scale, with 1 being LOW and 10 or 5 being HIGH) for Likelihood (chances it will occur) and Impact (financial, operational, economic, human resource cost). Likelihood x Impact = Key Risk Indicator (KRI). KRI is, therefore, 1–25 or 1–100 depending on which scale the user chooses to use.

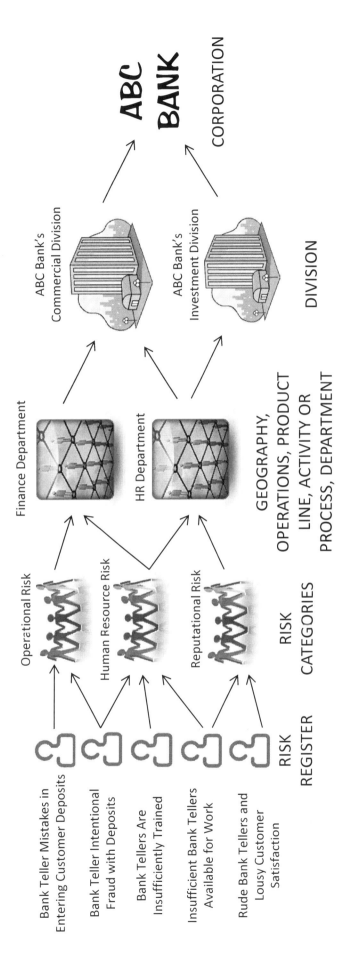

Risk KRI: Global Settings of Risk Categories (1-5 or 1-10) with Customizable Color Coding of KRI

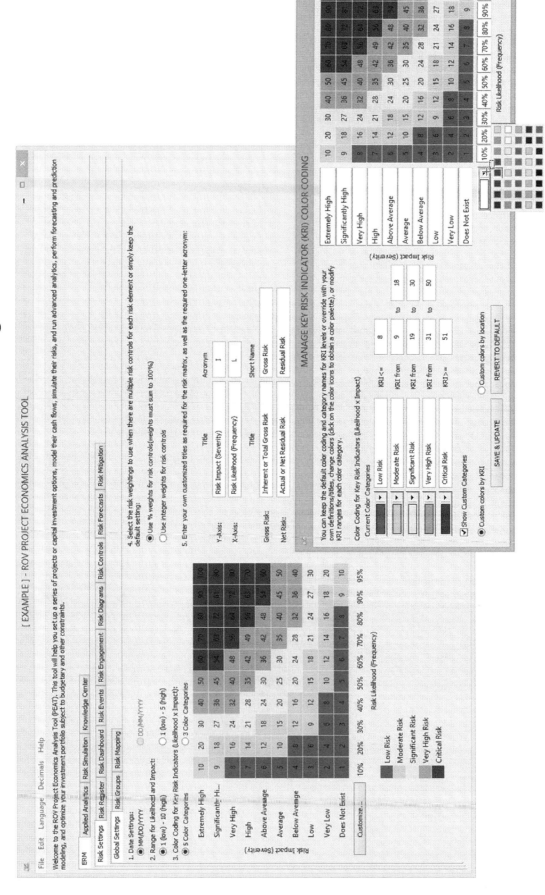

Global Settings allows customization of Risk Categories (1-5 or 1-10) with Customizable Color Coding of KRI, etc.

Real Options Valuation

Risk Divisions, Risk G.O.P.A.D., Risk Categories, and Risk Managers

[EXAMPLE] - ROV PROJECT ECONOMICS ANALYSIS TOOL

File   Edit   Language   Decimals   Help

Welcome to the ROV Project Economics Analysis Tool (PEAT). This tool will help you set up a series of projects or capital investment options, model their cash flows, simulate their risks, and run advanced analytics, perform forecasting and prediction modeling, and optimize your investment portfolio subject to budgetary and other constraints.

ERM

Applied Analytics | Risk Simulation | Knowledge Center

Risk Settings | Risk Register | Risk Dashboard | Risk Engagement | Risk Diagrams | Risk Controls | Risk Forecasts | Risk Mitigation

Global Settings | Risk Groups | Risk Mapping

Choose the risk level/hierarchy you would like to either manually add and edit individual items or copy/paste multiple entries at once in the data grid below. You should start by adding Divisions followed by G.O.P.A.D., then Risk Category and Risk Manager. Select the risk level to manage, then add a new or edit/search for an existing entry.

○ DIVISION
Division Name:
Acronym:
Location:
Notes:

○ G.O.P.A.D.
Type: Products
Item Name: BRG 225 Retail Development
Acronym: P-Croydon
Location: London, U.K.
Notes: Development of 225 retail units by the end of 2017

◉ RISK CATEGORY
Risk Category Name: Competitive Risk
Acronym: Competition
Status: Active
Notes:

[Load Risk Inventory Library]

○ RISK MANAGER
Risk Manager Name:
Acronym:
Title/Position:
Department:
Direct Dial:
E-mail:
Location:
Notes:

[Report]   [Save As New]   [Save Edits]   [Delete]

Edit	Name	Acronym	Notes	Status	Create Date
✓	Client Risk	Client		Active	3/13/2014
✓	Competitive Risk	Competition		Active	3/13/2014
✓	Compliance Risk	Compliance		Active	3/13/2014
✓	Concentration Risk	Concentration		Active	3/13/2014
✓	Cost Risk	Cost		Active	3/13/2014
✓	Credit Risk	Credit		Active	3/13/2014
✓	Cultural Risk	Cultural		Active	3/13/2014
✓	Economic Risk	Economy		Active	3/13/2014
✓	Financial Risk	Financial		Active	3/13/2014
✓	Foreign Exchange Risk	Forex		Active	3/13/2014
✓	Human Resource Risk	Human		Active	3/13/2014

Creation of multiple Divisions within the Company allows the company can manage multiple risk profiles for each division. Creation and assignment of G.O.P.A.D. categories (geographic, operations, products, activity or process, and department) provides the ability to slice-and-dice the company's risk profile from multiple points of view, select from and create queries of specific G.O.P.A.D. to analyze, etc. Customized Risk Categories or use our library of predefined risk categories. Creation of persons in charge of certain risks, complete with contact information

Risk Mapping: Creation and Linking of Risk Categories to one or more G.O.P.A.D.s and on to one or more Divisions.

Welcome to the ROV Project Economics Analysis Tool (PEAT). This tool will help you set up a series of projects or capital investment options, model their cash flows, simulate their risks, and run advanced analytics, perform forecasting and prediction modeling, and optimize your investment portfolio subject to budgetary and other constraints.

Based on previously created Risk Categories, G.O.P.A.D.; and Divisions, you can now map and link these hierarchies. Each Risk Category can be mapped to one or more G.O.P.A.D. and Divisions. Hold down CTRL key to select multiple items.

Edit	Risk Category	GOPAD Assignment	Division Assignment	Status
	Client Risk	P-Croydon	Europe	Active
	Competitive Risk	P-Dublin	USA	Active
	Cost Risk	D-Finance	USA	Active
	Cost Risk	D-Risk	USA	Active
	Cost Risk	P-Dublin	USA	Active
	Economic Risk	P-Saudi	ME	Active
	Financial Risk	D-Finance	USA	Active
	Human Resource Risk	P-Saudi	ME	Active
	Inflation Rate Risk	P-Saudi	ME	Active
	IT Risk	D-IT	USA	Active
	Legal Risk	P-Croydon	Europe	Active
	Operational Risk	P-Croydon	Europe	Active

This allows the analyst the ability to view how a certain risk permeates through the organization as well as how a specific risk element may touch multiple departments, divisions, processes, and so forth.

Risk Registers: Creation of Multiple Risk Registers

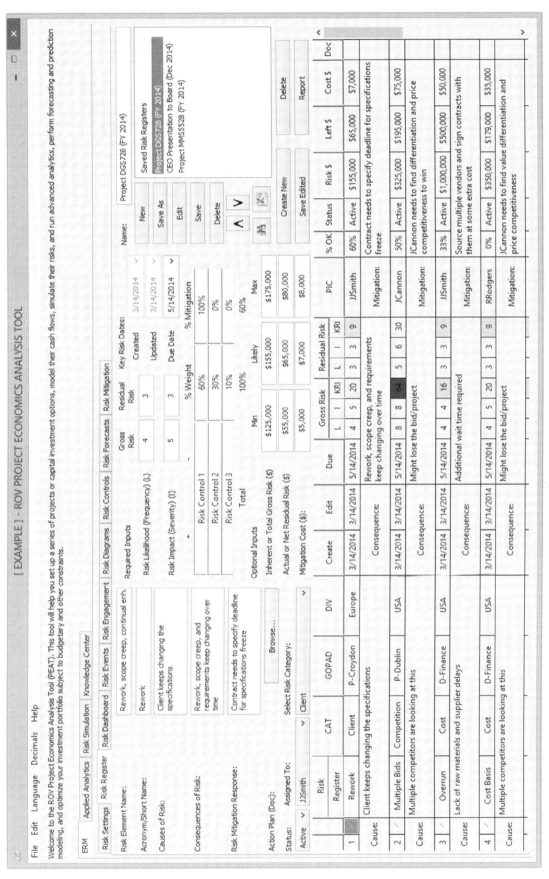

We allow the creation of Multiple Risk Registers where each Risk Register has multiple Risk Elements consisting of Causes of Risk, Consequences of Risk, Risk Mitigation Response, Risk Manager Assignments, Risk Category, Risk Status, Likelihood, Impact, Key Risk Indicators (KRI), Risk Dates (Creation, Edit, and Due Dates), Total $ Risk Levels, Residual $ Risk Levels, Mitigation Cost, and so forth.

Risk Dashboards: Risk Elements (Viewing KRIs and Pareto Charts)

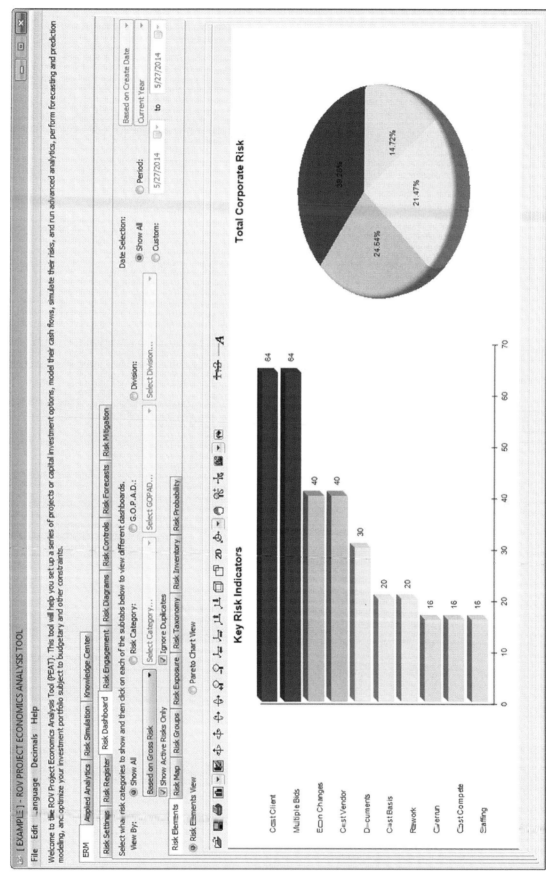

Creation of customized Risk Dashboard views complete with reports, data grids, charts, and visuals, where analysts can select from a specific G.O.P.A.D., Division, Risk Category, or Risk Dates.

Risk Dashboard: Risk Maps (Risk Heat Maps of KRI Counts)

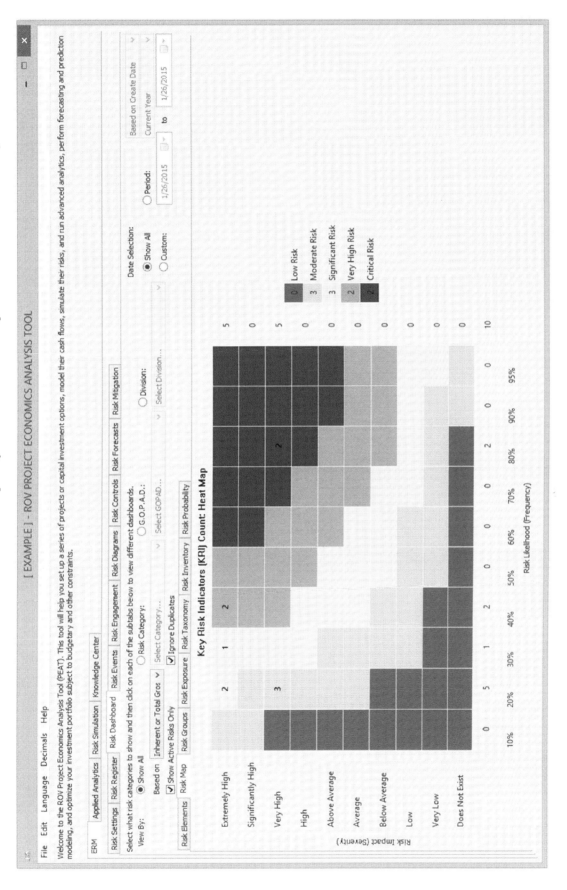

Risk Heat Maps of 5 x 5 or 10 x 10 matrices can be automatically created with customizable risk heat zones.

Risk Dashboard: Risk Groups (Risk Accumulation by G.O.P.A.D.)

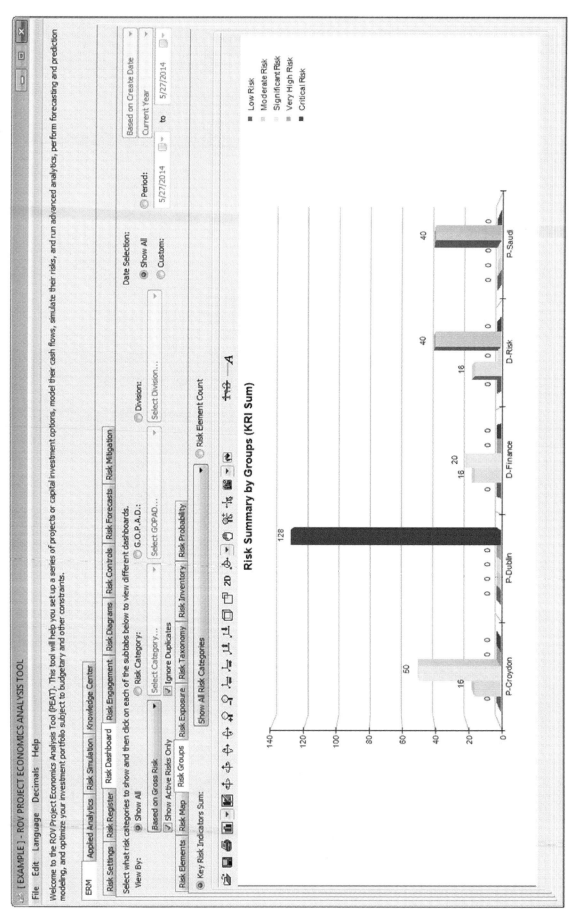

A bird's eye view of all G.O.P.A.D.s accumulated by KRI Sum and Risk Element Count within the active Risk Register

Risk Dashboard: Risk Exposure (Selected Category versus the Company)

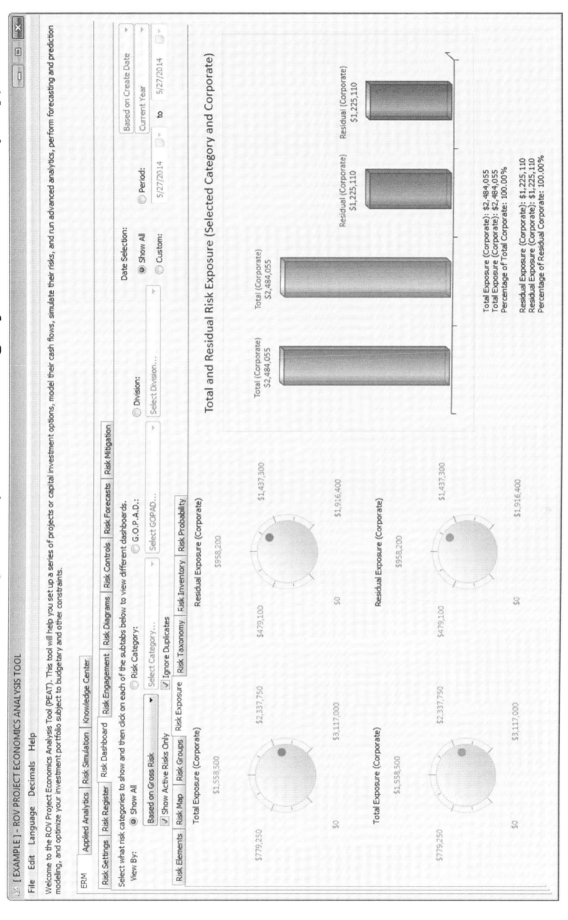

Risk Exposure provides a visualization using risk dials and dashboards of the selected category versus the entire Company.

Risk Dashboard: Risk Taxonomy

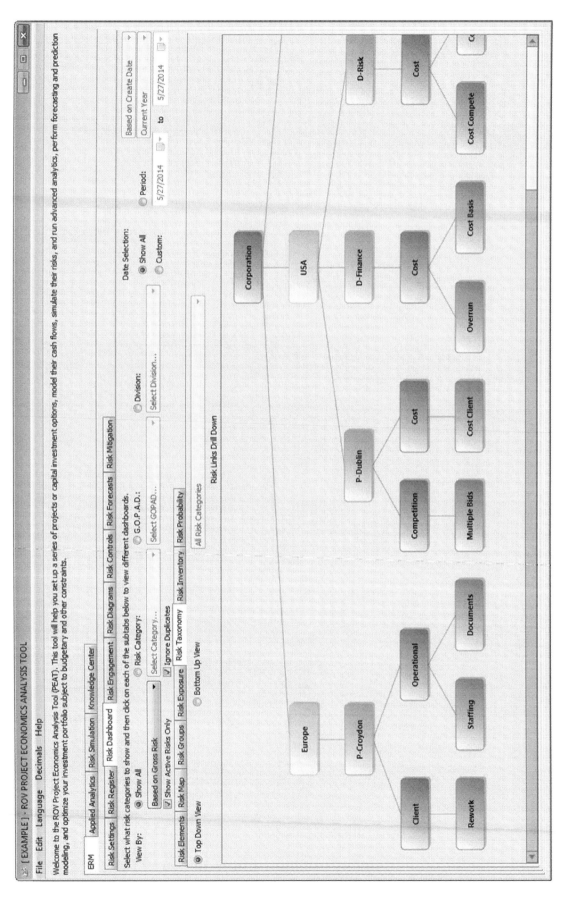

Risk Taxonomy (top-down view to drill-down and see the structure of the corporation and its risk associations, versus a bottom-up view of how a specific risk permeates throughout the corporation)

Risk Dashboard: Risk Inventory (SQL Queries)

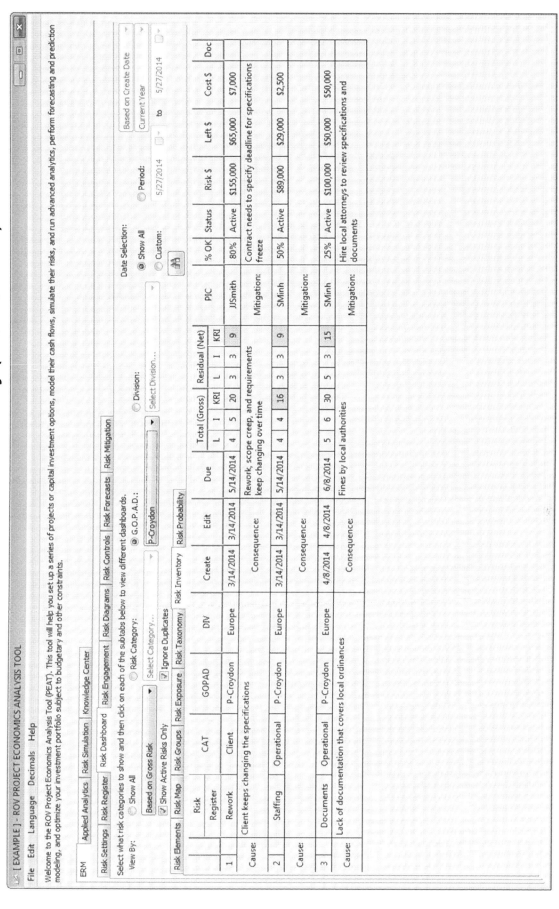

Risk Inventory (running SQL queries to obtain the customized risk profiles and risk reports by Division, G.O.P.A.D., Risk Category, Risk Dates, and so forth)

Risk Dashboard: Risk Probability (PDF, CDF, ICDF)

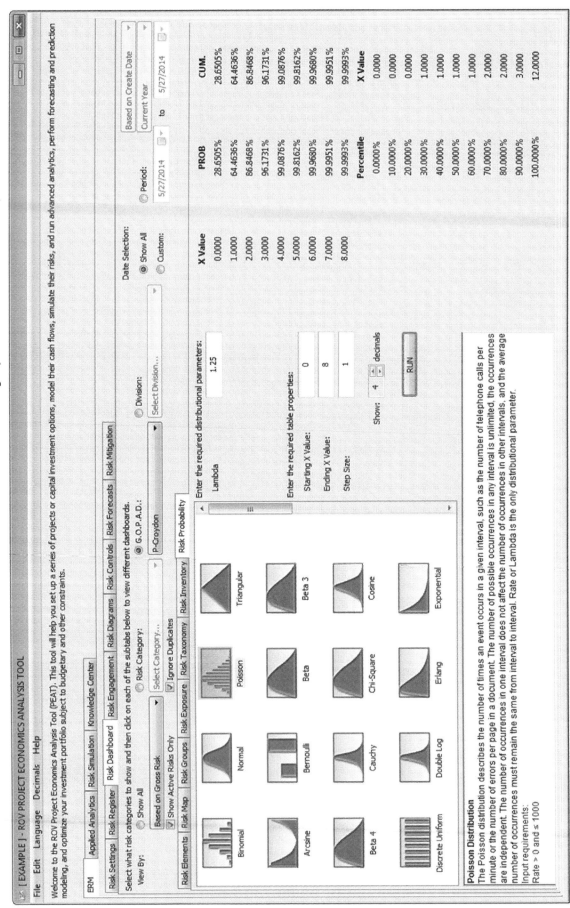

Risk Probability (computing PDF and CDF of the probability of a discrete risk event occurring or continuous risk amounts based on historical experience)

Risk Events: Simple and Customizable Risk Event Inputs

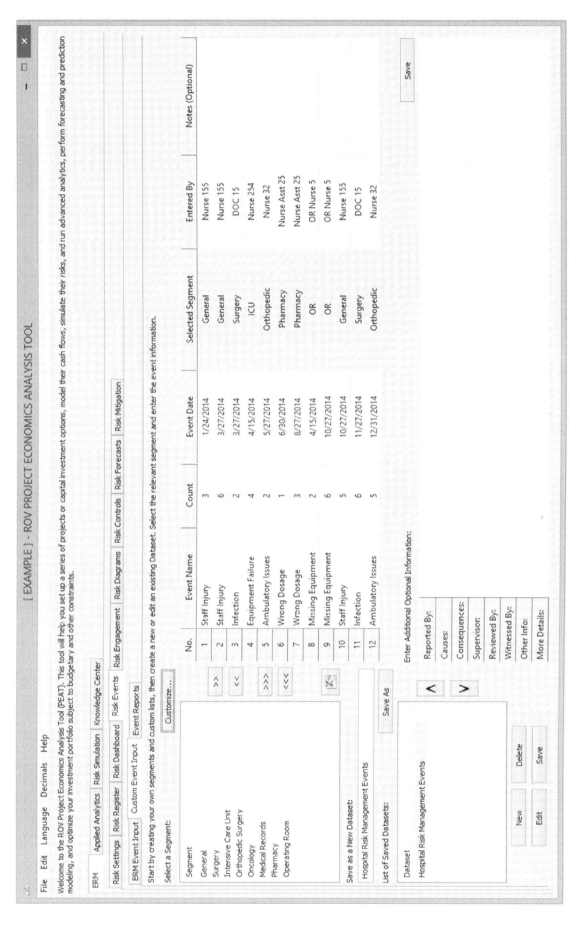

[EXAMPLE] - ROV PROJECT ECONOMICS ANALYSIS TOOL

File   Edit   Language   Decimals   Help

Welcome to the ROV Project Economics Analysis Tool (PEAT). This tool will help you set up a series of projects or capital investment options, model their cash flows, simulate their risks, and run advanced analytics, perform forecasting and prediction modeling, and optimize your investment portfolio subject to budgetary and other constraints.

ERM | Applied Analytics | Risk Simulation | Knowledge Center

Risk Settings | Risk Register | Risk Dashboard | Risk Events | Event Reports

ERM Event Input | Custom Event Input

Risk Engagement | Risk Diagrams | Risk Controls | Risk Forecasts | Risk Mitigation

Start by creating your own segments and custom lists, then create a new or edit an existing Dataset. Select the relevant segment and enter the event information.

Select a Segment: Customize...

Segment
General
Surgery
Intensive Care Unit
Orthopedic Surgery
Oncology
Medical Records
Pharmacy
Operating Room

`>>` `<<` `>>>` `<<<` `X`

No.	Event Name	Count	Event Date	Selected Segment	Entered By	Notes (Optional)
1	Staff Injury	3	1/24/2014	General	Nurse 155	
2	Staff Injury	6	3/27/2014	General	Nurse 155	
3	Infection	2	3/27/2014	Surgery	DOC 15	
4	Equipment Failure	4	4/15/2014	ICU	Nurse 254	
5	Ambulatory Issues	2	5/27/2014	Orthopedic	Nurse 32	
6	Wrong Dosage	1	6/30/2014	Pharmacy	Nurse Asst 25	
7	Wrong Dosage	3	8/27/2014	Pharmacy	Nurse Asst 25	
8	Missing Equipment	2	4/15/2014	OR	OR Nurse 5	
9	Missing Equipment	6	10/27/2014	OR	OR Nurse 5	
10	Staff Injury	5	10/27/2014	General	Nurse 155	
11	Infection	6	11/27/2014	Surgery	DOC 15	
12	Ambulatory Issues	5	12/31/2014	Orthopedic	Nurse 32	

Save as a New Dataset: Save As
Hospital Risk Management Events

List of Saved Datasets:

Dataset
Hospital Risk Management Events

New   Edit   Delete   Save

Enter Additional Optional Information:

`<` `>`

Reported By:
Causes:
Consequences:
Supervisor:
Reviewed By:
Witnessed By:
Other Info:
More Details:

Save

Risk events can be inputted as simple counts and segregated by departments

Real Options Valuation

Risk Events: Month to Month and Year Over Year Comparisons of Risk Events

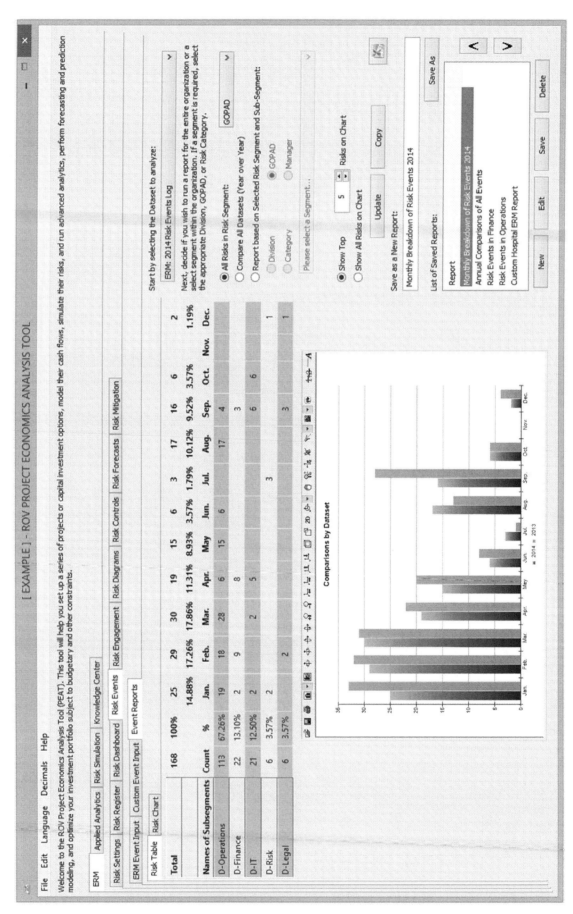

Comparisons of counts by month, year, of different datasets can be generated

Risk Engagement: Pre-Engagement Risks

[EXAMPLE] - ROV PROJECT ECONOMICS ANALYSIS TOOL

File   Edit   Language   Decimals   Help

Welcome to the ROV Project Economics Analysis Tool (PEAT). This tool will help you set up a series of projects or capital investment options, model their cash flows, simulate their risks, and run advanced analytics, perform forecasting and prediction modeling, and optimize your investment portfolio subject to budgetary and other constraints.

ERM | Applied Analytics | Risk Simulation | Knowledge Center

Risk Settings | Risk Register | Risk Dashboard | Risk Engagement

Pre-Engagement or Pre-Bid | Engagement or Bid Assessment | Lessons Learned | Risk Diagrams | Risk Controls | Risk Forecasts | Risk Mitigation

Project Name: Project Saturn: Residential Housing Developm
Project ID #: RH-563162
Updated: 3/11/2014

Name: Project Synecor 2015
Notes: Development of 1000 residential units in the outskirts of Croydon, London, anticipated bid

Save As | Save | Edit | Delete

Engagement
John Smith
Project Synecor 2015

Custom Categories | Copy | Report

Show: 30 rows | Risk Library | ∧ ∨

RISK CRITERIA

ITEM	CATEGORIES	EXPLANATIONS & DETAILS	DATA SOURCE	Low Risk	Significant Risk	Critical Risk	NOTES
Client Profile	Experience dealing with client (integrity, ontime payment, frequent	We have dealt with the client before in the past and they are very picky on technical details and keep changing	Past Experience		Manageable risk if our contracts are air tight on scope creeps		
Partnerships	Potential partners and subcontractors available to reduce project risk	We can mitigate any technical risks with our pool of partners		We have a pool of existing partners			
Project Profile	Insufficient information on bid order, RFP has limited details, future	RFP has some technical issues missing such as who will implement the architectural changes to plots C-DE	RFP		We can state this in the contract that client's responsibility		
Competitors	Key competitors for the project	HHSC and RMBH are two main competitors in the bid that we foresee	Competitive Database	We can significantly outprice them			
Financial Profitability	Potential for financial losses if resource, cost, and schedule risks are not	Lowered pricing will cause profits to shrink and if overrun happens, we may make losses on early phases	Pricing Model			Pricing is a significant risk	
Internal Capabilities	Potential lack of expertise and experience in executing and						
Contractual Obligations	Potential complex contract negotiations and loopholes						
Cost Risk	Potential for cost and budget overruns from human resources and raw						

This section allows the creation of multiple Risk Engagement projects where each saved project has multiple Risk Elements

Real Options Valuation

Risk Engagement: Engagement Risks

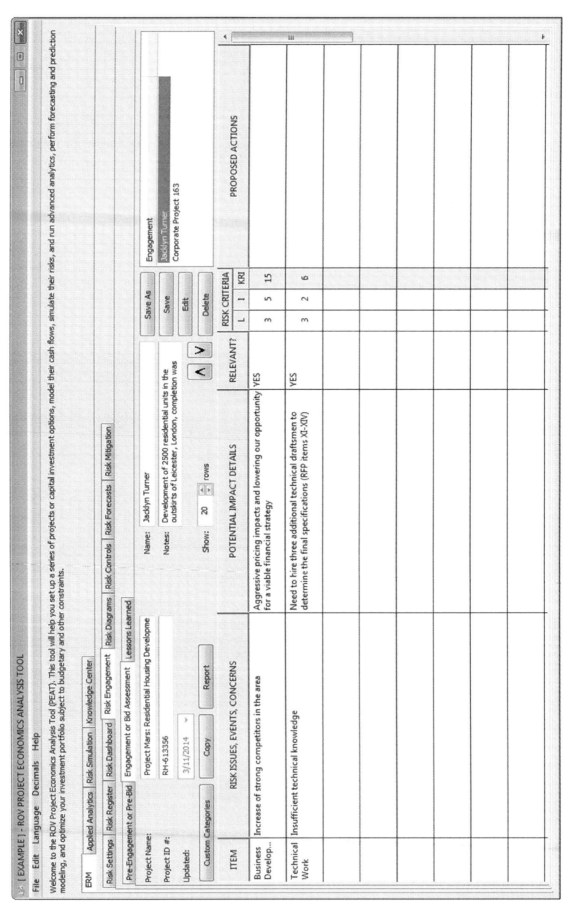

Variable categories (columns) can be customized to include or exclude certain categorical items

Risk Engagement: Lessons Learned (Post-Engagement)

Welcome to the ROV Project Economics Analysis Tool (PEAT). This tool will help you set up a series of projects or capital investment options, model their cash flows, simulate their risks, and run advanced analytics, perform forecasting and prediction modeling, and optimize your investment portfolio subject to budgetary and other constraints.

Tabs: ERM | Applied Analytics | Risk Simulation | Knowledge Center

Risk Settings | Risk Register | Risk Dashboard | Risk Engagement | Risk Diagrams | Risk Controls | Risk Forecasts | Risk Mitigation

Pre-Engagement or Pre-Bid | Engagement or Bid Assessment | Lessons Learned

Project Name: Project Mars: Residential Housing Developme
Project ID #: RH-613356
Updated: 3/11/2014

Name: Jaddyn Turner
Notes: Development of 2500 residential units in the outskirts of Leicester, London, completion was

Engagement
Jaddyn Turner

[Save As] [Save] [Edit] [Delete]

Show: 20 rows [A] [V]

[Custom Categories] [Copy] [Report]

ITEM	CATEGORIES	ISSUES (WHAT)	CAUSE (WHY)	IMPACT (CONSEQUENCES)	ACTIONS TAKEN & RECOMMENDATIONS	IMPACT AREAS	NOTES
Project Management	Technical staff required	Need project managers who are more technical or have a technical	Schedule overruns was in part due to bad project management	Cost and budget overruns causing losses	Hire and train better PMs	Operations and PM	
Cost Analysis	Cost analysts required	Cost calculations are high level estimates and were highly inaccurate	Cost overruns was in part due to bad forecasting of costs	Cost and budget overruns causing losses	Risk Simulation with Monte Carlo cost risk models are required	PM and Cost Anlaysis	
Schedule Modeling	Senior management oversight	Schedule on bid was too optimistic	Schedule overruns was in part due to bad project management	Cost and budget overruns causing losses		PM and Cost Anlaysis	
Schedule Modeling	Technical training required	Schedule calculations are high level estimates and were highly inaccurate	Schedule delays were in part due to bad forecasting of time to	Cost and budget overruns causing losses	Risk Simulation with Monte Carlo schedule risk models are required	PM and Cost Anlaysis	

Maintain a library of lessons learned from past projects (good and bad)

Risk Diagrams

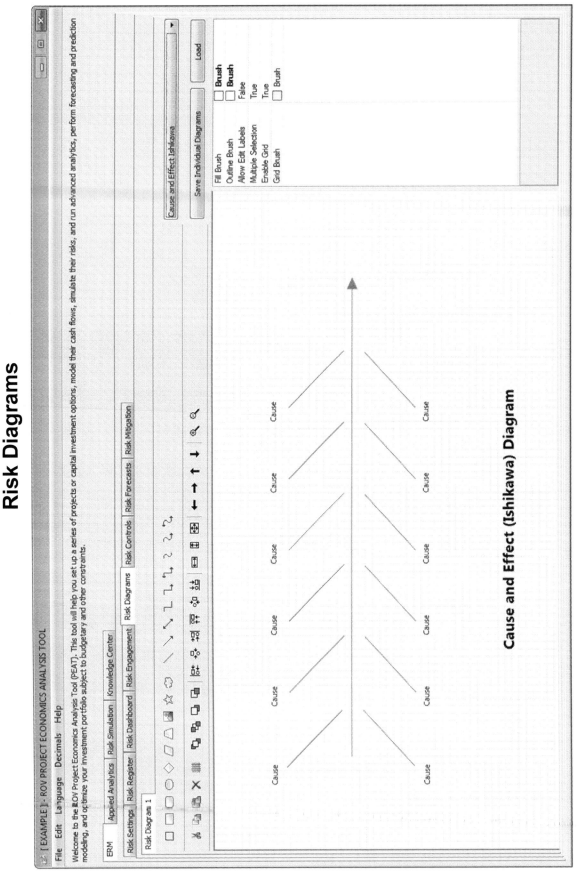

Cause and Effect (Ishikawa) Diagram

Custom creation of your own Risk Diagrams with ready-made templates on Bowtie Hazard Diagrams, Cause and Effect Ishikawa Fishbone Diagrams, Drill Down Diagrams, Influence Diagrams, Mind Maps, and Node Diagrams. Users can create multiple custom risk diagrams using this tool.

Risk Control

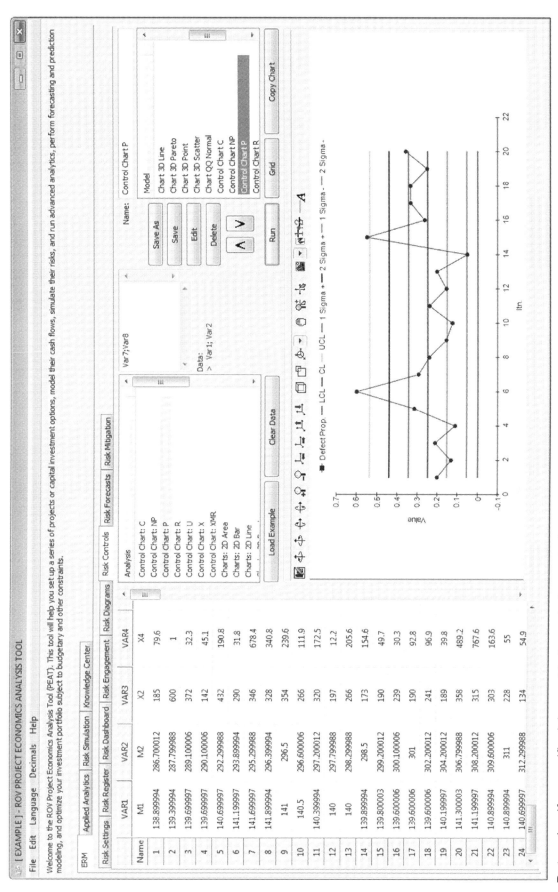

Determine if a specific risk event is in-control or out-of-control... For instance, if the number of risk events such as a plant accident spikes within a certain time period, was that set of events considered expected under statistically normal circumstances or an outlier requiring more detailed analysis?

Risk Forecast

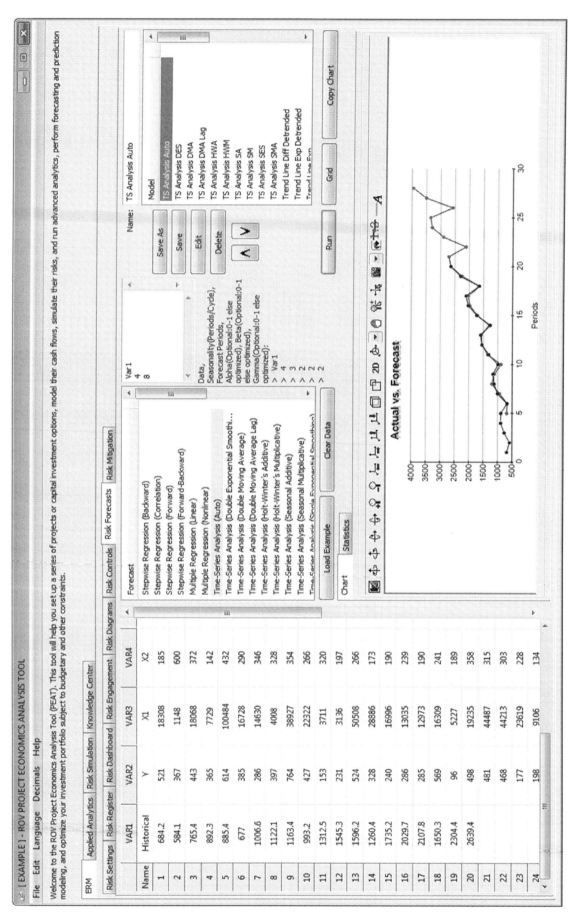

Using historical risk data, analysts can now apply predictive modeling to forecast future states of risk

Risk Mitigation

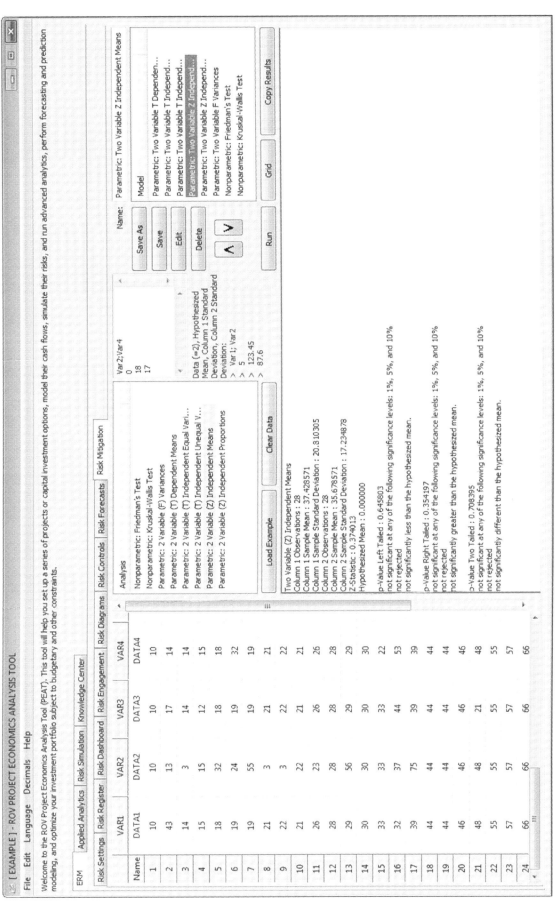

Determine if a specific risk mitigation strategy or technique is working, at least statistically speaking... Collect data from before and after a risk mitigation strategy is implemented and determine if there is a statistically significant difference between the two..

Risk Sensitivity: Tornado Analysis

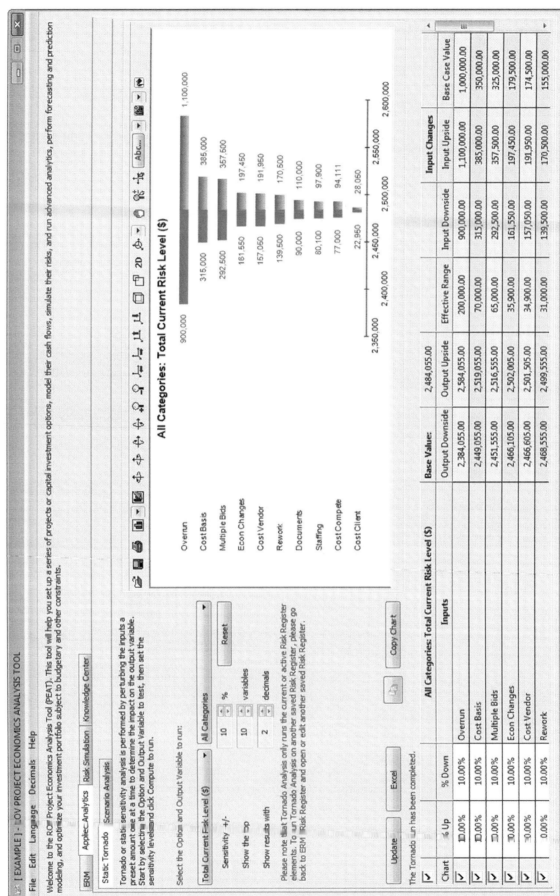

Identify the critical success factors or which risk element contributes the most to the bottom line risk profile of the company (or risk segment) by statically perturbing each of the risk element's financial risk levels

Risk Scenarios: Multiple Scenario Analysis

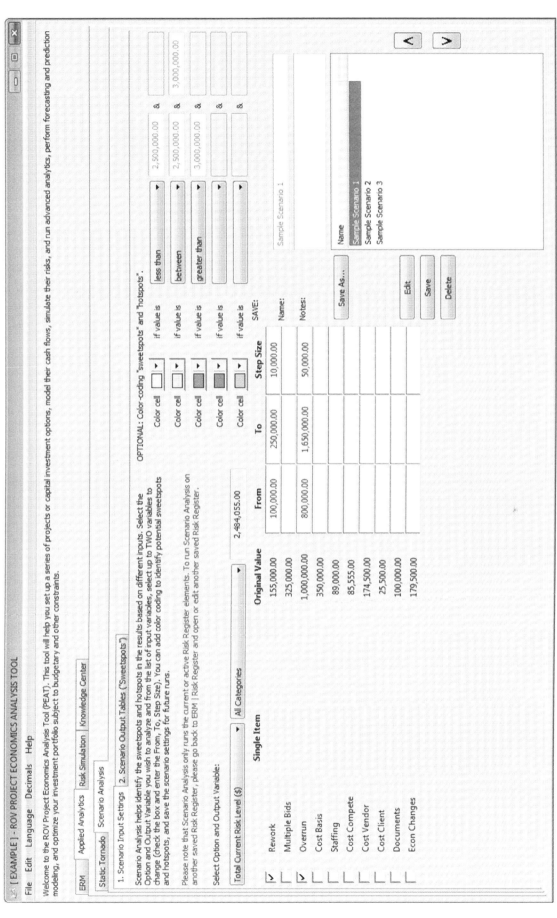

Create multiple risk scenarios of your current or total risk amounts of individual risk elements to determine the impact on the corporate risk profile and create scenario heat maps

Real Options
Valuation

Risk Scenarios: Scenario Heat Maps

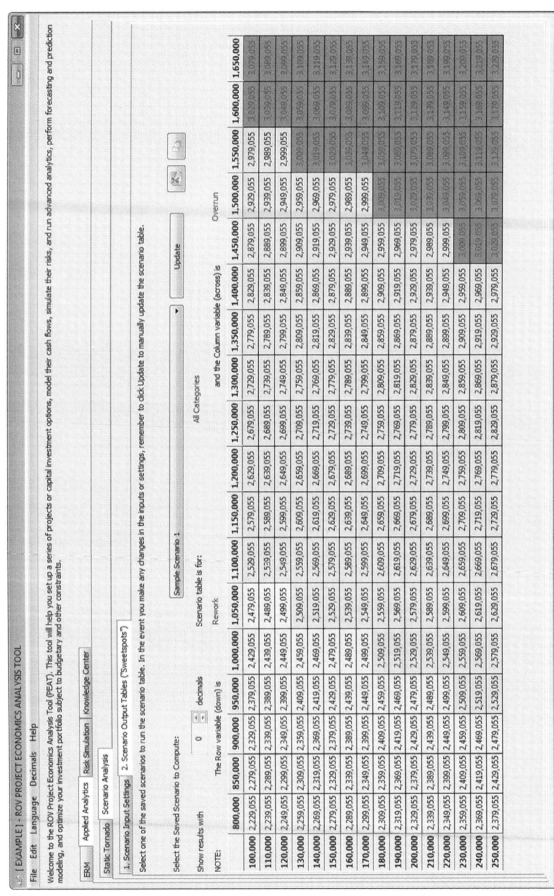

Scenario heat maps help identify the impact of each risk element and its corresponding effect on the organization's risk profile

Risk Simulation: Simulation Assumptions

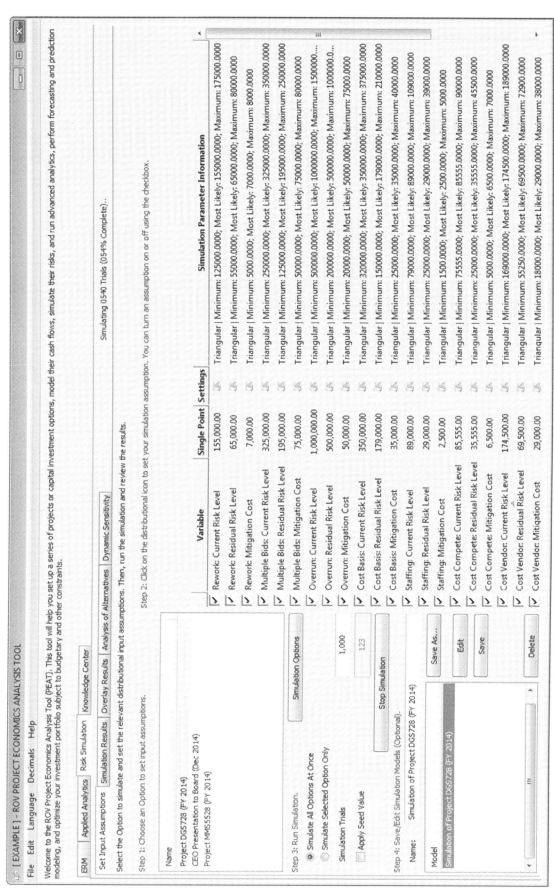

Run Monte Carlo Risk Simulations on your risk elements thousands to hundreds of thousands of times to generate probabilistic distributions and quantitative risk profiles

Risk Simulation: Simulation Results

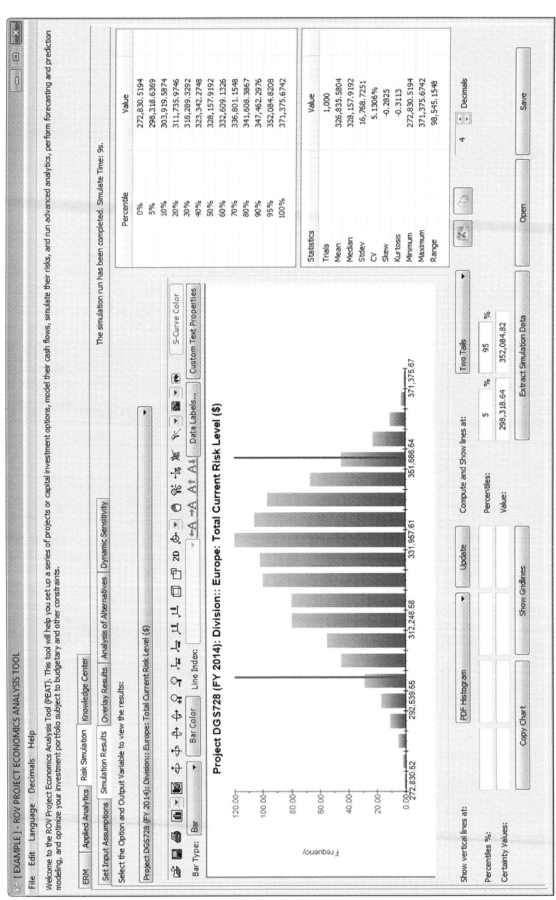

Results from the Monte Carlo Risk Simulation run thousands to hundreds of thousands of times are presented as probability distributions and statistical moments, percentiles, and confidence intervals

Risk Simulation: Overlay Results

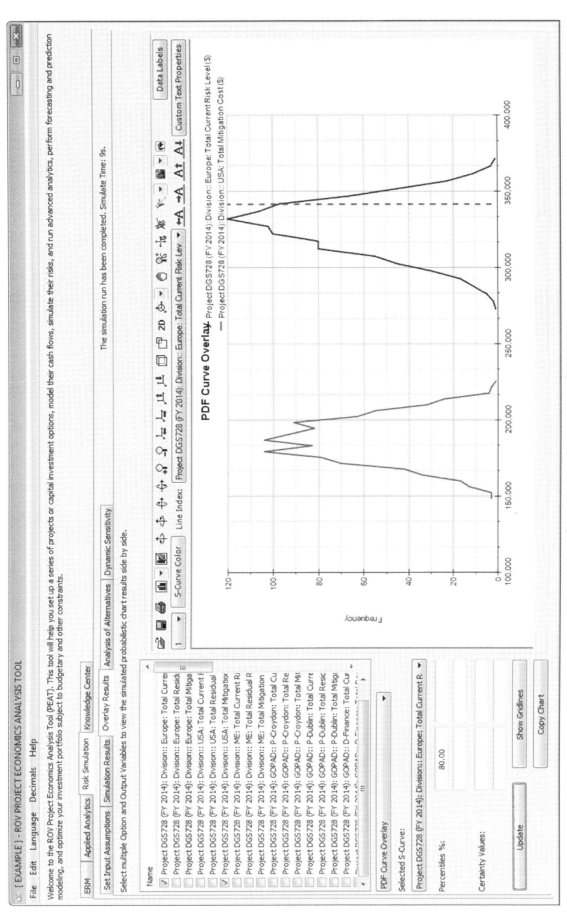

Overlay multiple risk profiles side by side to determine their respective impacts and uncertainty effects on the corporate risk profile

Risk Simulation: Analysis of Alternatives

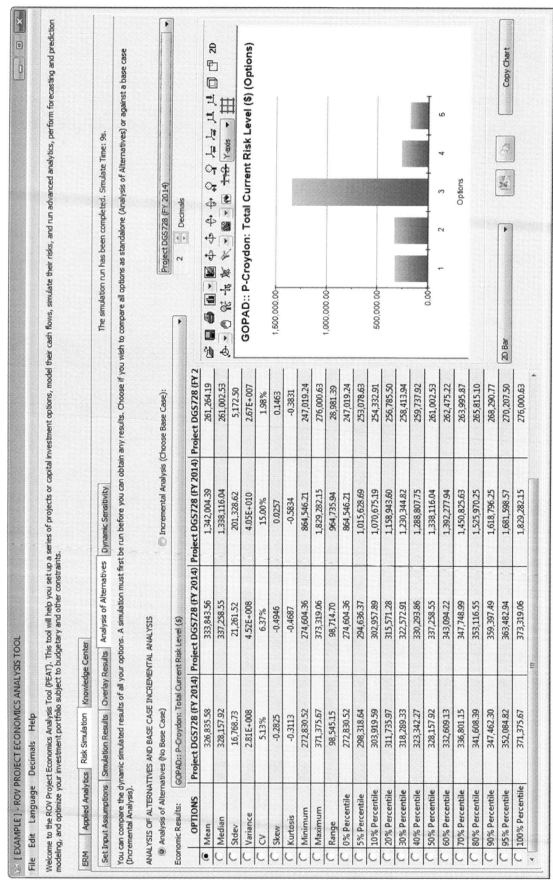

Compare the simulated results of various risk profiles

Risk Simulation: Dynamic Sensitivity

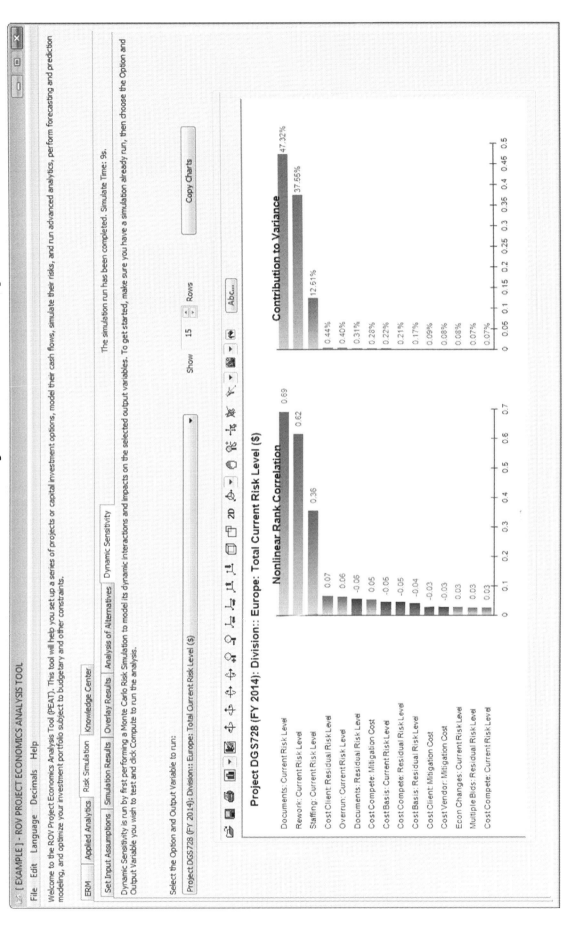

Identify the contribution to variance and uncertainty of each risk element to the corporate, division or G.O.P.A.D. total as well as rank and identify the critical success factors or which risk element contributes the most to the bottom line risk profile when dynamically simulated

Risk Reports

Project MMS5528 (FY 2014)

Risk Register Item	Acronym	Risk Category	G.O.P.A.D.	Division	Create Date	Edit Date	Due Date	Total Gross Risk L	KRI	I	Residual Net Risk L	KRI	I	Person in Charge	% OK	Status	Total Risk Level $	Residual Risk Level $	Mitigation Cost $	Cause	Consequence	Mitigation
Rework, scope creep, continual enhancement requests	Rework	Client	P-Croydon	Europe	3/14/2014	3/14/2014	5/14/2014	4	20	5	3	9	3	JJSmith	80%	Active	$0	$0	$0	Client keeps changing the specifications	Rework, scope creep, and requirements keep changing over time	Contract needs to specify deadline for specifications freeze
Multiple bids from main competitors like RHS and CCB	Multiple Bids	Competition	P-Dublin	USA	3/14/2014	3/14/2014	5/14/2014	8	44	8	5	30	6	JCannon	0%	Active	$0	$0	$0	Multiple competitors are looking at this	Might lose the bid/project	JCannon needs to find differentiation and price competitiveness to win
Cost overrun due to raw material delay and price hikes	Overrun	Cost	D-Finance	USA	3/14/2014	3/14/2014	5/14/2014	4	16	4	3	9	3	JJSmith	50%	Active	$1,000,000	$500,000	$50,000	Lack of raw materials and supplier delays	Additional wait time required	Source multiple vendors and sign contracts with them at some extra cost
Cost overrun due to raw material delays and price hikes	Overrun	Cost	D-Risk	USA	3/14/2014	3/14/2014	5/14/2014	4	16	4	3	9	3	JJSmith	50%	Active	$1,000,000	$500,000	$50,000	Lack of raw materials and supplier delays	Additional wait time required	Source multiple vendors and sign contracts with them at some extra cost
Cost overrun due to raw material delays and price hikes	Overrun	Cost	P-Dublin	USA	3/14/2014	3/14/2014	5/14/2014	4	16	4	3	9	3	JJSmith	50%	Active	$1,000,000	$500,000	$50,000	Lack of raw materials and supplier delays	Additional wait time required	Source multiple vendors and sign contracts with them at some extra cost
Cost pressures from competitors	Cost Compete	Cost	D-Finance	USA	3/14/2014	3/14/2014	5/14/2014	4	20	5	3	9	3	RRodgers	50%	Active	$0	$0	$0	Multiple competitors are looking at this	Might lose the bid/project	JCannon needs to find value differentiation and price competitiveness
Cost pressures from competitors	Cost Compete	Cost	D-Risk	USA	3/14/2014	3/14/2014	5/14/2014	4	20	5	3	9	3	RRodgers	50%	Active	$0	$0	$0	Multiple competitors are looking at this	Might lose the bid/project	JCannon needs to find value differentiation and price competitiveness
Cost pressures from competitors	Cost Compete	Cost	P-Dublin	USA	3/14/2014	3/14/2014	5/14/2014	4	20	5	3	9	3	RRodgers	50%	Active	$0	$0	$0	Multiple competitors are looking at this	Might lose the bid/project	JCannon needs to find value differentiation and price competitiveness
Missing critical subcontractors in the region	Staffing	Operational	P-Croydon	Europe	3/14/2014	3/14/2014	5/14/2014	4	16	4	3	9	3	SMinh	50%	Active	$0	$0	$0			
Cost pressures from competitors	Cost Compete	Cost	D-Finance	USA	3/14/2014	3/14/2014	5/14/2014	4	16	4	3	9	3	SMinh	50%	Active	$0	$0	$0	Multiple competitors are looking at this	Might lose the bid/project	JCannon needs to create price competitiveness to win
Cost pressures from competitors	Cost Compete	Cost	D-Risk	USA	3/14/2014	3/14/2014	5/14/2014	4	16	4	3	9	3	SMinh	50%	Active	$0	$0	$0	Multiple competitors are looking at this	Might lose the bid/project	JCannon needs to create price competitiveness to win
Cost pressures from competitors	Cost Compete	Cost	P-Dublin	USA	3/14/2014	3/14/2014	5/14/2014	4	16	4	3	9	3	SMinh	50%	Active	$0	$0	$0	Multiple competitors are looking at this	Might lose the bid/project	JCannon needs to create price competitiveness to win

Auto generating Reports and extraction to Excel capabilities.

Risk Training: Knowledge Center – Step-by-Step Procedures

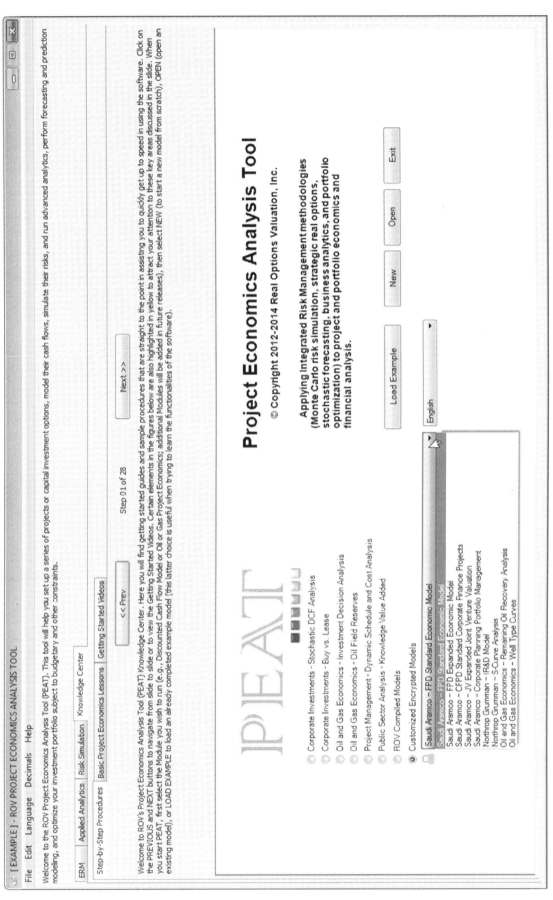

All step-by-step procedures are customizable (text, slides, graphics, etc.) and can include high-level or detailed descriptions as desired. We can create custom lessons for your users or you can do it yourself!

Risk Training: Knowledge Center – Basic Project Economics Lessons

All lessons are customizable (text, slides, graphics, etc.). We can create custom lessons for your users or you can do it yourself!

[EXAMPLE] - ROV PROJECT ECONOMICS ANALYSIS TOOL

File   Edit   Language   Decimals   Help

Welcome to the ROV Project Economics Analysis Tool (PEAT). This tool will help you set up a series of projects or capital investment options, model their cash flows, simulate their risks, and run advanced analytics, perform forecasting and prediction modeling, and optimize your investment portfolio subject to budgetary and other constraints.

ERM | Applied analytics | Risk Simulation | Knowledge Center

Step-by-Step Procedures | Basic Project Economics Lessons | Getting Started Videos

Lesson 01. Welcome to the Basic Project Economic Lessons. In this series of slides, we cover the basics of project economics and key financial indicators, as well as interpretation of risk simulation results. Specifically, the Project Economics Analysis Tool (PEAT) computes various project economics and financial results including Net Present Value (NPV), Internal Rate of Return (IRR), Modified Internal Rate of Return (MIRR), Profitability Index (PI), Return on Investment (ROI), Payback Period (PP), and Discounted Payback Period (DPP). Payback measures liquidity, NPV measures direct dollar benefit, IRR measures percentage return with a safety margin built in, MIRR measures a percentage return considering a better reinvestment rate, and PI measures bang for the buck. However, NPV is the best single measure, and almost all firms now use NPV. These results are available in the Economic Results subtab (results for a single Option) as well as in the Portfolio Analysis tab, where the results from multiple Options are compared at once within a portfolio.

<< Prev   Lesson 01 of 20   Next >>

Applied Analytics | Risk Simulation | Options Strategies | Options Valuation | Forecast Prediction | Portfolio Optimization | Knowledge Center

Discounted Cash Flow

Custom Calculations | Option 1... | Option 2... | Option 3... | Option 4... | Option 5... | Portfolio Analysis

1. Discounted Cash Flow Model (DCF) | 2. Cash Flow Ratios | 3. Economic Results | 4. Information and Details

Select the Discounting Convention to Use: ● Discrete   ○ Continuous

Select the Cash Flow to Use: NET CASH FLOW (NCF)

Terminal Period Annualized Growth Rate (%):   2.00%   □ Discount out-year capital investments at IRR

Economic Indicators	Results		Economic Indicators	Results
Net Present Value (NPV)	78.28		Profitability Index (PI)	3.45
Net Present Value (NPV) with Terminal Value	148.87		Return on Investment (ROI)	244.62%
Internal Rate of Return (IRR)	73.16%		Payback Period (PP)	1.5723
Modified Internal Rate of Return (MIRR)	31.95%		Discounted Payback Period (DPP)	1.9007

Show NPV: 50   % to   100   %   Update   Net Present Value Profile ►   Copy Results   Copy Chart

Discount Rate	NPV ($M)
15.00%	78.28
50.00%	12.00
51.00%	11.26
52.00%	10.54
53.00%	9.85
54.00%	9.19
55.00%	8.55
56.00%	7.93
57.00%	7.33
58.00%	6.76

Risk Training: Knowledge Center – Getting Started Videos

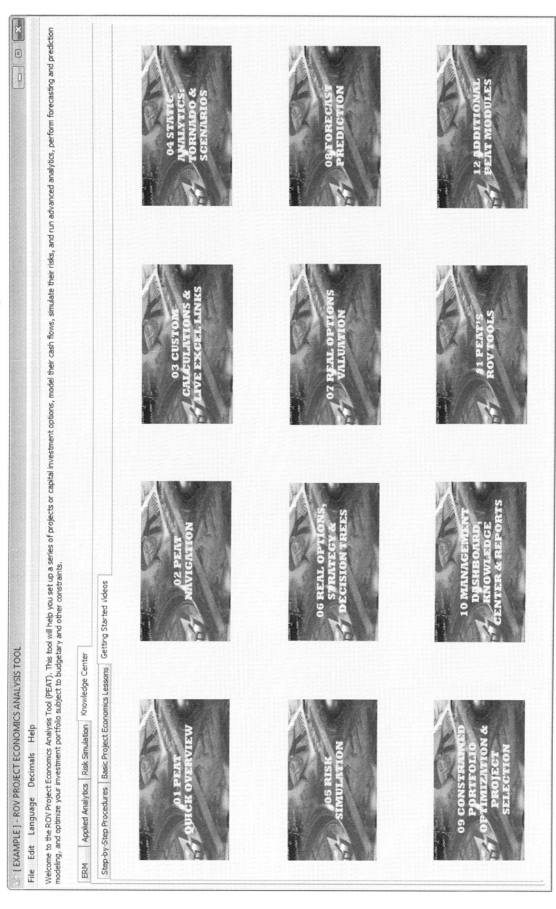

All video lessons are customizable

Real Options Valuation

Data Encryption and Foreign System Support

[EXAMPLE] - ROV PROJECT ECONOMICS ANALYSIS TOOL

File | Edit | Language | Decimals | Help

New
Open
Save
Save As...

Password Protect and Encryption

Load Example

Owner 1: Save Current Profile as Unencrypt File

Owner 2: Load Profile from Unencrypt File

Owner 3: Encrypt Current Profile to Example

Exit

○ North America (1,000.50)
○ Europe and Latin America (1.000,50)

et up a series of projects or capital investment options, model their cash flows, simulate their ris
straints.

Risk Diagrams | Risk Controls | Risk Forecasts | Risk Mitigation

Required Inputs

	Total (Gross)	Current (Net)

Likelihood of Occurrence (L):

1 ——————— 10

Possible Financial Impact (I):

1 ——————— 10

% Risk Mitigation Currently Completed: %

Optional Inputs

Total Risk Level ($):

Residual Risk Level ($):

Mitigation Cost ($):

Min	Likely	Max

Browse....

Risk Mitigation Response:

Action Plan (Doc):

Assigned To: Select Risk Category:

Status: | Created | Updated | Due Date |

The software comes with a 256-bit encryption protocols to encrypt your Risk Database and supports foreign decimal settings (e.g., USA settings for one thousand dollars and fifty cents is $1,000.50 versus a Latin American peso of P1.000,50 with interchangeable decimal and thousand separators)

User Manuals, Quick Getting Started Guides, and White Papers

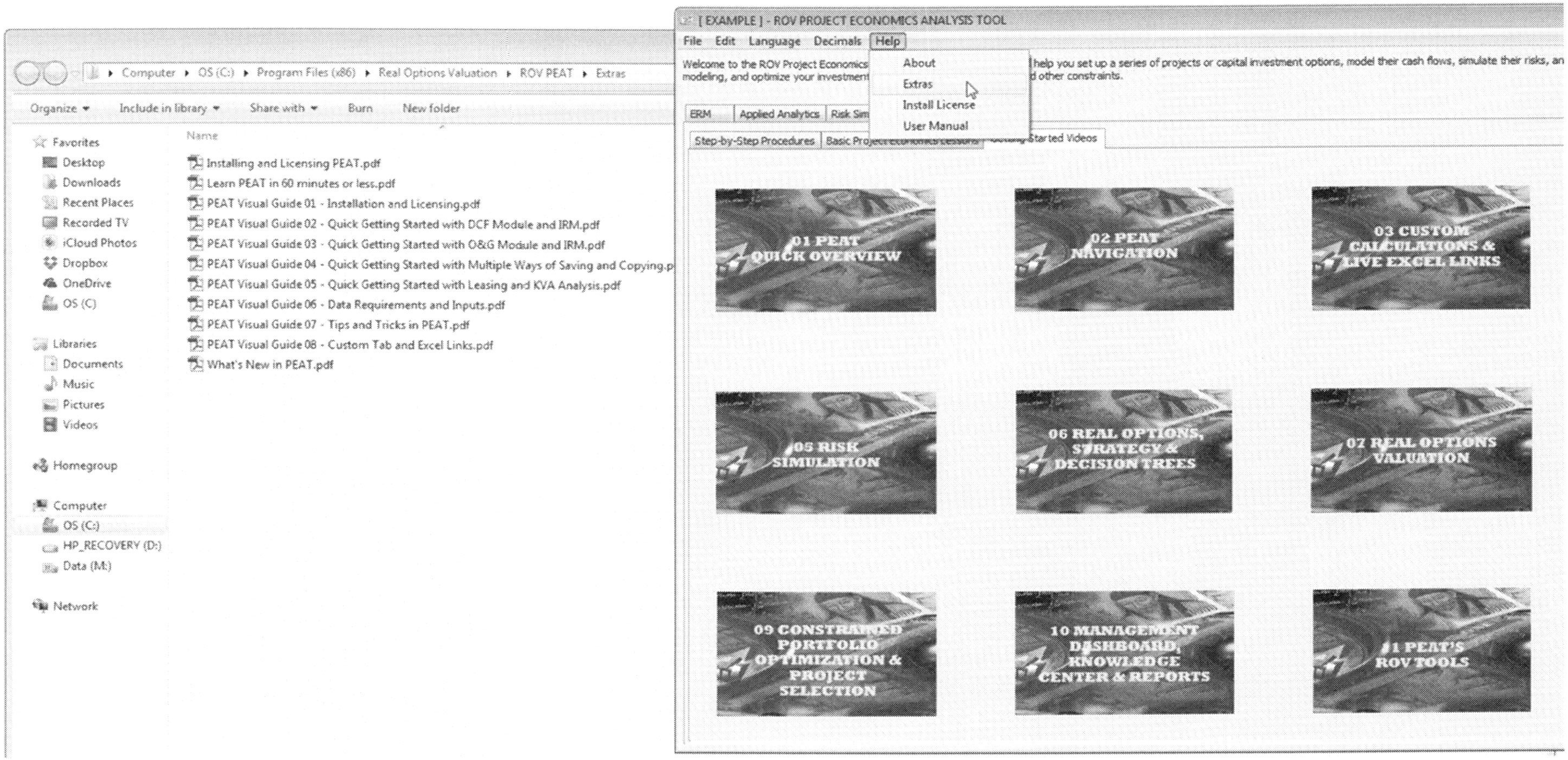

Computer ▸ OS (C:) ▸ Program Files (x86) ▸ Real Options Valuation ▸ ROV PEAT ▸ Extras
Organize ▾ Include in library ▾ Share with ▾ Burn New folder
Favorites
Desktop
Downloads
Recent Places
Recorded TV
iCloud Photos
Dropbox
OneDrive
OS (C)
Libraries
Documents
Music
Pictures
Videos
Homegroup
Computer
OS (C:)
HP_RECOVERY (D:)
Data (M:)
Network
Name
Installing and Licensing PEAT.pdf
Learn PEAT in 60 minutes or less.pdf
PEAT Visual Guide 01 - Installation and Licensing.pdf
PEAT Visual Guide 02 - Quick Getting Started with DCF Module and IRM.pdf
PEAT Visual Guide 03 - Quick Getting Started with O&G Module and IRM.pdf
PEAT Visual Guide 04 - Quick Getting Started with Multiple Ways of Saving and Copying.p
PEAT Visual Guide 05 - Quick Getting Started with Leasing and KVA Analysis.pdf
PEAT Visual Guide 06 - Data Requirements and Inputs.pdf
PEAT Visual Guide 07 - Tips and Tricks in PEAT.pdf
PEAT Visual Guide 08 - Custom Tab and Excel Links.pdf
What's New in PEAT.pdf
[EXAMPLE] - ROV PROJECT ECONOMICS ANALYSIS TOOL
File Edit Language Decimals Help
About
Extras
Install License
User Manual
ERM Applied Analytics Risk Sim
Step-by-Step Procedures
01 PEAT QUICK OVERVIEW
02 PEAT NAVIGATION
03 CUSTOM CALCULATIONS & LIVE EXCEL LINKS
05 RISK SIMULATION
06 REAL OPTIONS, STRATEGY & DECISION TREES
07 REAL OPTIONS VALUATION
09 CONSTRAINED PORTFOLIO OPTIMIZATION & PROJECT SELECTION
10 MANAGEMENT DASHBOARD, KNOWLEDGE CENTER & REPORTS
11 PEAT'S ROV TOOLS

The Help menu provides multiple Visual Guides, Whitepapers, and User Manuals to quickly get you started using the software

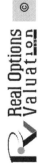

© Copyright 2005-2015 Dr. Johnathan Mun. All rights reserved. REAL OPTIONS VALUATION, Inc. www.realoptionsvaluation.com

Additional Advanced Modules and Foreign Language Support

PEAT

- Corporate Investments - Stochastic DCF Analysis
- Corporate Investments - Buy vs. Lease
- Oil and Gas Economics - Investment Decision Analysis
- Oil and Gas Economics - Oil Field Reserves
- Project Management - Dynamic Schedule and Cost Analysis
- Public Sector Analysis - Knowledge Value Added
- ROV Compiled Models
- Customized Encrypted Models

Saudi Aramco – FPD Standard Economic Model

Saudi Aramco – FPD Standard Economic Model
Saudi Aramco – FPD Expanded Economic Model
Saudi Aramco – CFPD Standard Corporate Finance Projects
Saudi Aramco – JV Expanded Joint Venture Valuation
Saudi Aramco – Corporate Planning Portfolio Management
Northrop Grumman – iR&D Model
Northrop Grumman – S-Curve Analysis
Oil and Gas Economics – Remaining Oil Recovery Analysis
Oil and Gas Economics – Well Type Curves
Enterprise Risk Management (ERM) - Risk Register
Health Economics Analysis Tool (HEAT)
ROV HQDM Rapid Economic Justification (REJ)

Project Economics Analysis Tool

© Copyright 2012-2014 Real Options Valuation, Inc.

Applying Integrated Risk Management methodologies (Monte Carlo risk simulation, strategic real options, stochastic forecasting, business analytics, and portfolio optimization) to project and portfolio economics and financial analysis.

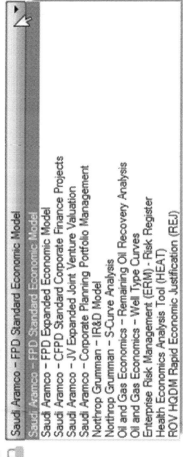

| Load Example | | New | Open | Exit |

English
English
Arabic
Korean
Portuguese
Russian
Simplified Chinese
Spanish
Traditional Chinese

Multiple advanced analytical and decision analysis models accompany the PEAT software and complements the existing ERM module, including the Corporate Investment module, Project Management (Cost and Schedule Risk), and other relevant applications. The software also comes with multiple foreign language user interface.

ADDITIONAL ROV REFERENCE BOOKS

 *Modeling Risk: Applying Monte Carlo Risk Simulation, Strategic Real Options, Stochastic Forecasting, Portfolio Optimization, Data Analytics, Business Intelligence, and Decision Modeling, 3rd Edition*
1112 Pages (2015)
ISBN: 9781943290000
Thomson-Shore & ROV Press

 *Modeling Risk: Applying Monte Carlo Simulation, Real Options Analysis, Stochastic Forecasting, and Optimization*
610 Pages (2006)
ISBN: 0471789003
Wiley Finance

 *Modeling Risk: Applying Monte Carlo Risk Simulation, Strategic Real Options Analysis, Stochastic Forecasting, and Portfolio Optimization, 2nd Edition*
986 Pages (2010)
ISBN: 9780470592212
Wiley Finance

 *Valuing Employee Stock Options: Under 2004 FAS 123*
320 Pages (2004)
ISBN: 0471705128
Wiley Finance

 *Real Options Analysis: Tools and Techniques for Valuing Strategic Investments & Decisions, 2nd Edition*
670 Pages (2005)
ISBN: 0471747483
Wiley Finance

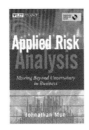 *Applied Risk Analysis: Moving Beyond Uncertainty*
460 Pages (2003)
ISBN: 0-471-47885-7
Wiley Finance

  Credit Engineering for Bankers (With Morton Glantz)
1000 Pages (2010)
ISBN: 9780123785855
Elsevier Academic Press

 *Real Options Analysis Course: Business Cases and Software Applications*
360 Pages (2003)
ISBN: 0471430013
Wiley Finance

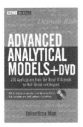 *Advanced Analytical Models: Over 800 Models and 300 Applications from Basel II Accords to Wall Street and Beyond*
1000 Pages (2008)
ISBN: 9780470179215
Wiley Finance

 *Real Options Analysis: Tools and Techniques for Valuing Strategic Investments & Decisions*
416 Pages (2002)
ISBN: 0-471-25696-X
Wiley Finance

 *The Banker's Handbook on Credit Risk: Implementing Basel II (With Morton Glantz)*
420 Pages (2008)
ISBN: 9780123736666
Elsevier Science

See Dr. Mun's other books, articles, whitepapers, technical papers, and academic journal publications on his company's website at www.rovusa.com and www.realoptionsvaluation.com.

Made in the USA
Columbia, SC
18 August 2023

21822644R00191